EVALUATING TRANSFER AND DISPOSITION

Focusing on juvenile transfer and disposition evaluations, this volume provides an up-to-date integration of current law, science, and practice with respect to juvenile risk assessment, treatment needs/amenability, and sophistication-maturity. Included are perspectives relating to international practices, the use of specialized assessment tools, and a separate chapter on resentencing following US Supreme Court decisions on juveniles sentenced to mandatory life without parole. This text will be a useful and comprehensive reference for forensic psychologists and other mental health professionals engaged in juvenile evaluation, as well as legal professionals, juvenile and criminal justice professionals, and others involved with juvenile assessment, decision-making, and rehabilitation.

Kirk Heilbrun, PhD, is a professor in the Department of Psychology at Drexel University. He directs the forensic assessment clinic and the Reentry Project, both based in the department. He has published a number of books, articles, and chapters in the areas of forensic mental health assessment, diversion, and juvenile delinquency.

David DeMatteo, JD, PhD, is an associate professor of psychology and law at Drexel University, and director of Drexel's JD/PhD Program in law and psychology. His research interests include psychopathic personality, juvenile and adult offenders, forensic mental health assessment, and offender diversion. He is currently president of the American Psychology-Law Society (AP-LS; APA Division 41).

Christopher King, JD, PhD, is an assistant professor of psychology at Montclair State University.

Sarah Filone, MS, is a doctoral candidate in clinical psychology at Drexel University.

International Perspectives on Forensic Mental Health

A Routledge Book Series

Edited by Ronald Roesch and Stephen Hart,
Simon Fraser University

The goal of this series is to improve the quality of health care services in forensic settings by providing a forum for discussing issues related to policy, administration, clinical practice, and research. The series will cover topics such as mental health law; the organization and administration of forensic services for people with mental disorder; the development, implementation and evaluation of treatment programs for mental disorder in civil and criminal justice settings; the assessment and management of violence risk, including risk for sexual violence and family violence; and staff selection, training, and development in forensic systems. The book series will consider proposals for both monographs and edited works on these and similar topics, with special consideration given to proposals that promote best practice and are relevant to international audiences.

Published Titles

Case Studies in Sexual Deviance: Toward Evidence Based Practice
Edited by William T. O'Donohue

Forensic Psychological Assessment in Practice: Case Studies
Corine De Ruiter and Nancy Kaser-Boyd

Sexual Predators: Society, Risk and the Law
Robert A. Prentky, Howard E. Barbaree and Eric S. Janus

Forthcoming Titles

Handbook of Forensic Social Work with Children
Edited by Viola Vaughan-Eden

EVALUATING JUVENILE TRANSFER AND DISPOSITION

LAW, SCIENCE, AND PRACTICE

Kirk Heilbrun, David DeMatteo, Christopher King, and Sarah Filone

Routledge
Taylor & Francis Group
NEW YORK AND LONDON

First published 2017
by Routledge
711 Third Avenue, New York, NY 10017

and by Routledge
2 Park Square, Milton Park, Abingdon,
Oxon, OX14 4RN

Routledge is an imprint of the Taylor & Francis Group, an informa business

Library of Congress Cataloging in Publication Data
A catalog record for this book has been requested

ISBN: 978-1-138-95795-4 (hbk)
ISBN: 978-1-138-95794-7 (pbk)
ISBN: 978-1-315-66144-5 (ebk)

Typeset in MinionPro
by Cenveo Publisher Services

To the many dedicated legal and mental health professionals who work with justice-involved youth

KH, DD

To Sarah, and our families and mentors

CK

To my mother-in-law, Susan, for all her work with justice-involved youth. And to my husband, for his ever-present support.

SF

CONTENTS

FOREWORD

The International Association of Forensic Mental Health Services (IAFMHS) is an interdisciplinary professional society representing forensic professionals engaged in research and practice in forensic mental health. Its membership includes psychologists, psychiatrists, social workers, nurses, and lawyers representing over 22 countries worldwide. Its goals are to promote education, training, and research in forensic mental health and to enhance the standards of forensic mental health services in the international community. The IAFMHS holds an annual conference, and publishes a journal (*International Journal of Forensic Mental Health*) and a book series (International Perspectives on Forensic Mental Health).

The goal of the book series is to improve the quality of healthcare services in forensic settings by providing a forum for discussing issues related to policy, administration, clinical practice, and research. The series covers topics such as mental health law; the organization and administration of forensic services for people with mental disorder; the development, implementation and evaluation of treatment programs for mental disorder in civil and criminal justice settings; the assessment and management of violence risk, including risk for sexual violence and family violence; and staff selection, training, and development in forensic mental health systems.

I am delighted to add *Evaluating Juvenile Transfer and Disposition: Law, Science, and Practice* to the list of books in this series. Kirk Heilbrun, David DeMatteo, Chris King, and Sarah Filone have produced an outstanding book that provides a comprehensive analysis of forensic assessments of juveniles in the context of juvenile transfer and disposition. Transfer of juvenile offenders to adult court has been an important focus of a considerable amount of literature in the last 25 years or so. The use of transfer, including the automatic transfer of 16- and 17-years-olds charged with violent offenses, saw a dramatic increase in the 1990s. This continued into the early part of the century but notably, the use of transfers has been on the decline in many jurisdictions across the US. This is due in part to research showing that transfers are counterproductive in the long term due to the research findings that recidivism rates may actually be higher for those youth incarcerated as adults. As well, there is evidence of increased risk of sexual and physical abuse in prison for these youth.

Attitudes toward transfer of youth to adult court, and indeed the treatment of young offenders generally, has been influenced by a series of US Supreme Court cases (*Roper v. Simmons*, *Graham v. Florida*, *Miller v. Alabama*, *Montgomery v. Louisiana*) that referred heavily to the growing body of developmental research showing that juveniles are immature, impulsive, irresponsible, and highly susceptible to peer influences compared to adults. Importantly, the Supreme Court also recognized that juveniles are more amenable to change. The Supreme Court's opinions in these cases supported the view that adolescents should be considered less culpable than adults and also reinforced the perspective that the juvenile justice system should move away from the punitive approach of the last few decades to the more rehabilitation focus that was the rationale for the juvenile justice system when it was created well over 100 years ago.

Forensic psychologists provide assessments of youth being considered for transfer to adult court. Many states make this transfer automatic for 16- or 17-year-old youth charged with violent offenses so no hearing or evaluation takes place. However, a reverse transfer is possible and an evaluation would be conducted if this were considered. For youth not subject to automatic transfer, a hearing is always held, and forensic psychologists can contribute evaluations that may assist the court in reaching a decision about whether to retain a youth in the juvenile system or order a transfer to adult jurisdiction. Another Supreme Court case, *Kent v. United States*, provides the court with criteria to consider in these cases. There are eight Kent criteria that can guide the court in its decision, three of which are relevant to the expertise of forensic psychologists: risk and protection of the public, sophistication and maturity, and the likelihood of reasonable rehabilitation of the juvenile (if the youth is found to have committed the alleged offense) by the use of procedures, services, and facilities currently available to the Juvenile Court. Heilbrun and his colleagues present a model to conduct these evaluations, with a particular focus on how an assessment of risk, treatment needs and amenability can be used to evaluate rehabilitation potential. Following a thorough review of the developmental research and its implications for the evaluation of juvenile transfer and disposition, separate chapters provide a framework for the assessment of risk, treatment needs and amenability, and sophistication-maturity. These chapters provide a clear roadmap for evaluators who conduct these assessments.

The evaluation framework alone makes this a valuable book for forensic evaluators. But there is much more. Some youth who had been transferred to adult court over the past several decades were convicted and automatically sentenced to life without parole. The series of Supreme Court cases noted earlier in this Foreword has ruled that these automatic sentences are unconstitutional and thus nullified all prior mandatory life without parole sentences. These offenders, some of whom have already spent decades in prison, are now eligible for either a parole hearing or a resentencing hearing. It is estimated that more than 2,000 offenders nationally are affected by this decision. Heilbrun and colleagues present a framework for how these evaluations can be conducted, with a particular focus on the five factors that *Miller v. Alabama* identified that can be considered in deciding the sentence of an individual convicted of a violent offense as a juvenile. These include the juvenile's age and maturity at the time of the offense; the circumstances of familial dependency and vulnerability that are a part of adolescence, as well as the susceptibility to peer influences and environmental pressures; the circumstances of the offense, with special attention to the youth's role in the offense; the youth's capacity to waive arrest rights or competence to stand trial; and the potential for rehabilitation. The authors review forensic assessment instruments and other psychological tests that can be helpful in evaluating these five factors.

A welcome feature of this book, particularly since it is published in the International Perspectives on Forensic Mental Health book series, is its chapter on international juvenile justice models and trends. This chapter applies the developmental research and assessment model to the evaluation of disposition and transfer in other countries, with a particular focus on Canada, Europe, Australia, and New Zealand.

This is the first book to focus solely on the transfer of youth to adult court. It provides a framework for best practices in assessing youth charged with serious offenses that comprehensively integrates relevant law and policy, developmental and other relevant research, forensic assessment instruments, and practice guidelines. As such, it will be a valuable resource for forensic evaluators, researchers, legal scholars, and students.

Ronald Roesch
International Perspectives on
Forensic Mental Health Series Editor

PREFACE

We decided to write this book because it fills an important gap in the literature. The forensic evaluation of justice-involved youth for the purposes of assisting the court in the decisions of transfer, reverse transfer, and disposition is important and complex. There have been very significant developments over the last two decades in areas such as US Supreme Court decisions, research in human development, the emergence of specialized risk-need measures, and the clarification that many adults sentenced to life without parole for crimes committed as juveniles would need resentencing. Yet there was no book available that sought to integrate relevant law and policy, research, and practice considerations at the time we began this project.

That has changed for the better. But our goals for this book—the review of a large but uneven literature; the distillation of the important components of these evaluations; the discussion of relevant law, science, ethics, and practice standards; the integration of this material toward meaningful "next steps" in law, policy, practice, and research; and the provision of international comparisons of juvenile justice—make it an unusual and helpful contribution, to the extent that we have succeeded.

We are grateful for the congenial environment provided by Drexel University, particularly the Department of Psychology and the Thomas R. Kline School of Law, that allowed the four of us to collaborate. We are equally grateful for the many contributions to this area provided by researchers, scholars, legal and forensic practitioners, and policy advocates.

Kirk Heilbrun and David DeMatto, Philadelphia, PA
Christopher King, Montclair, NJ
Sarah Filone, Durham, NC

CHAPTER ONE

The Juvenile Justice System in The United States: History Relevant to Disposition, Transfer, and Reverse Transfer

Our society has an important interest in juvenile justice. If the juvenile justice system is to meet its primary goals of rehabilitating youth who commit crimes and protecting the public, then legal decision-making about juveniles must be well informed. This means that judges and attorneys must receive juvenile forensic evaluations that are relevant, understandable, practical, based on scientific data, and guided by best practice. It also means that policy-makers and clinical administrators must insist on making such information available to the courts, and the forensic mental health professionals who provide them must be sufficiently informed and thorough to offer such evaluations to legal decision-makers. One of our goals in writing this book is to provide detailed, balanced, and relevant information on the questions of juvenile disposition, transfer, and reverse transfer. We also discuss the resentencing of adolescents who originally received mandatory life sentences as adults—such resentencing is now required under recent United States Supreme Court decisions. We review evidence suggesting that there is considerable room for improvement in the evaluations now being provided to courts making decisions about juveniles, despite important advances in our capacities to assess and rehabilitate justice-involved youth. We hope that by assembling, critically reviewing, and distilling the relevant evidence, we can provide a resource to improve the clinical forensic evaluation of juveniles—and enhance the information available to courts and attorneys who request them.

DEFINING DISPOSITION, TRANSFER, AND REVERSE TRANSFER

When a juvenile judge considers the question of where, how long, and under what conditions a youth adjudicated as delinquent should be placed, that is a question of *disposition*. It is the juvenile equivalent of sentencing in the adult system. The decision has also been called *commitment* or *placement*. In other cases, there is a question of whether a youth should be moved from juvenile court to adult criminal court. This is a decision regarding *transfer*. It has also been called *certification*, *waiver*, *remand*, or *bindover*. Finally, a youth who has been initially placed in criminal court because of relevant statutes or prosecutorial discretion has, in some states, the right to petition the criminal court for a return to juvenile court. This is a question of *reverse transfer*. These are the three juvenile forensic issues addressed in this book.

There are other legal questions facing juvenile court judges regarding justice-involved youth, of course. Indeed, there are numerous points along the juvenile justice continuum where assessments conducted by different professionals, both informally and formally, affect how youths are subsequently treated. These points have been described as follows: pre-arrest diversion, arrest procedures, filing of criminal charges, pretrial detention, transfer to and from adult court, competency to stand trial, adjudication, disposition, sentencing, rehabilitation intervention planning, and supervision planning (Hoge, 2012). The issues of competence to proceed, and the defendant's capacity to waive *Miranda* rights prior to making an inculpatory statement while in police custody, have been discussed in detail elsewhere (Goldstein, Kelley *et al.*, 2016; Kruh & Grisso, 2009). There are also juvenile placement and rehabilitation-planning evaluations, as well as progress and outcome evaluations (Grisso, 2013). But we focus on disposition because there has been surprisingly little book-length attention centered on this frequent decision by juvenile courts, and on transfer and reverse transfer because of their relevance to whether youth will be rehabilitated in the juvenile or adult system.

There have been a number of chapters and articles on disposition and transfer, however. According to Chen & Salekin (2012), there have been a variety of important contributions in this area over the last 30 years (see Brannen, Salekin *et al.*, 2006; Ewing, 1990; Grisso, 2000, 2013; Kalogerakis, 1992; Kruh & Brodsky, 1997; Melton, Petrila *et al.*, 2007; Salekin, 2004a; Salekin & Grimes, 2008; Salekin, Rogers *et al.*, 2001; Salekin, Yff *et al.*, 2002; Schetky & Benedek, 2002; Weiner & Hess, 2006; and Witt, 2003). Further recommendations for guidance on juvenile transfer evaluations (Grisso, 2013) include Barnum (1987, 1990), Grisso (2010–11), Loving & Patapis (2007), Penney & Moretti (2005), Salekin (2002b), and Witt & Dyer (1997).

All provide valuable perspectives on this topic. To date, however, there has been only one book on juvenile disposition and transfer (see Salekin, 2015a). Finally, a number of chapters and texts have addressed the role of forensic professionals in delinquency matters in general, often as evaluators of different risks and needs (e.g. Borum, 2006; Conroy, 2012; Conroy & Murrie, 2007; Grisso, 2013; Heilbrun *et al.*, 2005; Hoge & Andrews, 2010a).

As we discuss in detail throughout this book, the question of "juvenile versus adult system" is important for the individuals involved, and for society and public policy more broadly. We focus on disposition, transfer, and reverse transfer in part because several of the criteria for these decisions across most jurisdictions—public safety, treatment needs and amenability, and sophistication-maturity—are similar.

Mental health professionals in the early twentieth century served newly-developed juvenile courts by offering holistic and multidisciplinary evaluations of youths that were consistent with the era's broad and exclusive focus on rehabilitation. As times and legal policies changed, evaluators began to incorporate information relevant to public safety, juveniles' rights, and mental health and trauma-related needs (Grisso, 2013). The primary areas addressed in contemporary juvenile evaluations have been described as mental health, maturity, risk for violence and offending, adjudicative competence, and treatment effectiveness (Otto & Douglas, 2010).

Models including risk, and needs that are relevant to both criminality and behavioral health, have been usefully applied to the core questions in disposition and transfer. There are, of course, other juvenile justice questions beyond disposition and transfer that can be informed by such models. Risk and risk–need assessment are useful for pre-adjudication decision-making to help determine: (1) the appropriateness of early-stage diversion; (2) whether secure detention is warranted at intake and leading up to the adjudication hearing; (3) whether a juvenile is likely to harm other youths while in custody; and (4) what services may be necessary to manage acute needs or crises. Risk assessment services are also useful at various steps following the disposition decision. First, these services help inform juvenile corrections about initial placement, and whether less secure placements are appropriate based on risk and need. Second, in some jurisdictions, risk assessment services help to inform decisions about whether to extend juvenile jurisdiction past the usual maximum age for an individual who presents an ongoing high risk. Advances in rehabilitation-oriented evaluations for justice-involved youth—addressing domains such as re-offense risk, physical and mental health, family and social support, schooling and work, finances and housing, recreation, and spirituality, and monitoring response to interventions—are important in delivering rehabilitative services (Grisso, 2013). Although such post-disposition rehabilitative evaluations are beyond the scope of this book, it is important to note that risk and need assessment—and interventions provided in accordance with such assessment—may provide valuable information for rehabilitation planning and implementation.

There is an important question that will recur throughout this book. Certainly the evaluation of justice-involved youth includes both clinical/behavioral domains and legal domains (Otto & Douglas, 2010). But the questions of public safety, treatment needs and amenability, risk, and risk reduction raise several important considerations. Risk of what? Are youth receiving interventions to improve their clinical functioning and behavioral effectiveness? Should the interventions primarily target risk factors for offending, with the goal of making re-offending less likely? Can interventions do both? In an era of limited resources for such interventions, it is important to ask such questions, and make decisions according to the best evidence available.

The decision-making criteria are similar across the issues of disposition and transfer, but the outcomes can be quite different. The rehabilitative goals of juvenile disposition can be implemented through options ranging from home-based community intervention and probation to intermediate security residential placements to higher security, more remote facilities. In the criminal system, which handles youth who are transferred, there is more exposure to inmates who are 18 or older—and a criminal conviction that is part of that individual's record permanently (Elrod & Ryder, 2011). These are potentially very important differences. Review of the empirical evidence on the outcomes associated with the juvenile and criminal systems (in Chapter 8, this volume) will clarify how important.

JUVENILE JUSTICE, DISPOSITION, AND TRANSFER: RELEVANT HISTORY

In this section, we focus on the aspects of juvenile justice history providing the most important context for juvenile disposition and transfer evaluations. We summarize (1) how the juvenile system developed as a separate entity from the criminal justice system and how its major goals have shifted over time, and (2) where the system now stands on disposition, transfer, and reverse transfer. We provide this history to contextualize the law that is described in Chapter 2 (this volume), and the forensic questions that form the basis for evaluations of transfer and disposition.

THE JUVENILE SYSTEM: ORIGINAL DEVELOPMENT AND PHILOSOPHY

Youth are considered differently than adults in many areas of the law (McPherson, 2012). Prior to the end of the nineteenth century, juveniles were considered and adjudicated within the criminal law. There were distinctions between young children and other defendants, however. For instance, in the tenth century, Anglo-Saxon and English law exempted children under the age of 15 who committed robbery from death sentences—and even from imprisonment—if their families assured the authorities that their children would desist from illicit conduct (Dattilio & Fromm, 2011). Under common law, infancy was a defense against criminal charges until a certain age (which varied between seven and ten, depending on the jurisdiction). Children up to the age of 14 were presumed incapable of forming criminal intent, although this could be rebutted by a showing of maturity (see Melton, Petrila *et al.*, 2007).

In the late nineteenth century, the common law tradition of full application of the law to relatively young children began to be replaced by a new system of segregating youth (Melton, Petrila *et al.*, 2007). The newly-defined period of "adolescence" allowed an extended period for socializing youth. This lengthier period of socialization was intended to buffer them from baser instincts and undesirable "lower"/working/immigrant-class influences, and prepare them for more complex industrial-age jobs. More detailed coverage of the social construction of childhood and adolescence, the social welfare model, their foundational role in the history of the early juvenile court, and the tension between the social welfare model and criminal social model is beyond the scope of this book, but available elsewhere (Feld, 2006; Jensen, 2006). The creation of the juvenile court was one of numerous legal changes of the early twentieth century, developed in response to changing conceptions of childhood and adolescence. It was established in the larger context of other social structures and practices, and continues to interact with them (Bartol & Bartol, 2009; Chen & Salekin, 2012; Dattilio & Fromm, 2011; Dupée, 2002; Elrod & Ryder, 2011; Gardner, 2014; Guerra, Hoge *et al.*, 2008; Heilbrun *et al.*, 2005; Salekin, 2015; Weithorn, 2006). These related institutions and mandates include child labor laws (Jensen & Arnett, 2012); schools and compulsory school attendance requirements (Dohrn, 2002; Jensen & Arnett, 2012); child welfare (Grossberg, 2002); institutional care for welfare, correctional, mental health, or substance abuse purposes (Lerman, 2002); and politics (Edelman, 2002). A summary of many of these developments is provided in Table 1.1.

The early juvenile court philosophy emphasized that the interests of the state and the youth were reciprocal: the state was to act on behalf of the juvenile to ensure proper socialization, so the youth could overcome age-related uncivilized tendencies and problematic socio-cultural influences that had culminated in illegal behavior. The juvenile court ideal was rehabilitative. Legal protections and adversarial procedures were deemed unnecessary due to the absence of retributive goals, and the potential of such protections to impede treatment. Proceedings and records were

Table 1.1 The Juvenile Court and Related Social-contextual Institutions and Policies

Social institution or policy	**Historical relevance to the juvenile court**
Social control of children before the juvenile court	• *Medieval view of childhood in developing Europe and the role of the family in the early social control of children* (e.g. harsh conditions for children and views of them as miniature adults and personal property started to change around 1300 to 1400 to emerging conceptions of childhood and adolescence, loving parent–child relations, etc.). • *Social control of children in Europe in the 1500s and 1600s and in early America* (e.g. state and local control; treating children like all other dependent persons; child labor, including binding out and apprenticeship systems; family responsibility and limiting public funding; harsh parenting practices; religious morality; early youth welfare and correctional institutions, such as houses of refuge and facilities styled after English bridewells; public reprimands and warnings; fines; whippings; brandings; placements in stocks or pillories; banishment; capital punishment for a variety of infractions). • *Children and family in the 1800s* (e.g. developments in hybrid public and private agencies to provide assistance to different groups of children, including early juvenile welfare and correctional institutions, such as houses of refuge; non-institutional placements, called *placing out;* probation; and reform, industrial, and training school).
Early juvenile court	• *Antecedents/social context prompting the juvenile court movement* (e.g. prolongation of childhood and concerns about the moral socialization of young persons perceived to be in need; shift from an agricultural to an industrial economy, and from a rural to an increasingly urban society). • *The parens patriae era from 1899 to 1965* (e.g. retrofitting developing juvenile courts with a complaint system, broad and exclusive jurisdiction up to at least the age of majority, chancery-style proceedings, confidential records and private hearings, detention, probation, and psychiatric clinic services; handling mothers' petitions from the 1910s to 1930).

Social construction of childhood and adolescence, the government, and the politics concerning youths	• *Early twentieth century* (e.g. emergence of *youth* and *adolescence* as distinct periods; extending childhood through Progressive Movement focus on child labor laws, compulsory education, socialization organizations and moral legislation, and the juvenile court; the precursor to family–child welfare such as family foster care, and other solutions to large orphanages and other residential institutions for children). • *Depression era* (e.g. first national youth policy in the form of the National Youth Administration and the de facto youth policy of World War I military mobilization). • *Post-World War II era* (e.g. commitment to high-school graduation, steep decrease in job availability for those without a high school diploma; urbanization and job discrimination; suburbanization, deindustrialization, technological advancement, and globalization). • *1960s and 1970s: liberalism era* (e.g. major youth participation in the civil rights movement, urban violence and militant race-based groups, Vietnam War, lowered voting age, delinquency prevention and the war on poverty, progressive and conservative Supreme Court decisions concerning children and youth in the 1960s and 1970s, respectively). • *Late-twentieth century* (e.g. changes in economic, educational, family structure; violent crime increases in the 1970s and 1980s, particularly for minority youths of low socioeconomic status; public cry for tougher law enforcement and criminal justice, which disproportionately affected poor, minority youths; educational requirements for jobs continued to rise while the availability of good jobs decreased; increase in immigrant youths; restrictions on welfare benefits). • *Looking forward* (e.g. policies for family socioeconomics, education and activities for the non-schooling hours, youths with psychosocial problems, and youths with involvement in crime).

(Continued)

Table 1.1 The Juvenile Court and Related Social-contextual Institutions and Policies (Continued)

Social institution or policy	Historical relevance to the juvenile court
Schools	• *Historic overlap between school and juvenile court* (e.g. early juvenile court reformers also interested in reforming child labor and education; the juvenile court conceived of as a type of social instruction for parents and children, and operated as an educator to the public about wayward and needy children; school attendance was a primary performance metric for the juvenile court). • *Referrals from schools to the juvenile court* (e.g. truancy and parental schools; deinstitutionalization of truants and other status offenders; distinct treatment of girls, often due to sexual activity concerns or gender-specific offending; within-school offending and violence, traditional school discipline strategies, children with disabilities and the advent of special education and accommodations, increased school security, in-school policing, and zero tolerance policies; and abuse and neglect). • *Juvenile court programs concerning community schooling* (e.g. school attendance disposition conditions; probation, social work, and court clinic; and court-created community schools and later classes as an alternative disposition option). • *Schooling while detained* (e.g. early reform and training schools, education in juvenile correctional facilities and complications). • *Return to public schools following release from custody and related complications.*
Systems of institutional care for youths with psychosocial problems	• *Child welfare* (e.g. home care situation prior to 1935; federal assistance program and deinstitutionalization from 1935 to 1962; reforms in federal policies and funding regarding home care from the 1960s to 1990s; types of placements, lengths of stays). • *Juvenile corrections* (e.g. deinstitutionalization situation and scientific treatment of delinquency from the 1900s to 1950s, situation concerning alternatives to training schools in the 1950s to 1970s, federal involvement in the 1970s to 2000s; census and length-of-stay data and facility counts over time; atmospheres of public versus private facilities; interstate variability versus a national vantage; gender and racial disparities).

	• *Mental health system* (e.g. increasing recognition of childhood mental disorders; general hospital mental health units; public and private psychiatric hospitals; residential treatment centers; hybrid inpatient/outpatient organizations; psychoactive drugs; diverse funding; differential service utilization by demographic factors). • *Substance abuse system* (e.g. detoxification and residential treatment in hospitals and private settings; processing of juvenile drug offenders in the juvenile justice system versus the substance abuse system).
Public perceptions	• *Myths: beliefs held without knowledge of or concern for accuracy* (e.g. severity of delinquency in the past relative to today's delinquency; juvenile violence epidemic of the late 1980s and early 1990s; juveniles as chiefly responsible for the increase in violence in the United States between the 1980s and 1990s; juvenile super-predators; juvenile crime as the leading crime problem facing the United States; juvenile possession and use of firearms, juvenile perpetrated school shootings as a more recent crime wave, increasing violence among younger juveniles, the juvenile justice system is a failure or cannot handle serious, violent, and chronic juvenile offenders; the juvenile justice system currently prioritizes punitive approaches over rehabilitative ones; juvenile correctional systems are a failure in terms of recidivism; juvenile transfer to adult court will reduce juvenile delinquency; public support has waned for juvenile offender rehabilitation; nothing works with juvenile offenders; community-based programs for juvenile offenders are ineffective) • *Moral panic—exaggerated perception of a threat from a group or situation* (e.g. twentieth-century moral panics concerning juvenile delinquents in 1920s, 1932, 1946, 1954, 1977, late 1990s). • *Harsh–lenient pendulum in juvenile justice.*

Adapted chiefly from Elrod & Ryder (2011), Howell (2009), and Rosenheim, Zimring *et al.* (2002). See also Bartol & Bartol (2009), Chen & Salekin (2012), Dattilio & Fromm (2011), Gardner (2014), Grisso (2003a, 2013), Guerra, Hoge *et al.* (2008), Heilbrun, Goldstein *et al.* (2005), Howell, Lipsey *et al.* (2014), Jensen (2006), Otto, Borum *et al.* (2012), Salekin (2015a), and Weithorn (2006).

closed and sealed to avoid stigma; civil terminology and procedures were used to distinguish the juvenile system from the criminal justice system; dispositions were intended to be responsive to the offender rather than the offense; the category of "status offense" was created to expand the jurisdiction of the court; and the primary actors were to be clinicians and caseworkers rather than legal professionals.

Beginning around the early twentieth century, dependency courts began to extend their jurisdiction to include youths who committed crime, or non-criminal but unruly behavior (e.g. status offenses) (Weithorn, 2006). The underlying assumptions were that minors were (1) less responsible and blameworthy for their misconduct than were adult offenders due to lack of mature reasoning and self-control abilities, and (2) more amenable to intervention because they were still developing. These courts exercised substantial discretion over the remaining minor years for the children and adolescents who appeared before them, regardless of the initial grounds for jurisdiction. Their less adversarial approach and purportedly non-punitive means were used to justify their failure to provide adult-level procedural protections in the areas of due process, standards of proof, and participatory capacities (Weithorn, 2006).

The Illinois Juvenile Court Act of 1899 established the first juvenile court in the United States, in Cook County (Chicago), Illinois (Levick & Feirman, 2016). Among its designated purposes were enhancing the emphasis on rehabilitation, establishing a less formal setting for decision-making that was also separate from that used with adults, and limiting the consequences of juvenile misconduct (Zimring, 2005). The specialized juvenile court, and the larger juvenile justice system of which it was a part, expanded rapidly following the establishment of the first juvenile court. Nearly every state in the US had established a separate juvenile justice system by 1925 (Dattilio & Fromm, 2011; Snyder & Sickmund, 1999). Some of the differences in the newly-established juvenile courts were linguistic: crimes became "offenses," trials were "proceedings," youth were "adjudicated delinquent" rather than found guilty, and received "dispositions" rather than sentences (Shulman & Steinberg, 2016). Because the overwhelming priority of the juvenile system was rehabilitative, these courts featured (1) fewer due process protections, (2) "individualized" decisions with disposition determined by the needs of the youth rather than the nature of the offense, and (3) jurisdiction over "status" offenses (e.g. incorrigibility, unruliness) that would not have been illegal but for the age of the youth (Melton, Petrila *et al.*, 2007).

Although the original rehabilitative goals of the juvenile court were admirable, the reality of the system's operation over its first 65 years of existence was different for many justice-involved youth. They were subject to limited due process, lengthy detention, and inconsistent rehabilitation (Weithorn, 2006). These considerations played a prominent part in a series of United States Supreme Court decisions between 1966 and 1970, during what has been termed the rights reform or due process era (Grisso, 2003, 2013). Discussed in more detail in Chapter 2 (this volume), these decisions enhanced the due process protections applicable in juvenile court (*Kent v. United States*, 1966), the more specific rights to counsel, notice of charges, protection from self-incrimination, and confrontation (*In re Gault*, 1967), and proof beyond a reasonable doubt (*In re Winship*, 1970).

There was a legal and policy shift from a primarily rehabilitative emphasis before 1966 to a greater focus on retribution following *Kent*, *Gault*, and *Winship* (Slobogin, 2016). The growing emphasis on public safety was seen in US Supreme Court decisions establishing no right to a jury trial for juveniles (*McKeiver v. Pennsylvania*, 1971), no expectation that asking to speak with a probation officer rather than an attorney would suffice to halt interrogation following the provision of *Miranda* rights (*Fare v. Michael C.*, 1979), and no bar to preventive detention of a juvenile charged but not yet adjudicated on the grounds of public safety and protecting the juvenile from committing further offenses (*Schall v. Martin*, 1984). The growing emphasis on retribution was accompanied by increased emphasis on public safety during a period featuring punishment reform and shrinkage of the juvenile court (Grisso, 2003, 2013).

The impact of these changes became clearer during the 1980s and 1990s, as many states responded to higher rates of offending by expanding the list of covered offenses to include those that were less serious (Griffin, 2008).

Prior to 1970, the overwhelming majority of juveniles in criminal court arrived via judicial waiver (Griffin *et al.*, 2011). But expanded prosecutorial discretion (allowing the prosecutor to choose whether charges would be filed in the criminal or juvenile court), and more frequent passage of statutes specifying "direct filing" in the criminal court for certain offenses, yielded an increase in the number of juveniles handled in the adult system. That number is now estimated at more than 200,000 annually in the United States (Griffin *et al.*, 2011). With the increase in automatic and prosecutorial discretion transfer laws, there has been an accompanying decrease in judicial waiver evaluations but an increase in reverse transfer evaluations (Grisso, 2013). In light of the *Miller v. Alabama* (2012) and *Montgomery v. Louisiana* (2016) decisions, there will be need for a new juvenile evaluation informing courts deciding whether adolescents who received mandatory life-without-parole sentences following criminal convictions should receive a different sentence. This is discussed in Chapter 10 (this volume).

Because the emphasis in juvenile courts during the first half of the twentieth century was rehabilitative, the forensic evaluations conducted to assist in disposition decision-making were focused almost entirely on rehabilitative needs (Grisso, 2003). They were forensic evaluations in the sense that they were provided in a legal context; otherwise, they were essentially child-clinical/developmental evaluations that incorporated the limited knowledge base about delinquent youth. In contrast, requests for risk- and amenability-focused juvenile forensic evaluations began to increase gradually with the rights and punishment reforms within juvenile justice during the latter half of the twentieth century. Such referrals became more prominent in the 1980s, challenging the field to develop new psycho-legal constructs and corresponding assessment methods that would guide these evaluations in providing more relevant and empirically supported information to decision-makers (Grisso, 2003).

One noteworthy problem with the original juvenile court model: it was philosophically commendable but not empirically supported. The movement away from rehabilitation as the single goal of juvenile court was facilitated by the reality that there was little scientific support for the effectiveness of such rehabilitative efforts (Melton, Petrila *et al.*, 2007). In addition, the limited availability of community-based services for juveniles meant that many youth were placed in remote settings for indeterminate periods of time (DeMatteo, Wolbranski *et al.*, 2016). This dearth of data and services characterized the "rehabilitative" period up to 1966 and much of the post-1966 "rights and retribution" period following *Kent*, *Gault*, and *Winship*.

This began to change around 1990, when a number of important scientific developments in juvenile rehabilitation began to emerge. The "rediscovery of psychology" as applied to correctional classification (Andrews, Bonta *et al.*, 1990) described the early Risk-Need-Responsivity (RNR) model, which currently has significant theoretical and empirical application to the assessment of juvenile disposition and transfer (Hoge, 2008, 2012, 2016; Hoge & Andrews, 2010a, 2010b; Vincent, Guy *et al.*, 2012a). Building on the growing awareness of the contributions of particular risk factors to offending risk, and the associated risk-reduction value of interventions targeting those risk factors, researchers have focused on domains such as substance abuse (Chassin, Mansion *et al.*, 2016), education (Cornell & Heilbrun, 2016; Daly, Hildebrand *et al.*, 2016), and family (Henggeler, Schoenwald *et al.*, 2009). Research in these and other areas was most valuable when characterized by careful attention to "what works?" Gathering outcome data involving re-arrest and other justice involvement promoted the development of juvenile evaluations that could meaningfully address questions of risk and risk-relevant need on a more empirically-supported basis (Viljoen, Brodersen *et al.*, 2016).

Advances in forensic mental health assessment were also seen around this same time. Scholars (e.g. Grisso, 1986; Melton, Petrila *et al.*, 1987) advocated careful attention to the functional-legal capacities prescribed by law (what an individual must be able to do to satisfy the legal test), with implications for juvenile evaluations. Rather than assuming that youths should be evaluated for clinical treatment needs, there emerged a greater focus on the crime-related rehabilitation needs just described. These were needs that, if improved, would reduce the likelihood of further offending. These advances continued into the 1990s, culminating in a description of model practices in evaluating adolescents (*Understanding Adolescents: A Juvenile Court Training Curriculum*, Youth Law Center, Juvenile Law Center, & American Bar Association, 2000) and FMHA foundational principles applicable to a wide range of mental health evaluations (Heilbrun, 2001). Each of these early-2000 efforts was revised later in the decade with the strong interest and continuing developments in best practices in evaluating juveniles (National Juvenile Defender Center & Juvenile Law Center, 2009) and foundational principles of forensic mental health assessment (Heilbrun, Grisso *et al.*, 2009) driving the push for updates.

While the emphasis on public safety continued at the turn of the century, there were signs of growing interest in accountability of both offenders *and* courts. The federal Omnibus Crime Control and Safe Streets Act 2002 provided graduated sanctions for juvenile offenders, and for improved tracking and provision of alternatives to standard prosecution within the juvenile justice system. The expanding influence of organizations such as the MacArthur Foundation (Models for Change), the Annie E. Casey Foundation (Juvenile Alternatives to Detention), and the Council of State Governments (Justice Project) served to counterbalance a growing emphasis on public safety at the cost of rehabilitation (see Koocher & Kinscherff, 2016).

These influences presaged a third shift in legal policy—toward considering juveniles less culpable—that was seen in a series of US Supreme Court decisions beginning in 2005 (*Roper v. Simmons*, 2005; *Graham v. Florida*, 2010; *J.D.B. v. North Carolina*, 2011; *Miller v. Alabama*, 2012). The roots of this shift appeared even earlier, however, with the American Bar Association's Juvenile Justice Standards (ABA, 1980; see also Feld, 1988; Scott & Steinberg, 2008). This shift coincided with the evolving research on adolescent development and brain science, clarifying important developmental differences (Steinberg & Scott, 2003) that were directly applied by the Supreme Court on the issue of culpability.

More relevant to re-offense risk was research on desistance (Mulvey, Steinberg *et al.*, 2004) suggesting that only a very small percentage of adolescent offenders (5–6 percent) persisted into adulthood in significant criminal misconduct. But although delinquent-to-criminal persistence appears infrequent, the proportion of youth with behavioral health disorders in the juvenile justice system seems high. This prevalence has consistently been estimated at levels as high at 65–75 percent during the last 15 years (Shufelt & Cocozza, 2006; Wasserman, McReynolds *et al.*, 2010), including high rates of cognitive and learning disabilities (Quinn, Rutherford *et al.*, 2005) and trauma-related disorders (National Child Traumatic Stress Network, 2008; Zelechoski, 2016).

This third shift in the late 1990s and 2000s has been referred to as the developmental era, reflecting a shift in juvenile forensic evaluation that adopted a neo-paternalistic developmental view (Grisso, 2003, 2013; Melton, Petrila *et al.*, 2007). This developmental era arose after the increase in rates of youth violence (particularly homicides involving firearms) observed in the 1980s and into the 1990s (Redding, Goldstein *et al.*, 2005; see Howell, 2009) subsided, leaving harsher juvenile laws from the 1990s that appeared extreme to some. (This perception is apparently not held by the majority of the general public in the United States, however. See Howell, 2009; Redding, Goldstein *et al.*, 2005; Zottoli, Daftary-Kapur *et al.*, 2015.)

Developmental neuroscientific research of this era yielded new evidence on how the brains of adolescents are developing. It had earlier been believed that the structural and connectivity organization of the brain was mostly completed by around age 3, and adolescents were comparable to adults by about age 16. However, these views have been largely discarded. Data have demonstrated that there is a second important neurodevelopmental period, peaking around age 11 for girls and 12 for boys, in which the brain overproduces gray matter before undergoing a pruning process, which increases the brain's efficiency by strengthening neuronal connections while eliminating the lesser-used white matter tracts. Rather than relying on frontal lobe functioning, a portion of the brain that has strong associations with higher-level and more complex cognitions such as planning, reasoning, judgment, and behavior control, adolescents are believed to rely more heavily on parts of the brain related to emotions rather than logic. The parts of the brain associated with future-oriented planning, anticipation of consequences, judgment, impulsivity, and other characteristics relevant to moral culpability continue to mature through the early 20s (see Howell, 2009, for a detailed summary).

These data supported the view that adolescents differ from adults in legally relevant ways, particularly in their impulse control and other executive cognitive functions. This in turn raised the issue of regarding adolescents as less culpable for developmental reasons. This was the one important aspect of amicus briefs filed by the American Psychological Association in the US Supreme Court *Roper* case, and continued to influence the majority in *Graham, J.D.B., and Miller*. In particular, the Court endorsed three rationales for categorically invalidating application of the most extreme punishments to juveniles (Howell, 2009). The first is the evidence-based but also common-sense understanding that juveniles are more immature and irresponsible than adults. States already treat juveniles differently with respect to a variety of rights, including voting, jury service, and marriage. Second is the reality that youths are particularly susceptible to the influence and pressure of their peers, and have less control over their social environments. The third is that youth identity and personality are less fixed than they are in adults. The high court decisions, in turn, slowed the long-term American trend toward a more punitive approach to justice-involved adolescents.

Additional arguments for reform have included that juveniles are experientially immature but cannot be fully accountable for that, as society affords them few opportunities for occupying positions of responsible decision-making, and they face assorted challenges to their full and meaningful participation in the legal process (Bishop, 2009; Melton, Petrila *et al.*, 2007). Research has also demonstrated the higher rates of behavioral health disorders in justice-involved youth, underscoring the important point that developmental research focusing on adolescents in general must be considered in light of additional challenges experienced by many juveniles. Others argued for reform on more pragmatic grounds, including the high costs and effects of processing juveniles in the adult system.

Since 2000, there has been increasing attention to expanding the scope of juvenile forensic evaluations to include behavioral health and substance use needs as well as trauma and adversity history (Abbott & Barnett, 2015; Grisso, 2003). This attention has included several very detailed works (Grisso, Vincent *et al.*, 2005; Kessler & Kraus, 2007; see also Ribner, 2002). Not only was there a high rate of mental health disorders among justice-involved youths, but that rate also seemed to be rising (Grisso, 2003).

The Crossover Youth Practice Model (CYPM) (Abbott & Barnett, 2015) defines relationships among influences such as childhood poverty, maltreatment (abuse and neglect), trauma, mental health, substance use, and delinquent behavior. It specifies that any youth who experiences maltreatment and engages in delinquency is a *crossover youth*. These youths may have *dual involvement*–contact with both the child welfare and juvenile justice systems. Some youths' involvement may be as a participant in formal court proceedings, termed *dual adjudication* within the model. From a systems perspective, crossover youths may experience involvement or adjudication within numerous systems, including behavioral health, juvenile justice, education, child welfare, and low-income social health care. The model recommends that systems collaborate and share information at all levels throughout case processing, assisted by the execution of consent forms, and that mental health and substance use professionals be involved in multidisciplinary team meetings to facilitate assessment, coordinated intervention planning, and evidence-based treatment interventions for youths' mental health and substance use needs, including trauma-informed and gender-specific practices and services.

A fourth wave of legal policy and practice has been proposed. As part of what they call "preventive justice," Slobogin & Fondacaro (2011) suggest that the next major priority for the juvenile justice system should involve reducing and managing public safety risk presented by juveniles. This proposal would drastically reduce or eliminate transfer, on the grounds that retribution (the strongest justification for treating juvenile offenders as adults) does little to improve public safety, but that capitalizing on advances in risk assessment and improvements in empirical support for juvenile interventions to reduce offense risk does. This, they argue further, is best accomplished within the juvenile system and through enhancing the use of community-based interventions and providing rehabilitation that is narrowly focused on reducing criminogenic risk. This proposal is consistent with two contemporary trends in evidence. First, the advances in risk–need assessment with juveniles have been considerable; it can now be done with strong empirical support (DeMatteo, Wolbransky *et al.*, 2016). Second, there is a firmly-established body of evidence showing that rehabilitation of certain kinds (Multisystemic Therapy, Functional Family Therapy, and Multidimensional Treatment Foster Care) provided to juveniles in the community is effective in reducing re-offense risk, controlling costs, and providing less disruption in family and educational contexts (Henggeler, 2016).

This proposal for preventive justice is a valuable perspective that will inform the discussion in this book. If the frequency of transfer is reduced, it seems likely that public safety would be enhanced through more effective community-based interventions that reduce risk. But the areas of risk, treatment needs and amenability, and sophistication-maturity would be important even under a substantially altered juvenile system prioritizing preventive detention. Accordingly, we anticipate that much of the material presented in this book would remain relevant even if the juvenile system were operated differently.

THE CONTEMPORARY JUVENILE SYSTEM: SALIENT ISSUES

In this section, we provide an overview of important considerations in the contemporary juvenile system that will be incorporated into much of the discussion throughout this book.

MULTICULTURAL CONSIDERATIONS

The problem of continuing racial and ethnic bias in the juvenile justice system is troubling (McPherson, 2012). Youth who are white enter the juvenile justice system in response to unlawful behavior at lower rates than do youth who are minorities (Stagman & Cooper, 2010). This is particularly true for youth who come from families with lower incomes. This raises three important points. First, legal and mental health professionals should be aware of this larger trend and be determined to make decisions and conduct evaluations, respectively, with careful attention to the enumerated criteria that are appropriate for these tasks (McPherson, 2012). Second, those who work with justice-involved youth should be culturally competent—aware of important values, trends, and practices in families and communities in all youth but particularly those minorities who are overrepresented in the juvenile justice system. Third, it would be valuable to expand the availability of preventive (Rich, Harris *et al.*, 2016) and diversionary services to those at risk for justice involvement due to trauma, minority status, low incomes, or some combination of these influences.

International perspectives (see Chapter 11, this volume) may also influence change in the US juvenile justice system. Broader sources of authority on children's rights (e.g. the United Nations Convention on the Rights of the Child) and the experience of other counties in addressing the problem of juvenile offending (Jensen & Jepsen, 2006; Junger-Tas & Dünkel, 2009; Rosenheim, Zimring *et al.*, 2002) will be discussed in greater detail in Chapter 11.

ETHICAL AND LEGAL ISSUES

There are numerous ways in which the evaluation of juvenile transfer and disposition are complicated by ethical and legal considerations. These are addressed throughout this book. They include the impact of the assessment on the judicial process, confidentiality/informed consent, and assessment quality and integrity (Hoge, 2008). Complications include the improper consideration of risk–need information by decision-makers at criminal sentencing (e.g. if a youth is assessed for transfer or reverse transfer, but subsequently convicted in criminal court), ensuring compliance with legal privilege and ethical confidentiality standards (which differ depending on whether the evaluation is court-ordered or attorney-requested), and questions about whether such evaluation material should ever be shared beyond the immediate context in which it was requested (Hoge, 2012). General and specialized ethical guidelines developed by professional associations (e.g. the American Academy of Psychiatry and the Law, the American Bar Association, the American Psychological Association, the American Psychiatric Association) can provide helpful guidance to evaluators on such questions.

Referrals may call for multiple questions to be answered by a single evaluation (e.g. transfer and disposition). Consequently, forensic evaluators need to know the pertinent laws in the jurisdiction(s) in which they practice so that they focus on all of the relevant issues in their assessments (Dupée, 2002).

These complications affect youths, their families, those who would be victims of future offending, and our society more broadly. When forensic evaluators perceive that juvenile justice practice is harming such individuals unnecessarily, they must consider whether this should be addressed with referring parties or decision-makers—or whether evaluators should decline to provide such services unless the harmful practice is revised (Grisso, 2013; McPherson, 2012).

BEHAVIORAL HEALTH

Juveniles with certain kinds of behavioral health disorders (e.g. neurodevelopmental problems such as attention-deficit hyperactivity disorder, other executive dysfunctions, intellectual developmental disorders, and specific learning disorders; post-traumatic stress disorder and complex trauma; conduct disorder and other disruptive disorders of childhood; and childhood psychopathy) are more likely to become involved with the juvenile justice system (Weithorn, 2006). This is due in part to overlapping populations in children's mental health and juvenile justice contexts, which results from shared risk factors, unmet rehabilitation needs, and inconsistent use of legal leverage to mandate treatment (Melton, Petrila *et al.*, 2007; Shoenberg, 2012). It has been suggested that the number of justice-involved juveniles with significant behavioral health problems increases when there is limited availability of behavioral health services for youths in the community (Weithorn, 2006).

The integration of behavioral health services into juvenile justice is not straightforward. There are conflicts between the goals and values of behavioral health versus juvenile justice, centering generally around the promotion of individual wellbeing versus justice more broadly. But there are also converging values: avoiding deceit, exploitation and harm; competence; respect for persons; and accuracy, honesty, and informed consent. In some instances, forensic psychology ethics guidelines promote accommodating legal values, such as affirmatively acknowledging competence and evaluation limitations, specifying the factual bases underlying opinions, generally avoiding service provision until a litigant has legal representation, and minimizing reliance on inadmissible information (Melton & Kimbrough-Melton, 2006).

Relative to traditional clinical assessments, transfer and disposition evaluations have a broader scope, considering the numerous influences that contribute to risk, need, amenability, and sophistication-maturity. To offer realistic recommendations, however, the forensic evaluator must be aware of the availability of services in the community and regionally, not just the range of options that have been described in the literature (e.g. Heilbrun, Goldstein *et al.*, 2005). Forensic evaluators must also be careful in making recommendations regarding family and neighborhood conditions, as these may be (1) influenced by legal and moral opinions properly in the province of the legal decision-maker, (2) subject to considerable error, and (3) often beyond the control of the court (Melton & Kimbrough-Melton, 2006).

The interpretation of behavioral health and criminogenic findings from juvenile evaluations is particularly challenging because of developmental influences. This is discussed in some detail throughout this book. Among the developmental factors that must be considered are the influence of physical development on others' (e.g., legal decision-makers, peers) perceptions of a youth, peer influences, the role of independence-seeking and identity-formation tasks, intellectual functioning, knowledge and skills, and the anticipated trajectories of antisocial conduct over time as youths age (Dupée, 2002). Developmental considerations also complicate the interpretation of neuropsychological assessment results, for reliability and validity reasons, in forensic evaluations of transfer and disposition (McPherson, 2012). Recently, brain development research has had an increasing impact on juvenile justice policy (Shoenberg, 2012).

CONTEMPORARY JUVENILE JUSTICE: AN OVERVIEW

A number of sources provide overviews of the wide range of available statistics on trends in juvenile justice (e.g. Bartol & Bartol, 2009; Chen & Salekin, 2012; Godwin & Helms, 2002; Grigorenko, 2012; Howell, 2009; Howell, Lipsey *et al.*, 2014; Krisberg & Wolf, 2005; Marsh, 2007; Otto, Borum *et al.*, 2012; Parker, Negola *et al.*, 2008; Williams, Tuthill *et al.*, 2008; Woolard, Vidal *et al.*, 2015). These are generated from both official data (e.g. concerning arrests) and unofficial data (e.g. elicited via self-report methods). Examples of both domains and sources may be seen in Table 1.2. Acquiring contextual knowledge from different sources and datasets is challenging but important in providing the kinds of evaluations we discuss in this book. Among the cautions suggested in association with reviewing such data are awareness that: (1) large percentage increases may actually reflect small absolute increases; (2) timeframes affect outcome rates; (3) it is inadvisable to select the lowest point in a data series as the basis for comparison; and (4) there are differing limitations and interpretive caveats for the various sources of available data.

Table 1.2 Example Sources of Juvenile Justice Statistics Relevant to Juvenile Evaluations

- Numerous data sources compiled in the Office of Juvenile Justice and Delinquency Prevention's interrelated Statistical Briefing Book (n.d.) website, Compendium of National Juvenile Justice Data Sets (n.d.) website, and Juvenile Offenders and Victims reports (e.g. Sickmund & Puzzanchera, 2014) address topics including the following (with results often stratified by demographic factors):
  - characteristics of juveniles, justice-involved or not;
  - juvenile as victims;
  - juveniles as offenders and law enforcement;
  - structure and process of the juvenile justice system and juveniles in court (see also the National Center for Juvenile Justice (n.d.) and its Juvenile Justice Geography, Policy, Practice, and Statistics website for additional useful information about transfer and disposition);
  - juvenile dispositions (community supervision and corrections, including reentry and aftercare);
  - individual state juvenile and justice profiles.
- The National Gang Center's National Youth Gang Survey (n.d.) website addresses topics including:
  - prevalence and extent of the issue;
  - demographics; and
  - gang-related offenses.
- Other useful resources for locating juvenile justice data (e.g. non-governmental data addressing the aforementioned topics as well as other topics) are the Office of Justice Program's National Criminal Justice Reference Service website (specifically, the Juvenile Justice topic section; n.d.) and the National Archive of Criminal Justice Data (n.d.) website, the latter being maintained at the University of Michigan.

In its present form, the *juvenile justice system* is a set of institutions that make serial and interrelated decisions regarding state intervention into the lives of youth. It includes the police, the juvenile courts, their intake and probation staffs, the attorneys for the state and for the child (and sometimes his or her parents), juvenile detention centers, juvenile correctional facilities, and social agencies that accept youth in placement following disposition and order of the juvenile court. Each group has a particular set of responsibilities and expectations. They operate in a climate in which other child-service agencies, such as schools, claim an important share of public attention and public resources, and in a political environment in which the views of citizens and the attention of mass media contribute to public perception and political influence (Rosenheim, 2002).

Juvenile court referrals consist primarily of delinquency and status offense cases, and three times more males than females. There is some relationship between the volume of court referrals and the size of the youth population at risk at any given time, although there is more variability in crime rates than in population shifts (Rosenheim, 2002). The decision points along the juvenile justice continuum have been summarized as follows:

- approximately 20 percent of all police stops result in the arrest of a juvenile;
- approximately 70 percent of juvenile arrestees are referred to juvenile court;
- approximately 50 percent of juvenile court referrals are resolved by intake staff and prosecutors without filing a formal petition;
- a sizable portion of the remaining cases are dismissed in court;
- a very small number of cases will be transferred to criminal court;
- the remaining cases result in a finding of delinquency via entrance of a guilty plea or after an adjudicatory hearing;
- these cases are disposed of through:
  - continuance and eventual dismissal without entering a formal disposition or order;
  - placement on probation;
  - orders to pay restitution, perform community service, or attend counseling; and
  - occasional orders for placement (to public or private agencies) or commitment to a juvenile correctional facility.

(Rosenheim, 2002)

Other data suggest that about 20 percent of all juvenile justice system participants are detained pretrial, 60 percent of all delinquency cases are referred by law enforcement to the juvenile courts, and two-thirds of all juvenile court referrals result in delinquency adjudications (Howell, Lipsey *et al.*, 2014).

A fundamental difference between the juvenile justice system and adult criminal justice system is the former's focus on rehabilitation and the latter's prioritization of retribution to promote law-abiding behavior. In addition, juvenile courts are civil courts. Historically they were meant to be non-adversarial, fact-finding, and informal in terms of rights and process. They are presided over by judges who consider extralegal factors bearing on delinquency (e.g. family conditions), societal interests, child development principles, and the best interest of the child. Different terminology is used (e.g. delinquency versus guilt, dispositions rather than sentences). They tend to involve mental health professionals, childcare specialists, and social workers (Howell, 2009).

Juvenile justice involvement is sometimes assumed to have only minor consequences in the life of an individual because juvenile records are protected. This assumption is not accurate. A recent 50-state review concluded that most states have insufficient confidentiality and sealing/expungement provisions to adequately protect juveniles from the harm that can result if delinquency records are revealed (Juvenile Law Center, 2014a, 2014b). Such harm can include problems for youths in obtaining housing, receiving public benefits, being admitted into and funding higher education, serving in the military, and obtaining employment (Juvenile Law Center, 2014a, 2014b). Although a community-protection rationale has been offered for retaining and sharing such information, public safety can actually be impeded if rehabilitation opportunities are limited through disclosure of such information. In recognition of these problems, the American Bar Association's House of Delegates unanimously adopted the Model Act Governing the Confidentiality and Expungement of Juvenile Delinquency Records (American Bar Association, 2015).

Mental health professionals who conduct transfer and disposition evaluations fit into this system in one of three ways. They may be jurisdiction employees responsible for a juvenile court's evaluation needs (court clinic model), employees of an organization under contract to provide court evaluations (community mental health model), or private practitioners who provide evaluations to courts and attorneys as requested in exchange for a fee (private practice model) (Chapman, 2012). In addition, mental health professionals employed by state or private juvenile corrections agencies to provide assessment and treatment services are also frequently involved in post-adjudication court hearings and agency decision-making (e.g. about treatment progress and changes in placement and supervision) (Grisso, 2013).

ROLES OF COMMITMENT, TRANSFER, AND REVERSE TRANSFER IN THE JUVENILE SYSTEM

Three kinds of jurisdiction have been exerted historically by the juvenile court: act jurisdiction over those committing crimes before age 18, dispositional jurisdiction over those adjudicated guilty up to age 21, and transfer jurisdiction over those over age 14 or 15 (Slobogin, 2016). Many states have changed age requirements, lowering the maximum age for juvenile jurisdiction over acts and disposition, and also lowering the minimum age for transfer jurisdiction (Redding & Mrozoski, 2005). In 16 states, for example, the lower age limit for transfer is 14, while another 21 states have no lower age limit for certain offenses (OJJDP, 2012).

The criteria that typically apply to legal judgments on juvenile disposition, transfer, and reverse transfer have included re-offense risk, treatment needs and amenability, and sophistication-maturity—sometimes aggregated under the broad rubric of "treatment amenability." These appear to be derived from multiple sources, including the original rehabilitative ideals of the 1899 juvenile court, the US Supreme Court decisions in the 1960s and 1970s, the American Bar Association (1982) Juvenile Justice Standards Project, and public concern about juvenile crime in the 1980s and 1990s (Melton, Petrila *et al.*, 2007). The term "treatment" may be misleading to behavioral health professionals who consider symptom reduction and improved global functioning to be the main goals. Four particularly important questions regarding amenability to treatment in juvenile justice have been posed as follows: (1) What are the characteristics of the youth that are important? (2) Which among these must change?

(3) What interventions could change them? (4) If these interventions are provided, how likely is such change to occur? (Grisso, 1998). Seen in this light, "treatment" in the juvenile justice system should be conceptualized broadly to include domains such as educational, vocational, family, peers, and leisure time, with the primary goal of improved functioning that is directly related to reduced re-offense risk (Kinscherff, 2016). Discussion of "treatment" in this book will almost always refer to these broader domains and re-offense-relevant outcomes.

Disposition and transfer have both been part of the process since the inception of the juvenile system. Transfer to the adult system was rare and almost always at the discretion of the court prior to 1970. Since then, however, states have added two mechanisms facilitating the movement of juveniles into criminal court. These mechanisms are *automatic transfer* (in which a statute specifies specific charges that are filed directly in criminal court for youth of a certain age) and *prosecutorial discretion* (allowing prosecutors to decide whether charges will be filed initially in criminal or juvenile court) (Griffin, Addie *et al.*, 2011). Paralleling the rise of violent offending among juveniles, the number of transfers via judicial waiver peaked in 1994 and decreased by about 35 percent as of 2007. This decrease may be smaller than it appears, however, since other transfer mechanisms—prosecutorial discretion and statutory exclusion implemented during this period in many states—may have initially placed juveniles in criminal court, so they were not subject to judicial waiver. This means that the 9/1,000 (about 1 percent) of cases transferred in 2007 via judicial waiver may underestimate the number of juveniles who are treated as adults (Griffin, Addie *et al.*, 2011).

STATUS OFFENDERS

Reviews of the juvenile justice system often include discussion of status offenders (Melton, Petrila *et al.*, 2007). Because a status offense is illegal only because it was committed by a minor (Elrod & Ryder, 2011), it cannot be the basis for juvenile transfer to adult court—the act would not be unlawful in the adult system. However, such offenses are typically included in a youth's juvenile history. To ensure appropriate use of these offenses as part of such history, a brief review of status offenses and offenders is useful.

A large number of youths are brought before the juvenile court through status offense jurisdiction. (This is sometimes called "children in need of supervision" or "person in need of supervision.") Common status offenses include incorrigibility, unruliness, and truancy. Research has indicated that status offenders are a heterogeneous group: some are also delinquent youths, some are exclusively and non-chronically involved in status offenders, and a few are chronic status offenders. Certain groups of status offenders appear to have social and psychological needs that are more pronounced than in the general population of juvenile delinquents.

As in delinquency, the basis of status offense jurisdiction is the *parens patriae* doctrine. Consequently, it has been suggested that juvenile courts have traditionally found little reason or practical utility in distinguishing status offenders from delinquent offenders (Elrod & Ryder, 2011). *Parens patriae* arguments in favor of status offense jurisdiction include: (1) the potential for antisocial youth conduct to escalate into delinquency; (2) enforcing compulsory school laws and parental exercises of authority; (3) facilitating access to and overseeing treatment services; (4) the unique needs of some status offenders relative to delinquent youths; and (5) carrying out the juvenile court's historic mission to advance children's best interests. On the other hand, some (e.g. Melton, Petrila *et al.*, 2007) have raised concerns that status offense jurisdiction too often involves quasi-punishment (e.g. restrictive dispositions, referral to ineffective juvenile justice services) for children who are often different from non-status juvenile offenders, embroiled in family dysfunction and conflict, and maltreated. Youth victims of abuse and neglect may be detained on status offense charges because no alternative emergency placement is available. Similarly, status offense petitions may be misused to access services for a child and the child's family. Juvenile court jurisdiction may be more properly invoked via child protection petitions in many cases, and adequate investment in child welfare agency staffing and services may limit the need for juvenile court jurisdiction. Critics of status offense jurisdiction have advocated its elimination, relying on a number of arguments that are summarized in Table 1.3. It has been recommended that forensic mental health evaluators involved in the diversion or disposition of status offenders focus especially on issues of family dysfunction, and identify available extra-familial resources for reducing conflict at home and school (Melton, Petrila *et al.*, 2007).

Table 1.3 Critical Arguments Against Status Offense Jurisdiction

1. The language of status offenses statutes is often vague.
2. Status offense jurisdiction often raises concerns about equal protection and the ban on cruel and unusual punishment.
3. The assumption that non-treated status offending will escalate to delinquent behavior is not well supported.
4. There is limited evidence that juvenile courts are efficacious in improving the circumstances of and outcomes for status offenders.
5. Social agencies are better equipped to deal with the problems of status offenders.
6. Institutional placements are appropriate only for a violation of the criminal law.
7. Youths held to a higher standard of conduct than adults may come to lose respect for the law.
8. Labeling may lead to antisocial identity development.
9. Interfamily problems are not particularly amenable to juvenile court intervention, and such over-intervention often weakens parental responsibility.
10. Since juvenile courts often lack resources and expertise; they are likely to prove ineffective, and will therefore be likely to utilize coercive strategies.
11. Schools and social agencies might avoid responsibility for developing solutions for family and community problems.
12. Poor and female children are disproportionately impacted by status offense laws.
13. Status offenders are assigned undue burden and responsibility when adults (e.g. parents, guardians, school personnel) often are partially responsible for the development of the problematic behavior.
14. A status offender may experience removal from the home and placement in detention, foster care, or some other out-of-home setting as punitive regardless of whether the stated purpose is protection or correction.

Adapted from Elrod & Ryder (2011).

In the early to mid-1970s, deinstitutionalization of status offenders started to occur in some states, and a nationwide movement was encouraged by the federal Juvenile Justice and Delinquency Prevention Act of 1974 and its progeny, which has used grant money to encourage states to divert status offenders from the juvenile justice system and avoid placing them in detention or adult correctional facilities. Some states abolished status offender institutionalization in response to lawsuits, while others passed legislation to facilitate deinstitutionalization. With calls from different directions to focus more on serious juvenile delinquents, juvenile courts in some jurisdictions have directed attention away from status offense jurisdiction. For instance, some have stopped accepting parental or school complaints as the sole basis for court intervention. Moreover, encouraged by sources such as the American Bar Association's Juvenile Justice Standards Project, which proposed to eliminate general juvenile court jurisdiction over status offenders, many juvenile justice practitioners have acknowledged the lack of resources and expertise for dealing with status offenders. Consequently, they have called for other agencies to play a larger role in responding to child and family problems in the community, and declined involvement with a status offender until he or she escalates to delinquent conduct. Many European countries, such as the Netherlands, Germany, and Sweden, do not recognize status offenses; the same is true for a few US states, such as Delaware and Maine.

However, juvenile courts in most American jurisdictions continue to exercise authority over status offenders, with nearly 151,000 status offense cases having been handled in 2005—an increase of nearly 30 percent since 1995 (Elrod & Ryder, 2011). Also, local practices have developed to continue status offense jurisdiction. These include referring status offenders to a secure mental health facility, developing low-security status-offender-only facilities, creating or awaiting delinquency jurisdiction, or using the contempt power to detain youth for failing to obey a court order rather than the original status offense. The latter strategy has been permitted by some state courts in some, typically extreme, circumstances, while other jurisdictions have rejected it altogether.

THE IMPORTANCE OF FORENSIC MENTAL HEALTH ASSESSMENT

There are different ways in which forensic mental health professionals involved in juvenile transfer and disposition proceedings can influence legal and public policy (Grisso, 2000; Salekin, 2015a). Forensic mental health evaluators who use best-practice approaches in their reports and testimony can favorably influence how courts apply legal standards. They can help ensure that important considerations are not overlooked, for example by offering good evidence about rehabilitation and sophistication-maturity when courts might be primarily concerned with public safety (Chen & Salekin, 2012). This might be particularly applicable in decisions guided by additional statutes and for which there is great emphasis on public safety (e.g. juvenile sexual offenses) (McPherson, 2012).

Forensic mental health reports and testimony in juvenile transfer and disposition proceedings further help to individualize the juvenile justice system's response to youths. For instance, forensic mental health evaluators help appraise re-offense risk and associated rehabilitation needs, providing broader program- and system-level information as well as case-specific evidence. They can also help identify juveniles with behavioral health symptoms for whom treatment might also be provided on humanitarian grounds. Fortunately, many behavioral health services are likely to have a positive impact on both behavioral health symptoms and re-offense risk, so it is unnecessary to make sharp distinctions between mental health and criminogenic rehabilitation.

Accurate appraisal of amenability to rehabilitation can potentially increase the effective allocation of resources. But risk, need, and sophistication-maturity are all dynamic constructs, so multiple assessments over time in these areas may better serve to appraise them accurately than are impressions gathered at a single time.

Some evidence suggests that certain components of forensic evaluations have moderate predictive utility for transfer outcomes. One study described the following as most accurate in predicting whether youth were decertified: younger age, lower risk-need total score, fewer prior dispositions, and less antisocial personal characteristics and behavioral history (Marczyk, Heilbrun *et al.*, 2003). In the Netherlands, there is evidence that unstructured professional risk judgments are related to disposition decision-making in the following way. Low-risk youths received more detention dispositions while high-risk youths received more detention *with treatment* dispositions—suggesting that courts paid particular attention to specifying how risk might be reduced in the latter category (Lodewijks, 2008).

The emphasis on evidence-based practice has been applied in juvenile justice contexts. Measures and tools that apply particularly in the evaluation of transfer and disposition will be discussed throughout this book. Other broader measures, applicable to program-level development using evidence-based practice, have also been advocated. These include structured decision-making tools for assessing risk and need, intake screening, comprehensive treatment planning, classification, case management, quality assurance, information management, and performance for courts and agencies (Dishion, 2012; Howell, Lipsey *et al.*, 2014).

A MODEL FOR EVIDENCE-BASED JUVENILE JUSTICE

A comprehensive framework for evidence-based juvenile justice practice (Howell, 2009; Howell, Lipsey *et al.*, 2014) provides a useful model for juvenile forensic evaluators considering disposition recommendations. Incorporating psycho-social history, behavioral health assessment, and risk-need assessment, it includes prevention, early and immediate intervention, and behavioral health treatment for youths in primary prevention programs or secondary prevention programs encountered in diversionary contexts. It also includes youths who are formally adjudicated along a graduated sanctions continuum that includes intermediate sanctions, community confinement, secure residential placements, and aftercare. The model's stages can be applied to generating recommendations for services that are specific to the stage within the juvenile system, the needs of the youth, and the planning, implementation, and evaluation steps that will be necessary.

CONCLUSION

The juvenile system was developed distinctively from the larger criminal justice system in the attempt to rehabilitate adolescent offenders. During the period since the first appearance of a specialized juvenile court, there has been a growing emphasis on influences that extend beyond rehabilitation—particularly re-offense risk and sophistication-maturity—with such emphasis also consistent with greater due process protections for youth following US Supreme Court decisions in *Kent*, *Gault*, and *Winship*. To properly conduct a forensic mental health assessment on the issue of juvenile disposition, transfer, or reverse transfer, it is important to incorporate relevant law, science, ethics, and best practice standards. Our focus in this book incorporates these sources of authority into evaluations that can provide good evidence for legal decision-makers who consider risk, risk-relevant needs, amenability to treatment, and sophistication-maturity in their adjudication of justice-involved youth. Contemporary theory—in particular Risk-Need-Responsivity and Preventive Justice—will provide foundational support for the discussion of juvenile disposition, transfer, and reverse transfer in subsequent chapters.

CHAPTER TWO

Legal Context of Transfer, Reverse Transfer, and Disposition

This chapter describes the laws—legal cases, statutes, and constitutional provisions—that are relevant to juvenile transfer, reverse transfer, and disposition decisions. We focus on both procedural due process, which involves the mechanical aspects of the law and the manner in which cases proceed through the juvenile justice system, and substantive due process, which refers to the content of the legal rights that have been provided to juvenile offenders (Marsh, 2007). We begin by discussing several influential cases from the Supreme Court of the United States that have shaped the substantive and procedural aspects of transfer and disposition decisions, including several recent cases that recognized the distinctiveness of adolescents in certain legal contexts. We also discuss several specific aspects of the juvenile justice system, including juvenile court jurisdiction and the procedural and substantive aspects of transfer, reverse transfer, adjudication (for context), and disposition. Finally, we discuss the role of forensic mental health professionals in the processing of juvenile offenders.

SUPREME COURT JURISPRUDENCE

The development of the first juvenile court in Cook County, Illinois in 1899 marked a paradigm shift in how the law handled juvenile offenders. As described in Chapter 1 (this volume), juvenile courts were based on the principle of *parens patriae*—the state acting as a parent—and the juvenile court was developed with an emphasis on rehabilitation rather than punishment. In practice, however, juvenile courts often provided limited due process rights and very little rehabilitative intervention (Weithorn, 2006). Beginning in the mid-1960s, juvenile courts began providing more due process protections to juvenile offenders. However, the enhanced due process protections were accompanied by a philosophical, legal, and policy shift from a primarily rehabilitative orientation to a more retributive focus (Grisso, 2013; Slobogin, 2016). The shift in focus of juvenile courts and in the juvenile justice system more broadly is reflected in several key decisions from the Supreme Court of the United States that impacted juvenile offenders.

The Supreme Court has addressed the rights of juveniles and the functioning of the juvenile justice system in numerous cases over the past 50 years. Although the Supreme Court has held in a series of cases that juveniles are entitled to many (but not all) of the procedural and substantive due process rights that are afforded to adults, it has also held, particularly more recently, that adolescents are fundamentally different from adults. As will be discussed, these differences have important implications for the rights and available dispositions of juvenile offenders.

RIGHTS OF JUVENILE OFFENDERS

The first notable case in the modern era of the juvenile justice system was *Kent v. United States*, which was decided by the Supreme Court in 1966. In *Kent*, a 16-year-old juvenile offender, Morris Kent, challenged the transfer of his case to criminal court and his subsequent conviction on the grounds that he was not provided with adequate due process rights prior to the transfer. After a series of appeals, the Supreme Court overturned Kent's transfer, holding that juvenile courts cannot act with procedural arbitrariness and engage in indiscriminate decision-making in the exercise of their *parens patriae* power (Loving & Patapis, 2007). The Supreme Court highlighted several due process deficiencies in Kent's case, including that Kent was transferred to criminal court without receiving a hearing, without access to an attorney, without access to the records that were considered by the juvenile court, and without a statement of reasons for the transfer decision. In a highly influential appendix to the majority opinion, the Supreme Court suggested that juvenile court judges use the following eight criteria when determining whether the court should waive jurisdiction and transfer the juvenile to criminal court:

1. The seriousness of the alleged offense to the community and whether the protection of the community requires waiver.
2. Whether the alleged offense was committed in an aggressive, violent, premeditated or willful manner.
3. Whether the alleged offense was against persons or against property, greater weight being given to offenses against persons especially if personal injury resulted.

4. The prosecutive merit of the complaint, i.e. whether there is evidence upon which a Grand Jury may be expected to return an indictment (to be determined by consultation with the United States Attorney).
5. The desirability of trial and disposition of the entire offense in one court when the juvenile's associates in the alleged offense are adults who will be charged with a crime in the US District Court for the District of Columbia.
6. The sophistication and maturity of the juvenile as determined by consideration of his home, environmental situation, emotional attitude and pattern of living.
7. The record and previous history of the juvenile, including previous contacts with the Youth Aid Division, other law enforcement agencies, juvenile courts and other jurisdictions, prior periods of probation to this Court, or prior commitments to juvenile institutions.
8. The prospects for adequate protection of the public and the likelihood of reasonable rehabilitation of the juvenile (if he is found to have committed the alleged offense) by the use of procedures, services, and facilities currently available to the Juvenile Court.

(*Kent*, 1966, pp. 566–7)

The *Kent* decision is significant for at least three reasons. First, the Court explicitly recognized the importance of the transfer decision, which underscored the need for procedural rights. Juvenile offenders adjudicated in juvenile court could only be subject to certain dispositions, while juvenile offenders tried in criminal court could be subjected to punishments that far exceeded the age of majority (see del Carmen & Trulson, 2006). Second, *Kent* greatly enhanced the due process protections applicable in juvenile court, which provided juvenile offenders with a range of rights that was previously reserved for adult offenders. Prior to the *Kent* decision, very few states took steps to protect juvenile offenders from the arbitrariness of the transfer process in juvenile courts (del Carmen & Trulson, 2006). Third, *Kent* signified (albeit unofficially) the beginning of the end of the *parens patriae* approach. Juvenile courts were no longer viewed as being purely rehabilitative, and it was accepted from that time forward that juvenile courts were indeed adversarial in nature. The recognition that juvenile courts were adversarial forums was reflected in several Supreme Court decisions that followed *Kent*; the demise of the *parens patriae* approach followed shortly thereafter (see del Carmen & Trulson, 2006).

The Supreme Court's landmark decision in *In re Gault* in 1967 is perhaps the most important case regarding the rights of juvenile offenders. In *Gault*, the Supreme Court held that juvenile offenders in delinquency proceedings enjoy many of the same legal rights as adults in criminal court, including the right to an attorney, the right to remain silent, the right to notice of the charges, and the right to a full hearing on the merits of the case. *Gault* is properly viewed as a significant turning point regarding the rights of juvenile offenders because it essentially constitutionalized the juvenile justice process (Marsh, 2007). Although *Gault* provided considerable due process protections to juvenile offenders, it also implicitly reaffirmed that juvenile proceedings are inherently adversarial. With the incorporation of constitutional due process into the juvenile court proceedings, some have noted that the proceedings have become more similar—perhaps too similar—to the criminal process, with a noticeable loss in the previously non-adversarial nature of juvenile court proceedings; conversely, others have asserted that the procedural reforms have not changed the fundamental focus of juvenile courts (see Davis, 2016; del Carmen & Trulson, 2006).

Several subsequent decisions from the Supreme Court continued to diminish the differences between proceedings in juvenile court and criminal court. For example, three years after deciding *Gault*, the Supreme Court held in *In re Winship* (1970) that the standard of proof for delinquency adjudications in juvenile court is the same standard that is used for convictions in criminal court: beyond a reasonable doubt. In *Winship*, the Supreme Court recognized that juvenile courts, despite still being ostensibly rehabilitative, needed to provide juvenile offenders with fuller legal protection. As stated in *Gault* (1967), "civil labels and good intentions do not themselves obviate the need for criminal due process safeguards in juvenile courts" (p. 36).

Kent, *Gault*, and *Winship* marked efforts by the Supreme Court to provide heightened due process protections to juvenile offenders, with the Court providing juvenile offenders with many of the same rights as adult offenders. However, several Supreme Court cases that followed the 1970 *Winship* decision underscored the growing emphasis on public safety, which resulted in the imposition of certain limits on the rights of juveniles. For example, in *McKeiver v. Pennsylvania* (1971), the Supreme Court held that the Due Process Clause of the 14th Amendment of the United States Constitution did not guarantee juvenile offenders the right to a jury trial in delinquency adjudication proceedings. This was the first Supreme Court case after *Gault* to hold that juvenile offenders were not entitled to the same due process rights as adult offenders:

> We do not mean by this to indicate that the hearing to be held must conform with all of the requirements of a criminal trial or even of the usual administrative hearing; but we do hold that the hearing must measure up to the essentials of due process and fair treatment. (*McKeiver*, 1971, pp. 533–4; quoting *Kent v. United States*, 1966, p. 562)

In *McKeiver* (1971), the Supreme Court noted that juries are not necessary to ensure adequate fact-finding, and thus not a necessary element of due process, noting that providing for jury trials in juvenile courts would eliminate one of the remaining distinctions between juvenile delinquency hearings and criminal trials—a distinction that was tolerable to the Court.

> If the formalities of the criminal adjudicative process are to be superimposed upon the juvenile court system, there is little need for its separate existence. Perhaps that ultimate disillusionment will come one day, but for the moment we are disinclined to give impetus to it. (p. 551)

With that said, some jurisdictions (e.g. Oklahoma) provided a right to a jury trial at adjudicatory hearings, even if that right was not extended to disposition hearings (see "Juvenile Right to Jury Trial Chart," 2014, for a recent state-by-state listing).

While *Kent*, *Gault*, and *Winship* narrowed the differences between juvenile and adult proceedings, *McKeiver* recognized that constitutional due process requirements are not always the same for juvenile and adult offenders (see Slobogin, 2016). There were, however, limits on the due process distinctions the Supreme Court was willing to recognize. For example, in *Breed v. Jones* (1975), the Supreme Court held that it is a violation of the Double Jeopardy Clause of the 5th Amendment to try a juvenile offender in criminal court after his or her case has been adjudicated in juvenile court.

In *Schall v. Martin* (1984), the Supreme Court addressed the important question of whether a finding of probable cause permits juveniles to be detained without bail while waiting for an adjudicatory hearing. *Schall* involved the detention of a 15-year-old who was accused of committing a serious offense. The Supreme Court held that such detention was constitutional because it served the dual purposes of protecting both the juvenile and society from the dangers of pretrial crime. The Court also noted that the statute in question provided adequate procedural protections against unnecessary confinement. The Supreme Court subsequently upheld the constitutionality of the preventive detention of adult offenders in *United States v. Salerno* (1987), another example of how the Supreme Court has held that juvenile and adult offenders can be treated similarly.

More recently, in *J.D.B. v. North Carolina* (2011), the Supreme Court addressed whether age was a factor in determining whether a juvenile was in custody for *Miranda* purposes. The youth, aged 13, was questioned at school by the assistant principal, a school administrator, and a police investigator regarding several recent burglaries. J.D.B. was not given his *Miranda* rights prior to the questioning, and his legal guardians were not notified about the questioning. After he incriminated himself in the burglaries, J.D.B. was reportedly told that he was free to leave. The Supreme Court held that because a child's age can affect how a reasonable person in the suspect's position would perceive his or her freedom to leave, age is a factor that must be considered when determining whether an individual is in custody for *Miranda* purposes. *J.D.B.* is one of several recent Supreme Court cases that recognizes that juveniles are fundamentally different from adults.

DISPOSITION OF JUVENILE OFFENDERS

In recent years, the Supreme Court has addressed the constitutionality of various dispositions for juvenile offenders. The dispositions that have received the most attention—the death penalty and sentences of life without parole—have taken center stage in the Supreme Court's jurisprudence and drawn the most attention from legal scholars. The Supreme Court's decisions addressing both the death penalty and life without parole for juvenile offenders reflect the recognition that the differences between juveniles and adults make certain dispositions constitutionally inappropriate.

Death Penalty

The execution of offenders who committed murder while under the age of 18 has drawn considerable attention from courts and legal scholars over the past 40-plus years. Although capital punishment statistics indicate that executions of juvenile offenders were rarely carried out, it remained constitutionally permissible in many jurisdictions. Given the obvious finality of a death sentence and the growing national opposition to the death penalty, courts have grappled with whether such a disposition is appropriate for someone who committed murder before becoming an adult.

The Supreme Court addressed the constitutionality of executing juvenile offenders in several cases in recent decades, reaching different conclusions regarding whether such a punishment was constitutional. The Supreme Court's first opportunity to address the constitutionality of executing juvenile offenders was *Eddings v. Oklahoma* (1982). At the age of 16, Eddings shot and killed a police officer, and the juvenile court, which had initial jurisdiction over Eddings because of his age, granted the prosecution's motion to have the case transferred to criminal court. The youth was subsequently convicted of first-degree murder and sentenced to death. On appeal, the Supreme Court vacated Eddings' death sentence and remanded the case for a new sentencing hearing. The case was not reversed because of concerns about the constitutionality of executing juvenile offenders, however, but rather because the sentencing judge had refused to consider information regarding Eddings' background that could potentially have mitigated the death sentence.

In the modern era of the death penalty, which began in 1976 when the Supreme Court ended the four-year moratorium of capital punishment with its decision in *Gregg v. Georgia*, the first Supreme Court cases to directly address the constitutionality of executing juvenile offenders were decided several years after *Eddings*. In *Thompson v. Oklahoma* (1988), a four-member plurality of the Supreme Court held that imposing a death sentence on anyone who was under age 16 at the time of the offense was cruel and unusual punishment in violation of the 8th Amendment. In a theme that would continue for many years, Justice O'Connor asserted that the propriety of imposing a death sentence on offenders under age 16 should be left to the legislatures as opposed to the courts. One year later, in *Stanford v. Kentucky* (1989), the Supreme Court held via a five-member majority that executing offenders who were aged 16 or 17 at the time of the offense did not violate the 8th Amendment's prohibition against cruel and unusual punishment. In the aftermath of *Stanford*, the debate regarding the appropriateness of executing juvenile offenders moved from the courts to the legislatures (Davis, 2016).

The Supreme Court's decision in *Stanford* permitted the execution of juvenile offenders who were aged 16 or 17 at the time of the offense, and this remained a constitutionally permissible practice for over 15 years until the Supreme Court next addressed the constitutionality of executing juvenile offenders in *Roper v. Simmons* (2005). Christopher Simmons was tried as an adult, convicted of capital murder, and sentenced to death for murdering his neighbor when he was age 17. Following his sentence and several failed post-conviction relief efforts, Simmons filed a petition for state post-conviction relief based on the Supreme Court's then-recent decision in *Atkins v. Virginia* (2002), which had prohibited the execution of offenders who are intellectually disabled. Simmons argued that the same reasoning that led to the exclusion of offenders with intellectual disabilities from the death penalty, which focused on their general reduced culpability stemming from their relative cognitive deficits, also applied to juvenile offenders and the typical deficits they display relative to adults. On appeal, the Supreme Court of Missouri set aside Simmons's death sentence and resentenced him to life in prison without the possibility of parole. Dissatisfied with the Supreme Court of Missouri's decision, the Missouri Attorney General sought review of the case in the Supreme Court of the United States.

Given changes in the national legislative landscape and increasing opposition to the death penalty among the general public and several prominent organizations, the Supreme Court granted certiorari to address the issue it had decided 15 years earlier in *Stanford*—whether it is constitutionally permissible to execute an offender who was older than age 15 but younger than age 18 at the time of the murder. In a narrow 5–4 decision, the Supreme Court held that imposing the death penalty on offenders who were younger than age 18 at the time of the offense violated the 8th Amendment's ban on cruel and unusual punishment. Justice Kennedy (who earlier voted with the majority in *Stanford* to uphold the death sentence for offenders aged 16 or 17 at the time of the offense) was joined by Justices Stevens, Souter, Ginsburg, and Breyer in the majority decision. The Supreme Court relied on three factors in reaching its decision in *Roper*: (1) emerging evidence of a national consensus against capital punishment for those who were juveniles at the time they committed the otherwise qualifying offense (which is the factor that primarily convinced Justice Kennedy to vote against the juvenile death penalty); (2) international practices concerning juveniles and the death penalty, noting that the United States was the only developed country at that time to still sanction juvenile death sentences; and (3) the lesser culpability of juvenile offenders. The first two factors are commonly considered in 8th Amendment cases because the Supreme Court looks to evidence of evolving standards of decency that mark the progress of a maturing society, which is an 8th Amendment standard established in *Trop v. Dulles* (1958). The third factor, however, was explicit recognition that juveniles are fundamentally different to adults and, therefore, deserving of a lesser punishment for the same offense.

In terms of the lesser culpability of juvenile offenders, the Supreme Court in *Roper* highlighted three significant differences between juveniles and adults which demonstrated that juveniles could not be classified among those offenders who are most deserving of being executed: (1) juveniles lack maturity and have an underdeveloped sense of responsibility, which can lead to poor decision-making and behavior; (2) juveniles are more susceptible to negative influences and outside pressures, including peer pressure, which can affect their behavior; and (3) juveniles' characters are not yet fully formed, which suggests that they have a greater opportunity for rehabilitation. Of note, these are similar to the factors the Supreme Court considered when deciding *J.D.B. v. North Carolina* (2011). Given the resulting reduced culpability of juvenile offenders, the Supreme Court concluded that the primary penological justifications for the death penalty—retribution and deterrence—would not be served by executing those who were juveniles at the time of the index offense. The immediate effect of the *Roper* decision was that 72 offenders across 12 states who were awaiting execution for murders they committed as juveniles were removed from death row and resentenced to the harshest punishment available in that state, which was typically life without parole.

In reaching its decision in *Roper*, the Supreme Court relied on a good deal of social science research, which was offered to the Court in the form of amicus curiae briefs from several different organizations, including the American Psychological Association (APA). The APA's amicus brief, filed in support of Simmons, argued that developmentally immature decision-making combined with incomplete neurological development diminishes a juvenile offender's blameworthiness (Brief for Amicus Curiae of the American Psychological Association and Missouri Psychological Association, 2004). Therefore, according to the APA, executing juvenile offenders would not further the constitutional purposes of the death penalty.

In a strong dissent in *Roper*, Justice Scalia (joined by Chief Justice Rehnquist and Justice Thomas) asserted that the Supreme Court's decision simply reflected the moral judgment of the five-member majority.

He disagreed that a national consensus against juvenile capital sentencing existed, as fewer than half of the states with the death penalty at that time prohibited the sentence for juveniles (18 of 38 states), and only four states had banned it in the more than 15 years since *Stanford* had been decided. Justice Scalia also argued that the majority selectively picked the social science evidence that supported its position without explaining "why those particular studies are methodologically sound" (*Roper*, 2005, p. 617), and concluded that the conflicting social science research regarding juvenile development provided "scant support" for the majority's categorical prohibition against juvenile executions (*Roper*, 2005, p. 618). In a separate dissent, Justice O'Connor argued against a categorical age-based rule, advocating instead for a case-by-case approach in which sentencing juries would be required to give appropriate mitigating weight to the juvenile's youth and immaturity when deciding whether death is an appropriate sentence.

Life Without Parole

The Supreme Court's decision in *Roper v. Simmons* (2005) marked the beginning of a new era of Supreme Court jurisprudence in which the differences between juveniles and adults played an influential role in determining which dispositions are constitutionally appropriate for juvenile offenders. Some of the concerns relating to the execution of juvenile offenders—lack of maturity, susceptibility to peer pressure, and lack of a fully formed character—are also relevant when considering the constitutionality of sentencing a juvenile offender to life without parole. Several researchers and legal scholars have opposed life without parole sentences for juvenile offenders based on the developmental limitations associated with adolescence (e.g. Berkheiser, 2005; Feld, 2003), and lower courts have reached different conclusions about the constitutionality of life without parole sentences for juvenile offenders.

The Supreme Court has addressed the constitutionality of life without parole sentences for juvenile offenders in several recent cases. In *Graham v. Florida* (2010), the Supreme Court held that imposing a sentence of life without parole on an offender who was convicted of a non-homicide offense that was committed under age 18 constitutes cruel and unusual punishment in violation of the 8th Amendment. Of note, at the time *Graham* was decided, courts in several states had already prohibited sentences of life without parole for juvenile offenders. The Supreme Court based its decision on the lesser culpability of juvenile offenders, particularly in those cases in which the juvenile was not convicted of a homicide offense:

> It follows that, when compared to an adult murderer, a juvenile offender who did not kill or intend to kill has a twice diminished moral culpability. The age of the offender and the nature of the crime each bear on the analysis. (*Graham*, 2010, p. 69)

Following *Graham*, it was unclear if it was constitutional to sentence a juvenile offender to life without parole when the juvenile was convicted of a homicide offense. Fortunately, the Supreme Court resolved this issue two years after *Graham*. In *Miller v. Alabama* (2012), the Supreme Court held that a statutory scheme that requires a mandatory sentence of life without parole for an offender who was a juvenile at the time of the offense, even if it was a homicide offense, violates the 8th Amendment's prohibition against cruel and unusual punishment. As will be discussed more thoroughly in Chapter 10 (this volume), the Supreme Court's decision in *Miller* did not create an absolute ban on sentences of life without parole for juvenile offenders; instead, it held that life without parole sentences are unconstitutional if the sentence is mandatory rather than discretionary, even if the juvenile offender has been convicted of homicide. Unless the Supreme Court imposes a categorical ban on all life without parole sentences for juvenile offenders in a future case, *Miller* leaves open the possibility that some juvenile offenders can be constitutionally sentenced to life without the possibility of parole. The *Miller* decision, while not creating an absolute ban, observed that life without parole sentences imposed at the discretion of the court should be rare, which suggests that the Court perhaps sees little justification for such sentences.

Finally, the Supreme Court recently addressed the important question of whether the ban on mandatory life without parole established by the *Miller* decision applies retroactively to juveniles who received such sentences prior to the 2012 ruling. In the years following the *Miller* decision, several states had reached different conclusions about whether *Miller*'s ban should be applied retroactively. While several state courts held that *Miller* should be retroactive, the Supreme Court of Pennsylvania, for instance, held that *Miller*'s constitutional ban on mandatory life without parole sentences did not apply retroactively to cases that were final at the time *Miller* was decided (*Pennsylvania v. Cunningham*, 2013). However, in *Montgomery v. Louisiana* (2016) the Supreme Court held by a 6–3 decision that *Miller* applied retroactively and nullified all prior mandatory life without parole sentences for juvenile offenders. As a result of the *Montgomery* decision, offenders who received a mandatory sentence of life without parole for offenses they committed as juveniles must either be provided with a parole hearing or resentenced. The Supreme Court stated:

> Extending parole eligibility to juvenile offenders does not impose an onerous burden on the States, nor does it disturb the finality of state convictions. Those prisoners who have shown an inability to reform will continue to serve life sentences. The opportunity for release will be afforded to those who demonstrate the truth of *Miller*'s central intuition—that children who commit even heinous crimes are capable of change. (*Montgomery*, 2016, slip op., p. 21)

The Supreme Court's recognition of the malleability of juvenile offenders clearly influenced their decisions relating to capital punishment (*Roper*) and sentences of life without parole (*Graham*, *Miller*, and *Montgomery*).

Other Dispositions for Juvenile Offenders

The Supreme Court's recent jurisprudence relating to sentences of life without parole for juvenile offenders raises the question of whether extremely lengthy sentences that include the possibility of parole should also be considered unconstitutional. The essential question is whether lengthy prison terms that amount to de facto life sentences for juvenile offenders violate the United States Constitution (and specifically the 8th Amendment). Given the Supreme Court's recognition that juvenile offenders differ from their adult counterparts in important and fundamental ways, one could argue that de facto life sentences are inconsistent with the thrust of the Supreme Court's recent decisions. Some courts have apparently agreed with this idea. For example, an appellate case from California held that sentencing a 16-year-old offender to a period of incarceration from 84 years to life was unconstitutional because it constituted cruel and unusual punishment (*People v. Mendez*, 2010). The California court noted that its decision was not required by *Graham*, but that it was nonetheless guided by the principles articulated in *Graham*. Conversely, another California appellate case held that a sentence of 30 years to life for a juvenile convicted of a non-homicide offense was not the equivalent of a sentence of life without parole and was therefore constitutionally permissible (*People v. Perez*, 2013). More recently, the Supreme Court of Florida held that a lengthy prison sentence can be functionally equivalent to a sentence of life without parole and is therefore a violation of the 8th Amendment (*Gridine v. Florida*, 2015). Courts in several other states (e.g. Iowa, Missouri, Louisiana, Minnesota) have reached similar conclusions.

Finally, several courts have addressed the constitutionality of committing a juvenile offender until age 21 without the possibility of parole or another form of early release. This form of sentencing is available in several states (e.g. Illinois, Louisiana) and is sometimes referred to as "juvenile life," or life without parole until age 21 (Davis, 2016). We are not aware of any court decisions to date that have held such a sentencing scheme to be unconstitutional (cf. *In re Deshawn G.*, 2015; *State ex rel. D.Y.*, 2011).

JUVENILE COURT JURISDICTION

Jurisdiction involves the question of whether a particular court has the legal authority to decide a particular case. Jurisdictional questions often appear straightforward, but they can be deceptively complex. For a court to have proper authority to hear a case, the court must have both *subject matter jurisdiction*, which relates to the nature of the alleged offense (in criminal contexts) or wrongdoing (in civil contexts), and *personal jurisdiction*, which relates to various aspects of the parties involved in the case. A court's jurisdiction can be based on several factors, including the subject matter of the case or dispute, the location of the parties, the age of the offender, and the amount of money in controversy. Jurisdictional disputes are not uncommon in both civil and criminal contexts.

Many factors can be relevant in determining whether a specific court has jurisdiction over a particular case, but juvenile courts have jurisdiction over juvenile offenders based on only two: the age of the offender (which provides the court with personal jurisdiction) and the nature of the alleged offense (which provides the court with subject matter jurisdiction) (Marsh, 2007). If a case originates under the proper jurisdiction of the juvenile court, the court may have discretionary authority to either retain jurisdiction or transfer jurisdiction to criminal court (46 Am. Jur. 2d. *Juvenile Courts and Delinquent and Dependent Children* § 46, 2016). Of note, in locales that utilize exclusive jurisdiction, criminal courts do not have jurisdiction over a juvenile offender who is properly within the jurisdiction of the juvenile court unless a properly executed transfer has taken place (e.g. 46 Am. Jur. 2d. *Juvenile Courts and Delinquent and Dependent Children* § 46, 2016). However, in other locales, the juvenile court and criminal court can have concurrent jurisdiction (e.g. Davis, 2016). For example, some states provide concurrent jurisdiction based on the offender's age (typically older) or the nature of the offense (more serious) (Davis, 2016). Generally, however, juvenile courts have jurisdiction over offenders of a certain age who have committed certain types of offenses.

AGE

Juvenile proceedings based on acts of delinquency and status offenses, as opposed to juvenile dependency proceedings, apply to offenders above and below certain statutorily-defined ages. With respect to the minimum age for juvenile court jurisdiction, some states designate an age below which a child is presumed to be incapable of possessing the requisite intent to commit a delinquent act. Stated differently, these individuals may have committed an act that violates the law (*actus reus*), but they are considered to be legally incapable (which is often called *de jure* incompetence) of forming the intent (*mens rea*) that is a required element of the offense. Adolescents below this minimum age cannot be adjudicated delinquent (see Juvenile Justice Geography, Policy, Practice & Statistics [GPS], n.d., for a state-by-state review). Not all states have a minimum age, and in those jurisdictions children of any age could theoretically be adjudicated delinquent or even prosecuted criminally if the offense is sufficiently severe (see Juvenile Justice GPS, n.d., for a state-by-state review). Given the importance of age in determining whether an offender should be adjudicated in juvenile court or prosecuted in criminal court, jurisdictions have developed precise rules for determining age. For example, according to the Invisible Day Rule, the court considers an individual to be a certain age at the beginning of the day of that person's birthday, regardless of the actual time of day when the person was born (Marsh, 2007).

At the other end of the continuum, every state has identified an age at which juvenile court jurisdiction ends, and the maximum age is often different in transfer and disposition contexts (see Juvenile Justice GPS, n.d., for a state-by-state review). For example, in Pennsylvania, offenders older than age 14 but younger than age 18 can be adjudicated as a juvenile or prosecuted as an adult, depending on several factors, including the seriousness of the offense, but juvenile court jurisdiction ends for disposition purposes when the offender reaches age 21. When a juvenile offender becomes ineligible for the juvenile system based on age, he or she can no longer be lawfully detained unless the jurisdiction has a blended sentence option that permits the disposition to extend beyond the period of juvenile minority (Marsh, 2007) (see Juvenile Justice GPS, n.d., for a state-by-state review).

SUBJECT MATTER

Juvenile courts have original jurisdiction over most unlawful acts committed by minors, including both acts of delinquency and status offenses (Marsh, 2007) (see Juvenile Justice GPS, n.d., for a state-by-state review). There are, however, several exceptions to the juvenile court's jurisdiction. For example, juveniles can be prosecuted in criminal court in some jurisdictions based on the seriousness of the alleged offense. Another exception is when a case involving a juvenile offender is handled in a family court or domestic relations court. In this section, we focus on the juvenile court's jurisdiction over delinquency and status offenses.

Delinquency

Although definitions vary by jurisdiction, an act is generally considered delinquent if the act committed by a juvenile would have been a crime if committed by an adult (Marsh, 2007). Most jurisdictions do not consider a delinquent act to be a crime (i.e. a violation of the jurisdiction's criminal code), although some states have adopted more punitive legislation that enables them to treat the delinquent act as a crime in certain circumstances. Juveniles who are alleged to have committed a delinquent act are subject to the jurisdiction of juvenile courts, which can order a range of dispositions if the juvenile is adjudicated delinquent. Gardner (2014) suggests that the foundation of the juvenile court's delinquency jurisdiction has been weakened by several factors, including the erosion of the juvenile court's rehabilitative focus, the perception that juvenile crime is increasing, and social science research suggesting that adolescents are not fundamentally different from adults in some respects.

Status Offenses

In contrast with acts of delinquency, which often involve behavior that can cause harm to other people or to society more generally, status offenses are only considered offenses because of the status—typically the age—of the person who committed the conduct. Stated differently, these acts would not have been considered unlawful except for the age of the person who committed them (see Melton, Petrila *et al.*, 2007). Examples of status offenses include curfew violations, truancy, running away from home, and alcohol consumption. Legally emancipated minors are not subject to status offender laws because they are considered adults for legal purposes. The process of adjudicating a juvenile as a status offender—with common synonymous terminology such as being unruly, unmanageable, incorrigible, and the like (see Juvenile Justice GPS, n.d., for a state-by-state review)—is similar to that of delinquency cases; however, the extension of the earlier discussed procedural due process rights enjoyed by youths in delinquency proceedings is not as clear for youths in status offense cases (e.g. "The Right to Counsel in Status Offense Cases," 2010). Youths adjudicated for status offenses are generally subject to the same range of dispositions used in cases of delinquency (43 C.J.S. *Infants* §§ 156–7, 2016), although secure confinement is discouraged (43 C.J.S. *Infants* § 156, 2016; Development Services Group, Inc., 2015; Gardner, 2014). Some have argued that status offense jurisdiction is only acceptable if the juvenile court system is actually helping the troubled youths brought within its reach, while others have asserted that status offense jurisdiction is overly paternalistic (Gardner, 2014).

TRANSFER, REVERSE TRANSFER, AND ADJUDICATION

As discussed in Chapter 1 (this volume), all states have procedural mechanisms that enable them to prosecute a juvenile offender's case in criminal court (Davis, 2016; Griffin, Addie *et al.*, 2011; see generally Grigorenko, 2012; Heilbrun, DeMatteo *et al.*, 2016). There are several ways this can be accomplished, and many states use more than one approach. Most states provide for an automatic waiver of the juvenile's case to criminal court if specific age and offense criteria are met, or if a youth was previously prosecuted as an adult (43 C.J.S. *Infants* § 42, 2016; Gardner, 2014; see Juvenile Justice GPS, n.d., for a state-by-state review). Some states provide prosecutors with the discretion to file certain cases directly in criminal court (enabled by the juvenile court and criminal court having concurrent jurisdiction) (Juvenile Justice GPS, n.d.), and this decision is often based on the offender's age, delinquency–criminal background, and seriousness of the current offense (Davis, 2016; see Juvenile Justice GPS, n.d., for a state-by-state review). The majority of states also allow the juvenile court judge to waive the juvenile court's jurisdiction in certain cases, either discretionarily, presumptively (shifting the burden of proof to the defense), or mandatorily (with the juvenile court simply ensuring that the exclusion criteria are met) (Gardner, 2014; Marsh, 2007; see Juvenile Justice GPS, n.d., for a state-by-state review).

According to the Model Juvenile Court Act, issued by the National Conference of Commissioners on Uniform State Laws in 1968 (and subsequently adopted by North Dakota and Pennsylvania), a juvenile court should ideally be able to transfer a case to criminal court if the offender is aged 16 or older at the time of the alleged offense and if, after a hearing, the court finds that there are "reasonable grounds" to believe the juvenile committed the offense, the juvenile is not amenable to treatment in the juvenile justice system, and concerns relating to public safety ("the interests of the community require that the child be placed under legal restraint or discipline") require the juvenile to be in a more secure setting (Model Juvenile Court Act § 34, 2016). As such, it endorses the judicial waiver procedure, and in a comment expressed concern about the constitutional basis for the prosecutorial-discretion approach. Of note, most states also have a legal mechanism for allowing juveniles whose cases are in criminal court, typically via prosecutorial direct-file, to petition for a return of the case to juvenile court, and these decisions are usually based on the criteria of risk for future danger, amenability to treatment, and sophistication-maturity (46 Am. Jur. 2d. *Juvenile Courts and Delinquent and Dependent Children* § 45, 2016; Davis, 2016; Griffin, Addie *et al.*, 2011).

Depending on the context, a juvenile's case may involve several hearings. For example, there may be a hearing on the transfer issue, followed by the adjudication hearing, and then the disposition hearing. In terms of the transfer issue, the Supreme Court's decision in *Kent v. United States* (1966) enhanced due process protections for juvenile offenders by articulating eight criteria that juvenile court judges could use in determining whether to waive jurisdiction and transfer the juvenile to criminal court. The Supreme Court's decision in *Kent* did not require states to use these criteria, but most states adopted identical (or very similar) criteria for use in their jurisdiction. Other states, however, have either not set a clear standard for transfer decisions or have adopted a general standard, which is typically focused on the rehabilitative potential of the juvenile (Davis, 2016). Generalized standards, which essentially leave the transfer decision to the discretion of the juvenile court judge, have been upheld as constitutional (43 C.J.S. *Infants* § 41, 2016; Davis, 2016). A transfer decision cannot be made without a hearing, at which the juvenile offender has certain rights (see *In re Gault*, 1967; see also 43 C.J.S. *Infants* § 41, 2016; 46 Am. Jur. 2d. *Juvenile Courts and Delinquent and Dependent Children* § 47, 2016). The evidentiary rules at a transfer hearing are relaxed (e.g. hearsay is admissible) because it is not an adjudicatory procedure (Davis, 2016). In that regard, it is similar to a preliminary hearing in the criminal process.

As noted, most states vest original jurisdiction in criminal court for juveniles who meet specific age and offense criteria, or for youth who have been prosecuted as an adult in a previous matter; cases involving older offenders who have committed serious offenses originate in criminal court by way of legislative exclusion from juvenile court or mandatory waiver by the juvenile court (43 C.J.S. *Infants* § 42, 2016; Gardner, 2014). For juveniles whose cases originate in criminal court, most jurisdictions offer the possibility of having the case transferred to the juvenile court system. In these reverse transfer contexts, the juvenile (defense) must prove at a hearing in criminal court that the case is more appropriate for the juvenile court system (Juvenile Justice GPS, n.d.). The judge's decision in reverse transfer contexts is discretionary, and the court's decision will not be reversed on appeal unless there is an abuse of discretion. The criteria employed in reverse transfer contexts are typically the same criteria that are used in transfer contexts—i.e. risk, sophistication-maturity, and treatment amenability (Davis, 2016) (see Table 2.1).

The allocation of the burden of proof in juvenile proceedings is governed by state law. The presumption in most circumstances is that juvenile offenders should be rehabilitated in the juvenile system, so most states place the burden on the state (prosecution) to prove that the juvenile should be in criminal court (46 Am. Jur. 2d. *Juvenile Courts and Delinquent and Dependent Children* § 102, 2016). Such proof involves showing that

Table 2.1 States with Reverse Transfer Laws: Status of Risk, Sophistication–Maturity, and Treatment Amenability Criteria

State	R(e)	R(i)	S–M(e)	S–M(i)	A(e)	A(i)	Residual	Same
1. Arizona		X		X	X		~	~
2. Arkansas		X	X		X		X	X
3. California			X		X		X	X
4. Colorado		X	X		X		~	~
5. Connecticut					X		X	
6. Delaware					X		X	
7. Georgia		X	X		X		X	X
8. Iowa					X		X	X
9. Maryland		X		X	X		~	~
10. Mississippi		X	X		X			X
11. Montana		X					X	
12. Nebraska		X		X	X		X	X
13. Nevada							X	
14. New York		X					X	X
15. Oklahoma		X	X		X			X
16. Pennsylvania	X		X		X		X	X
17. South Dakota		X		X	X		~	X
18. Tennessee		X		X	X		X	X
19. Vermont							X	
20. Virginia		X	X		X		X	X
21. Wisconsin		X			X			
22. Wyoming							X	
Total	1	14	8	5	17	0	19	15

Notes: R(e) = risk explicitly referenced (e.g. "threat to the safety of the public or any individual posed by the child"); R(i) = risk implicitly referenced (e.g. "protection of the community"); S–M(e) = sophistication–maturity explicitly referenced (e.g. "sophistication or maturity of the juvenile"); S–M(i) = sophistication–maturity implicitly referenced (e.g. "mental and physical condition of the child"; A(e) = treatment amenability explicitly referenced (e.g. "amenability of the child to treatment in an institution, facility, or program available to delinquent children"); A(i) = treatment amenability implicitly referenced (no example is available since no such provision was identified); Residual = catch-all factor, indication that additional unspecified factors may be considered, or a general or vague factor or standard; Same = transfer and reverse transfer were considered in the same provision with indications that the same factors apply, or the same factors were endorsed by cross-reference in separate provisions, or the same factors were listed in separate provisions; ~ = statute vague as to whether a residual factor is included, but statute could be read as including such a factor (residual), or transfer and reverse transfer factors are similar but not identical, or if identical, there is a different general standard.

the juvenile cannot be rehabilitated in the juvenile system or poses too much of a risk of danger to the community. However, as noted, in many jurisdictions, cases involving serious offenses require a presumptive or mandatory transfer of the juvenile to criminal court—or the case against the juvenile originates in criminal court—and then the juvenile (defense) bears the burden of proving that the case should be transferred to the juvenile court (Juvenile Justice GPS, n.d.). Also, the degree of proof required in transfer decisions is typically a preponderance of the evidence or clear and convincing evidence, standards which are easier to meet than beyond a reasonable doubt (46 Am. Jur. 2d. *Juvenile Courts and Delinquent and Dependent Children* § 104, 2016; see also Marsh, 2007). Finally, when ruling on a motion to transfer a juvenile, the court can assume that the juvenile is guilty of the alleged offense (Davis, 2016).

An appeal procedure for juvenile court decisions is not clearly guaranteed by the US Constitution (46 Am. Jur. 2d. *Juvenile Courts and Delinquent and Dependent Children* § 126, 2016); the Supreme Court in *In re Gault* (1967) did not provide any guidance as to whether due process requires a right of appeal (Davis, 2016). It is noteworthy that the Supreme Court has never held that due process requires a right of appeal in criminal cases, either—but all states provide such a right. The foreseeable legal logic is that if a state provides a right of appeal to criminal offenders, then it must provide a right of appeal to all offenders or it would be denying equal protection to certain offenders.

Despite the current absence of a clear constitutional requirement for an appeal, states typically allow for appeals of juvenile court orders (46 Am. Jur. 2d. *Juvenile Courts and Delinquent and Dependent Children* § 126, 2016). However, there is considerable variation in who may appeal (defense versus prosecution), which court hears the appeal, and which types of juvenile court orders are appealable (43 C.J.S. *Infants* § 59, 2016; 46 Am. Jur. 2d. *Juvenile Courts and Delinquent and Dependent Children* § 127, 2016; Davis, 2016). There are even jurisdictional variations on whether juveniles have a right to counsel when appealing a decision of the juvenile court, although some authorities indicate that juvenile offenders are indeed guaranteed a right to counsel on appeal (see Davis, 2016). Most authorities indicate that juvenile court orders denying or granting the state's motion to refer the juvenile's case to criminal court are appealable by either party, but some authorities indicate that juvenile court decisions not to waive jurisdiction are not appealable (43 C.J.S. *Infants* §§ 59–60, 2016). A juvenile court's decision will be reversed on appeal if the appellate court determines that the juvenile court judge abused his or her discretion to waive jurisdiction of the juvenile offender (43 C.J.S. *Infants* § 60, 2016; 46 Am. Jur. 2d. *Juvenile Courts and Delinquent and Dependent Children* § 127, 2016; Davis, 2016). Finally, there is no constitutional right to a jury trial in delinquency adjudication proceedings (*McKeiver v. Pennsylvania*, 1971), and so, by extension, neither is there for transfer hearings.

The transfer and adjudication process in federal courts is guided by the Juvenile Justice and Delinquency Prevention Act, which was codified in Chapter 403 (Juvenile Delinquency) of Title 18 of the United States Code (18 U.S.C. §§ 5031–42, 2016). This law applies to individuals who committed a federal criminal violation prior to their eighteenth birthday, although the law retains jurisdiction over the offender until age 21 for purposes of proceedings and dispositions. Further, an offender who commits a qualifying offense, but who is not indicted until after age 21, must be prosecuted as an adult. The law also provides prosecutorial discretion regarding whether an offender will be tried as an adult even if the offense qualifies as an act of juvenile delinquency. The government can make a motion to have an offender transferred to adult (criminal) court to be tried as an adult if he or she is age 15 or older, and is alleged to have committed one or more of certain enumerated offenses (43 C.J.S. *Infants* §§ 38, 381, 2016; 46 Am. Jur. 2d. *Juvenile Courts and Delinquent and Dependent Children* §§ 25–33, 2016).

DISPOSITION

After an adjudication of delinquency, the juvenile court can immediately determine a disposition or hold a separate disposition hearing within a statutorily-defined period of time (43 C.J.S. *Infants* § 143). Davis (2016) notes a trend toward a bifurcated process in which the adjudicative and disposition hearings are separate; such a bifurcated process is required in federal delinquency hearings. Holding a separate hearing at a later date can be beneficial because it permits the juvenile offender to obtain an evaluation and report from a forensic mental health professional that informs the court about the juvenile's amenability, sophistication-maturity, and risk to public safety (see 43 C.J.S. *Infants* § 143). The court's primary focus at the disposition phase is imposing a disposition that will address the juvenile's areas of need, but the court also considers a range of factors, including any risk to public safety presented by the juvenile and the least restrictive alternative (43 C.J.S. *Infants* § 142, 2016).

The Supreme Court in *In re Gault* (1967) did not address whether constitutional due process rights apply during the disposition phase of delinquency proceedings (Davis, 2016). While the adjudication hearing is analogous to a criminal trial and therefore requires certain procedural safeguards, the disposition hearing is focused exclusively on making an individualized determination of which disposition is most appropriate for a given juvenile (43 C.J.S. *Infants* § 142, 2016); such procedures do not require the provision of full procedural rights and protections. However, states have carved out certain rights that are afforded to juveniles during the disposition phase, although these rights vary across jurisdictions (Gardner, 2014). As a starting point, all states provide, either via statute or simply as a matter of due process, that juveniles have a right to counsel at the disposition hearing (Davis, 2016). In some jurisdictions the juvenile's parents or guardians must be permitted to be present during the hearing (43 C.J.S. *Infants* § 142, 2016). The juvenile also typically has a right to be present and to provide evidence that may inform the court's decision regarding an appropriate disposition, although this right is not universal (43 C.J.S. *Infants* § 144, 2016). Moreover, if the juvenile received a full evidentiary hearing during the adjudication proceeding, he or she may not be entitled to a second evidentiary hearing during the disposition phase of the proceedings (43 C.J.S. *Infants* § 144, 2016). Similar to the adjudication phase, there is no right to have a jury present during the disposition hearing

(43 C.J.S. *Infants* § 142, 2016; Davis, 2016). At the disposition stage, the juvenile has no constitutional right under the 6th Amendment or analogous state constitutional provisions to confront witnesses (43 C.J.S. *Infants* § 145, 2016), although some states have established via statute and case law that juveniles can cross-examine witnesses during the disposition hearing (Davis, 2016). Further, the 5th Amendment right against self-incrimination is not applicable at this stage of the proceedings because the juvenile has already been adjudicated delinquent (43 C.J.S. *Infants* § 144, 2016).

To make an informed and individualized disposition decision, juvenile courts generally consider information about the juvenile across several domains, including family, school, home environment, peers, and clinical and behavioral health needs. This process takes time, so disposition can be delayed for many months. Under a continuance mechanism, the court informs the juvenile that the disposition decision will be delayed, and that if the juvenile is arrested before the hearing, he or she will be committed to the state's youth authority on the offense for which the juvenile was found delinquent (Grisso, 2013; see also 43 C.J.S. *Infants* § 143, 2016). During the continuance, the juvenile court monitors the juvenile through regular status hearings. Much of the information about the juvenile that informs the court's disposition decision will be contained in a predisposition report provided to the court, and forensic mental health professionals can also provide such information through their evaluations. If the court orders a predisposition report, the report must be provided to the juvenile in advance of the disposition hearing so the juvenile can respond to the factual findings in the report. Standard evidentiary rules typically do not apply during disposition hearings, and any evidence that is relevant to the disposition decision is typically admitted (Davis, 2016). Juvenile court judges generally have broad discretion in fashioning an appropriate disposition (46 Am. Jur. 2d. *Juvenile Courts and Delinquent and Dependent Children* § 59, 2016; Gardner, 2014; Marsh, 2007), although certain dispositions may be required by statute in some jurisdictions (43 C.J.S. *Infants* § 142, 2016). Further, dispositions that are not specified in the governing statute may not be imposed by the juvenile court (43 C.J.S. *Infants* § 142, 2016), which limits the discretion of the judge and protects the juvenile from arbitrary or abusive dispositions. Moreover, there is precedent that a custodial commitment must be adjudged the least restrictive alternative (i.e. the only appropriate option), taking into account the same or similar factors involved in transfer decisions (46 Am. Jur. 2d. *Juvenile Courts and Delinquent and Dependent Children* § 63).

The majority of states follow the disposition guidelines found in the Model Juvenile Court Act (also referred to as the Uniform Juvenile Court Act) (Model Juvenile Court Act 2016), which was promulgated by the National Conference of Commissioners on Uniform State Laws in July 1968 in response to the Supreme Court's decision in *In re Gault* (1967). It was adopted by the American Bar Association the same year. Because it is model legislation, the Model Juvenile Court Act has no authority unless it is adopted by a particular jurisdiction. Substantively in regard to juvenile dispositions, it provides for a range of dispositions after a youth is adjudicated delinquent, including permitting the juvenile to remain with his or her family subject to the court's supervision; probation; placement in an institution, camp, or other facility; and commitment of the juvenile to a relevant state department or state institution (see Davis, 2016; see also Juvenile Justice GPS, n.d., for recent [2013] data regarding the frequency of different disposition outcomes based on a large sample of 123 counties, amounting to 16 percent of the total number of local juvenile justice jurisdictions nationwide).

In general, the facility in which a juvenile might be placed is legally responsible for the juvenile's care and rehabilitation, although there may be some ongoing judicial oversight (43 C.J.S. *Infants* § 475, 2016; see Juvenile Justice GPS, n.d., for a state-by-state review of operating agencies, agency and systems integration, and state or local operation of services). Any facility—correctional or rehabilitative—must comply with applicable statutes regarding the care, punishment, and treatment of juvenile offenders, and all detained or committed juveniles are entitled to minimally adequate care (43 C.J.S. *Infants* §§ 397, 475, 2016; see also Gardner, 2014, for a discussion). The development of a rehabilitation/treatment plan for a committed juvenile is guided by the best interests of the juvenile and the safety interests of the public (43 C.J.S. *Infants* § 475, 2016; see Juvenile Justice GPS, n.d., for a state-by-state review regarding evidence-based practices). The facility should notify the court if there is a poor fit between the juvenile and the services offered by the facility (43 C.J.S. *Infants* § 475, 2016). If a juvenile is being transferred to or from a correctional or rehabilitative facility, judicial approval is not required if it is considered an administrative (as opposed to judicial) act, but some states nevertheless provide for a transfer hearing (43 C.J.S. *Infants* § 477, 2016). If, however, a juvenile is being transferred to a fundamentally distinct facility, some jurisdictions require that a hearing be held in which the juvenile receives a number of procedural safeguards (Davis, 2016). The decision to provide a hearing is typically based on *Baxstrom v. Herold* (1966), in which the Supreme Court held that individuals who are being transferred to a fundamentally distinct facility are entitled to certain procedural safeguards. Some courts have relied on *Baxstrom* to require a hearing before a juvenile can be lawfully transferred to a functionally distinct facility (e.g. *Shone v. Maine*, 1969).

When a juvenile reaches the maximum age of juvenile court jurisdiction, the juvenile typically must be discharged (46 Am. Jur. 2d. *Juvenile Courts and Delinquent and Dependent Children* § 65, 2016). There are, however, several exceptions (see Grisso, 2013, for a discussion). For example, in some jurisdictions juveniles can request a continuance of their commitment for a limited time so they can continue receiving services. Other jurisdictions use youthful offender sentences that call for commitment that extends beyond the statutory maximum age. Finally, in many jurisdictions, the state's youth authority can petition the juvenile court for an extension of juvenile court jurisdiction upon the showing of special circumstances (e.g. the discharge of the juvenile would present a serious danger to the public) (Grisso, 2013).

Juveniles who are committed to a correctional or rehabilitative institution are typically not sentenced for a specific term (43 C.J.S. *Infants* § 476, 2016; 46 Am. Jur. 2d. *Juvenile Courts and Delinquent and Dependent Children* § 65, 2016). The timing of the discharge of a juvenile who has been committed to a rehabilitative facility is a decision often made by the facility (see Juvenile Justice GPS, n.d., for a state-by-state review), although the facility must comply with applicable statutory requirements (43 C.J.S. *Infants* § 478, 2016). In many jurisdictions, juveniles can be released upon showing good behavior (43 C.J.S. *Infants* § 476, 2016).

States may approve of a variety of other dispositions. For example, some states permit the juvenile to be housed by the state's department of corrections (see 43 C.J.S. *Infants* § 166, 2016; see also 46 Am. Jur. 2d. *Juvenile Courts and Delinquent and Dependent Children* § 64, 2016). However, consistent with the least restrictive alternative principle, juvenile courts are somewhat reluctant to impose dispositions involving a deprivation of liberty unless it is deemed absolutely necessary for the juvenile and society (46 Am. Jur. 2d. *Juvenile Courts and Delinquent and Dependent Children* § 63, 2016). Along those lines, alternative dispositions (e.g. day programs, community service, and family treatment) are becoming more common (Davis, 2016). Other dispositions include restitution by the juvenile offender (either as a disposition or condition of probation) and fines (Gardner, 2014; Marsh, 2007). As may be evident in some of the dispositions used in juvenile courts, the focus is often less rehabilitative and more punitive.

In states with blended sentencing, a juvenile court may be empowered to impose both a juvenile disposition and an adult sentence, or even just the latter (Cheesman, 2011). However, the adult sentence is typically stayed as long as the juvenile successfully completes the terms of the juvenile disposition (Salekin, 2015a). If the juvenile fails to complete the juvenile disposition or commits another offense, the stay may be revoked and the adult sentence imposed (Davis, 2016). Blended sentencing laws may also authorize criminal court judges to remand to the juvenile court for juvenile sanctions, directly impose juvenile dispositions, or issue hybrid juvenile–adult sanctions (see Juvenile Justice GPS, n.d., for a state-by-state review).

If a juvenile is convicted of a crime in criminal court, the juvenile can be punished in the same manner as adults, although certain punishments, such as the death penalty (*Roper v. Simmons*, 2005) and mandatory life without parole (*Miller v. Alabama*, 2012), are not available if the offender committed his or her crime as a juvenile. Under youthful offender statutes, which apply to offenders of a young age who are convicted in criminal court, courts have relatively broad authority in imposing sentence (Gardner, 2014; Marsh, 2007). Sentences that are not in conformity with statutory applicable requirements can be set aside, and sentences that are considered an abuse of the judge's discretion can be modified or reduced (43 C.J.S. *Infants* §§ 389–93, 2016). Under some circumstances, the offender may receive a new sentence (43 C.J.S. *Infants* § 389, 2016).

Like transfer and adjudication, dispositions in federal court are guided by the Juvenile Justice and Delinquency Prevention Act (codified in Chapter 403 of Title 18 of the United States Code; 18 U.S.C. §§ 5031–42, 2016). If the federal court adjudicates the juvenile delinquent, a disposition hearing must be held within 20 days, although extensions are permitted if the court has ordered an investigation or evaluation to inform the court's disposition decision (43 C.J.S. *Infants* § 395, 2016). When courts need more information, the youth can be committed to the custody of the United States Attorney General after a hearing at which the juvenile is represented by counsel (43 C.J.S. *Infants* § 395, 2016). The purpose of the commitment is to allow an evaluation of the juvenile, and the Attorney General must submit a report to the court and attorneys within 30 days of the commitment unless the court grants an extension upon a motion of the government (43 C.J.S. *Infants* § 395, 2016).

In terms of a disposition in federal courts, the court may suspend the findings of juvenile delinquency, order probation, or commit the juvenile to a detention facility (43 C.J.S. *Infants* § 396, 2016). The term of detention cannot extend beyond the lesser of the date upon which (1) the juvenile turns age 21, (2) the maximum of the statutorily-set guideline range for a similarly sentenced adult defendant, or (3) the maximum length of incarceration authorized under the Federal Sentencing Guidelines if the juvenile had been convicted as an adult (43 C.J.S. *Infants* § 396, 2016). A court can, however, deviate from the guideline range if it finds aggravating factors that justified an upward departure (43 C.J.S. *Infants* § 396, 2016). Upon a finding of delinquency, a juvenile may not be placed or retained in a facility in which the juvenile would have regular contact with incarcerated adults who have been convicted or are awaiting trial (43 C.J.S. *Infants* § 397, 2016). Federal law also provides that committed juveniles must have adequate food, heat, light, sanitary facilities, bedding, clothing, recreation, counseling, education, training, and medical care (which includes mental health care) (43 C.J.S. *Infants* § 397, 2016).

ROLE OF FORENSIC MENTAL HEALTH PROFESSIONALS

There are various decision points in the juvenile justice process at which forensic mental health professionals may be asked to provide information to legal decision-makers (see Salekin, 2015a, for a discussion). After a juvenile has been arrested and charged, decisions must be made about whether the juvenile should be detained while awaiting the next step in the process. These decisions are based on a number of factors, some of which (e.g. risk to public safety) can be addressed by forensic mental health professionals. As noted, the issue of whether the juvenile should be processed in juvenile court or criminal court is a preliminary question that must be addressed before there is any judgment on the merits of the case against the juvenile. Forensic mental health professionals are often asked to evaluate the juvenile in an effort to help the court make a better-informed decision about whether the juvenile should be adjudicated in juvenile court or tried in criminal (adult) court. During the disposition phase after a finding of delinquency, forensic mental health professionals can assist courts in making disposition decisions that take into account the strengths and needs of juvenile offenders and courts' desire to protect the public from violent offenders (Salekin, 2015a). Finally, forensic mental health professionals may be called on to evaluate a juvenile's progress during his or her commitment. Several chapters in this book focus on the role of forensic mental health professionals at some of the points in the processing of a juvenile's case.

CONCLUSION

Although the juvenile court system was initially developed with an exclusive focus on rehabilitation, concerns about public safety and rising juvenile crime rates led to a gradual shift to a dual focus on rehabilitation and punishment. As the juvenile system became increasingly adversarial, courts and legislatures recognized the importance of providing rights and procedural safeguards to juvenile offenders. The result is a juvenile justice system that is complex and nuanced. Through a series of legislative enactments and court decisions, juveniles have been provided with a range of due process rights that were previously reserved for adults. Although the Supreme Court has addressed several aspects of the juvenile court system, many issues remain unaddressed. As a result, there is noticeable variability across jurisdictions.

One of the more noteworthy developments in recent years is the Supreme Court's recognition that adolescents are fundamentally different from adults. Many of the Supreme Court's decisions were informed by relevant social science research. These differences, according to the Supreme Court, have important implications for the rights and available dispositions of juvenile offenders, although some state courts have explicitly distinguished these cases—all of which dealt with particularly extreme sentences—so as to narrow the import for transfer and most dispositions (e.g. *People v. Patterson*, 2014). Nevertheless, some of the remaining chapters in this book will highlight identified developmental differences, with a discussion of how such differences affect the roles of forensic mental health professionals who work with juvenile offenders.

CHAPTER THREE

Foundations of Evaluations

This chapter addresses the nature of forensic mental health assessment (FMHA), and the underlying models associated with it. The evaluation of juveniles in a legal context, for the purpose of either transfer or disposition, is a form of mental health evaluation for the courts that is similar in important respects to the evaluation of other individuals involved in different kinds of criminal and civil litigation. Our discussion in this chapter clarifies how this kind of juvenile FMHA is consistent with other kinds of forensic mental health assessment—but also addresses some distinctive aspects of transfer and disposition evaluations.

FORENSIC MENTAL HEALTH ASSESSMENT

FMHA, which provides mental health evaluation in legal contexts, encompasses a wide variety of legal questions. These include criminal, civil, administrative, and juvenile court contexts (Heilbrun, Grisso *et al.*, 2012). Forensic mental health professionals may be asked to evaluate an individual by focusing on different time periods:

- past functioning—addressing the mental state, motivations, behaviors, thoughts, and attitudes of the evaluee at a previous time (e.g. mental state at the time of the offense; sentencing addressing culpability);
- present functioning—assessing current functioning and abilities in relation to a specific present-stated legal question (e.g. competence to stand trial); and
- future functioning—gauging the likelihood of some specific and legally relevant future outcome (e.g. reoffending; favorable response to intervention).

(Heilbrun, Grisso *et al.*, 2012)

It is useful to review briefly how FMHA differs from evaluations conducted for diagnosis and treatment-planning ("therapeutic assessment"). There are important differences in several areas, including the following.

1. *Purpose*—FMHA is conducted to assist a legal decision-maker or attorney, while therapeutic assessment is performed to diagnose and treat behavioral health disorders.[1]
2. *Examiner–examinee relationship*—in FMHA, the relationship is more detached and quasi-objective, while in therapeutic assessment the evaluator plays a helping role.
3. *Notification of purpose*—such notification is formal and explicit in FMHA, while the shared assumptions about purpose associated with therapeutic assessment means that the notification does not need to be as explicit or extensive.
4. *The "client"*—varies with FMHA, but typically is the court or the attorney; in therapeutic assessment, it is the individual being evaluated.
5. *Nature of standard*—legal standards as well as behavioral health standards are incorporated into FMHA, while in therapeutic assessment the standard is almost exclusively behavioral health (psychiatric, psychological, and/or medical).
6. *Data sources*—in addition to the self-report, psychological testing, behavioral assessment, and medical procedures are typically employed in both FMHA and therapeutic evaluations; FMHA also routinely uses the observations of others that appear in records and are elicited through third-party interviews.
7. *Response style*—with the litigation-related incentive for distortion of self-reported information in FMHA, self-report is not assumed to be accurate. Therapeutic assessment, by contrast, may use the assumption that the individual is typically making a reasonable attempt to report accurately, without the complication of deliberate exaggeration or minimization.
8. *Clarification of reasoning and limits of knowledge*—a very important part of FMHA, but much less important in therapeutic assessment.
9. *Written report*—lengthy and detailed, documenting the findings, reasoning, and conclusions in FMHA; often briefer and more conclusory in therapeutic assessment.
10. *Court testimony*—always anticipated as a possibility in FMHA; not anticipated as a possibility in therapeutic assessment (Heilbrun, 2001).

It might appear initially that juvenile FMHA bears a closer resemblance to therapeutic evaluation than does adult FMHA, considering the important role of "treatment needs and amenability" as a frequently considered aspect of juvenile evaluations—and the more rehabilitative orientation of the juvenile system. In one sense, this is accurate. FMHA with juveniles on the topics of transfer and disposition must routinely incorporate the consideration of "treatment needs." But such "treatment" is not only for the improvement of an adolescent's behavioral health. As we discuss throughout this book, the interventions of major interest to legal decision-makers are those that reduce the risk of future offending—or both reduce re-offense risk and improve behavioral health. In a larger sense, however, the distinctions between therapeutic and forensic assessment apply nearly as well to evaluating juveniles as they do to evaluating adults. With the exception of the first distinction (purpose), these considerations, when applied to juvenile evaluations, suggest that such evaluations are indeed a form of FMHA, distinct from therapeutic assessment with adolescents.

MODELS OF FORENSIC MENTAL HEALTH ASSESSMENT

In Grisso's original *Evaluating Competencies* (1986), detailed attention was paid to describing a model for FMHA. This discussion began with the delineation of the sources of the law's discontent with FMHA circa 1986: (1) insufficient legal knowledge on the part of the FMHA practitioner; (2) intrusion into the purview of legal decision-makers (e.g. addressing the ultimate legal question but saying little about the relevant psycho-legal constructs); and (3) overreliance on insufficient data or speculation rather than data-driven findings. To avoid these problems, Grisso suggested that forensic mental health practitioners be familiar with relevant legal concepts (e.g. statutes and case law) and "operationalize" legal competency constructs into ""functional abilities." In addition, his model called for empirically based data (rather than clinical impressions or isolated observations). It also was designed to promote description of the evaluee's functional abilities in a way that is congruent with the relevant legal standard. The model's components included a *functional characteristic* (that which an individual can do or accomplish, as well as the specific knowledge, understanding, or beliefs that may be necessary for the accomplishment), a *contextual characteristic* (a class of external situations to which a person must respond), a *causal characteristic* (focusing on personal control and probable change with regard to relevant functional abilities), an *interactive characteristic* (person–context interaction—does level of ability meet the demands of the specific situation), *judgmental characteristics* (person–context incongruency is sufficient to warrant a finding of legal incompetency), and *dispositional characteristics* (what will happen following such a judgment).

Consistent with this model, there is much agreement in the literature that FMHA should be guided by relevant legal statutes and case law, incorporate standardized testing and validated measures whenever possible, and gather data from multiple sources (e.g. clinical interview, records, collateral sources) (Goldstein, 2003, 2007; Heilbrun, 2001; Heilbrun, Grisso *et al.*, 2012; Melton, Petrila *et al.*, 2007; Otto, Slobogin *et al.*, 2007). Models of FMHA can generally be divided into two distinct types. One approach identifies specific types of FMHA based on the relevant legal question(s), case law and statutory guidelines, practice literature, and ethical guidelines. An alternative approach posits that all types of FMHA share a common foundation, and can thus be described using common elements that recur across assessment types (see, for example, Grisso, 2003; Heilbrun, Grisso *et al.*, 2012).

Several scholars have combined these two FMHA approaches in providing guidelines for FMHA practitioners. For example, some provide descriptions of various types of FMHA in addition to discussing commonalities and guidelines that apply to each type of assessment (see, for example, Melton, Petrila *et al.*, 2007; Simon & Gold, 2004). Brodsky (1991, 1999, 2004, 2013) has also published FMHA guidelines related to the provision of expert testimony.

A Proposed Model for Juvenile Disposition and Transfer Evaluations

Models applicable to many kinds of forensic evaluation can be useful in their breadth and overview. But they invariably lack specificity, particularly when the legal question is primarily focused on future functioning rather than previous mental state or current capacity. In constructing a model specifically for juvenile disposition and transfer, it is useful to adapt Grisso's (1986, 2003a) broad models of competencies to focus on the specific elements of the evaluation and its future orientation.

We propose such a model (see Figure 3.1). It incorporates risk and needs, treatment amenability, and sophistication-maturity—with the conclusion involving an integration of information in these domains to yield an opinion about rehabilitation potential. We describe the basic operation of this proposed model in the present section, and elaborate on each of these domains in other chapters in this book.

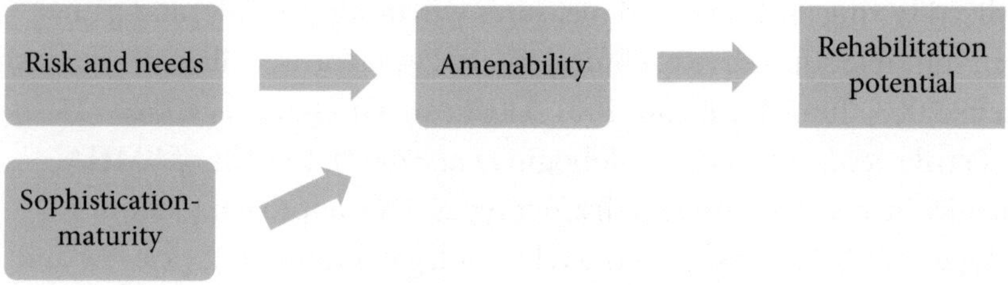

Model 1. Sophistication-maturity and risk and needs both relevant to amenability

OR

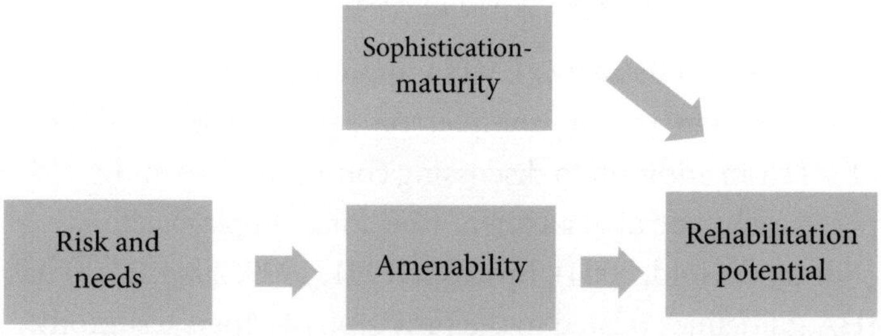

Model 2. Sophistication-maturity is relevant to rehabilitation potential but not amenability

Figure 3.1 Proposed Models for Juvenile Evaluation of Transfer and Disposition.

It is clear that both re-offense risk and criminogenic needs should be important parts of this model. Many jurisdictions explicitly cite public safety as a consideration, which translates fairly directly into the question of whether the youth is likely to engage in future offending and other antisocial conduct. (Even when this does not appear directly in the relevant statute, it remains fundamental and very likely to be of interest to the legal decision-maker.) The question of needs is less directly relevant, but has logical and common-sense justification. One cannot be clear about a youth's amenability to treatment without specifying what is being treated—the risk-relevant deficits that need improving, or the protective factors that must be strengthened. Including both risk and needs in the model links it as well with the Risk-Need-Responsivity model, a strong and well-supported theoretical model of correctional rehabilitation planning and provision for adults and juveniles (Hoge & Andrews, 2010a). While treatment of youths' behavioral health needs that are unrelated to re-offense risk is one consideration for juvenile judges, it is useful to consider the two primary components of risk-need assessment: (1) static risk factors for re-offending (unchangeable through planned intervention); and (2) dynamic risk factors relevant to re-offense risk (potentially changeable through planned intervention; including some behavioral health problems such as substance abuse, as well as generally recognized criminogenic influences such as antisocial peers, criminal thinking, and family dysfunction). In a world with unlimited resources, courts could focus on all needs regardless of their relationship to re-offense risk. Given the limitations on resources and funding evident in many juvenile justice systems, however, we suggest that courts are most interested in risk factors for re-offending—and evaluators are most useful to the courts when they focus on these areas, distinguishing between clinical needs that are also relevant to re-offending and clinical needs that are not.

Amenability to treatment is another element that must be included in this model. The link between risk, needs, and treatment amenability is as follows: both level of re-offense risk and nature of the relevant needs can help answer questions such as what program, with what services, at what level of security, in what location, and (in the case of transfer and reverse transfer) in what system? It is also important to contextualize this analysis with information involving previous placements, response to previous interventions, expressed motivation for change, availability of such programs, and other considerations that will be discussed in Chapter 6 (this volume).

What is less clear, however, is how sophistication-maturity should fit into this model. Since one important goal of such juvenile evaluations is to reach well-informed conclusions about the youth's potential for rehabilitation within the time remaining under the juvenile system's jurisdiction, the model guides the evaluator to appraise risk, need, and amenability to treatment. But there are three ways in which sophistication-maturity might fit into the evaluation process. Two are depicted in Figure 3.1. First, sophistication-maturity findings could be applied, in conjunction with risk and need findings, to informing the evaluator's conclusions about treatment amenability. Second, it could be applied more directly to informing the conclusion about rehabilitation potential without being considered as part of the treatment amenability findings. Third (not covered in Figure 3.1), sophistication-maturity findings could be applied directly to the court's ultimate decision about disposition or transfer, much as other extra-evaluation influences are considered. Using this approach, sophistication-maturity would not be a part of the evaluation—but still considered by the court in its reasoning or conclusions regarding rehabilitation potential.

This model has the potential to inform the conceptual, data collection, interpretation, and communication stages of the evaluation of juvenile disposition and transfer. We will apply it throughout this book, and consider which of the three applications of sophistication-maturity seems best indicated.

PRINCIPLES OF FORENSIC MENTAL HEALTH ASSESSMENT APPLICABLE TO JUVENILES

A set of foundational principles of FMHA (Heilbrun, 2001; Heilbrun, Grisso *et al.*, 2009) has been applied to specific types of FMHA. These more specific forms include neuropsychological assessment (Heilbrun, Marczyk *et al.*, 2003) and capital sentencing (Heilbrun, DeMatteo *et al.*, 2005).

In addition, these guidelines have recently been adapted for use in juvenile forensic contexts (Heilbrun & DeMatteo, 2012; Heilbrun & Locklair, 2016).

When conducting any kind of FMHA, it is important to consider the relevant sources of authority. Juvenile evaluations conducted to assist legal decision-making are FMHAs. Accordingly, the broad sources of authority for FMHA described elsewhere (Grisso, 2003; Heilbrun, 2001; Heilbrun, Grisso *et al.*, 2009; Melton, Petrilo *et al.*, 2007) should be applied to juvenile FMHA. These foundational sources are law, science, ethics, and practice.

Law as a Source of Authority in Juvenile FMHA

The first important source of authority is law. Evaluations of transfer and disposition are conducted in a legal context, so they must incorporate the guidance and structure provided by the substantive and procedural law outlined earlier. Using statutes, case law, and administrative codes to help define the referral question and the particular criteria to be addressed is essential. It is also important that contributing legal standards be *explicitly acknowledged*, thereby enhancing both ecological validity and credibility. These legal sources of authority have been discussed in detail in Chapter 2 (this volume).

Science as a Source of Authority in Juvenile FMHA

The findings of scientific research are an essential resource for any FMHA practitioner. It can also be valuable to use the scientific process involved in designing, executing, and interpreting research by applying that process to FMHA (see Heilbrun, 2001). Throughout this book, we review relevant research and apply findings to the evaluation of juvenile disposition and transfer. Areas of particular focus include specialized measures for the evaluation of juvenile forensic questions, adolescent development and its implications for juvenile capacities and behavior, juvenile risk assessment, adolescent treatment needs and amenability, and sophistication and maturity. When aggregate reviews and meta-analyses are available, we have emphasized them in the attempt to capture trends and quantify effect sizes.

Ethics as a Source of Authority in Juvenile FMHA

Professional ethics are a third source of foundational authority for juvenile evaluations of disposition and transfer. Moving from the broad to the specific, and from the enforceable to the aspirational, we begin with the *Ethical Principles of Psychologists and Code of Conduct* (EPPCC) for psychology (American Psychological Association, 2010), and the *Principles of Medical Ethics* (American Medical Association, 2001) and the *Principles of Medical Ethics with Annotations Especially Applicable to Psychiatry* (American Psychiatric Association, 2013b) for psychiatrists. These are the enforceable codes to which psychologists and psychiatrists, respectively, must adhere in their practice. (Since these are the major professional groups involved in the evaluation of juvenile disposition and transfer, the present discussion will focus on ethics authority for these disciplines.)

The EPPCC is intended to guide ethical practice in a variety of areas: resolving ethical issues, competence, human relations, privacy and confidentiality, advertising and public statements, record-keeping, education and training, research and publication, assessment, and therapy. Standard 9 (Assessment) is particularly relevant to juvenile FMHA, and practitioners should be familiar with the components of the standard. Important highlights include: (1) basing professional opinions on sufficiently rigorous techniques and data; (2) utilizing appropriate and relevant assessment measures; (3) obtaining informed consent; (4) interpreting assessment results within the context of the evaluation and client-specific factors; and (5) maintaining test security (American Psychological Association, 2010).

The *Specialty Guidelines for Forensic Psychology* (SGFP) (American Psychological Association, 2013) is a revised version of the original SGFP (Committee on Specialty Guidelines for Forensic Psychologists, 1991). Both versions address the differences between the practice of forensic psychology and the practice of psychology in other contexts. This was recognized earlier in an ethical guidelines book for forensic, police, and correctional psychology entitled *Who is the Client?* (Monahan, 1980). The 2013 revision of the SGFP provides updated material on issues such as competence, diligence, relationships, fees, conflicts in practice, privacy/confidentiality, and assessment. The assessment guidelines within the SGFP are particularly relevant to juvenile

FMHAs, and (by design) include several that are similar to those provided by the EPPCC. However, others are more specifically applicable to FMHA, including those guiding FMHA practitioners to focus on legally relevant factors (Guideline 10.01), provide appropriate documentation in response to a subpoena or court order (Guideline 10.07), and retain documentation related to a case until all appeals have been exhausted (Guideline 10.08).

Practice as a Source of Authority in Juvenile FMHA

The literature on practice comprises guidance provided by individuals and organizations that is relevant, but does not fall into the categories of law, science, or ethics. Practice contributions to foundational principles of FMHA have been summarized by various commentators (Heilbrun, 2001; Heilbrun, Grisso *et al.*, 2009; Melton, Petrila *et al.*, 1987, 1997, 2007). One particularly important component of the practice literature involves the development of practice standards (descriptions of desirable, best, or empirically supported practices) that is carried out by professional organizations and summarized in the form of standards. For example, the American Academy of Psychiatry and Law has developed a series of practice guidelines on topics such as the evaluation of insanity (Giorgi-Guarnieri, Janofsky *et al.*, 2002), competence to stand trial (Mossman, Noffsinger *et al.*, 2007) and disability (Gold, Anfang *et al.*, 2008). These represent the consensus of a respected national professional organization on these questions, and are particularly valuable for that reason. Such guidelines apparently do not exist at present for juvenile forensic evaluations, however.

PRINCIPLES OF FMHA AND THEIR APPLICATION TO JUVENILE FORENSIC EVALUATIONS

While these foundational principles were constructed to be broad, they can be applied to the evaluation of juvenile forensic cases in a fairly straightforward way. Some of these principles require special considerations when working with juvenile justice populations, while others apply the same to both adult and juvenile contexts. As noted in Table 3.1, 30 of the 38 principles apply to juvenile justice contexts without modification

Table 3.1 Expanded Principles of Forensic Mental Health Assessment Applied to Juveniles

FMHA Principle	Juvenile Application
GENERALLY	
1. Be aware of the important differences between clinical and forensic domains.	1. Similar. There is somewhat more overlap between clinical and forensic domains with youth than with adults, given the rehabilitative focus of the juvenile system.
2. Obtain appropriate education, training, and experience in one's area of forensic specialization.	2. Similar. Also need to have specific training and experience with youth.
3. Be familiar with the relevant legal, ethical, scientific, and practice literatures pertaining to FMHA.	3. Same.
4. Be guided by honesty and striving for impartiality, actively disclosing the limitations on as well as the support for one's opinions.	4. Same.
5. Control potential evaluator bias in general through monitoring case selection, continuing education, and consultation with knowledgeable colleagues.	5. Same.
6. Be familiar with specific aspects of the legal system, particularly communication, discovery, deposition, and testimony.	6. Same.
7. Do not become adversarial, but present and defend your opinions effectively.	7. Similar. Those presenting expert testimony should be prepared for more active questioning by the judge and more relaxed procedural rules relative to criminal court.

IN SPECIFIC CASES: PREPARATION	
8. Identify relevant forensic issues.	8. Same.
9. Accept referrals only within area of expertise.	9. Same.
10. Decline the referral when evaluator impartiality is unlikely.	10. Same.
11. Clarify the evaluator's role with the attorney.	11. Same.
12. Clarify financial arrangements.	12. Same.
13. Obtain appropriate authorization.	13. Same.
14. Avoid playing the dual roles of therapist and forensic evaluator.	14. Same.
15. Determine the particular role to be played within FMHA if the referral is accepted.	15. Same.
16. Select the most appropriate model to guide data gathering, interpretation, and communication.	16. Models including a description of "clinical condition" should be broadened to include developmental maturity and age-appropriate clinical and educational functioning.
IN SPECIFIC CASES: DATA COLLECTION	
17. Use multiple sources of information for each area being assessed. Review the available background information and actively seek important missing elements.	17. Same.
18. Use relevance and reliability (validity) as guides for seeking information and selecting data sources.	18. Same.
19. Obtain relevant historical information.	19. Same.
20. Assess clinical characteristics in relevant, reliable, and valid ways.	20. Similar. "Clinical" should be defined to include developmentally appropriate clinical and behavioral functioning.
21. Assess legally relevant behavior.	21. Same.

(Continued)

22. Ensure that conditions for evaluation are quiet, private, and distraction-free.	22. Same.
23. Provide appropriate notification of purpose and obtain appropriate authorization before beginning.	23. Same.
24. Determine whether the individual understands the purpose of the evaluation and the associated limits on confidentiality.	24. Similar. Expectations for understanding should be developmentally appropriate.
IN SPECIFIC CASES: DATA INTERPRETATION	
25. Use third-party information in assessing response style.	25. Same.
26. Use testing when indicated in assessing response style.	26. Same.
27. Use case-specific (idiographic) evidence in assessing clinical condition, functional abilities, and causal connection.	27. Same.
28. Use nomothetic evidence in assessing clinical condition, functional abilities, and causal connection.	28. Same.
29. Use scientific reasoning in assessing causal connection between clinical condition, functional abilities, and causal connection.	29. Same.
30. Carefully consider whether to answer the ultimate legal question. If it is answered, it should be in the context of a thorough evaluation clearly describing data and reasoning, and with the clear recognition that this question is in the domain of the legal decision-maker.	30. Similar. There may be particular interest on the part of the juvenile judge in having the expert directly answer the ultimate legal question, so the expert should be prepared to carefully consider the request to do so.
31. Describe findings and limits so that they need change little under cross examination.	31. Same.

IN SPECIFIC CASES: WRITTEN COMMUNICATION	
32. Attribute information to sources.	32. Same.
33. Use plain language; avoid technical jargon.	33. Same.
34. Write report in sections, according to model and procedures.	34. Same.
IN SPECIFIC CASES: EXPERT TESTIMONY	
35. Base testimony on the results of the properly performed FMHA.	35. Same.
36. Prepare.	36. Same.
37. Communicate effectively.	37. Same.
38. Control the message. Strive to obtain, retain, and regain control over the meaning and impact of what is presented in expert testimony.	38. Similar. If there is more direct responding to questions posed by the judge, however, such questions should be assumed to be inquisitorial rather than adversarial—and controlling the meaning of responses becomes less important.

Note: Reprinted with permission from Heilbrun & Locklair (2016).

(Heilbrun & Locklair, 2016). The remaining eight principles, however, require some modification for juvenile evaluations.

Several of these modifications stem from the differences between the juvenile and criminal justice systems. For example, Principle 1 ("Be aware of the important differences between clinical and forensic domains") is relevant to juvenile cases—but the distinction between forensic and clinical evaluation is less pronounced, given the rehabilitative focus of the juvenile justice system. Similarly, modifications to Principles 7 ("Do not become adversarial, but present and defend your opinions effectively"), 30 ("Carefully consider whether to answer the ultimate legal question. If it is answered, it should be in the context of a thorough evaluation clearly describing data and reasoning, and with the clear recognition that this question is in the domain of the legal decision-maker"), and 38 ("Control the message. Strive to obtain, retain, and regain control over the meaning and impact of what is presented in expert testimony") underscore differences between expectations and procedures in juvenile versus criminal court. These include more active questioning by the judge, less stringent procedural rules, and a tendency to request that the expert provide an opinion on the ultimate legal question—all of which are more typical in juvenile court (Heilbrun & Locklair, 2016).

Other FMHA principle modifications for juvenile contexts are related to the incorporation of developmental differences. For example, Principle 2 ("Obtain appropriate education, training, and experience in one's area of forensic specialization") is comparable in the juvenile context but would also include education and training related to child and adolescent development and youth-specific issues (Heilbrun & Locklair, 2016). Similarly, Principle 16 ("Select the most appropriate model to guide data gathering, interpretation, and communication"), Principle 20 ("Assess clinical characteristics in relevant, reliable, and valid ways"), and Principle 24 ("Determine whether the individual understands the purpose of the evaluation and the associated limits on confidentiality") are modified to incorporate information about developmental maturity and age-appropriate clinical, behavioral, and educational functioning (Heilbrun & Locklair, 2016).

SPECIALIZED MEASURES

Kent v. United States (1966) held that judges should consider several specific factors before transferring a youth to or from the adult criminal justice system. These factors included seriousness of the offense, nature of the offense (e.g. whether it was violent, premeditated, and the like), the juvenile's level of sophistication and maturity, the juvenile's previous arrest and adjudication record, and the juvenile's likelihood of rehabilitation by means of treatments and services available within the juvenile system (Loving & Patapis, 2007). Forensic mental health professionals typically assess sophistication and maturity, and likelihood of rehabilitation within the juvenile system, as part of these evaluations, as these factors are cited directly in *Kent*. Risk to public safety is not cited directly, but implied by some of the other factors that are cited (nature and seriousness of the offense, previous record of offending). Specialized measures designed to assist in these areas specifically are reviewed in this section.

Sophistication and Maturity Assessment Measures

There are several measures that can assist with the assessment of sophistication-maturity. One is the Consideration of Future Consequences Scale (CFCS) (Strathman, Gleicher *et al.*, 1994). This 12-item self-report scale is designed to gauge a youth's ability to weigh short- and long-term consequences of behaviors and assesses how perceived outcomes may influence decision-making (Salekin, MacDougall *et al.*, 2016). Higher scores are associated with greater consideration of future consequences. The CFCS has demonstrated adequate retest-reliability and internal consistency (Petrocelli, 2003; Strathman, Gleicher *et al.*, 1994), and has been shown to correlate with at least one other measure of future directedness (Salekin, MacDougall *et al.*, 2016)—the Stanford Time Perspective Inventory (Zimbardo, 1990a).

A second measure is the Weinberger Adjustment Inventory (WAI) (Weinberger & Schwartz, 1990). The WAI is a self-report measure that gauges the presence of emotional distress and self-restraint. The self-restraint subscale is perhaps most useful in juvenile disposition evaluations and comprises four subscales: suppression of aggression, temperance, consideration of others, and impulse control (Salekin, MacDougall *et al.*, 2016). The WAI has demonstrated predictive and concurrent validity (e.g. Feldman and Weinberger, 1994; Weinberger and Gomes, 1995), although it has been suggested that the WAI may be more useful in the assessment of antisocial behavior risk and less associated with the construct of developmental maturity (Salekin, MacDougall *et al.*, 2016).

The Psychosocial Maturity Inventory Form (PSMI) (Greenberger, Josselson *et al.*, 1975) is a 30-item self-report measure designed to assess levels of personal responsibility. It includes three subscales: *self-reliance* (ability to make independent decisions and perception of internal control); *identity* (sense of self, self-esteem); and *work orientation* (sense of accomplishment associated with goal attainment) (Salekin, MacDougall *et al.*, 2016).

The PSMI has demonstrated acceptable validity and reliability (e.g. Cauffman & Steinberg, 2000; Colwell, Cruise *et al.*, 2005). It has been used to assess sophistication-maturity constructs such as autonomy and maturity of judgment (Salekin, MacDougall *et al.*, 2016).

The Resistance to Peer Influence (RPI) (Steinberg & Monahan, 2007) is a 10-item self-report measure that gauges the ability to resist peer-influence. Respondents select one of two statements to describe their behavior, then rate how closely the statement approximates their behavior in life. The RPI has been used to measure autonomy in relation to sophistication and maturity, and has been used in combination with the PSMI to provide supplemental information (Monahan, Steinberg *et al.*, 2009).

The Stanford Time Perspective Inventory (STPI; Zimbardo, 1990a) is a 56-item self-report inventory designed to assess the tendency to consider future and long-term consequences. It consists of five subscales: future, present-hedonistic, present-fatalistic, past-positive and past-negative (Salekin, MacDougall *et al.*, 2016). Several studies have demonstrated the reliability and validity of the STPI (e.g. Zimbardo & Boyd, 1999).

The Future Outlook Inventory (FOI) (Cauffman & Woolard, 1999) was developed by using items from the STPI, the CFCS, and the Life Orientation Task (Scheier & Carver, 1985), and is intended to gauge both future orientation and perspective taking (Salekin, MacDougall *et al.*, 2016). FOI respondents are asked to indicate to what extent each of 15 items describes them on a four-point scale.

The Risk-Sophistication-Treatment Inventory (RSTI) is available as both a structured interview (Salekin, 2004b) and a self-report measure (RSTI-SR) (Salekin & Iselin, 2010). The RSTI interview-based measure consists of 45 items, 15 of which are associated with developmental maturity. Clinical interviewers rate the presence of each item on a three-point scale. The developmental maturity scale of the RSTI consists of three subscales: cognitive skills, autonomy, and emotional skills. The RSTI has demonstrated adequate inter-rater reliability and convergent validity (Salekin, MacDougall *et al.*, 2016). The self-report version of the RSTI (the RSTI-SR) contains a similar developmental maturity subscale and clusters corresponding to cognitive skills, autonomy, and emotional skills. Respondents rate the presence of each item on a three-point scale.

Treatment Amenability Measures

There are few measures that directly assess treatment amenability in a way that is relevant to the corresponding legal construct. Evaluators often use measures of clinical treatment needs to inform discussions related to the legal construct of treatment amenability. Examples include clinical and personality measures (e.g. the Minnesota Multiphasic Personality Inventory–Adolescent version) (Butcher, Williams *et al.*, 1992); substance use evaluation tools; antisocial and psychopathic trait measures; and trauma screening tools (Kinscherff, 2016). Such measures are most helpful when the evaluator specifies the need identified by the measure, and this need is relevant to re-offending risk reduction as well as clinical improvement.

One specialized measure that includes a specific treatment amenability scale is the RSTI. The RSTI and RSTI-SR include subscales pertaining to treatment amenability. The three subscales of the amenability scale are (1) responsibility and motivation to change (e.g. takes responsibility for actions); (2) psychopathology degree and type (e.g. insight into cause of problems); and (3) consideration for and tolerance of others (e.g. considers and generally cares about others) (Salekin, 2015a). The treatment amenability subscale of the RSTI is associated with older age of criminal behavior onset and has been observed to be negatively correlated with symptoms of conduct disorder (Salekin, MacDougall *et al.*, 2016).

Risk and Need Measures

The three measures reviewed in this section are discussed in more detail in Chapter 4. The RSTI and RSTI-SR include subscales pertaining to risk: (1) planned and extensive criminality (e.g. premeditated crimes); (2) violent and aggressive tendencies (e.g. aggression toward others); and (3) psychopathic features (e.g. lack of remorse or guilt) (Salekin, 2015a). The risk subscale of the RSTI has been associated with younger age of criminal behavior onset, symptoms of conduct disorder, and violent crimes (Salekin, MacDougall *et al.*, 2016).

The Structured Assessment of Violence Risk in Youth (SAVRY) (Borum, Bartel *et al.*, 2005) is a structured professional judgment tool designed to assess violence risk by focusing evaluators on risk and protective factors. It includes 24 risk-relevant items covering three risk domains (individual, historical, and social/contextual), and six items relevant to protective factors, such as pro-social activities and positive relationships with pro-social adults. The forensic evaluator rates each risk-relevant item as low, moderate, or high based on the scoring guidelines. Examples of risk factors that are assessed using the SAVRY include history of violence (historical), peer delinquency (social), and anger management problems (individual). The SAVRY includes both static and dynamic risk factors, which facilitates identification of treatment targets and progress. Protective factors are rated as either absent or present. The SAVRY has been associated with scores on other violence risk measures, and has demonstrated good reliability and validity (Borum, Bartel *et al.*, 2005; Spice, Viljoen *et al.*, 2010).

The Youth Level of Service/Case Management Inventory (YLS/CMI) (Hoge, 2005) was designed to assess risk factors in young offenders as well as to assist with treatment planning and placement recommendations. The risk assessment section comprises 42 questions that constitute eight subscales: family circumstance/parenting (e.g. inconsistent parenting); prior/current offenses/dispositions (e.g. prior probation); education/employment (e.g. disruptive classroom behavior); substance abuse (e.g. chronic drug use); peer relations (e.g. some delinquent friends); personality/behavior (e.g. poor frustration tolerance); attitudes/orientation (e.g.   social attitudes); and leisure/recreation (e.g. limited organized activities). A revised version of the YLS/CMI was published in 2010 (YLS-CMI 2.0) (Hoge & Andrews, 2010b) using a standardization sample that was demographically representative of the contemporary juvenile justice population. The YLS/CMI has demonstrated predictive validity in relation to recidivism (Marczyk, Heilbrun *et al.*, 2005) and is the clearest example of a specialty measure designed consistent with Risk-Need-Responsivity (RNR).

CONCLUSION

This chapter focused on the foundational aspects of FMHA that are important for evaluations of juvenile disposition and transfer. Such juvenile evaluations differ from other kinds of FMHA in certain respects, particularly regarding a greater emphasis on developmental and rehabilitative considerations. Despite these differences, a principles-based analysis (considering law, science, ethics, and practice as the major sources of authority) demonstrates that disposition and transfer evaluations are a kind of FMHA, as they are consistent in most respects with other kinds of forensic evaluations. As part of the fundamental description of juvenile evaluations of disposition and transfer, we propose a model containing risk, needs, treatment amenability, and sophistication-maturity. There are different ways in which these model components could interact. Sophistication-maturity could combine with risk and needs to yield a conclusion about amenability. Alternatively, sophistication-maturity could be considered along with amenability to reach a broader conclusion about rehabilitation potential. Each possibility is considered in subsequent chapters to determine which is better supported by available theory and evidence. Specialized measures of risk-need and sophistication-maturity are reviewed. Such a review is also provided for amenability, but there are few available ways to measure this construct. Discussion in subsequent chapters will provide more detail on risk, need, amenability, and sophistication-maturity, with a more in-depth consideration of the supporting research and related practice implications.

NOTE

1. We use the term "behavioral health disorders" to include mental, emotional, behavioral, and substance abuse disorders, as well as intellectual dysfunction.

CHAPTER FOUR

Developmental Aspects of Evaluation

One of the important differences between FMHA with juveniles and that with adults involves the developmental influences on various capacities in youth. This chapter reviews the developmental research that is particularly relevant to the domains included in risk, treatment needs and amenability, and sophistication-maturity. It also addresses the evidence concerning culpability, which has been the focus of much of the relevant developmental research to date.

ADOLESCENT DEVELOPMENT

Adolescence is a tumultuous period involving considerable change, as youth mature in social, biological, cognitive, self-perception, and moral domains (Barbot & Hunter, 2012). It is also a time that is associated with a greater likelihood of behavior involving rules violation, risk-taking, conflict with authority, and other antisocial conduct. Numerous behavioral health disorders first emerge during adolescence (Kessler, Berglund *et al.*, 2005). Neither developmental maturity nor behavioral health functioning is sufficient to answer the questions posed by the law as part of juvenile FMHA, of course. But they are part of the larger picture. It is important that such juvenile forensic evaluators consider relevant scientific evidence in the areas of brain development, cognitive development, biological changes, identity development, social development and peer influence, psycho-social maturity, and developmental maturity. These areas help to explain why adolescents act as they do—including adolescents who are involved in antisocial behavior. But this discussion must also consider the risk of expecting more from developmental data than they can provide. One important advantage of having a separate juvenile justice system is that decisions involving young offenders' evaluation and rehabilitation are made in the context of a system that *should* consider developmental maturity, as all evaluees are adolescents. Developmental differences become more pronounced and influential when justice-involved youth are being considered for transfer into the criminal system, or have already been placed there and are considered for transfer back to the juvenile system.

The vast majority of those in the criminal justice system are adults—and the system is not designed to accommodate developmental immaturity in the way that the juvenile system is.

THE ADOLESCENT BRAIN

Changes in the brain occur during adolescence in both structural and functional respects, as summarized in a recent detailed review (see Luna & Wright, 2016). Among the structural changes are synaptic pruning, which eliminates unused connections between neurons and strengthens those that remain (Rauschecker & Marler, 1987). Such pruning continues in the prefrontal cortex through adolescence (Petanjek, Judaš *et al.*, 2011). Significant influences on brain development during this period include exposure to increased levels of hormones such as estrogen, testosterone, and gonadotropin releasing hormone (Sisk & Zehr, 2005). Brain development during adolescence (particularly the maturation of prefrontal executive functioning and limbic motivational/emotional processes) may be associated with a tendency toward sensation-seeking that may lead to greater risk-taking, particularly in the presence of peers (Luna & Wright, 2016).

Two neurobiological systems have been recognized as most relevant to adolescent behavior control and offending: the cognitive control system and the socio-emotional system (Casey, Jones *et al.*, 2008). The cognitive control system typically refers to the lateral prefrontal and parietal cortices, and it is associated with executive functions such as planning, behavior regulation, judgment, working memory, and impulse control (Johnson, Blum *et al.*, 2009). Executive functioning capacities allow mature individuals to assess a situation, weigh potential options, develop a plan of action, and respond accordingly. Executive functioning is associated with the following areas:

- attention and concentration;
- understanding, processing, and communicating information;
- planning, organizing, and initiating thoughts and behavior;
- understanding others' reactions;
- abstracting and reasoning;

- controlling impulses, stopping behavior, and regulating emotions;
- inhibiting unsuccessful, inappropriate, or impulsive behaviors;
- using knowledge to regulate behavior;
- behavioral flexibility to changing contingencies;
- modulating behavior in light of expected consequences;
- distraction from persisting with appropriate behavior;
- appreciation of the impact of behaviors on others;
- manipulation of learned and stored information when making decisions.

(Fabian, 2011: 742)

The cognitive control system evolves gradually through adolescence, with some areas of the prefrontal cortex only reaching maturity between the ages of 20 and 25 (Gogtay, Giedd *et al.*, 2004).

The socio-emotional system refers to brain structures and functions that facilitate the processing and integration of emotional and social stimuli. Neural structures such as the amygdala, orbitofrontal cortex, insula, medial prefrontal cortex, ventral striatum, and superior temporal sulcus are included in the socio-emotional system (Nelson, Leibenluft *et al.*, 2005). This system is closely associated with the brain's reward pathways, linked with seeking pleasure, avoiding unpleasant experiences, and regulating the expression of emotion. It evolves quickly after the onset of puberty, and is typically considered mature in youth by the ages of 15 or 16 (Barbot & Hunter, 2012).

These neurobiological changes are accompanied by discernible behavioral changes in areas such as judgment and planning, risk-taking, and decision-making (Cohen & Casey, 2014). They may be related to a well-known phenomenon called the "age-crime curve." This refers to the increased prevalence of criminal behavior that peaks at around age 17 and subsequently diminishes (Landsheer & van Dijkum, 2005). Some suggest that the higher rates of impulsivity and risk-taking in adolescence reflect the gap between the earlier maturation of the brain's emotion-processing system and the later maturation of the cognitive control system (e.g. Steinberg, 2007). More specifically, the limited development of skills related to executive control (an underdeveloped cognitive control system) coupled with a strong orientation toward pleasurable and social influences (a more fully developed socio-emotional system) can yield poorer judgment, planning, and decision-making relative to adults—particularly in the context of highly emotionally or socially salient circumstances (Barbot & Hunter, 2012).

Prominent neurobiological theories of adolescence suggest that dynamic and asymmetric trajectories in structural and functional development of limbic and prefrontal circuitry are implicated in motivated behavior and its control, respectively, and may lead to a propensity toward risky and impulsive actions (Casey, 2015; Ernst, Pine *et al.*, 2006; Mills, Goddings *et al.*, 2014; Steinberg, 2010). Phylogenetically older brain regions, such as the subcortical limbic regions, show non-linear developmental changes and appear to be functionally sensitized during adolescence (Galvan, Hare *et al.*, 2006; Hare, Tottenham *et al.*, 2008; Raznahan, Shaw *et al.*, 2014), whereas development of the prefrontal cortex exhibits a roughly linear trajectory (Galvan, Hare *et al.*, 2006; Gogtay, Giedd *et al.*, 2004; Sowell, Thompson *et al.*, 2004). Resting-state functional-connectivity data show prolonged development of long-range cortical connectivity that does not stabilize until the twenties (Dosenbach, Nardos *et al.*, 2010; Fair, Dosenbach *et al.*, 2007). Together, these results suggest continued refinement of brain circuitry, particularly prefrontal cortical circuitry, into young adulthood—but the behavioral implications of this protracted brain development remain unclear.

The possibility that adolescents engage in risk-taking behavior because they are deficient in assessing risk has not been supported, however. Most studies in this area have not reported age differences in perceptions of risk associated with a variety of high-risk behaviors (Beyth-Marom, Austin *et al.*, 1993; Millstein & Halpern-Felsher, 2001; Steinberg, 2008). Adolescents appear to understand the nature and seriousness of risks about as well as adults, but their behavior does not reflect a comparable reluctance to take such risks. How might this be understood?

One alternative to the risk-insensitivity hypothesis involves the neurochemistry of reward-seeking behavior, the so-called "reward deficiency syndrome" (Steinberg, 2008). Research suggests that dopamine receptors, which are involved in the reward pathways, tend to diminish rapidly in number around the onset of puberty (Chambers, Taylor *et al.*, 2014; Spear, 2000). With this substantial decrease in receptors for the transmission of pleasurable sensation, the adolescent brain may require more intense stimulation to activate dopaminergic neurons (Steinberg, 2008). Behaviorally, this may manifest as intense sensation-seeking behavior (e.g. reckless driving, impulsive sexual activity), as the surge of dopamine associated with risk-taking behaviors is strong enough to activate the weakened adolescent reward system (Barbot & Hunter, 2012.) This is analogous to substance use tolerance, with individuals who abuse substances often needing more to achieve the same "high" (in this case, more stimulation to yield comparable dopaminergic activation of the reward system).

However, several studies have reported findings that are inconsistent with the reward deficiency syndrome hypothesis, including the observation of *increased* prefrontal cortex dopaminergic activity (despite the loss of receptors) and subcortical activation in response to rewards during adolescence (Ernst, Nelson *et al.*, 2005; Rosenberg & Lewis, 1995). Some suggest, therefore, that greater risk-taking during adolescence is not related to an increased threshold for dopaminergic stimulation, but rather to the development of a more sensitive and efficient dopaminergic system—which may increase reward salience by making the experience of potentially rewarding stimuli even more intense (Ernst & Spear, 2009; Steinberg, 2008).

COGNITIVE DEVELOPMENT

Current conceptions of cognitive development in adolescence include a range of capabilities. Planning, self-governance, goal-directed behavior, values, and principles are among the domains that have been included (Steinberg, Dahl *et al.*, 2006). In addition, such capacities include selective inhibition, inductive reasoning, and epistemic understanding (Kuhn, 2009; Moshman, 2005). Adolescents must also learn to think about how to organize their understanding of events in the world (Chandler, Lalonde *et al.*, 2003; Fischer & Bidell, 2006).

Studies of cognitive development lend themselves to laboratory research. This is valuable in some respects, as it allows the careful control of confounding variables and implementation of controlled designs. But it is limiting as well. Much of what we know about adolescent cognitive development comes from an artificial laboratory environment. We know less about the development of self-regulation in school, family, peer, and community contexts (Rogoff, Baker-Sennett *et al.*, 1994). For instance, much is known about adolescent motivation—but little about how it changes and develops (Wigfield, Eccles *et al.*, 2006).

On simple cognitive tasks, the speed and accuracy with which adolescents (particularly those aged 15 and older) perform is comparable to that of adults (Luna, Marek *et al.*, 2015). But the maturation in the cognitive performance of adolescents is less straightforward than it once appeared. There is evidence that it is affected by contextual variables such as incentives (Galvan, Hare *et al.*, 2006; Geier, Terwilliger *et al.*, 2010; Somerville, Hare *et al.*, 2011; Van Leijenhorst, Zanolie *et al.*, 2010), threats (Cohen-Gilbert & Thomas, 2013; Dreyfuss, Caudle *et al.*, 2014; Grose-Fifer, Rodrigues *et al.*, 2013; Hare, Tottenham *et al.*, 2008), and peers (Chein, Albert *et al.*, 2011; Gardner & Steinberg, 2005). In a recent study, Cohen, Breiner *et al.* (2016) compared the cognitive performance of adolescents (13–17 years old), young adults (18–21 years old), and adults (22–25 years old) on a go/no go task under conditions of negative arousal (expecting a loud noise), positive arousal (expecting a prize), or neutrality (no expectations). Under the negative arousal condition, young adults performed similarly to the younger adolescent group, in that both groups made significantly more errors than the adults. Under the neutral and positive arousal conditions, however, the young adults performed like adults—and better than the adolescents. The investigators concluded that young adult cognitive performance under negative emotional conditions was adversely affected in a way that it was not under emotionally neutral or positive conditions. The implications of this study for understanding the cognitive functioning of 18–21 year olds, for either psychological evaluation or policy-making purposes, underscore the contextual effects on cognitive functioning, even among individuals who are older than most youth evaluated for disposition or transfer. Individuals of this age differ in some important respects from younger boys and girls. Such differences were part of the argument made by prominent developmental scholars *against* increasing the age of eligible participants in the juvenile system from 18 to 21 (Steinberg, Grisso *et al.*, 2016).

It has also been shown that the capacity to weigh risk and rewards continues to develop some time after the ability to simply recognize risk (Scott & Steinberg, 2008). The former is a more complex cognitive task akin to "dynamic systems" decisions, while the latter is a simpler recognition and understanding task. Cognitive development continues throughout adolescence, but relative maturity is seen at different ages depending on the nature and complexity of the demands and the influence of context. The ability to recall a previous face does not improve past age 12 or 13, for example, but the ability to remember several pieces of information and use them in problem-solving improves through ages 16 and 17 (Luciana, Conklin *et al.*, 2005). Moreover, cognitive development may be slowed by a variety of influences, including the presence of various behavioral health disorders—particularly important because justice-involved youth have a relatively high prevalence of more limited intellectual functioning, learning disorders, brain dysfunction, and other behavioral health challenges (Nagel, Guarnera *et al.*, 2016).

IDENTITY DEVELOPMENT

One of the important tasks of adolescence involves developing a clearer understanding of one's own identity (Erikson, 1968). Developing a mature sense of self is often associated with conflict between opposing influences: the need for independence and individuation versus the need for affiliation and social connection. This struggle represents a major challenge for adolescents (Kroger, 2003). Identity formation has been described as the primary developmental task of adolescence, during which individuals mature in their personal, gender, ethnic, sexual, and social identities (Barbot & Hunter, 2012). The development of maladaptive coping strategies as part of identity-related struggles may be linked in some instances with delinquent behavior. Research related to Erikson's (1968) theory of adolescent identity has demonstrated that identity formation is characterized by extensive experimentation and exploration during adolescence (Steinberg & Scott, 2003). Although identity-seeking typically occurs most intensively during middle adolescence, its resolution and integration of personally relevant elements of identity into a cohesive "developed self" usually does not occur until late adolescence or early adulthood (Waterman, 1982). Often the exploration associated with identity formation includes risk-taking behaviors such as substance use, sexual experimentation, and antisocial behavior (Steinberg & Scott, 2004). However, the failure to develop in the self-identity domain is not clearly linked to either risk or treatment needs in juveniles. There is limited evidence suggesting that it is associated with low motivation (Waterman, 2004), earlier first arrests, and more total arrests (White & Jones, 1996).

SOCIAL DEVELOPMENT AND THE INFLUENCE OF PEERS

Research in social development indicates that actively seeking peer approval and acceptance is a frequent component of adolescent development (Cohen & Casey, 2014). Peer influence (including negative influence) is particularly potent during this stage of life (Haynie, 2002). Such peer influence involves two related processes: social comparison (assessing one's own behavior by observing the behavior of others) and social conformity (the tendency to imitate the behavior of peers). Social conformity is particularly important in adolescence, as the tendency to model one's behavior on that of peers peaks around 14 or 15 years of age and then slowly declines during mid and late adolescence (Scott & Steinberg, 2008). Further, perceived peer rejection during adolescence often results in greater risk-taking behavior associated with efforts to gain acceptance from peers (Cohen & Casey, 2014; Steinberg & Monahan, 2007).

Relative to adults, adolescents tend to commit more group-based crimes (Steinberg & Scott, 2003). Social pressures can influence adolescent offending behavior either directly (e.g. an adolescent is pressured into engaging in behavior that he or she would not typically display), or indirectly (e.g. an adolescent's fear of peer rejection and desire for acceptance leads to engaging in offending behavior) (Scott & Steinberg, 2008). It has been suggested that the offending behavior of adolescents who become justice-involved but do not continue offending into adulthood is frequently motivated by a desire to imitate antisocial peers of higher social status (Moffitt, 1993). Consistent with this, a study involving measuring brain activation (with fMRI) during a driving simulation task showed that when adolescents performed the task under peer observation, they were more likely to exhibit activation in the region of the brain related to the reward system, and to engage in risk-taking behavior, than when the task was performed without peer observation (Chein, Albert *et al.*, 2011). This effect was not seen with adult participants.

The need for affiliation may be particularly problematic for adolescents immersed in subcultures (e.g. gangs) where so-called "delinquent reputations" are promoted as desirable (Jennings & Gonzalez, 2016). In light of research on peer influence in adolescence, it has been suggested that the motivation for the behavior of juvenile offenders differs from that of typical adult offenders in that justice-involved adults are more likely to act according to more stable personal characteristics and values. By contrast, adolescent offending behavior is more likely to be shaped by the social influences that are present during this developmental stage (Steinberg & Scott, 2003).

PSYCHO-SOCIAL MATURITY

The evaluation of juvenile transfer often incorporates constructs such as sophistication and maturity (Borum & Grisso, 2007). These constructs could refer to at least four aspects of the evaluee's appearance and functioning: (1) physical appearance—the extent to which the individual physically resembles an adult; (2) intellectual and cognitive functioning—the maturity of thinking, as affected by both developmental maturity and strengths or deficits in areas such as IQ, and basic academic skills such as reading, spelling, and math; (3) psycho-social maturity, as discussed in this section; and (4) criminal sophistication, or the extent to which planning, skill, and motivation are more typical of adult offenders than juveniles. The United States Supreme Court, in *Kent*, described sophistication and maturity as separate considerations, and states such as Pennsylvania indicate in relevant statutes that the maturity of a juvenile is different than the criminal sophistication. Maturity is likely to mean something akin to the first three considerations described in this paragraph, while sophistication apparently refers to the approach to offending. (See Chapter 6, this book, for a fuller discussion.)

The third of these may be related fairly closely to the construct of psycho-social maturity, which has been defined as the "complexity and sophistication of the process of individual decision-making as it is affected by a range of cognitive, emotional, and social factors" (Cauffman & Steinberg, 2000: 743). Three capacities contribute to the construct of psycho-social maturity. The first is *responsibility*, defined as the ability to make independent decisions and remain reasonably self-reliant in the face of external pressures. The second is *perspective*, or the ability to identify and weigh short- and long-term consequences of a decision (temporal perspective) *and* the ability to identify and understand another individual's position on an issue (interpersonal perspective). The third is *temperance*, or the capacity to exhibit self-control and restrain impulses. Each of these will be discussed in this section.

Responsibility

Research in the domain of responsibility indicates that typically developing juveniles tend to exhibit responsibility (as defined above) by late adolescence (Borum & Grisso, 2007). Research on the role of social influence in adolescence, addressing adolescents' ability to make independent decisions and demonstrate self-reliance when faced with external pressures, indicates that social conformity (the tendency to emulate the behavior of peers) peaks around 14 or 15 years of age and then gradually declines during mid to late adolescence (Scott & Steinberg, 2008). The need to conform behavior to that modeled by peers is often at odds with the development of independence and the capacity to resist external pressures (particularly peer pressure). Adolescents' tendency to seek peer approval through risky behavior, and to commit more group-based crimes, can slow the maturation of responsibility. Relative to adolescents, adults tend to engage in consistent decision-making whether alone or with peers, suggesting that difficulty with independent decision-making typically declines by adulthood (Gardner & Steinberg, 2005).

Temporal Perspective

Both temporal and interpersonal perspectives change during adolescence. When perspective is less mature, adolescents may display poor judgment in part because they assign greater value to short-term consequences (Borum & Grisso, 2007). The relationship between less mature temporal perspective and corresponding judgment errors is illustrated by rates of high-risk behaviors in adolescence. For instance, in one study involving a national sample of high-school youth, there were substantial endorsements of risky behaviors such as drinking alcohol (38.7 percent), having unprotected sex (38.5 percent of the students who reported that they were currently sexually active), and engaging in physical altercations (35.5 percent) (Eaton, Kann *et al.*, 2008).

There is also evidence that temporal perspective improves across age cohorts. When participants were instructed to complete a challenging puzzle in as few moves as possible, results showed linear increases in temporal perspective. Younger adolescents (aged 10–15) spent the least amount of time planning their moves, followed by older adolescents and young adults (aged 16–21), with adults (aged 22–30) spending the most time (Steinberg, Albert *et al.*, 2008). Another study suggests that this effect is more pronounced under emotionally salient circumstances, such as the ability to earn money based on performance. Adolescents engaged in less planning and considered less information than their adult counterparts during an emotionally arousing task—but when the monetary–emotional incentive was not present, they performed comparably to adults (Figner, Mackinlay *et al.*, 2009). However, other evidence suggests that such perspective does not develop in a straightforward linear fashion. For instance, a study considering temporal perspective, risk perception, and peer influence in detained versus non-detained youth yielded results consistent with a U-shape pattern: younger adolescents and older adolescents both exhibited greater maturity with regard to temporal perspective than those in middle adolescence (15–16 years of age) (Fried & Reppucci, 2001).

Interpersonal Perspective

Youths gain in the capacity to better understand and take the perspective of others during adolescence (Steinberg & Scott, 2003). Studying interpersonal perspective in over 1,000 participants ranging from 12–48 years old, investigators found an association between greater interpersonal perspective capacity and lower likelihood of self-reported antisocial or risky behavior in various age groups within adolescence and adulthood (Cauffman & Steinberg, 2000). They also noted an increase in interpersonal perspective capacity with age. This underscores not only the development of this capacity during adolescence, but the individual differences among individuals of comparable age, suggesting individual variability as well as developmental acquisition of greater interpersonal perspective.

Interpersonal perspective has also been studied in the context of juvenile justice as investigators have considered the relationship between empathy and outcomes such as aggression and antisocial behavior. Some research has suggested that lower empathy is related to greater risk for such outcomes (deKemp, Overbeek *et al.*, 2007; Kaukiainen, Björkqvist *et al.*, 1999; Richardson, Hammock *et al.*, 1994). This was also observed in a meta-analysis, although only one study included the specific outcome of offending (Miller & Eisenberg, 1988). Lower levels of empathy have also been described as associated with lower maturity in moral judgment (Barriga, Sullivan-Cosetti *et al.*, 2009). Youth with conduct disorder showed lower levels of empathy than did youth without such disorder

(Cohen & Strayer, 1996). When empathy is considered in two forms—cognitive and affective—then low cognitive empathy is strongly related to offending, while low affective empathy shows a more modest relationship. But the relationship between empathy and offending disappears when socioeconomic status (SES) and intellectual functioning is controlled, raising the possibility that SES and intellectual function are stronger risk factors than empathy for juvenile offending (Jolliffe & Farrington, 2004) (see Heilbrun, Shah *et al.* (2014) for a detailed discussion of the relationship between empathy and offending in justice-involved youth).

Temperance

Research related to temperance, or the capacity to exhibit self-control, indicates that individuals show stable levels of temperance from childhood to approximately 16 years of age (Steinberg, Cauffman *et al.*, 2009). Around age 16, impulsivity increases (and temperance decreases) for several years until approximately 19 years of age (Steinberg & Cauffman, 1996). Thus, older adolescents can be expected to display less developed temperance than younger evaluees in the context of juvenile FMHA (Borum & Grisso, 2007).

Temperance can be considered from both a neuropsychological and developmental perspective. The earlier maturation of the brain's emotion-processing system and the subsequent maturation of the cognitive control system have been implicated in the impulsive behavior of mid-to-late adolescents. The executive functions associated with the frontal lobes and cognitive control system are integral to the formation and utilization of temperance. Accordingly, research related to the developing brain is highly relevant to the understanding of this construct.

Research evidence on the temporal perspective, discussed earlier, is also relevant to developmental changes in temperance. For example, the results of Figner, Mackinlay *et al.*'s (2009) card game study suggest that under emotionally salient circumstances, adolescents tend to exhibit greater impulsivity and less temperance than adults. Similarly, Steinberg, Albert *et al.*'s (2008) puzzle task study is consistent with less temperance in adolescents, as reflected in more limited time spent planning prior to deciding on puzzle moves.

Although temperance is generally considered to be inversely related to risk of offending (see, for example, DeLisi, Beaver *et al.*, 2010), at least one study suggests the opposite. This study found that increased temperance (defined as the ability to think before acting and the control of impulsivity) was associated with total delinquent behavior, violence, and non-violent criminal behavior among boys (Cruise, Fernandez *et al.*, 2008). This may underscore the importance of considering the nature of the offending. Some crimes are committed after planning, which could mean that those with a greater capacity for self-control tend toward this type of offense when they do commit crimes.

Development of the psycho-social capacities discussed in this section continues throughout adolescence. Maturation in the areas of temporal perspective, interpersonal perspective, and temperance is accompanied by improvements in decision-making, self-control, and the understanding of others (Cauffman, Shulman *et al.*, 2010; Shulman & Steinberg, 2016; Steinberg, Cauffman *et al.*, 2009).

DEVELOPMENTAL MATURITY

The assessment of developmental maturity (a broader term encompassing both cognitive and psychosocial development) is a key component in any juvenile FMHA (Borum & Grisso, 2007). But forensic mental health professionals should not regard developmental maturity in dichotomous terms (either "developmentally mature" or "developmentally immature"). Rather, developmental immaturity should be conceptualized as a construct that (1) "refers to incomplete development (having not reached one's level of maturation) or delayed development (in relation to one's age peers)"; (2) "describes specific abilities or characteristics, not an overall condition of youth"; (3) "depends on actual functioning, not simply on age", and (4) "can be expressed in degrees in relation to one's peers" (Grisso, 2005: 18).

In addition, Borum & Grisso (2007) have underscored three basic principles of human development that can be applied when considering developmental maturity in juveniles.

First, normal development is a fluid concept and may vary greatly from one juvenile to another. The trajectory of normal or average development can be affected by variables within the environment, particularly poverty or low SES. Thus, published guides for "typical development" (usually standardized on Caucasian samples of middle-class children) may present an overestimate of expected developmental maturity in lower-SES or minority samples. Second, developmental domains (e.g. social, cognitive, and physical) may not progress along the same trajectory within an individual. A juvenile may exhibit normal cognitive functioning and present with socioemotional deficits, or show the opposite. Thus, it is important to assess all relevant developmental domains directly rather than inferring functioning in one domain from measured performance in another. Third, development does not always progress on a steady incline. Rapid developmental increases ("spurts"), developmental delays, and developmental regressions may be observed in juveniles.

DEVELOPMENTAL CONSIDERATIONS FOR CULPABILITY

There are several developmental capacities that may be particularly important to offending behavior and related decision-making. These include an inability to consider risks and consequences when faced with decisions, an inability to exhibit self- or impulse-control, difficulty resisting the influence of peers, and difficulty experiencing empathy (Borum & Grisso, 2007). These factors, which map onto Cauffman and Steinberg's (2000) conceptualization of psycho-social maturity fairly well, are all less developed in adolescents than they are in adults. It is this observation that has driven much of the legal decision-making regarding adolescent culpability in the *Roper*, *Graham*, *Miller*, and *Montgomery* cases. For example, Justice Kennedy, writing for the majority in *Roper*, pointed to three developmental differences between adolescents and adults that are relevant to diminished culpability for adolescents: (1) immaturity and an underdeveloped sense of responsibility, which impair decision-making; (2) greater susceptibility to peer pressure and other external influences, including less control over the environment; and (3) character that is still developing (Shulman & Steinberg, 2016). This is consistent with brain science research showing that the prefrontal cortex (the last region of the brain to mature) plays an important role in modulating emotions and behavioral impulses, gauging risk and reward, and anticipating longer-term consequences (see Steinberg, 2008, for a review).

IMPLICATIONS FOR ASSESSMENT

The application of neurodevelopmental research to juvenile FMHA is still in an early stage (Wynkoop, 2008). Neuropsychological functioning that is particularly relevant to juvenile evaluation includes areas such as IQ, language and verbal abilities, ADHD, and executive functioning (Fabian, 2011). But our search of the literature for research or clinical commentaries on juvenile offending and maturity (https://goo.gl/0Vzb5m) and identity (https://goo.gl/XfwBdk) revealed relatively little research—and no practice recommendations. There is a more general research literature on juvenile psycho-social maturation in social functioning (e.g. https://goo.gl/2bWc1F) and identity development (e.g. https://goo.gl/xyoj0c). But even when such a search yields promising possibilities, they should not be used in the field before they have been applied through research on the relevant population (justice-involved adolescents), questions (sophistication and maturity in conjunction with risk, needs, and treatment amenability), and contexts (juvenile and criminal courts, juvenile detention centers, and community-based and residential treatments).

One noteworthy exception for the assessment of sophistication and maturity in justice-involved adolescents is the Risk-Sophistication-Treatment Inventory (RSTI) (Salekin, 2004a; Iselin, DeCoster *et al.*, 2009; Salekin, 2015a). But as the present discussion makes clear, the translation from developmental research findings to the legally relevant areas of sophistication and maturity is not straightforward. This is attempted in the

15-item sophistication-maturity subscale of the RSTI (Salekin, Salekin *et al.*, 2005). Given the ongoing development of research in this area, it would be helpful to have others attempt a comparable translation. Until that is done, the RSTI remains the only specialized tool that offers a means of measuring this legally relevant construct. Evaluators who do not use the RSTI must be mindful of the translational difficulties between the developmental research and the legally relevant constructs of sophistication and maturity.

CONCLUSION

Evidence reviewed in this chapter has several important implications for the evaluation of juvenile transfer and disposition. First, there are some developmental influences—chiefly impulsivity and greater susceptibility to peer influence—that may be associated with certain kinds of offending. Second, this developmental evidence maps onto legal language regarding maturity and sophistication, although it is not synonymous. Third, even the development of cognitive capacity—once thought to be a fairly straightforward adult-like function achieved by adolescents around the age of 15 or 16—is now understood to be affected by contextual variables such as incentives, threats and other negative expectations, and peers. Much of the available developmental evidence should also be considered cautiously because it comes from the laboratory, using tasks that are much simpler than the thinking and feeling involved in delinquent behavior, and so it may not generalize well to justice-involved youth.

CHAPTER FIVE

Risk Assessment

This chapter will focus on risk assessment, addressing recidivism risk—one of the recurring criteria applicable to both transfer and disposition decisions. After identifying important conceptual considerations (e.g. risk of what, over what period), we describe the relevant research on juvenile risk assessment. We also discuss and critically consider specialized measures of such risk, and make recommendations for their use in light of the applicable research.

Risk analysis has dominated law in areas such as environment, health, and safety (Hamilton, 2015), but has been applied only more recently to criminal and juvenile law, despite the long-standing importance of public safety as a consideration in criminal sentencing. The emphasis on risk and public safety is explicit in the criteria for transfer and reverse transfer, while the disposition question is primarily focused on the youth's needs under relevant law (see Chapter 2, this volume). Most state statutes do not define the disposition "danger standard" beyond a brief phrase (e.g. "protection of the community") with possible modifiers (e.g. "substantial," "significant"), so there is much latitude for judicial discretion. But the job of the court in applying this consideration may be complex, considering risk of harming others in placement, persistent offending into adulthood, or likelihood of violence to others if placed under less controlled conditions (Grisso, 2013).

Using risk-relevant information can be very helpful in considering the needs at disposition of a youth who is adjudicated delinquent. There are several reasons for this: (1) such needs are relevant to re-offending, and (2) a youth's risk of re-offending has important implications for considerations such as the location, duration, and intensity of treatment, as (3) good information about risk promotes the diversion of low-risk offenders into community-based alternative interventions, that are (4) less disruptive to youth and their families, and minimize the "contagion effect" that can result from placing low-risk youth with higher-risk individuals. This can also promote accuracy while reducing crime. Using a structured decision-making tool incorporating risk to guide disposition, investigators found a recidivism rate of 19.4 percent in dispositions with placements within the prescribed range and a 38.7 percent recidivism rate for dispositions outside this range in a sample of 38,117 juvenile offenders (Baglivio & Epps, 2015). Crime severity is often used as a proxy for risk, with more serious offenses thought to indicate higher risk. In reality, the severity of the original offense does not predict later offending patterns—but risk assessment for re-offending does (Mulvey, Steinberg *et al.*, 2010).

Rehabilitative strategies that address the specific criminogenic needs of youth are less expensive and more effective in reducing re-offense risk, relative to punitive sanctions (Drake, Aos *et al.*, 2009; Lipsey, 2009; Vieira, Skilling *et al.*, 2009). The optimal use of risk assessment incorporates multiple stages within the juvenile (and possibly criminal) justice system, including disposition, placement, and community services. To the extent that similar rehabilitation targets can be identified early in this process, and receive continued attention over time and across settings, the potential for risk reduction and the efficiency of services are maximized.

It has been estimated that over 85 percent of judges consider formal risk assessment in the juvenile court process (Schwalbe, 2008a), and almost all states have some counties that use a risk assessment tool as part of juvenile probation services (Wachter, 2014). The National Academy of Sciences (2013) addressed the use of risk and need assessment in juvenile justice contexts: "Assessing the risk of re-arrest and the intervention needs of each youth is the necessary first step in achieving the overall goal of a more rational and developmentally appropriate array of preventive interventions in the juvenile justice system" (p. 5). But collecting risk-relevant information is only a first step. Unfortunately, research suggests that when risk assessment instruments are used to obtain such information, it is then often used improperly—or not at all (Shook & Sarri, 2007; Young, Moline *et al.*, 2006).

We suggest in this chapter, therefore, that appropriate, risk-relevant information be properly collected and appropriately conveyed in evaluations of disposition and transfer. (The construct of sophistication-maturity, by contrast, is largely applicable to transfer and reverse transfer, but not to disposition. The question of how "adult-like" the youthful offender appears is much less relevant in a juvenile disposition decision.) We prioritize re-offending risk in evaluating youth for disposition and transfer to a greater extent than some others. Salekin (2015a), for example, has described best practice in juvenile forensic assessment as appraising a young person's personality and possible pathology to the courts to ensure that effective decisions can be made regarding management and treatment of the child. This approach appears to incorporate the contributions of personality assessment and non-criminogenic psychopathology to a much greater extent than we do.

IMPORTANT CONSIDERATIONS IN RISK ASSESSMENT

Much of the value of risk assessment is drawn from the information that is considered, and the way in which this information is combined and interpreted. To use this process effectively, however, there are matters of definition, theory, and context that must be considered. Employing an effective strategy for risk assessment in juvenile evaluations has been analogized to being aware that a car is the best way to get across town: knowing how to operate the car will not get you to your destination most efficiently. One must know the context as well (Grisso, 2013).

PARAMETERS OF RISK ASSESSMENT

Risk assessment begins with questions that provide structure to this effort and make the results more meaningful. Important initial questions include target behavior, frequency, probability/risk category, settings, outcome period, and risk and protective factors (Heilbrun, 2009).

Target behavior is the outcome on which the process is focused. There are various outcomes that might be appropriate for evaluations of disposition and transfer: violent offending, violent behavior (including offending), general offending, and improvement in areas that are associated with offending (e.g. family dysfunction, school problems, substance abuse). Some evaluations also prioritize areas that are typically not associated with offending (e.g. self-esteem, life satisfaction). For reasons discussed in this chapter and throughout this book, we suggest that the outcome that is most consistent with relevant law and juvenile system precedent is re-offending—particularly serious re-offending. Secondary targets, such as risk factors that mediate the occurrence of re-offending and are appropriate aims of risk-reducing treatment intervention, are also reasonable targets. The particular target should be specified as part of risk assessment. However, outcomes that are distinct from re-offending (e.g. symptomatic improvement of behavioral health symptoms that nonetheless do not alter re-offense risk; increased self-esteem) may be useful as collateral improvements if they occur—but legal parameters, efficiency, and finite resources should dictate a primary focus on the outcome of re-offending. This is consistent with the specialized risk-need measures we describe later in this chapter.

Frequency refers to how often the target outcome is predicted to occur. Usually a single occurrence of an outcome such as crime or violence would be sufficient. This is a reasonable default assumption for the evaluator. It is also consistent with the guidelines for using specialized measures, which typically divide outcomes into "yes" or "no" based on such a single occurrence. Of course, if there is a clear basis for predicting that multiple occurrences of the target outcome are likely, this should be specified as part of the risk assessment.

Probability/risk category describes how the findings of the risk assessment will be combined, and how the conclusion will be conveyed. Three risk communication approaches have generally been used to convey the results of specialized risk measures: *probability* ("this youth is X percent likely to commit another offense following his release to the community"), *frequency* ("X percent of comparable youths will commit another offense following release to the community"), or *categorization* ("this youth appears at low risk relative to others under these circumstances for committing another crime following release to the community"). Unless the evaluator has a good empirical basis for framing a conclusion in probability or frequency terms—which means using a specialized measure that has been derived and validated to provide such information—then the appropriate form of risk communication is categorical.

Setting refers to the context in which the youth will be living. There are obvious and important differences between being confined in a secure residential placement, living in the community with intensive case management and day placement, or living at home under standard probation. Specialized risk measures typically distinguish only between confinement and community contexts, so further description of the youth's circumstances are appropriate when individualizing the results on evaluation using such specialized measures.

Over what period of time should the evaluation consider the youth's risk? The longer this outcome period, the less accurate will be the appraisal of risk. Longer outcome periods are associated with more influences that are difficult to anticipate: developmental maturation; response to interventions; changes in domains such as peers, family, school, and employment; changes in drug and alcohol use; and a variety of other influences may affect the likelihood of the target behavior's occurrence. A reasonable outcome period, consistent with research on specialized measures, would be 6–12 months.

Finally, risk and protective factors have been cited in much of the literature in this area (e.g. Grisso, 2010–11). In a useful discussion of precision-enhancing terminology, Monahan and Skeem (2015) note that risk factors function to directly increase the likelihood of an adverse outcome, promotive factors directly decrease the likelihood of an adverse outcome, and protective factors decrease the likelihood of an adverse outcome when risk factors are also present. It is helpful to communicate which risk, promotive, and protective factors have been identified in the course of a risk assessment. In addition, it is particularly useful to identify dynamic risk factors (subject to changing through planned interventions) as contrasted with static risk factors (largely historical influences that cannot change through such intervention). Dynamic risk factors can serve as rehabilitation targets and reflect change in risk level over time. But there is an important difference between variable risk factors (changing over time and showing an association with outcome) and causal risk factors (changing over time and causally related to outcome). Risk-reducing interventions are most likely to be effective when they focus on causal risk factors—although the research evidence for distinguishing between variable and causal risk factors is weak at present (Monahan & Skeem, 2015). Finally, Monahan and Skeem emphasize the importance of validation research—broadly, locally, and repeatedly—so there is reasonable assurance that the measure will perform as intended.

The approach to risk assessment that involves identifying risk, promotive, and protective factors is consistent with a public health perspective. There is a large and growing body of empirical research on juvenile risk factors (see Borum & Verhaagen, 2006). The aggregation of these influences is important, as there is no single risk factor that provides a high degree of accuracy in risk classification (DeMatteo, Wolbransky *et al.*, 2016.) The description of risk, promotive, and protective factors in this chapter is consistent with this assumption: the most effective approach to risk assessment currently relies on multiple factors, each of which has an established relationship to the outcome of interest. Of course, good forensic practice also involves informing the court of the logic underlying the conclusions of an evaluation—and disclosing limitations in logic or data (Grisso, 2010–11).

The broad principles of juvenile risk assessment are summarized in Table 5.1. Since this occurs in the context of juvenile or criminal proceedings, there must be an implication of each principle for best practice in a legal context. These implications are also described in Table 5.1 (drawn from Heilbrun, Brooks Holliday *et al.*, 2013). Among the most important is the value of the "individualization" of the assessment by using both nomothetic and idiographic approaches. In describing group-based research and specialized risk assessment measures, the present chapter focuses mostly on nomothetic approaches. But it is necessary (particularly in a legal context, where perceived accuracy is nearly as important as actual accuracy) to individualize the risk assessment by asking

Table 5.1 Principles of Risk Assessment and Implications for Best Practice

Principles of risk assessment	Implications for best practice
1. Identification of the task	Identify whether assessment of risk-relevant needs is required as well as prediction.
2. Specification of the context	Specify the setting in which the risk of the target behavior is being appraised (e.g. residential vs. community).
3. Specification of outcome	Clarify the outcome(s) for which risk is being assessed and consider outcome specification at every stage of the evaluation.
4. Identification of population	Match the use of specialized risk assessment tool(s) with the population to which the evaluee belongs.
5. Estimate of base rate	Consider base rates of the specific outcome(s) for the population to which the evaluee belongs.
6. Identification of risk factors and protective factors	Describe the factors that contribute to future risk of the target behavior.
7. Individualization of assessment	Use both nomothetic and idiographic approaches.
8. Communication of risk in probability, frequency, or relative terms	Express risk with probability- or frequencies-based statements when using actuarial tools, but only with terms of relative risk when using SPJ.
9. Description of risk-relevant needs	When indicated by the referral question, assess risk-relevant needs through the use of a specialized tool or other means.
10. Impact of values if the ultimate legal question is answered.	If answering the ultimate legal question, acknowledge the role of personal values in determining "dangerousness."

From Kirk Heilbrun, Stephanie Brooks Holliday, & Christopher King (2012) "Evaluation of Violence Risk in Adults," in Ronald Roesch and Patricia A. Zapf (eds), *Forensic Assessments in Criminal and Civil Law: A Handbook for Lawyers.* Oxford: Oxford University Press. By permission of Oxford University Press, www.oup.com.

detailed questions regarding the person's history of the target behavior, and the "who/what/when/where/why" of previous occurrences of such behavior, as would be expected using an idiographic approach. A specific approach to such individualization in risk assessment has been termed "anamnestic," and it provides a useful complement to nomothetic risk assessment (see Melton, Petrila *et al.*, 2007). Such individualization also promotes the use of "conditional" risk estimates, specifying the variation in risk that may occur in different settings, across different time periods, and with different target outcomes (Grisso, 2010–11). Hart and Logan (2011) provide a review of forensic risk formulation approaches.

RNR AS A MODEL: RISK AND NEED

The Risk-Need-Responsivity (RNR) model is the leading contemporary theory involving the application of behavioral science to correctional classification and rehabilitation. It was developed by Andrews, Bonta *et al.* (1990) and has undergone a number of refinements since (Andrews & Bonta, 2010a; Hoge, 2016), with applications to juvenile offenders developed as well (Hoge, 2001; Hoge & Andrews, 2011). RNR has good empirical support when applied to juveniles in its potential to promote risk reduction (Andrews & Bonta, 2010a, 2010b; Lipsey, 2009) and cost-effectiveness (Drake, Aos *et al.*, 2009; Vincent, 2015) when compared with more punitive sanctions. Combining risk-need measurement with intervention, RNR can provide a more balanced and accurate appraisal of risk and needs, even among experienced corrections professionals (Perrault, Paiva-Salisbury *et al.*, 2012). It offers a good conceptual fit for measuring considerations relevant to disposition (particularly treatment needs relevant to recidivism risk) and transfer (re-offense risk, treatment needs, and treatment amenability). It does so by measuring risk for re-offending, need (changeable risk factors for re-offending), and responsivity (including specific factors affecting an individual's likelihood of responding favorably to interventions, and general considerations such as whether the intervention is relevant and empirically supported). Developmental considerations can be part of the responsivity domain; a given intervention would be most likely to be considered favorably under general responsivity if it were targeted toward adolescents, with outcome research demonstrating its effectiveness with youth. Recent discussion of responsivity has proposed a modified definition: "matching the correct type (behavioral target and intensity) of programming to an individual based on his or her risk and needs profile" (Crites & Taxman, 2013: 144).

RNR can also provide a structure for informing the court about treatment needs by incorporating risk data. It has not been applied to juvenile assessment as long as it has to adult correctional classification, so perhaps with increasing interest and research will come the development of additional validated risk-need measures beyond those discussed in this chapter (see Brogan *et al.*, 2015; Hoge & Andrews, 2010b).

A major advantage to using RNR as a structure for assessing risk and need in adolescents involves its linkage of assessment with intervention. Developed originally as an approach to classifying justice-involved individuals according to criminogenic risk reduction needs, RNR offers a structure for considering interventions through their adherence to the principles of risk (more intensive interventions for higher-risk individuals), need (identified criminogenic needs targeted specifically by the interventions selected), and responsivity (deliver interventions that are generally empirically supported, and specifically tailored to the individual's capacities). Adherence to these principles has been associated with decreased re-offending rates, with the most significant reductions observed when all three principles are observed (Andrews & Bonta, 2010a; Dowden & Andrews, 1999; Koehler, Lösel *et al.*, 2013)—although more research is needed on individual responsivity, the least well-researched aspect of RNR. This means that RNR has the potential to inform the court and subsequent decision-makers at the stages of transfer consideration, disposition, placement, discharge, and community reentry regarding empirically-supported information on risk, need, and responsivity.

EMPIRICAL EVIDENCE ON JUVENILE RISK ASSESSMENT

A detailed review of this topic has recently been provided (see DeMatteo, Wolbransky *et al.*, 2016). Considering dynamic risk, promotive, and protective factors by domain (e.g. individual factors, social factors such as family and peers, contextual factors) is a good way to be comprehensive, specific, and developmentally informed (Hoge & Andrews, 2010a).

RISK FACTORS

Certain individual characteristics in adolescents—particularly anti-social attitudes and beliefs, callousness, deficits in self-control, and susceptibility to peer influence—have been associated with general and violent re-offending (Cottle, Lee *et al.*, 2001; Hawkins, Herrenkohl *et al.*, 1998; Mulvey, Steinberg *et al.*, 2010). Research on psychopathic traits in adolescence, which overlap with several of those just mentioned but fit into a single disorder that has been associated strongly with crime and violence in adults, has shown mixed results in its association with delinquent behavior (see DeMatteo, Edens *et al.*, 2010; DeMatteo, Haney-Caron *et al.*, in press; Vincent, Kimonis *et al.*, 2016). If it were possible to accurately identify adolescents with psychopathy, such identification would provide useful information about increased risk over a much longer outcome period. The difficulty, however, is that some adolescents involved in crime and violence may resemble those with genuine emerging psychopathy—but do not go on to manifest the disorder. The field has not yet reached the point at which we can accurately distinguish emerging psychopathic personality disorder from other influences that will not persist, although there has been some progress in this regard. This is discussed more in the next section.

There are high rates of trauma and adverse experience in juvenile offender populations (Abram, Teplin *et al.*, 2013). It is becoming increasingly clear that previous physical or sexual abuse is associated with general and violent re-offending (Zelechoski, 2016), although the causal role in trauma's impact on offending is less clear. Behavioral health disorders such as post-traumatic stress disorder (PTSD), learning disorders, depression, and attention-deficit/hyperactivity disorder may not be directly related to offending outcomes. They are, however, more directly related to an adolescent's capacity to function effectively in school—and ineffective school performance is a much stronger risk factor for offending (Daly, Hildebrand *et al.*, 2016). In addition, some recent research (Zara & Farrington, 2013) suggests that disorders such as depression and anxiety, experienced during adolescence, are associated with offending that begins after age 21. This provides a somewhat stronger basis for the argument that such symptoms should be part of the intervention targets when treating justice-involved adolescents.

Other risk factors for juvenile offending with strong empirical support include deficits in school (particularly attendance, behavior, and performance), problems with family and parenting, antisocial peers, and poorly structured leisure time (Hawkins, Herrenkohl *et al.*, 2000; Hoge, 2013; Lipsey & Derzon, 1998; Resnick, Ireland *et al.*, 2004). Early onset and more intensive school problems are more predictive of later juvenile offending. Family problems can enhance risk in different respects. Parents who are themselves justice-involved may model criminal behavior. Absent parenting is associated with antisocial behavior in adolescents, as is family conflict (Cottle, Lee *et al.*, 2001; Wasserman, Keenan *et al.*, 2003).

Adolescents are particularly susceptible to the influence of peers (Shulman & Steinberg, 2016), so it is not surprising that adolescent antisocial behavior is often influenced by peers who themselves are antisocial or even justice-involved (Hawkins, Herrenkohl *et al.*, 1998; Hoge, 2013). Low socioeconomic status (SES) has been associated with offending (Lipsey & Derzon, 1998; Loeber, Farrington *et al.*, 1998), possibly mediated by influences such as violent neighborhoods and the absence of structured pro-social leisure time.

Much of the evidence regarding the impact of trauma on the risk of juvenile offending is relatively recent. This includes one very large-scale study of delinquent youth in Florida ($N = 22{,}575$) in which the relationship between serious, violent, and chronic (SVC) offending and the history of adverse events was considered. Controlling for other risk factors for criminal offending, the investigators reported that each additional adverse event in a youth's history (measured by the Adverse Childhood Experiences scale, or ACE) increased the risk of becoming an SVC offender by a substantial magnitude (Fox, Perez *et al.*, 2015). This observation of higher rates of adverse childhood experiences in juveniles, and their relationship with re-offense risk, is consistent with other evidence as well (Baglivio & Epps, 2015; Zelechoski, 2016), and suggests that evaluators should incorporate trauma-related needs into their evaluation of youth for transfer and disposition.

PERSISTENCE OF OFFENDING

Research on factors associated with general, violent, and sexual offending among youth has yielded much information about the persistence of such offending (Farrington & Welsh, 2006; Hoge & Andrews, 2010a; Thornberry & Krohn, 2003). A history of delinquent behavior is associated with future recidivism, with younger age of first contact consistent with higher risk (Cottle, Lee *et al.*, 2001; Hawkins, Herrenkohl *et al.*, 1998; Hoge, 2013). The distinction between adolescent-limited and life-course persistent antisocial behavior refers to the time-limited nature of such behavior for most adolescents who engage in it (Moffitt, 1993), as they "desist" during their early 20s—even youth who commit violent offenses (Elliott, Huizinga, *et al.*, 1986). The younger an adolescent at the time of onset of significant antisocial behavior, the more likely it is that this behavior will persist into adulthood (Moffitt, 2003). Other risk factors for general offending include number of prior arrests, commitments and out-of-home placements, recency and length of prior commitments, seriousness of prior offenses, and prior substance use (Cottle, Lee *et al.*, 2001; DeMatteo & Marczyk, 2005; Hoge, 2013; Lipsey & Derzon 1998; see DeMatteo, Wolbransky *et al.*, 2016, for a fuller discussion).

This theoretical and empirical distinction—adolescent-limited versus life-course persistent—has recently been called into question, however. A detailed review of the research literature from 1993 to 2013 casts some doubt on the sharp, qualitative distinction between these categories of offending. Reviewing 61 empirical studies that either focused on one of these forms of misconduct or compared both directly, Guerra, Williams *et al.* (2008) described strong empirical support for life-course persistent antisocial behavior as a neurodevelopmental disorder associated with emotion processing deficits, changes in brain structure and cortisol secretion, and certain personality traits (e.g. callous/unemotional). However, these investigators also noted growing evidence that adolescent-onset antisocial behavior ("desistant") may be a comparable neurodevelopmental disorder that differs from the early-onset form in quantity rather than quality. They proposed that the quality of the child's early environment moderates the relationship between individual characteristics and the age of onset of antisocial behavior. This conclusion would not apply to all adolescent antisocial behavior, of course. However, it is important given the empirical support for the prospect that some later-onset aggression in adolescence is affected by the same factors that influence early-onset aggression, but is delayed because of the support provided in these youths' environments.

These data are consistent with findings from a recent series of multi-level meta-analyses on the contributions of various risk domains to life-course persistent versus adolescence-limited offending (Assink, van der Put *et al.*, 2015). Relatively large effects (for life-course persistent offending relative to adolescence-limited offending) were noted for criminal history, aggressive behavior, and alcohol/drug abuse, with small effects seen for family, neurocognitive, and attitude domains—and no effects for physical health and neighborhood domains. These investigators concluded that risk domains (particularly those with large effects) contributed to the development of life-course persistent offending, and the differences between life-course persistent and adolescence-limited patterns are quantitative rather than qualitative.

This conclusion appears consistent with the findings of a study following adolescent offenders into adulthood, over a ten-year period, using the Hare Psychopathy Checklist: Youth Version (PCL:YV) (Forth, Kosson *et al.*, 2003), Structured Assessment of Violence Risk in Youth (SAVRY) (Borum, Bartel *et al.*, 2006; Borum, Lodewijks *et al.*, 2010), and Youth Level of Service/Case Management Inventory 2.0 (YLS/CMI 2.0) (Hoge & Andrews, 2011). Each of these studies showed predictive efficacy of moderate effect size (YLS/CMI *AUC* = 0.66) to large effect size (SAVRY *AUC* = 0.74; PCL:YV *AUC* = 0.79) (Schmidt, Campbell *et al.*, 2011). This suggests that these standard juvenile risk assessment measures, which aggregate risk factors to produce an overall risk estimate, are providing estimates that are reasonably stable over a ten-year period. This is further evidence for the revised notion that desistance versus life-course persistence is better depicted by a quantitative difference than by two separate categories.

Developmental Influences

The impact of risk, promotive, and protective factors on adolescent offending varies according to developmental influences. The biological, psycho-social, and cognitive changes associated with human development make it difficult to determine whether offending propensities are stable personal characteristics or transient aspects of functioning that will change as the individual moves from adolescence into adulthood. Accordingly, one aspect of risk assessment for adolescents includes an appraisal of whether applicable risk factors are developmentally influenced—and whether the adolescent is likely to age out of these influences. An important consideration for the evaluator as part of any such risk assessment, therefore, is whether a given criminogenic need is (1) likely to change in the short term, with appropriate intervention, (2) likely to change over the longer term in the course of developmental maturation, or (3) unlikely to change as a result of either. There is also a moderating age effect within adolescence on the relationship between risk factors and offending; both risk and protective factors have a stronger relationship with offending in younger adolescents (van der Put, van der Laan *et al.*, 2011).

There is evidence that the majority of delinquent behavior does not persist into adulthood, with a minority of offenders continuing to commit increasingly serious violence and other offending (Hoge & Andrews, 2010a). It was once estimated that only 5–10 percent of justice-involved youth become life-course-persistent offenders (Moffitt, 2003). This subgroup may be larger if a certain proportion of adolescent "desistant" offenders are actually "deferred life-course persistent" offenders

(Guerra, Williams *et al.*, 2008), but it remains common for youth to desist in their antisocial behavior by early adulthood—even youth who appear to be high risk during adolescence (Mulvey, Steinberg *et al.*, 2010).

Gender Influences

Many of the risk factors discussed earlier apply to female adolescent offenders, although there have been noteworthy gender differences in delinquent trajectories (Moretti, Odgers *et al.*, 2004). Some of the important gender differences have involved higher rates of abuse, particularly sexual abuse, among females (Abram, Teplin *et al.*, 2013; Begle, Hanson *et al.*, 2011). Girls who are involved with the juvenile justice system also have even higher rates of family problems (although this is a strong risk factor for delinquent boys as well), and females also show higher levels of behavioral health problems (Cauffman, Lexcen *et al.*, 2007; Gammelgard, Weizmann-Henelius *et al.*, 2012; Odgers, Moretti *et al.*, 2005). Gender-informed risk assessment should take into account that most risk factors from specialized risk measures apply to females as well as males. One meta-analysis concluded that using risk assessment instruments that are not gender-specific results in comparable levels of predictive validity for male and female offenders (Schwalbe, 2008b); another study noted that the internal structure of the SAVRY did not vary across gender (Childs, Frick *et al.*, 2016). However, the differences between the abuse histories and the behavioral health symptom prevalence across genders should inform interventions with justice-involved females. It would be useful to develop a gender-specific measure for use with female juveniles to gauge its incremental validity over that of validated measures that are not gender-specific. In the absence of such a measure and such comparative data, however, the recommended strategy for evaluators at present involves using a good measure that is not gender-specific (e.g. YLS/CMI, SAVRY) and gathering additional information in areas including family, trauma, abuse, and behavioral health problems.

Some data suggest that gender differences may reside more in the response to interventions than in the impact of risk factors. One study with a relatively small sample (39 males and 37 females) (Vitopoulos, Peterson-Badali *et al.*, 2012) suggests that RNR risk assessment is comparably accurate for males and females—but re-offense risk reduction is associated with "matching" criminogenic need to intervention for boys, but not for girls.

JUVENILE RISK ASSESSMENT INSTRUMENTS

The development of risk assessment instruments has been described in three generations (Schwalbe, 2007). The first involves impressionistic assessments without the assistance of structured assessment devices, an approach that has also been called "unstructured clinical judgment." Over 60 years, this approach has consistently been found to be less accurate than structured approaches (Dawes, Faust *et al.*, 1989; Grove & Meehl, 1996; Grove, Zald *et al.*, 2000). The second generation is grounded in statistical associations between the risk assessment instrument and specified outcomes such as violent offending or general offending, but is limited to prediction and risk classification. The third generation of risk assessment is also structured, but includes the assessment of criminogenic needs to help inform intervention planning.

Within these three generations, there have been two particular approaches to risk assessment that have been used to develop specialized risk assessment instruments for juveniles: actuarial assessment and structured professional judgment (SPJ). The research literature suggests that these two approaches are comparably accurate with respect to the prediction of future behavior such as violence and other offending (Heilbrun, Yasuhara *et al.*, in press). More detailed research evidence on particular instruments is discussed later in this section.

Actuarial assessment "uses an equation, a formula, a graph, or an actuarial table to arrive at a probability, or expected value, of some outcome" (Grove & Meehl, 1996: 294). It uses predictors that can be reliably measured or classified. Such predictors are empirically validated using the specified outcome that is also reliably measured or classified. It is this objective, reliable combination of predictive factors, empirically validated against known outcomes, that is the essence of actuarial assessment.

SPJ uses risk factors that are usually identified from a literature review rather than drawn from a particular database. As with actuarial assessment, these risk factors must be clearly defined and reliably rated. The process of using such a structured tool involves having the user gather information from multiple sources and apply it to rating each factor. But the scored factors are not combined into an overall total. Rather, the evaluator is asked to consider all this information by rating overall risk in the context of needs and any relevant idiosyncratic information. This promotes the use of dynamic risk factors, which have the potential to change through planned intervention, rather than static risk factors, which do not.

Actuarial and SPJ risk assessment approaches are similar in certain ways. Both employ factors that are empirically related to the particular outcome (typically violent or general offending). Both provide structure by specifying the variables that are used, and both have variables that are classified or rated reliably, minimizing the influence of evaluator judgment at the variable-rating level. But the two approaches differ in how they combine data. Actuarial approaches employ scoring that has been validated using known outcomes, while SPJ does not combine item scores. Rather, it has the user consider the collected information and make a professional judgment about risk level.

On balance, empirical evidence does not support a meaningful difference in predictive or incremental validity between SPJ and actuarial assessment (Heilbrun, Douglas *et al.*, 2009; Heilbrun, Yasuhara *et al.*, in press; Olver, Stockdale *et al.*, 2009), nor in inter-rater reliability between these approaches (Vincent, Guy *et al.*, 2012a). However, both specific training and adhering to standardized procedures are necessary for evaluators to obtain optimal accuracy in risk classification using measures of either kind (Vincent, Guy *et al.*, 2012b).

EMPIRICALLY SUPPORTED MEASURES

There are many juvenile risk assessment instruments currently available, but few have significant empirical support. Fortunately, there have been a number of reviews of these measures (see, for example, Grisso, 2013, Grisso *et al.*, 2005; Hoge & Andrews, 2010a; Otto & Douglas, 2010; Vincent, Terry *et al.*, 2009). Three of the juvenile risk measures with considerable empirical support (see, for example, Olver, Stockdale *et al.*, 2009; DeMatteo, Wolbransky *et al.*, 2016) are the PCL:YV, the SAVRY, and the YLS/CMI. The SAVRY and the YLS/CMI were selected for an evaluation of the usefulness of evidence-based juvenile risk assessment measures in the context of probation (Vincent, Guy *et al.*, 2012a). Both of these measures, when used in juvenile disposition or transfer evaluations, can provide continuity over time and across interventions when they are also employed in juvenile placements or in the community under conditions of parole or probation for justice-involved youth.

RESEARCH ON VALIDITY OF JUVENILE RISK MEASURES

Perhaps the most important evidence concerning specialized risk assessment measures is the accuracy of such measures in classifying the risk of re-offending. At one time, researchers focused on predictive accuracy as the most applicable form of validity for such measures. However, the risk-relevant considerations for youth being evaluated for transfer or disposition do not align cleanly with prediction as the only goal of risk assessment. The questions are not simply who is at risk and how great the risk might be. Rather, the questions also include who might be rehabilitated through intervention (meaning that they do not re-offend during the outcome period). More specifically, who might become less likely to re-offend through a combination of developmental maturation, increased propensity for responsible behavior, fewer adverse situational influences, improved skills, and different thinking?

Meta-analyses have evaluated the predictive and incremental validity of risk assessment instruments. Three measures (the PCL:YV, SAVRY, and

YLS/CMI) were reported to have comparably strong associations with the outcomes of violent and non-violent offending (Olver, Stockdale *et al.*, 2009). The YLS/CMI reportedly has incremental validity over the PCL:YV (Viljoen, Elkovitch *et al.*, 2009), but the PCL:YV may not have incremental validity over the YLS/CMI or SAVRY (Viljoen, Elkovitch *et al.*, 2009; Welsh, Schmidt *et al.*, 2008). In another meta-analysis, the PCL:YV (the adult PCL with "youth modifications") was significantly associated with general and violent recidivism in male justice-involved youth, but not with sexual recidivism. Effect sizes for female samples were mostly small and non-significant, and psychopathy was a weaker predictor of violent recidivism in more racially mixed samples (Edens, Campbell *et al.*, 2007).

There are additional considerations in using the PCL:YV as a risk assessment measure in disposition and transfer evaluations. Because the PCL was developed to measure psychopathy, a personality disorder in adults, there are questions about whether such a disorder exists for most adolescents.[1] Unlike the SAVRY and YLS/CMI, the PCL:YV was not developed for assessing risk. Moreover, given the possible stigmatization of the psychopathy label, using the PCL:YV may have unintended negative consequences.

Jurisdictional-specific risk assessment instruments have also found some empirical support. The Washington State Juvenile Court Assessment (WSJCA) (Barnoski, 2004) is a comprehensive SPJ measure that also includes a screening component, and research supports its predictive validity (Barnoski & Markhussen, 2005). Other states have modeled risk assessment tools after the WSJCA, including the Positive Achievement Change Tool (PACT) (Baglivio & Jackowski, 2013), implemented in Florida for case management, and the Youth Assessment and Screening Instrument (YASI) (Orbis Partners, 2007), which is currently used in New York State to predict recidivism and guide case management. North Carolina has also developed a risk screening instrument (the North Carolina Assessment of Risk (NCAR)), and research has yielded mixed support for its predictive validity across subgroups (Schwalbe, Fraser *et al.*, 2006).

The Risk-Sophistication-Treatment Inventory (RSTI) (Salekin, 2004a) is a promising measure that includes the major constructs associated with transfer decisions (risk, sophistication-maturity, and treatment). Its major drawback as a risk assessment measure is that it does not appear to have been validated using the outcome of future offending (see Salekin, 2015a, for a more detailed description). It does have the intriguing potential to serve as a measure of change for relevant interpersonal targets of juvenile treatment such as motivation, positive emotion, and interpersonal callousness (Salekin, Tippey *et al.*, 2012). This kind of study design, involving response to specific interventions, provides a model for the field to better inform courts on juvenile responsiveness to interventions in risk-relevant areas.

There is not yet good, consistent empirical evidence that the risk of juvenile sexual offending can be appraised accurately (Olver, Stockdale *et al.*, 2009; Viljoen et al., 2009). Examining risk assessment measures used with male adolescents with a history of sexual offending, investigators (Viljoen, Scalora *et al.*, 2008; Viljoen, Elkovitch *et al.*, 2009) reported that none of the measures that have been reasonably good with violent and with general offending risk appraisal (PCL:YV, SAVRY, YLS/CMI) and none of those designed specifically to predict sexual recidivism among adults (Estimate of Risk of Adolescent Sexual Offense Recidivism (ERASOR), Juvenile Sex Offender Assessment Protocol-II (J-SOAP-II), Juvenile Sexual Offense Recidivism Risk Assessment Tool–II (J-SORRAT-II), Static-99) were significantly associated with sexual re-offending in this population—although the YLS/CMI, PCL:YV, SAVRY, and J-SOAP-II were all significantly associated with non-sexual re-offending (Viljoen, Scalora *et al.*, 2008; Viljoen, Elkovitch *et al.*, 2009). The ERASOR, J-SOAP-II, and J-SORRAT-II did perform somewhat better in predicting sexual offending than the more general risk measures (SAVRY and PCL:YV), but with substantial variability in *AUC* values from outcomes studies on the J-SOAP-II (0.44 to 0.86), J-SORRAT-II (0.50 to 0.79), and ERASOR (0.50 to 0.86), the predictive performance of these measures ranges from chance to quite good (Hempel, Buck *et al.*, 2013). Aggregating these effect sizes using meta-analysis, Viljoen, Mordell *et al.* (2012) documented moderately sized effects for the J-SOAP-II (*AUC* = 0.67), ERASOR (*AUC* = 0.66), and J-SORRAT-II (*AUC* = 0.64). Clearly additional research and careful scrutiny by evaluators using these measures are indicated.

BEST-SUPPORTED MEASURES OF RISK AND NEED

The SAVRY and YLS/CMI, the major juvenile risk assessment tools discussed in this section, are good examples of the exceptional progress that has be seen in this area over the last 20 years. Both the strong push for evidence-based practice and the development and validation of such specialized measures have improved the practice of juvenile risk assessment considerably (Grisso, 2010–11).

The YLS/CMI is an actuarial instrument designed for use by probation officers or mental health professionals with minimal specialized training. Both the YLS/CMI and its revision (YLS/CMI 2.0) incorporate eight major risk factors for juvenile offending: history of conduct disorder or crime; family or parental dysfunction; education or employment deficits; antisocial peer associations; substance abuse; poor use of leisure time; dysfunctional personality or behavior traits; and antisocial attitudes, values, and beliefs. It can be re-administered over time, as the majority of domains are subject to change. The total score is associated with classification into one of four risk categories: low, moderate, high, and very high. There is the option for a professional override if the evaluator concludes that the total score does not accurately reflect the individual's risk level; this risk level can be adjusted by the evaluator.[2] These risk factors have considerable meta-analytic support (Cottle, Lee *et al.*, 2001; Farrington, 1998; Heilbrun, Lee *et al.*, 2005; Loeber & Farrington, 1998, 2000; Vincent, Terry *et al.*, 2009). Composites based on multiple risk factors from this list have an even stronger relationship with offending (Andrews & Bonta, 2010b). Most of this evidence has been obtained using North American Caucasian samples. But there is some evidence that these risk factors apply in both males and females, and for African American and Aboriginal youth in US and Canadian contexts (Gendreau, Little *et al.*, 1996; Jung & Rawana, 1999; Redding & Arrigo, 2005), and for those in the German youth correctional system (Grieger & Hosser, 2014). Indeed, larger effect sizes have been observed for the YLS/CMI's association with general offending with non-US samples (Canada and outside North America), although the association with violent re-offending was comparable across all jurisdictions (Olver, Stockdale *et al.*, 2014).

The SAVRY performed best in predictive accuracy among the nine commonly used risk assessment measures considered in a review and meta-regression analysis of 68 studies involving 25,980 participants from 88 independent samples (Singh, Grann *et al.*, 2011). In a subsequent review and meta-analysis, Fazel, Singh *et al.* (2012) considered 73 samples with 24,847 participants from 13 countries. They observed no difference in predictive accuracy between actuarial and SPJ measures. They also concluded that risk assessment tools generally are better at identifying low-risk individuals than they are at identifying high-risk individuals—suggesting that appraisals of individuals as high risk should not be the sole basis for decisions on transfer or disposition. SAVRY total scores were significantly predictive of adolescent re-offending, with some variability across racial-ethnic groups, over a five-year period (Vincent, Chapman *et al.*, 2011) with static factors most strongly predictive of non-violent re-arrest but social-contextual dynamic factors most predictive of violent re-arrest. The SAVRY (Borum, Bartel *et al.*, 2006) and the YLS/CMI (Hoge & Andrews, 2011) are the only juvenile risk assessment measures described as having a sufficient level of research support to place them in the category of "evidence-based" (Vincent, Guy *et al.*, 2012b; Vincent, Guy *et al.*, 2012c).

The SAVRY appears as accurate for younger adolescents as it does for older youth, and the dynamic risk factors contained in this measure provide incremental predictive validity over its static risk factors. Youth rated as moderate to high risk had greater odds of re-arrest, with static factors most strongly predictive of non-violent arrest, but social-contextual dynamic risk factors most predictive of violent re-arrest (Vincent, Chapman *et al.*, 2011). Tracking a large sample ($N = 674$) of youth in three age cohorts (12 and under, 13–15, and 16–18), several investigators (Vincent, Guy *et al.*,

2012b; Vincent, Guy *et al.*, 2012c) concluded that age did not moderate the association between SAVRY results and re-offending—and that dynamic risk factors provided incremental validity over static factors for violent and non-violent re-offending, but not probation violations.

Although the SAVRY and YLS/CMI are most often used for disposition or transfer in the course of juvenile proceedings (Urquhart & Viljoen, 2014), they have also been used later in the juvenile process by juvenile probation officers. Interviewed three and ten months after the use of one of these two measures was implemented, most juvenile probation officers perceived the tool as "somewhat" or "very" helpful for guiding case planning, with the majority preferring professional discretion to a score-based approach (Guy, Nelson *et al.*, 2014).

CONCLUSION

This chapter focuses on risk assessment as one of the three major criteria for transfer decisions, and a more implicit but nonetheless frequently considered aspect of disposition decisions. Risk analysis has become increasingly integrated into juvenile and criminal law, and is currently widely employed. Important parameters of risk assessment must be specified as part of this process to yield results that are meaningful and useful to the court. Such parameters include target behavior, frequency, probability/risk category, settings, outcome period, and risk and protective factors. The theory of RNR has a strong conceptual fit and good empirical support for its applicability to the risk and need questions associated with transfer and disposition evaluations. Reviewing the empirical evidence on adolescent offending, it is clear that most of the strongly supported risk factors for offending have been incorporated into specialized risk assessment measures. The strongest empirical support is seen for two specialized measures (SAVRY and YLS/CMI), at least one of which should be an integral aspect of risk assessment in juvenile forensic contexts. Significant evidence shows that a long-standing theory of adolescent antisocial behavior specifying two groups (adolescent-limited, or "desistant," versus life-course persistent) may need modification, as the difference between these two groups is now appearing more quantitative than distinctly qualitative. Principles of risk assessment and associated implications for FMHA are provided. As with any kind of FMHA, the interpretation of specialized measures and its integration with information from other sources is ultimately the responsibility of the evaluator.

NOTES

1. Antisocial Personality Disorder, the closest disorder in the *Diagnostic and Statistical Manual of Mental Disorders*, 5th edn (DSM-5) to psychopathy, cannot be diagnosed in individuals younger than 18 (American Psychiatric Association, 2013a: 648).
2. Two approaches to "adjusted actuarial" assessment have been discussed in the literature. The first is literally changing a score—adding or subtracting based on additional considerations—while the second involves interpreting a score differently. The former is discouraged in the strongest possible terms. The evaluator literally cannot know how much a score should be changed, and changing a score fundamentally violates the integrity of the actuarial process. The latter allows the evaluator to indicate why a score does not accurately reflect an individual's risk *at the interpretation stage*, which is consistent with the broader process in FMHA of considering multiple sources of information and making the evaluator (not a test or measure) responsible for the conclusions. Evaluators should remain aware that good actuarial measures are powerful tools for maximizing predictive accuracy over many cases, and that changing a risk measure's category (unless done rarely and for very good reasons) is likely to reduce accuracy in the long term.

CHAPTER SIX

Treatment Needs and Amenability

The primary major criteria applicable to both transfer and disposition decisions across jurisdictions are risk for recidivism and treatment needs, with additional criteria of treatment amenability and sophistication-maturity used in transfer cases. The previous chapter addressed risk to public safety, and the next chapter will address sophistication-maturity; the present chapter addresses treatment needs and amenability. Describing the role of treatment needs as a legal focus in both transfer and disposition decisions, this chapter reviews and integrates the relevant social science research in this area. We discuss the literature that defines treatment amenability—a construct that is more applicable to transfer than disposition—and describe best practices for conducting assessments of treatment amenability. We also review the research on treatment needs for justice-involved youth, and the factors that are empirically associated with amenability.

TREATMENT AMENABILITY: LEGAL CONTEXT

The landmark case relevant to juvenile waiver is *Kent v. United States* (1966). Morris Kent, aged 16, was interrogated by the police in connection with robbery and rape. After Kent admitted some involvement in the criminal activity, the juvenile court waived its jurisdiction over the case, which allowed Kent to be tried as an adult in criminal court (specifically, the federal trial court in the District of Columbia, where the offenses occurred). Kent moved to dismiss the indictment because the juvenile court did not conduct a full investigation before waiving jurisdiction, which he argued was legally required. Kent's motion was denied, and he was found guilty and sentenced to serve 30–90 years in prison. On appeal, the United States Court of Appeals for the District of Columbia Circuit affirmed the lower court's decision.

After granting certiorari, the United States Supreme Court overturned the waiver of Kent based on what was described as indiscriminate decision-making and neglect of Kent's due process rights (*Kent v. United States*, 1966) (Loving & Patapis, 2007). In a narrow five to four decision, the Court held that a waiver of jurisdiction from juvenile court to district court must be voluntary and knowing, and the Court noted that Kent did not receive a hearing regarding the potential waiver, was not given access to counsel, and was not permitted to access his record prior to the waiver. This was the first instance in which the United States Supreme Court rendered a decision about the operations and procedures of a juvenile court, and it represented a shift from viewing juvenile courts as purely rehabilitative to viewing them as adversarial forums in which due process is required.

A significant outcome of the *Kent* decision was that juvenile court judges were subsequently required to consider specific factors before transferring a youth *to* the adult criminal justice system (transfer) or *from* the adult criminal justice system (reverse transfer). The factors that judges were required to consider included the seriousness of the juvenile's offense; the nature of the offense (e.g. whether it was impulsive, violent, premeditated); the juvenile's level of sophistication and maturity; the juvenile's previous arrest and adjudication record; and the juvenile's likelihood of rehabilitation by means of treatments and services that are available within the juvenile system (*Kent v. United States*, 1966) (Loving & Patapis, 2007). As is evident, the three major criteria applicable to both transfer and disposition decisions across jurisdictions—risk for recidivism, treatment needs and amenability, and sophistication-maturity—stem from the *Kent* decision. The *Kent* factors emphasize the importance of weighing both community safety and the treatment needs and amenability of the juvenile when determining the appropriate forum in which to handle the case. Along those lines, the Supreme Court stated that "the prospects for adequate protection of the public and the likelihood of reasonable rehabilitation of the juvenile" should be evaluated when making transfer decisions (*Kent v. United States*, 1966, pp. 566–7).

After *Kent*, most states incorporated the *Kent* factors or similar criteria into their juvenile justice statutes to guide juvenile courts when making transfer and reverse transfer decisions. For example, the Pennsylvania Juvenile Act 2013, which provides statutory guidance for juvenile courts when making waiver and reverse waiver decisions, states that the following factors must be considered when determining whether the public interest can be served:

> (A) the impact of the offense on the victim or victims; (B) the impact of the offense on the community; (C) the threat to the safety of the public or any individual posed by the child; (D) the nature and circumstances of the offense allegedly committed by the child; (E) the degree of the child's culpability; (F) the adequacy and duration of dispositional alternatives available under this chapter and in the adult criminal justice system; and (G) whether the child is amenable to treatment, supervision or rehabilitation as a juvenile. (42 Pa. Cons. Stat. § 6355)

With respect to factor (G)—whether the juvenile is amenable to treatment, supervision, and rehabilitation as a juvenile—Pennsylvania courts must consider the following factors relating to the juvenile:

> (I) age; (II) mental capacity; (III) maturity; (IV) the degree of criminal sophistication exhibited by the child; (V) previous records, if any; (VI) the nature and extent of any prior delinquent history, including the success or failure of any previous attempts by the juvenile court to rehabilitate the child; (VII) whether the child can be rehabilitated prior to the expiration of the juvenile court jurisdiction; (VIII) probation or institutional reports, if any; [and] (IX) any other relevant factors. (42 Pa. Cons. Stat. § 6355)

Although the Pennsylvania Juvenile Act is only applicable in Pennsylvania courts, many states have enacted similar laws since the *Kent* decision.

In an early article relating to juvenile transfer, Ewing (1990) described three broad factors from the *Kent* decision that are relevant to the forensic mental health assessment of juveniles: (1) sophistication-maturity; (2) potential dangerousness; and (3) amenability to treatment. These three factors are widely regarded as the basis for FMHAs of juveniles in waiver and reverse waiver cases. Given the *Kent* decision and the contributions of scholars in the wake of *Kent*, it is clear that the assessment of treatment amenability is an essential component of any juvenile forensic mental health assessment relating to transfer or reverse transfer (Chen & Salekin, 2012).

Although *Kent* dealt with amenability to treatment in the context of waiver decisions, a juvenile's treatment amenability is relevant in almost all contexts in juvenile proceedings, which has led some scholars to conclude that treatment amenability is "the overriding question in the juvenile process" (Melton, Petrila *et al.*, 2007: 477). Treatment amenability is relevant at various times, including (1) the front end, when probation officers are deciding whether to release a juvenile with or without conditions or to pursue delinquency proceedings; (2) the dispositional bargaining stage, when attorneys for the state and defense are negotiating an appropriate disposition for the juvenile; (3) the dispositional hearing stage; and (4) the release stage (Melton, Petrila *et al.*, 2007).

DEFINING TREATMENT AMENABILITY

Given the central role of treatment amenability in forensic mental health assessments of juvenile offenders, defining treatment amenability is particularly important. Unfortunately, the research literature in this area has neither consistently operationalized the construct of treatment amenability nor shown any consensus on how it should be assessed. That notwithstanding, there is some agreement among researchers and scholars that certain characteristics and factors are relevant to the concept of treatment amenability among juveniles.

As a starting point, it is important to highlight three key differences between the concept of treatment amenability as used in the context of juvenile waiver, reverse waiver, and (possibly) disposition evaluations, and the concept of treatment amenability used in more traditional clinical contexts. First, the legal construct of treatment amenability is defined more broadly than clinical treatment (e.g. psychotherapy) (Kinscherff, 2006).

Specifically, assessment of treatment amenability in a legal context examines factors related to vocational, social, and educational domains that affect recidivism risk, in addition to the more traditional clinical factors such as mental health diagnosis (Kinscherff, 2006). Second, whereas treatment amenability in a clinical context typically refers to an individual's likelihood of responding favorably to psychotherapy, as shown by meaningful reductions in distressing symptoms and improvement in overall functioning, treatment amenability in a juvenile justice context is focused primarily on reducing the likelihood that the juvenile will re-offend. Given the historically child-centered approach of juvenile courts, some advocate for focusing on a juvenile's clinical needs even if there is no demonstrable relationship between the clinical needs and the juvenile's likelihood of re-offense (Melton, Petrila *et al.*, 2007). Finally, as noted by Melton, Petrila *et al.* (2007), given the broad scope of the construct of amenability in juvenile contexts, it should be understood as referring to amenability to *any* interventions that are available or even potentially available in the particular jurisdiction—not just to the likelihood that the juvenile will respond favorably to a specific intervention, such as individual psychotherapy or group treatment.

Turning to definitions of amenability, McGrath (1991) suggested that treatment amenability could be defined as acknowledgment of the offense, recognition of problematic behaviors, and willingness to engage in treatment. Although McGrath's conceptualization of treatment amenability was not specific to juvenile offenders, these three factors seem consistent with others' descriptions of juveniles' amenability to treatment. Taking a more nuanced approach specifically relating to juveniles, Salekin, Rogers *et al.* (2001) concluded:

> The general themes of the prototypical data for amenability to treatment indicate that keeping juveniles in juvenile court should be considered when youth (a) are motivated for treatment, (b) are aware of their difficulties and want to change them, (c) expect that they will benefit from treatment, (d) demonstrate remorse/guilt and empathy, (e) have knowledge of right from wrong, and (f) have a family that is stable and supportive. (p. 18)

More recently, Mulvey & Iselin (2008) noted that "amenability to interventions and sanctions is most often related to the adolescents' offense history, environmental and personality characteristics, willingness to engage in treatment, past treatments, availability of services, and age" (p. 38). This conceptualization of amenability highlights the importance of a broad focus when assessing amenability.

Part of the difficulty in defining the construct of treatment amenability is that it has not been extensively researched. This is an area that is considerably less developed than risk assessment. Much of the research that does exist involves factor analytic approaches or "prototypical" descriptions of treatment amenability (Chen & Salekin, 2012). For example, Salekin, Rogers *et al.*'s (2001) prototypical analysis study surveyed juvenile and forensic mental health professionals in an attempt to identify factors that are typically associated with the construct of treatment amenability. They identified four factors within the treatment amenability construct, including: (1) consideration and tolerance of others, with relevant characteristics including frustration tolerance, empathy, honesty, compassion, and self-involvement; (2) academic/work success and pro-social behavior, with relevant characteristics including goal-oriented and pro-social behavior in various domains (e.g. school, work, prior juvenile placements); (3) responsibility and motivation to change, with relevant characteristics including assumption of responsibility, acknowledgement of problems, motivation for treatment, and commitment to change; and (4) family cooperation, with relevant characteristics including family stability, family support, and familial involvement in relevant juvenile court processes (Salekin, Rogers *et al.*, 2001). Overall, the importance of treatment amenability in transfer decisions was rated moderately high and roughly as important as the risk to public safety and sophistication-maturity items (Salekin, Rogers *et al.*, 2001).

In a replication of this study with juvenile court judges as respondents, a slightly different factor structure was identified: (1) responsibility and motivation to change; (2) considerate and tolerant of others; (3) family cooperation; and (4) susceptible to peer influence, pro-social behavior, and good court conduct (Salekin, Yff *et al.*, 2002). The fourth factor was distinguishable from the "academic/work success and pro-social behavior" factor in the prior study in that it consisted of characteristics including gauging susceptibility to peer influence and involvement in an alcohol- or drug-related crime.

Researchers and scholars have identified several other factors that are relevant to the construct of treatment amenability among juveniles. For example, the age of the juvenile is relevant to the juvenile's treatment amenability. Developmental research suggests that younger offenders may be more amenable to treatment than older juveniles (Chen & Salekin, 2012; Loving & Patapis, 2007). With that said, continuity of offending from the juvenile years into the adult years is higher for individuals who start offending at an earlier age (e.g. Farrington & Hawkins, 1991; Loeber & Farrington, 2011; Tolan, 1987), so the prognosis for offenders who begin committing crimes at an earlier age may be worse than the prognosis for offenders who start at a later age (Hawkins, Herrenkohl *et al.*, 2000). As such, in an evaluation context, it is important for the evaluator to gauge whether the juvenile resembles an adolescent-limited offender or life-course persistent offender (Moffitt, 1993), with the former being the majority of juveniles who desist from offending behavior as they age and the latter being those who continue to engage in antisocial behavior into adulthood. This distinction highlights some of the complexity involved in assessing treatment amenability among juveniles. Further, because research suggests that younger offenders are typically perceived as more amenable to treatment (Chen & Salekin, 2012), it may be necessary for evaluators to educate the court about the complex relationship between a juvenile's age and his or her amenability to treatment.

Page and Scalora (2004) suggested that the concept of locus of control (Rotter, 1966) may be relevant when it comes to the treatment amenability of juvenile offenders. In general, an internal locus of control orientation—the belief that failures/successes are related to one's own decisions and behaviors—has been associated with increased treatment engagement, help-seeking behaviors, and positive treatment outcomes, whereas an external locus of control orientation—the belief that failures/successes are precipitated by fate, luck, or superiors—has been associated with poorer treatment engagement and outcomes (see Page & Scalora, 2004, for an informative review). An internal shift from an external locus of control to an internal locus of control is associated with improved treatment outcomes in a range of clinical settings with a variety of populations (e.g. Figurelli, Hartman *et al.*, 1994; Gaa, 1977; Kim, Omizo *et al.*, 1998; Weisz, 1986). With respect to juvenile offenders, it has long been observed that an external locus of control is associated with juvenile offending behavior (Parrot & Strongman, 1984). Accordingly, Page and Scalora (2004) asserted that juvenile offenders with an internal locus of control are more amenable to treatment than juvenile offenders with an external locus of control. They also noted that locus of control can be dynamic, which means that an external locus of control could be targeted during an intervention to improve outcomes and reduce recidivism risk.

ASSESSING TREATMENT AMENABILITY

Given the central role of treatment amenability in juvenile waiver and reverse waiver evaluations, a good deal of attention has been focused on the assessment of treatment amenability. The scope of the evaluation is guided by the legal definition of treatment amenability (which can differ depending on the stage of the proceedings), the dispositions that are available in the specific jurisdiction, and the likelihood that those dispositions will work (i.e. reduce the juvenile's risk of recidivism) (Melton, Petrila *et al.*, 2007). Given these evaluation parameters, various models, structures, and approaches have been developed for effectively assessing a juvenile's treatment amenability.

The Risk-Need-Responsivity (RNR) Model (Andrews & Bonta, 2010a; Andrews, Bonta *et al.*, 1990) can be a useful framework for the assessment of treatment needs and amenability. This model assists with the identification of specific risk factors, treatment targets, and responsivity factors for the individual being examined. Specific responsivity factors are particularly relevant to the concept of treatment amenability because they represent personal or environment characteristics that may function to promote or limit favorable treatment response. For example, negative responsivity factors are those conceptualized as potentially interfering with treatment. Possible negative responsivity factors include familial conflict, cultural/race/ethnic issues (e.g. limited cultural competence on the part of treatment providers), and behavioral health diagnoses based on symptoms of depression and anxiety (Hoge, 2013). Positive responsivity factors are those factors that are conceptualized as potentially helpful to treatment, such as pro-social interests (e.g. participating in organized sports), high levels of parental/familial involvement, and emotional maturity (Hoge, 2013). Using the RNR framework can assist evaluators in examining factors that are empirically relevant to a juvenile's treatment amenability.

Melton, Petrila *et al.* (2007) recommended that an assessment of a juvenile's amenability be broad because the range of dispositions open to judges is also typically broad in most jurisdictions. As an example, they suggest that a thorough assessment of a juvenile's treatment amenability should include an evaluation "not only of personality functioning, but also of cognitive, educational, vocational, and social needs in the context of the various systems (e.g. family, school, and neighborhood) of which he or she is a part" (Melton Petrila *et al.*, 2007: 480). Further, when addressing potential dispositions for a juvenile, the evaluator should consider alternatives that are easily available in the jurisdiction, alternatives that are available but more difficult to access, and alternatives that could be effective but are not presently available. As is evident, evaluators need to be familiar with the placements that are available or potentially available in their jurisdiction (see Chapter 9, this volume), and also with the literature regarding effectiveness in reducing a juvenile's risk for recidivism. Recommendations regarding dispositions that are detailed and specific are typically more useful to courts than are general recommendations (e.g. "youth would benefit from a structured treatment setting") (Melton, Petrila *et al.*, 2007). Once the evaluator presents disposition recommendations, the judge makes a determination of which disposition is most appropriate based on the specific circumstances of the case and the characteristics of the offender.

Grisso's (2013) guidelines relating to the assessment of a juvenile's treatment amenability suggest that forensic mental health professionals consider the following questions during the course of the assessment:

- What are the specific relevant characteristics of the juvenile?
- What needs to change?
- What types of intervention could accomplish these changes?
- How likely are changes to be enacted if appropriate interventions are applied?

These questions highlight the individualized assessment approach that is needed when evaluating a juvenile's treatment amenability.

Kinscherff (2006) offers a detailed conceptualization of treatment amenability evaluations that focuses on several factors. He recommends that evaluators assess for and identify any static (fixed) factors that may have contributed to the juvenile's offending behavior. Such factors might include the presence of prior offenses and the juvenile's age. Next, evaluators should identify and assess any dynamic (changeable) factors that may have contributed to offending behavior. Relevant considerations in this regard might include clinical, attitudinal, social, and environmental factors. Because dynamic factors are, by definition, changeable, they can be conceptualized as treatment targets in the context of amenability assessment. Evaluators should also gauge the presence of strengths and protective factors that may aid in treatment participation or outcome. Some examples include a high level of familial support, educational success, and the presence of pro-social attitudes. Finally, the evaluator should describe the recommended interventions based on the juvenile's risk and protective factors, and also describe the likely intervention-related outcomes (e.g. reduction in recidivism risk).

State statutes may also provide some guidance related to the construct of amenability. For example, as previously noted, the Pennsylvania Juvenile Act 2005 states that factors relevant to amenability include: age; mental capacity; maturity; the degree of criminal sophistication exhibited by the child; previous records, if any; the nature and extent of any prior delinquent history, including the success or failure of any previous attempts by the juvenile court to rehabilitate the child; whether the child can be rehabilitated prior to the expiration of the juvenile court jurisdiction; probation or institutional reports, if any; and any other relevant factors (42 Pa. Cons. Stat. § 6355). The Pennsylvania statute is relatively detailed, which contrasts with the more general approach taken in some other states. However, statutes are typically vague and occasionally silent when it comes to defining key concepts relating to amenability, such as sophistication-maturity.

TREATMENT NEEDS

The assessment of treatment needs is an important component of FMHA in disposition evaluations as well as transfer evaluations. The concept of treatment needs in the context of juvenile evaluations typically pertains to criminogenic needs within the RNR model because those are the factors associated with recidivism risk (Andrews & Bonta, 2010a; Andrews, Bonta *et al.*, 1990). However, treatment needs can also include the more traditional behavioral health symptoms or clinical needs. In light of the historically child-centered focus of juvenile courts, Melton, Petrila *et al.* (2007) recommend focusing on behavioral health symptoms even if there is no relationship between the clinical needs and the juvenile's offending behavior; the legal decision-maker can then determine whether the juvenile's clinical needs should be the focus of interventions. When such behavioral health symptoms are identified, it is useful to describe the extent to which treating them would reduce re-offense risk as well as improve behavioral health. Courts then have useful information to consider as part of the disposition decision.

Behavioral Health Treatment Needs

Juveniles with justice involvement are particularly vulnerable to mental health and behavioral health disorders. Research has demonstrated that approximately 70 percent of justice-involved youth meet criteria for at least one behavioral health diagnosis (Shufelt & Cocozza, 2006; Teplin,

Abram *et al.*, 2002; Wasserman, McReynolds *et al.*, 2002; Wasserman, McReynolds *et al.*, 2005). Shufelt and Cocozza's (2006) multi-state study indicates that disruptive disorders (e.g. conduct disorder) were the most prevalent (46.5 percent) among justice involved youth, followed by substance use disorders (46.2 percent), anxiety/obsessive-compulsive disorders (34.4 percent), and mood disorders (18.3 percent).

Although some clinical needs may have no relationship with a juvenile's offending behavior, other behavioral health treatment needs can indeed have a relationship with offense risk. The assessment of the latter type of clinical needs therefore has obvious importance. Salekin, Rogers *et al.* (2001) suggest that forensic mental health professionals conducting juvenile forensic mental health assessments should assess for psychopathology that may have influenced previous offending behavior, including serious mental illnesses such as mood disorders and psychotic disorders. Barnum (1987) also addresses treatment-needs assessment, suggesting that forensic mental health professionals attend to the treatability of symptoms that may have been related to offending behavior, such as those associated with post-traumatic stress disorder or depressive disorders.

Similarly, Kinscherff (2006) recommends that forensic mental health professionals routinely assess for several disorders in conducting juvenile evaluations: post-traumatic stress disorder, conduct disorder, mood disorder, substance use disorders, learning disorders, and impulse control disorders. Specifically, Kinscherff (2006) outlines important factors that should be addressed in the context of amenability assessment:

- early (preschool) onset of aggression;
- any established pattern of misconduct/rule-breaking behavior;
- childhood onset of conduct disorder;
- attention-deficit/hyperactivity disorder in the presence of persisting aggression;
- substance use or abuse (including the relationship between substance use and delinquent behavior);
- impulsivity;
- mood disturbance;

- anger control difficulties;
- juvenile's perception of alienation from others; and
- psychotic symptoms.

As is evident, the assessment approach must be broad so that it encompasses the range of clinical needs that could affect the juvenile's offending.

In addition to clinical symptoms and disorders, personality traits and disorders may be relevant to a juvenile's treatment needs and amenability. For example, personality traits related to the construct of psychopathy have often been associated with treatment difficulties (e.g. poor engagement and retention) or the lack of a meaningful treatment response (Cleckley, 1941; Hare, 2003; Ogloff, Wong *et al.*, 1990). Some of the relevant characteristics of psychopathy in this regard include lack of remorse, callousness, superficial charm, impaired judgment, egocentricity, lack of anxiety, and underdeveloped affective functioning. Since psychopathic characteristics among juveniles may be related to poor treatment amenability, the evaluators should assess for these characteristics. There is an ongoing debate regarding the appropriateness of diagnosing psychopathy among adolescents—however, the present focus is not diagnostic, but rather on identifying characteristics associated with psychopathy that may be relevant to treatment outcome. The research in this area is mixed, and Salekin's (2002c) review of 42 studies related to the treatment of psychopathy does not support the characterization of psychopathy as being an untreatable disorder.

Other behavioral treatment needs include medical disorders and conditions (e.g. head trauma, prenatal drug or alcohol exposure, epilepsy) and developmental disorders (e.g. autism spectrum disorders, attentional disorders) that could potentially be related to offending behavior (Kinscherff, 2006). Head trauma, in particular, is receiving increased attention from researchers and practitioners, and it is likely that our understanding of the relationship between head trauma and offending behavior will improve in the near future. Given the nature of some medical disorders, an evaluation by someone with neuropsychological or medical training may be useful, either as a stand-alone evaluation or in combination with an evaluation performed by a forensic psychologist.

Finally, intellectual functioning is also relevant to treatment needs and amenability in at least two ways. First, some juvenile placement facilities will not accept a juvenile if his or her intellectual functioning does not meet a particular threshold. As such, the available disposition options for juveniles with impaired intellectual functioning may be limited. Second, the juvenile's response to treatment may be affected by the juvenile's intellectual functioning (Kinscherff, 2006), so the evaluator should describe the relationship between intellectual functioning and treatment amenability. It is also important to note that high intellectual functioning serves as a protective factor that reduces the likelihood that the juvenile will engage in antisocial behavior (e.g. Kandel, Mednick *et al.*, 1988).

RNR Criminogenic Needs

The RNR model (Andrews & Bonta, 2010a; Andrews, Bonta *et al.*, 1990) identifies criminogenic risk factors (i.e. factors associated with increased risk for offending behavior) and classifies these risk factors as either static (unchangeable through planned intervention) or dynamic (potentially changeable through such intervention). For example, risk factors such as a history of early aggression, age at first adjudication, number of prior arrests, and number of out-of-home placements or institutional commitments—despite being empirically related to future risk for offending—are static risk factors because they cannot change (Hawkins, Herrenkohl *et al.*, 2000). By contrast, risk factors such as poor use of leisure time, high impulsivity, aggressiveness, substance use, risk-taking behaviors, pro-criminal attitudes, and associating with antisocial peers are dynamic risk factors because they may be responsive to targeted interventions (Hawkins, Herrenkohl *et al.*, 2000; Hoge, 2013). Dynamic risk factors are relevant to treatment needs/amenability assessments because they represent constructs that can (and should) be addressed during treatment in an attempt to decrease the juvenile's risk for future offending behavior.

Other Domains of Assessment

Several domains warrant assessment in addition to behavioral health and criminogenic needs, although many of the following areas can also be considered as static or dynamic needs within the RNR model.

Family Functioning

Family functioning is an important domain of assessment with regard to treatment amenability because it is often recognized as an influential factor in the success of juvenile offender treatment; see, for example, the Family Cooperation factor in Salekin, Rogers *et al.*'s (2001) conceptualization of treatment amenability. The most effective community-based interventions to reduce juvenile re-offending risk are family-centered (Henggeler, 2016). An evaluation of the juvenile's family can yield important data about the cause of the juvenile's behavior and provide important historical information. Family dysfunction is associated with poorer outcomes among adolescents. According to Patterson's (1982) "coercive family process" model, aggressive behavior among adolescents develops as the result of imitation of the parents and parental reinforcement (see Patterson, DeBaryshe *et al.*, 1989). As such, when evaluating a juvenile's treatment amenability, a variety of family-related factors should be examined. Some of the more important factors to include within this domain include the presence and adequacy of adult supervision; parental involvement in the juvenile's activities (e.g. school, home, play/leisure); family conflict, stress, and major transitions; high levels of hostility, conflict, and aggression within the family; abuse (physical, sexual, or emotional) or neglect within the family; inconsistent or poor boundary/rule-setting within the family; victimization of family members by the juvenile (e.g. sexual abuse of younger siblings); early parental loss; emotional deprivation; parental involvement with the criminal justice system; and parental substance use or abuse (DeMatteo & Marczyk, 2005; Kinscherff, 2006; Kumpfer & Alvarado, 2003; Monahan, Steadman *et al.*, 2001).

Social Functioning

Adolescents are developmentally primed to seek social inclusion and affiliation (see Chapter 4, this volume), and the literature suggests that the influence of peers supersedes the influence of the family as youths enter the teenage years (DeMatteo & Marczyk, 2005; Haynie, 2002). As such, it is important to assess a variety of social functioning factors that may be related to offending behavior and risk for recidivism, including the juvenile's association with delinquent peers (particularly those peers who use drugs or have anti-authority, pro-criminal, or rule-breaking attitudes), the social context of the juvenile's delinquent behavior (i.e. acting alone or with peers), gang affiliation, association with pro-social or non-delinquent peers, attitudes toward authority and authority figures, history of peer conflict (e.g. street fighting), and accessibility and interaction with one or more supportive adults (DeMatteo & Marczyk, 2005; Hawkins, Herrenkohl *et al.*, 2000; Kinscherff, 2006). One risk factor in particular—associating with negative peers—has received a great deal of attention from researchers (Haynie, 2002; Henggeler, 1989). Large-scale studies and meta-analyses have consistently demonstrated that exposure to deviant peers increases the likelihood that a juvenile will engage in delinquent behavior (e.g. Hawkins, Herrenkohl *et al.*, 2000; Keenan, Loeber *et al.*, 1995), and some researchers have estimated that adolescents with delinquent peers are ten times more likely to be involved in serious delinquent behavior than adolescents without delinquent peers (e.g. Bilchik, 1999).

Educational Functioning

There is a substantial empirical literature regarding the relationship between academic functioning and risk for recidivism among juveniles (see DeMatteo & Marczyk, 2005, and Melton, Petrila *et al.*, 2007, for reviews). Well-developed academic and vocational skills enable a juvenile to adapt to his or her environment, and those skills increase the likelihood that the juvenile will be able to secure meaningful employment, which is a protective factor for future recidivism. As such, any evaluation of a juvenile's amenability to treatment should include an assessment of relevant educational factors, which includes both individual-level and system-level variables. Some of the key factors to assess include early educational maladjustment (in elementary school); school infractions and disciplinary actions (detentions, suspensions, expulsions); the presence of special education planning; truancy; school achievement; withdrawal from school; multiple school transitions; and attitudes toward school, education, and vocational future (Hawkins, Herrenkohl *et al.*, 2000; Kinscherff, 2006). In earlier research, Hinshaw (1992) found that low academic achievement, poor academic performance, low commitment to school, and failing to complete school were associated with delinquent and violent behavior among juveniles. Even some system-level factors, such as school overcrowding, are associated with increased aggression among students (Kashani, Jones *et al.*, 1999).

Response to Past Interventions

Another factor relevant to treatment amenability is prior treatment adherence and response (Hoge, 2013). Some of the more important considerations in this area are the number of prior intervention attempts, prior treatment compliance (including types of non-compliance and reasons for non-compliance), factors that complicated the intervention (e.g. intellectual disability), and the juvenile's attitude toward current or future treatment possibilities (Kinscherff, 2006).

MAKING TREATMENT RECOMMENDATIONS AND IDENTIFYING OUTCOMES

Making treatment recommendations and identifying specific outcomes are important considerations in the context of transfer and disposition evaluations. With respect to the scope of the treatment recommendations, there is some disagreement regarding whether treatment recommendations should be broadly defined (any and all treatment options that would be recommended for the juvenile, regardless of whether the treatment is readily available in that jurisdiction) or narrowly defined (recommendations for treatment that are restricted to the currently available treatment options in that jurisdiction) (Chen & Salekin, 2012).

Melton, Petrila *et al.* (2007) support the broad recommendation approach, and assert that the evaluator should consider alternatives that are readily available in the jurisdiction, available but more difficult to access, and indicated but not available in the jurisdiction. However, state laws typically indicate that a juvenile may be prosecuted in criminal court if the juvenile system cannot reasonably be expected to rehabilitate the juvenile within that jurisdiction (Heilbrun, Leheny *et al.*, 1997). Accordingly, broad statements related to treatment amenability in the "perfect-world" treatment context may not be useful to legal decision-makers in juvenile courts (Chen & Salekin, 2012), and evaluators should focus more on the available resources in the jurisdiction in which they practice.

Focusing on the outcome of symptom reduction is of less interest to courts than focusing on the outcome of recidivism reduction (Grisso, 2013; Salekin, Rogers *et al.*, 2001). Several scholars have identified factors that could be considered when evaluators are making treatment recommendations in the context of juvenile FMHA. For example, Grisso (2013) describes several outcomes that should be considered in relation to the successful treatment of juvenile offenders, including a meaningful reduction in the risk of future harm to others, a significant reduction in the likelihood of future delinquency, development of the ability to adapt to family/school/community challenges, and changes in symptom-relevant or personality characteristics. Kinscherff (2006) suggests that forensic mental health professionals should address the following factors when considering treatment options and recommendations: whether the indicated interventions are available anywhere; if so, whether the indicated interventions are accessible within the juvenile justice system; if not, whether the required services could be accessed elsewhere (e.g. out-of-state placement); whether the quality of the available interventions in the jurisdiction is adequate; and whether the accessible programming is able to appropriately address any special considerations for the juvenile, including possible cognitive functioning and behavioral health impairment.

The RNR model, with its focus on risk, needs, and responsivity, delineates some guidelines related to treatment recommendations for juveniles.

The core premise of the risk principle is that treatment intensity should match risk level (Andrews & Bonta, 2010a). Essentially, high-risk juvenile offenders should receive higher intensity treatment than low-risk juvenile offenders. Moreover, the RNR model indicates that treatment should focus specifically on the individual treatment needs that are contributing to future offending risk (via specific criminogenic needs) as opposed to adopting a one-size-fits-all treatment approach. Finally, the RNR model holds that the treatment modality selected should account for both positive and negative responsivity factors of the youth as a way to maximize potential treatment effects and minimize barriers to improvement (Hoge, 2013).

FACTORS ASSOCIATED WITH TREATMENT OUTCOMES

Researchers have identified a variety of factors that are associated with both negative and positive treatment outcomes among justice-involved juveniles. For example, Salekin (2015a) notes that factors such as expectation, self-evaluation, engagement, cognition, and attention are associated with treatment outcomes in juveniles. Amenability in juveniles has also been associated with verbal abilities, intelligence, insight, acknowledgment of treatment targets, and motivation to change (Salekin, 2015a; Salekin & Grimes, 2008).

FACTORS ASSOCIATED WITH AMENABILITY DETERMINATIONS: A STUDY OF PENNSYLVANIA CASE LAW

As previously noted, the Pennsylvania Juvenile Act 2013 outlines several components of amenability, including age, mental capacity, maturity, the degree of criminal sophistication exhibited by the juvenile, and whether the juvenile can be rehabilitated prior to the termination of the jurisdiction of the juvenile court at age 21.

Loving and Patapis's (2007) case law analysis of relevant amenability factors is an informative framework for forensic mental health professionals who are interested in how amenability assessments have been viewed by Pennsylvania courts. Although their case law review was limited to Pennsylvania courts, courts in other jurisdictions have reached similar conclusions about these factors. With respect to age, Pennsylvania courts have typically characterized younger offenders as more amenable to treatment than their older counterparts, in part because older defendants have less available time within the jurisdiction of the juvenile justice system (Loving & Patapis, 2007). When the recommended treatment duration extends beyond the age of majority, it has historically been perceived as evidence against the juvenile's amenability (e.g. *Commonwealth v. Pyle*, 1975; *Commonwealth v. Rush*, 1989). Pennsylvania law related to mental capacity has been inconsistent. Although limited intellectual capacity is most often cited as an argument against amenability, a few decisions have asserted that greater mental capacity is related to criminal sophistication and thus may diminish treatment amenability (e.g. *Commonwealth v. Burley*, 1998).

Criminal sophistication is almost always conceptualized as a factor undermining treatment amenability, and both state and federal courts have helped to clarify the relationship between criminal sophistication and amenability. For example, offense-related variables such as premeditated violence (e.g. *Commonwealth v. Williams*, 1987; *Kent v. United States*, 1966) and unprovoked brutality (e.g. *United States v. H.M.M.S.*, 1993; *United States v. M.H.*, 1995) have been associated with greater criminal sophistication and more limited treatment amenability. Offender- and behavior-related variables have also been linked to criminal sophistication and amenability, including persistent and versatile criminal behavior, efforts to conceal offending behavior, successful evasion of authorities, lack of remorse (*Commonwealth v. Archer*, 1998), and disregard for victims (*Commonwealth v. Burley*, 1998).

Resource availability is an interesting component of amenability because (in theory) it suggests that a juvenile offender could be deemed less amenable to treatment based simply on system-related (rather than offense- or juvenile-related) characteristics. Federal case law indicates that the hypothetical treatability of an offender is irrelevant if the required treatment is not accessible to the offender (*United States v. Atkins*, 1997). Consistent with this view, Pennsylvania courts have consistently held that the inaccessibility of an indicated treatment argues against the juvenile's amenability (*Commonwealth v. Morningwake*, 1991; *Commonwealth v. Potts*, 1996).

FUTURE DIRECTIONS

Although treatment amenability is an important part of the *Kent* criteria, at least one study has demonstrated that amenability may be given less weight than the other two factors in the context of judicial decision-making (Brannen, Salekin *et al.*, 2006). Using a sample of 361 judges from the National Council of Juvenile and Family Court Judges, these investigators asked judges to make hypothetical transfer decisions based on vignettes describing juvenile offenders with varying levels of characteristics related to each of the three *Kent* criteria. The results indicated that sophistication-maturity and risk were statistically significantly related to judges' decision-making, but treatment amenability was not. This study sheds light on how judges view amenability in the context of juvenile court decision-making, but additional research is needed before firm conclusions can be drawn regarding how judges value treatment amenability.

In addition, research suggests that the inter-rater reliability of treatment amenability is poor, meaning that forensic mental health professionals often do not agree on an individual juvenile's level of treatment amenability (Page & Scalora, 2004). Possible explanations for limited clinician agreement include the absence of measures specifically designed to assess for treatment amenability, the lack of systematic information collection related to treatment planning (Quinsey, 1988), and the overreliance on non-clinical factors (Ashford, 1988). Of note, however, is that most research regarding the inter-rater reliability of treatment amenability estimates is based on adult offenders, so researchers should examine the reliability of amenability assessments among evaluators who work with juvenile offenders.

CONCLUSION

Treatment amenability is one of the three primary criteria applicable to transfer decisions across jurisdictions, with the other two being risk for recidivism and sophistication-maturity. In some ways, a juvenile's amenability is the most challenging criterion to evaluate. There are few instruments that even attempt to measure amenability; it is defined differently in clinical contexts (likelihood of favorable response to behavioral health interventions) than in juvenile justice contexts (reducing the likelihood that the juvenile will re-offend); and research on amenability is considerably less developed than research regarding risk for recidivism and sophistication-maturity. Nevertheless, researchers and scholars have developed models to guide the assessment of amenability and identified factors—behavioral health needs, criminogenic needs, and functioning in relevant domains—that are empirically related to amenability determinations. Such advances are of considerable use to forensic mental health professionals who conduct transfer and reverse transfer evaluations.

CHAPTER SEVEN

Sophistication-Maturity

This chapter focuses on the third criterion relevant to transfer and reverse transfer decisions: sophistication-maturity. After describing the legal context for sophistication-maturity, we review the empirical research that has examined this construct, with a particular emphasis on studies that have investigated correlates of sophistication-maturity and the predictive validity of the construct in the contexts of transfer and reverse transfer decisions. We then describe various approaches for assessing sophistication-maturity, and conclude with a synthesis of the practice literature and a focus on best practice.

LEGAL CONTEXT

The construct of sophistication-maturity is relevant in a number of legal contexts involving justice-involved adolescents, including adjudicative competence (e.g. Cox, Goldstein *et al.*, 2012; Dupée, 2002; Viljoen, Wingrove *et al.*, 2008), waiver of *Miranda* rights (e.g. Colwell, Cruise *et al.*, 2005), eyewitness testimony (e.g. Salekin, MacDougall *et al.*, 2016), and the treatment of detained youth with behavioral problems (e.g. Salekin, Tippey *et al.*, 2012). Both legal authorities and social science scholars have identified this construct as providing important and relevant information. In the present chapter, however, we focus on the relevance of sophistication-maturity in the context of transfer decisions. Legal decision-makers also may consider an adolescent's sophistication-maturity in terms of the likelihood that the adolescent will respond to an intervention, which is relevant to disposition decisions.

Similar to the construct of amenability to treatment (described in Chapter 6, this volume), the concept of sophistication-maturity has deep historical roots. The juvenile justice system was developed based on the assumptions that children and adolescents possess less developmental maturity and are more amenable to treatment than adults (Larson & Grisso, 2016; Salekin, MacDougall *et al.*, 2016). Two important implications flow from these assumptions. First, less maturity is associated with less culpability (or less blameworthiness), and less culpability suggests that the adolescent should receive a lesser punishment (see Grisso, 2010–11). This can be seen in several cases from the Supreme Court of the United States, including cases that excluded adolescent offenders from the death penalty (*Roper v. Simmons*, 2005) and from sentences of life without parole in certain circumstances (*Graham v. Florida*, 2010; *Miller v. Alabama*, 2012). Second, adolescents with less maturity are considered more appropriate for juvenile court; juvenile courts can order dispositions that provide interventions that are more consistent with the adolescent's developmental level and characteristics. By contrast, adolescents with heightened or "adult-like" maturity are considered more appropriate for criminal court because they are more likely to persist in their offending behavior and less likely to benefit from the interventions provided in the juvenile system.

The United States Supreme Court, in *Kent v. United States* (1966), described the construct of sophistication-maturity being considered in this chapter. *Kent* identified eight criteria that are relevant to judicial decisions regarding juvenile transfer and disposition. Although researchers and scholars have offered various interpretations of the *Kent* criteria (see Grisso, 2010–11, and Salekin, 2015, for discussions), it is generally accepted that the eight *Kent* criteria can be distilled into three psychological constructs that are relevant to transfer and disposition decisions, with sophistication-maturity being one of the three criteria (along with risk for future offending and treatment needs and amenability) (see Salekin & Grimes, 2008; Salekin, Price *et al.*, 2012). As we have noted, however, not every state requires a consideration of all three criteria in transfer and disposition decisions. According to one analysis, risk for recidivism is explicitly (or implicitly) a criterion in every state and treatment amenability is also a criterion in almost all states—but sophistication-maturity (or some variation thereof) is considered in fewer states (Chen & Salekin, 2012). Of the 22 states with reverse transfer statutes, all applicable statutes include a consideration of risk, 17 include amenability to treatment, and 13 include sophistication-maturity (King, 2016).

DEFINING SOPHISTICATION-MATURITY

Researchers and scholars have offered various conceptualizations of the defining elements of sophistication-maturity. Such efforts have important implications for forensic mental health professionals who seek to assess sophistication-maturity when working with justice-involved adolescents. Sophistication-maturity is a construct composed of several underlying and related characteristics, some of which may not be directly observable. Therefore, identifying the defining elements of sophistication-maturity provides guidance in the valid assessment of the construct, which ultimately provides greater assistance to legal decision-makers who work with justice-involved adolescents.

Some scholars have distinguished between the concepts of developmental maturity and sophistication-maturity. Salekin (2015a), for example, prefers the term "developmental maturity" because he contends that "sophistication-maturity," at least when used to signify criminal sophistication, is simply developmental maturity that has been modified by some other factor, such as psychopathic characteristics or antisocial thinking. Further, whereas developmental maturity has relevance in several contexts, it simply refers to an adolescent's maturity over time, regardless of whether the adolescent becomes involved with the law; by contrast, sophistication-maturity is the psycho-legal construct that is assessed when evaluating justice-involved adolescents in legal contexts (Salekin, MacDougall *et al.*, 2016). Because many aspects of developmental maturity are also important in sophistication-maturity, both concepts are discussed in this chapter. Unfortunately, however, the defining features of the concepts are not always clear.

In early research, Salekin, Rogers *et al.* (2001) examined the three constructs distilled from *Kent*—dangerousness, sophistication-maturity, and amenability to treatment—in decisions to transfer adolescents to criminal court. The researchers asked child psychologists ($n = 244$) and forensic psychologists board certified by the American Board of Professional Psychology ($n = 75$) to provide prototypical ratings of each of the three constructs with respect to juveniles they evaluated who had subsequently been transferred to criminal court. For the sophistication-maturity construct, results revealed that four items were rated high in prototypicality: criminal sophistication, capable of planned and premeditated criminal behavior, understanding of behavioral-societal norms, and ability to identify alternative actions. Salekin, Rogers *et al.* (2001) noted that the items of criminal sophistication and premeditated crime are reflected in relevant case law and juvenile statutes, whereas the items concerning behavioral norms and alternative actions reflect factors that are highlighted in the social science literature on developmental maturity.

In a related study, Ryba, Cooper *et al.* (2003a) surveyed 80 mental health professionals to examine how they conceptualize maturity in the specific context of juvenile competence to stand trial evaluations. The survey responses were grouped into seven categories of abilities that were considered relevant to adolescent maturity:

- *Cognitive skills* (endorsed by 51 percent of respondents). The most important abilities in this domain included intellectual functioning, cognitive abilities, and academic functioning. Other cognitive skills endorsed by respondents included verbal skills, thinking, planning, cognitive processing, evidence of formal operations, comprehension, memory, attention, concentration, executive functioning, problem-solving ability, and literacy.
- *Social skills* (endorsed by 40 percent of respondents). Some of the abilities noted in this domain included age-appropriate or adaptive social skills, social awareness, social age, level of socialization, and interpersonal skills.
- *Judgment/decision-making* (endorsed by 24 percent of respondents). The abilities reported in this domain included overall judgment, soundness of judgment, and social-moral judgment, with some respondents endorsing a combination of judgment and decision-making, or judgment and common sense.
- *Developmental level* (endorsed by 21 percent of respondents). Most of the responses that fell into this domain concerned the importance of assessing developmental age, the achievement of milestones, and adaptive functioning. Some respondents noted the importance of assessing an adolescent's ability to function autonomously, and other

respondents endorsed specific developmental characteristics such as psychosexual development, conceptual understanding, language use or sophistication of speech, manners, and life experiences.

- *Behavioral control* (endorsed by 18 percent of respondents). Self-control, age- and situation-appropriate behavior, and impulse control were the most commonly endorsed abilities in this domain.
- *Emotional control* (endorsed by 15 percent of respondents). The most commonly endorsed characteristics in this domain included overall emotional level, affect, and appropriate expression of emotions, followed by the less commonly endorsed abilities of adequately coping with stress, demonstrating empathy, minimal use of denial, and controlling anger.
- *Reasoning/moral reasoning* (endorsed by 15 percent of respondents). Respondents endorsed the importance of assessing general reasoning and abstract reasoning abilities, moral sophistication, and moral development when assessing an adolescent's maturity.

Of note, most survey respondents identified abilities that fell into more than one of these categories (64 percent), while some respondents listed characteristics that fell into only one category (30 percent) or none of the categories (6 percent).

Salekin (2015a) suggests that three factors underlie the concept of developmental maturity: (1) autonomy, (2) cognitive abilities-skills, and (3) emotional maturity (i.e. emotion regulation skills). Salekin, MacDougall *et al.* (2016) based this definition of developmental maturity on a synthesis of the research conducted over the previous 40 years (e.g. Greenberger & Sorensen, 1974; Salekin, 2002b; Salekin, Rogers *et al.*, 2001; Steinberg & Cauffman, 1996). Although there are differences in terminology, Salekin, MacDougall *et al.* (2016) note that the theoretical model of developmental maturity proposed by Steinberg and Cauffman (1996)—which includes the concepts of responsibility, perspective, and temperance—maps directly onto the empirically derived three-factor model of developmental maturity proposed by Salekin, Yff *et al.* (2002), with responsibility being similar to autonomy, perspective being similar to cognitive abilities-skills, and temperance being similar to emotional maturity. Salekin, MacDougall *et al.* (2016) prefer the terms autonomy, cognitive abilities-skills, and emotional maturity because they believe that these terms are most easily recognized by a range of professionals.

The core concepts of autonomy, cognitive abilities-skills, and emotional maturity identified by Salekin, Yff *et al.* (2002) include several subsumed characteristics, such as an internal locus of control, forethought, and planning, all of which can manifest in either antisocial or pro-social ways (Salekin, 2015a). On one hand, antisocial behavior may stem from deliberate premeditation and an ability to influence others into misconduct, both of which are associated with heightened sophistication-maturity. On the other, greater maturity can lead to strong academic performance, appropriate social skills, and participation in organized activities, which are associated with a decreased risk for engaging in antisocial behavior.

Grisso (2010–11) notes that the purpose, meaning, and intent of the law's interest in an adolescent's maturity are not clear—for example, whether the interest in an adolescent's maturity relates to security concerns or amenability considerations. Grisso (2013) focuses on two considerations in determining whether an adolescent demonstrates sufficient sophistication-maturity for his or her behavior to be considered "adult-like" in the context of transfer and disposition decisions. The first consideration is whether the youth's behavior is habitual, planned, and deliberate. These youth, according to Grisso (2013), have chosen a criminal lifestyle, and he referred to them as "criminal journeymen." In terms of transfer decisions, youth who fall into this category are less likely to desist in their offending behavior and are therefore more likely to be seen as appropriate for criminal court (Larson & Grisso, 2016). With respect to disposition, adolescents with greater levels of sophistication-maturity may be seen as requiring higher levels of security. The second consideration identified by Grisso (2013) is whether the youth's psychological immaturity is influencing his or her offending behavior. Often adolescent offending is due to poor self-control, limited foresight, and poorly developed perspective-taking. Adolescents who engage in antisocial behavior due to this type of psychological immaturity are seen as better candidates for being processed in the juvenile system because their deficits can be addressed through targeted interventions and the passage of time.

The natural maturation process that occurs over time is deserving of comment. Grisso (2010–11) summarized the effects of the passage of time by noting that

> maturation during adolescence proceeds from less to greater capacity to regulate impulses, less to greater likelihood of recognizing risks and weighing them meaningfully, less to greater capacity to consider options and their consequences before acting, and less to greater resistance to the influence of peers on making choices. (p. 182)

Importantly, adolescents mature at different rates, as do their skills and abilities. Although the science is continuing to develop, there is emerging and convincing evidence that brain development is related to developmental maturity. The processes of myelination and pruning are now thought to continue until individuals are in their mid-20s, and both processes appear to be related to decision-making and forethought (Gogtay, Giedd *et al.*, 2004), which are components of sophistication-maturity. Behavioral research appears consistent with the results of the brain research, demonstrating that adolescents as a class are less likely than adults to delay responses, more likely to engage in sensation-seeking behavior, and more likely to act based on perceptions of short-term gain rather than potential negative consequences.

Anything that substantially interferes with brain development or learning can affect developmental maturation. For example, several factors that are commonly seen among justice-involved adolescents, such as family dysfunction, mental illness, inadequate nourishment, ineffective learning environments, lower socioeconomic status, and substance abuse, have been associated with deficits in developmental maturity (see Salekin, 2015a, for a discussion). Impoverished environments (e.g. familial, academic, social) may stunt neural growth, which can hinder the development of maturity.

As will be discussed in more detail later in this chapter, these are among the many targets for evaluators when assessing an adolescent's sophistication-maturity.

Sophistication-maturity and the other two criteria distilled from *Kent* can also be conceptualized using the Risk-Need-Responsivity (RNR) model (Andrews & Bonta, 2010a). Salekin (2015a) noted that Risk maps onto the construct of risk for dangerousness, while Need and Responsivity map onto the concept of treatment amenability. He also noted that Responsivity, though most closely aligned with treatment amenability, is linked with developmental maturity because higher levels of maturity are related to better treatment outcomes.

There are alternative ways in which sophistication-maturity can be incorporated into the RNR model. For example, sophistication-maturity could be a specific risk factor for some adolescents, which is consistent with the idea that maturity can be applied in pro-social or antisocial ways, or it could be subsumed under antisocial cognition or antisocial personality style. If an adolescent's maturity is applied pro-socially, then sophistication-maturity could instead be considered a responsivity or strength factor. If not sufficiently developed, sophistication-maturity could represent a non-criminogenic need, responsivity factor, or specific (rather than general) risk factor, depending on the adolescent being evaluated. The role of sophistication-maturity for a particular adolescent—e.g. risk factor vs. strength—is contingent on a number of contextual and mediating factors that will be discussed later in this chapter.

RESEARCH ON SOPHISTICATION-MATURITY IN LEGAL CONTEXTS

Given the importance of the sophistication-maturity construct as distilled from the *Kent* criteria, researchers have examined whether there is indeed a relationship between developmental maturity and offending behavior among adolescents. In early research, Steinberg & Cauffman (1996) and Cauffman & Steinberg (2000) found that maturity was related to antisocial decision-making among adolescents, with the three components of their developmental maturity model—responsibility, temperance, and perspective—being inversely correlated with antisocial decision-making.

Subsequently, Cruise and colleagues (2008) examined whether there was a relationship between maturity and adolescent offenders' self-reported delinquent behavior. Among a sample of 136 juvenile offenders (106 male) recruited from two juvenile justice settings, Cruise, Fernandez *et al.* (2008) found significant correlations between psycho-social maturity variables and self-reported delinquent behavior over a one-year outcome period, with participant sex acting as a moderator. After controlling for participant age and setting, the psycho-social maturity variable of temperance consistently predicted self-reported total, violent, and non-violent delinquency for the male juvenile offenders (Cruise, Fernandez *et al.*, 2008). More specifically, they found that perspective and temperance—two of the components of the developmental maturity model proposed by Steinberg & Cauffman (1996)—were inversely related to frequency of delinquent acts, whereas the third component of the Steinberg & Cauffman model—responsibility—was not. Cruise, Fernandez *et al.* (2008) concluded that temperance was the maturity variable that most strongly predicted violent, non-violent, and total delinquent behaviors for male juvenile offenders; the results were less definitive for the female juvenile offenders. Considered with the research by Cauffman & Steinberg (2000), it appears that while perspective, temperance, and responsibility are all inversely related to antisocial decision-making, temperance is the most relevant factor in predicting antisocial behavior among adolescents.

Given the relationship between developmental maturity and adolescent offending, and the importance of sophistication-maturity in transfer and disposition decisions, several researchers have examined how juvenile court judges view sophistication-maturity relative to the other *Kent* criteria. For example, Brannen, Salekin *et al.* (2006) asked 361 judges from the National Council of Juvenile and Family Court Judges to examine a hypothetical case, varying levels of dangerousness, sophistication-maturity, and treatment amenability of a juvenile offender. Results revealed that nearly all of the judges reported that it would be useful for forensic mental health assessment reports to address dangerousness (98 percent), sophistication-maturity (97 percent), and amenability to treatment (97 percent). However, the judges reported that the evaluations they typically receive do not always address all three criteria, with 77 percent containing information on dangerousness, 84 percent including information on sophistication-maturity, and 86 percent containing information on amenability to treatment. Their results showed that dangerousness and sophistication-maturity, but not amenability to treatment, had a significant impact on the judges' dichotomous transfer decisions. When the dependent variable was judges' ordinal ratings of transfer likelihood (rather than a binary outcome), adolescents who were high in dangerousness and sophistication-maturity but low in treatment amenability were the most likely candidates to be transferred to criminal court, whereas adolescents low in dangerousness and sophistication-maturity but high in treatment amenability were the least likely to be transferred (Brannen, Salekin *et al.*, 2006).

Other investigators (Salekin, Yff *et al.*, 2002) surveyed 422 judges from the National Council of Juvenile and Family Court Judges regarding their perspective on the core *Kent* criteria of dangerousness, sophistication-maturity, and amenability to treatment in terms of their decision-making. Dangerousness was rated as the most important factor, followed by amenability to treatment and then sophistication-maturity. Notably, while the juvenile court judges described all three constructs as important to their juvenile waiver decisions, psychologists rated all three constructs as less important than did judges.

Some researchers have expressed concern regarding the relatively amorphous conceptualization of sophistication-maturity and the inconsistent application of the construct by some judges. One investigator (Harris, 2008), for example, examined juvenile court judges' decisions regarding adolescents in three juvenile courts in California. Results revealed that judges applied the concept of sophistication not only to the adolescent's offending behavior, but also to the adolescent's family, school, and lifestyle. For example, adolescents who were parents, affiliated with gangs, or performing poorly academically were considered by the judges to be more sophisticated and therefore more likely to be transferred to criminal court. This study also found that judges, prosecutors, and defense attorneys considered the offenders' remorse as being indicative of their level of sophistication because remorse is often an indicator of guilt and morality. The investigator concluded that the legal criterion of sophistication-maturity is ill defined, which provided judges with wide latitude to apply the construct to adolescents based on the judges' norms, morals, assumptions, and stereotypes. Other researchers and scholars (e.g. Grisso, 2010–11) have voiced similar concerns regarding the ambiguous conceptualization of sophistication-maturity in legal contexts.

Regardless of the clarity of the construct, it is apparent that a justice-involved adolescent's sophistication-maturity is an important consideration for juvenile court judges in transfer and disposition contexts (Chen & Salekin, 2012; Redding & Murrie, 2007). Sophistication-maturity is related to antisocial decision-making, likelihood of recidivism, and amenability to treatment, all of which are relevant considerations in transfer and disposition decisions. One study (Redding & Hensl, 2011) suggests a tendency of juvenile court judges to transfer juvenile offenders with higher levels of sophistication-maturity. In this study, judges were more likely to transfer juvenile offenders who were characterized by adult-like traits, prior court contact, low motivation, and less treatment amenability, whereas immature offenders were less likely to be transferred to criminal court.

ASSESSING SOPHISTICATION-MATURITY

Because of the importance of sophistication-maturity in transfer and reverse transfer decisions, a good deal has been written about the assessment of this construct. There are several options for measuring several key aspects of developmental maturity, such as intellectual functioning, cognitive development, emotional control, and social skills, and mental health professionals have a long history of assessing these constructs in both legal and non-legal contexts (Grisso, 2010–11). However, the assessment of adolescent sophistication-maturity presents some unusual challenges for forensic mental health professionals. Despite the availability of well-validated measures for assessing skills and abilities relevant to adolescent sophistication-maturity, it remains probably the most difficult of the *Kent* criteria for forensic mental health professionals (Salekin, Rogers *et al.*, 2001). This section reviews commonly used assessment approaches, synthesizes the practice literature, and describes the challenges faced by mental health professionals when assessing sophistication-maturity in transfer and disposition contexts.

Early recommendations for evaluating sophistication-maturity in transfer and disposition evaluations focused on assessing cognitive and emotional maturity (Ewing, 1990). To assess cognitive maturity, Ewing recommended using intelligence tests (e.g. Wechsler measures) and achievement tests (e.g. Wide Range Achievement Test). He recommended intelligence tests because those measures assess intellect and other factors, such as perception, processing speed, attention, and judgment, that are theoretically relevant to sophistication-maturity. His rationale for using achievement tests was that many justice-involved adolescents have learning disabilities that hinder the development of their maturity. Years later, the National Council of Juvenile and Family Court Judges (2005) similarly recommended that intellectual and developmental disabilities be considered part of the sophistication-maturity construct. Ewing (1990) recommended assessing emotional maturity through interviewing and psychological testing, including self-report personality measures and projective techniques, which he believed provide important information about the adolescent's internal controls, reality testing, and ability to organize thoughts. In the ensuing years, some researchers and scholars criticized these suggestions because some of the tests have complicated or unstandardized scoring systems, and also because there are better-validated methods for assessing maturity than projective tests (see Salekin, 2015a).

TEST BATTERIES

An early practitioner survey (Ryba, Cooper *et al.*, 2003a) focused on methods of assessing maturity in the context of juvenile competence to stand trial evaluations among 80 mental health professionals. Respondents reported using interviews (77 percent), psychological testing (68 percent), behavioral observation (35 percent), and record review (35 percent) to evaluate maturity, and 79 percent of the respondents reported using more than one assessment method. In terms of testing, 21 percent of the respondents reported that they do not use any tests when assessing maturity, while 79 percent reported using one or more of 34 different tests or assessment methods. The more commonly used tests included intelligence tests (e.g. earlier versions of the Wechsler Intelligence Scale for Children and the Wechsler Adult Intelligence Scale: 29 percent), the Vineland Adaptive Behavioral Scales (20 percent), the Minnesota Multiphasic Personality Inventory-Adolescent or Minnesota Multiphasic Personality Inventory-2 (12 percent), the Rorschach Inkblot Test (8 percent), the Thematic Apperception Test (8 percent), and the Human Figure Drawing Test (6 percent). A small portion of respondents (8 percent) also reported assessing maturity using a clinical interview.

As may be seen, respondents endorsed a wide variety of tools, including symptom checklists, intelligence tests, achievement tests, and personality measures (objective and projective) to assess maturity. Further, the measures included both clinical assessment instruments (i.e. tests developed for use in assessment, diagnosis, and treatment planning in therapeutic contexts) and forensically relevant instruments (i.e. tests that assess clinical constructs that are relevant to those involved in the justice system). Of note, this survey predated the development of a forensic assessment instrument for assessing sophistication-maturity, although some respondents endorsed using measures that included a scale or subtest that directly assessed maturity (e.g. Jesness Inventory-Maturity Scale, Missouri Children's Picture Series-Maturity Scale).

Although the investigators did not obtain data on *why* the mental health professionals endorsed using specific measures, they offered some informed speculation. They noted that intelligence tests, achievement tests, and measures of adaptive functioning yield data on an adolescent's cognitive abilities and level of independent functioning, while personality tests yield data relevant to an adolescent's social, emotional, and moral development. All of these abilities and characteristics are potentially relevant to assessments of maturity in multiple legal contexts. The use of personality tests to assess adolescent maturity is consistent with recommendations by Salekin (2015a), who noted that adolescents with higher levels of certain personality characteristics are likely to demonstrate greater autonomy, cognitive control, and emotion regulation, all of which are components of developmental maturity. He noted, for example, that adolescents high in conscientiousness, openness, and agreeableness demonstrate more amenability to treatment and a lower risk of engaging in antisocial behavior, which are relevant considerations in juvenile transfer contexts. Moreover, these personality characteristics can be targeted through specific interventions; this is relevant to disposition decisions.

Ryba, Cooper *et al.* (2003b) expressed some concern about the appropriateness of some of the tests endorsed by the survey respondents. There is a developed literature on test selection in forensic mental health assessment contexts (e.g. Melton, Petrila *et al.*, 2007; Otto and Heilbrun, 2002). Forensic mental health professionals should choose tests that have adequate psychometric properties, including validation on the population with which the measure is being used. Ryba, Cooper *et al.* (2003b) were particularly concerned about the use of projective tests, which they characterized as inappropriate measures for the assessment of juvenile competency. Salekin (2015a) has also expressed concerns regarding the use of projective tests in the assessment of adolescent developmental maturity, largely because of the specialized knowledge of administration and scoring that is needed for some projective tests (e.g. Thematic Apperception Test). Both Ryba, Cooper *et al.* (2003b) and Salekin (2015a) observed that projective tests may be appropriate if they are used to assess a specific aspect of the adolescent's developmental maturity. Salekin (2015a) noted, for example, that the scoring guidelines for the Thematic Apperception Test developed by Westen, Klepser *et al.* (1991) are useful for assessing developmental maturity because they provide information on internal representations, relationships, and social causality, which are theoretically related to maturity. Salekin (2015a) cautioned, however, that projective tests should not be used alone, and recommended that other tests that provide additional ("real-world") information on developmental maturity be included in the test battery. We would add that using projective testing in this context, even when it is scored, is problematic because of the absence of empirical data linking such theoretical constructs to behavioral outcomes in justice-involved youth.

More recently, Salekin and colleagues (2016) highlighted some of the most commonly used measures of adolescent developmental maturity, including the Psychosocial Maturity Inventory (Greenberger, Josselson *et al.*, 1975), the Weinberger Adjustment Inventory (Weinberger & Schwartz, 1990), the Consideration of Future Consequences Scale (Strathman, Gleicher *et al.*, 1994), the Stanford Time Perspective Inventory (Zimbardo, 1990a; Zimbardo & Boyd, 1999), the Criminal Decision Making Questionnaire (Fried & Reppucci, 2001), and the Resistance to Peer Influence (Steinberg & Monahan, 2007) measure. They noted that all of these self-report measures assess some aspect of developmental maturity, although most of them have been limited to use in research contexts. Synthesizing the practice literature, Salekin (2015a) suggested that forensic mental health professionals use a test battery that includes intelligence tests, achievement tests, measures of child and adolescent psychopathology, strengths-based measures, and a measure that specifically assesses the psycho-legal construct of sophistication-maturity (see Salekin, Tippey *et al.*, 2012).

RISK-SOPHISTICATION-TREATMENT INVENTORY

Noting the absence of a measure that specifically assesses sophistication-maturity among adolescents, Salekin (2004a) developed the Risk-Sophistication-Treatment Inventory (RSTI). The RSTI was developed using a three-step process. First, he generated items relating to dangerousness, sophistication-maturity, and treatment amenability through a search of relevant case law and the social science literature. Second, he solicited expert ratings from 75 forensic diplomates, 240 child and adolescent clinicians, and 430 juvenile court judges. The psychologists rated the items they considered to be central to dangerousness, sophistication-maturity, and treatment amenability; the forensic diplomates provided ratings of juveniles they had evaluated who had been transferred to criminal court; and the judges from the National Council of Juvenile and Family Court Judges rated core characteristics for all three constructs. Third, Salekin and colleagues conducted both exploratory factor analysis and confirmatory factor analysis of the prototypical ratings (Salekin, Rogers *et al.*, 2001; Salekin, Yff *et al.*, 2002).

The 45-item RSTI provides a structured basis for assessing developmental maturity, risk of dangerousness, and treatment amenability when juveniles are being considered for transfer or disposition (Salekin, 2004b), and the results can be used by mental health professionals, juvenile court judges, and parole officers in various contexts (Leistico & Salekin, 2003; Salekin, 2004b). One important limitation of this measure is the apparent absence of outcome data demonstrating the relationship between scale scores and future behavior in the domains that are measured. The RSTI is scored based on a semi-structured interview consisting of general background questions and several primary questions regarding dangerousness (risk), developmental maturity, and treatment amenability. To score the RSTI, information from the interview is combined with collateral information (e.g. academic records, arrest records, and treatment records; interviews with parents, guardians, teachers, probation officers, and treatment providers), with each item scored on a three-point scale using rating criteria outlined in the RSTI manual (Salekin, 2004b; Salekin, Salekin *et al.*, 2005). Consistent with Salekin's prior research (Salekin, Rogers *et al.*, 2001; Salekin, Yff *et al.*, 2002), the RSTI contains three scales (15 items each): Developmental Maturity, Risk, and Amenability. The Developmental Maturity scale consists of three subscales—Autonomy, Cognitive Skills, and Emotional Skills—that reflect the results of Salekin's conceptualization of the construct of developmental maturity. Each scale is then labeled descriptively as low, medium, or high. Salekin (2015a) recommends that clinicians have considerable professional knowledge, skill, and experience with juvenile offenders before using the RSTI.

The RSTI was normed on 690 juvenile cases (ages 9–18 years) from several juvenile justice facilities and settings, including both detained and non-detained youth (Salekin, 2004a). The normative analyses yielded sufficient psychometric data. The RSTI demonstrated adequate internal consistency, with alpha coefficients for the three RSTI scales ranging from 0.78 to 0.83, and no significant differences based on adolescent race, sex, or age (Salekin, 2004a). Intraclass correlation coefficients were 0.94 for Risk, 0.91 for Treatment Amenability, and 0.74 for Sophistication-Maturity, which suggests adequate interrater reliability (Leistico & Salekin, 2003; Salekin, 2004a).

In preliminary research on the RSTI, Leistico & Salekin (2003) examined the validity and reliability of the RSTI among a sample of 126 adolescent males incarcerated in the Mendota Juvenile Treatment Center. Besides reporting basic validity and reliability data, they examined the relationships among the three scales and several defining factors. They found that Risk was related to younger age of onset for criminal behavior, violent offenses, and violent and non-violent symptoms of conduct disorder. Sophistication-maturity and the Criminal Sophistication subscale correlated with non-violent offenses ($r = 0.28$ and $r = 0.30$, respectively). Interestingly, Sophistication-Maturity was not significantly related to aggression type, psychopathy, or transfer to adult court, but it was related to treatment amenability ($r = 0.36$). Of note, adolescents transferred to criminal court had significantly higher mean Risk and Developmental Maturity scores and lower mean Treatment Amenability scores than adolescents who remained in juvenile court, which supports the predictive validity of the RSTI for transfer decisions (Leistico & Salekin, 2003). Furthermore, Sophistication-Maturity was not significantly related to traditional measures of intelligence or academic achievement, which Leistico & Salekin (2003) interpreted as meaning that Sophistication-Maturity may involve "street-smart" abilities and other abilities/skills that are not traditionally assessed by standard intelligence and achievement tests.

In the years since the RSTI's publication, several researchers have examined the utility of the measure in juvenile transfer and disposition decisions. Taken together, the results are promising, which led Grisso (2010–11) to conclude that the RSTI can be an effective tool for clinicians who are evaluating adolescents in transfer and disposition contexts. A full review of all RSTI-related research is beyond the scope of this chapter, but several notable studies are described below.

One team of investigators (Spice, Viljoen *et al.*, 2010) examined the utility of the RSTI and the Structured Assessment of Violence Risk in Youth (SAVRY) among 74 Canadian adolescents considered for transfer to criminal court. They reported acceptable internal consistency and good to excellent inter-rater reliability, although the intra-class correlation coefficient of 0.60 for Sophistication-Maturity was considerably lower than the value (0.74) reported in the RSTI manual (Salekin, 2004b). Results revealed high correlations between SAVRY Risk scores and the RSTI Risk and Treatment Amenability scales, but weaker correlations between SAVRY scores and the RSTI Sophistication-Maturity scale. The Sophistication-Maturity scale was related to older age at first offense and fewer symptoms of conduct disorder, which Spice, Viljoen *et al.* (2010) interpreted as indicating that the Sophistication-Maturity scale is primarily measuring pro-social maturity. When compared to adolescents who received a juvenile sentence or no sentence, adolescents who received adult sentences had higher ratings of RSTI Risk, SAVRY Total, and RSTI Criminal Sophistication, and lower ratings of RSTI Treatment Amenability and SAVRY Protective Factors. RSTI Sophistication-Maturity scores did not significantly differ between the two groups. This latter finding contrasts with the findings reported by Leistico & Salekin (2003), which indicated that adolescents transferred to adult court had higher Sophistication-Maturity scores.

In terms of predictive validity, the results of ROC analyses conducted (Spice, Viljoen *et al.*, 2010) indicated that RSTI Risk, Treatment Amenability, and Criminal Sophistication scores and SAVRY Total, Protective, and Summary Risk scores significantly predicted an adult sentence, whereas RSTI Sophistication-Maturity scores were not significant predictors. The investigators also examined whether the RSTI and SAVRY added incremental predictive validity beyond other legal criteria for transfer, and reported that Treatment Amenability, Criminal Sophistication, and SAVRY Protective scores added significant predictive validity after controlling for age, offense type, and criminal history. Overall, Spice, Viljoen *et al.* (2010) concluded that the results supported the use of the RSTI in transfer decisions. However, the results also highlighted some of the ongoing confusion regarding the conceptualization of maturity, including the absence of a sufficiently detailed legal definition.

The RSTI also has utility in evaluating the effectiveness of juvenile dispositions. Salekin, Tippey *et al.* (2012) used the RSTI to measure incremental improvement in developmental maturity and treatment amenability after a 12-week treatment protocol among adolescents. Among other things, the intervention involved group treatment that focused on goal-setting, decision-making, the utility of positive emotions, and ways to increase positive emotion. Results revealed that the intervention yielded modest improvement in problem awareness, motivation to change, and consideration and tolerance of others, along with improvements in developmental maturity (Salekin, Tippey *et al.*, 2012).

A recent effort is the development and examination of an abbreviated version of the RSTI (RSTI-Abbreviated[A]) (Salekin, 2012). The RSTI-A is identical in content to the RSTI, but the accompanying semi-structured interview is shorter, which reduces the administration time by over 50 percent. In a recent study, investigators (Gillen, MacDougall *et al.*, 2015) examined the convergent validity of the RSTI-A among 63 adolescent offenders who were administered the RSTI-A, the RSTI-Self-Report (RSTI-SR) (Iselin & Salekin, 2008), and various other measures. Results revealed that the Sophistication-maturity scales of both RSTI measures were moderately correlated ($r = 0.31$). They concluded that the results supported the utility of the Sophistication-Maturity scale and its Autonomy and Criminal Sophistication subscales. However, despite favorable results, they concluded that the RSTI-A should be used exclusively for research purposes until more research can be conducted.

EVALUATION TARGETS AND CONSIDERATIONS

There is a variety of contextual factors that should be considered when assessing an adolescent's level of sophistication-maturity. Salekin (2015a) noted, for example, that when conceptualizing an adolescent's developmental maturity, an evaluator should consider the adolescent's developmental status, the adolescent's living environment, the adolescent's behavior during the evaluation, any potential psychopathology, and the context or situation in which the adolescent is required to make decisions. The assessment of some of the abilities and skills previously discussed should be done, to the extent possible, in the context of the adolescent's living situation and social environment. Intelligence provides an example of a construct that should ideally be assessed contextually because it can be viewed from pro-social, asocial, and antisocial perspectives. The contextual assessment of intelligence and maturity provides the court with more meaningful information about an adolescent's sophistication-maturity. In transfer contexts, evaluators should highlight contextual factors that are related to risk and treatment amenability, such as an adolescent's lack of trust in adults or exposure to negative role models, which are relevant considerations when determining whether a juvenile should be transferred to or from criminal court. In disposition evaluations, evaluators should highlight which contextual variables are changeable and which interventions are likely to be effective (Salekin & Grimes, 2008).

This discussion of contextual factors underscores the complex relationship between the adolescent and his or her environment. Developmental maturity may be mediated by a variety of environmental factors (Salekin & Grimes, 2008). If adolescents are in an environment in which they are supported and nurtured across domains—family, school, social, and health, for example—they are more likely to develop into pro-social members of society. In this context, an adolescent may use his or her heightened maturity in pro-social rather than antisocial ways. Maturity is also likely partially mediated by demographic characteristics. There is limited (but growing) research regarding how maturity differs between the sexes and across races/ethnicities, so the field currently lacks a thorough understanding of how these important factors relate to maturity.

It is also important to assess abilities relevant to sophistication-maturity, such as adult-like self-reliance, understanding behavioral norms, balanced decision-making, and moral development, that are not measured by traditional assessment instruments (e.g. intelligence tests, achievement tests). For example, some adolescents may have a substantial amount of practical knowledge that helps them survive outside of academic settings, but they may nevertheless score low on tests of intellectual functioning and academic achievement (Salekin & Grimes, 2008). Assessing these other relevant abilities provides the court with a more complete picture of the adolescent's level of sophistication-maturity.

Given the wide range of potential response styles among adolescent offenders, it is important to assess the adolescent's presentation during the evaluation and gauge the accuracy of self-reported information. During the evaluation, some adolescents may act more mature than they actually are because they believe it will be beneficial to their legal situation. Other adolescents attempt to hide their immaturity by giving overly brief answers to interview questions, which highlights the importance of asking open-ended questions that call for more detailed answers. Conversely, it is possible that an adolescent may act more immature than he or she actually is. Given the possibility that adolescents may provide a distorted presentation of their actual level of maturity, evaluators must be adept at using interview techniques that provide the richest information regarding an adolescent's maturity.

Grisso (2013) notes that courts have associated the elements of culpability, social maturity, and cognitive maturity with the sophistication-maturity standard, and offers some related considerations for assessment:

- *Culpability*—This element focuses on the adolescent's capacity to understand the nature of his or her offending behavior, which requires an assessment of whether the adolescent has at least a minimal understanding that certain behavior, such as assault or other aggressive behavior, can harm others. Almost all adolescents will have this threshold understanding.

- *Social maturity*—This element addresses whether the adolescent has sufficient maturity to understand societal norms, which calls for an assessment of whether the adolescent recognizes that behavior considered wrong from a societal perspective can lead to legal consequences. Courts are likely interested not only in whether the adolescent understands the concept of societal norms, but also whether the adolescent appreciates the concept. Examining the adolescent's daily behavior, and not just the alleged offense, can provide valuable data on whether the adolescent understands and appreciates societal norms.
- *Cognitive maturity*—This element focuses on whether the adolescent is capable of avoiding impulsive behavior. It can be challenging to assess this capacity because greater impulsivity is characteristic of adolescence. Evaluators should not focus on the adolescent's alleged offense, but instead on the adolescent's routine behavior, which will provide data on whether the adolescent can typically delay gratification and identify alternative options before acting.

There are differing views regarding the focus of assessments of an adolescent's sophistication-maturity. While Grisso (2013) asserts that assessments of developmental maturity should focus on the adolescent's maturity at the time of the evaluation, Salekin (2015a) suggests that evaluators should assess an adolescent's developmental maturity both at the time of the evaluation and around the time of the alleged offense, arguing that assessing developmental maturity only at the time of the evaluation provides an incomplete and potentially misleading picture of the adolescent's level of maturity because the adolescent's maturity may have been different around the time of the offense. (This would be particularly relevant to culpability. Its relevance to transfer is less apparent.)

The results of an evaluation of an adolescent's sophistication-maturity are typically conveyed in a written report. Evaluators are cautioned to avoid making conclusive, dichotomous statements regarding an adolescent's sophistication-maturity. Given the complexity of the sophistication-maturity construct, concluding that an adolescent is or is not sufficiently mature is not recommended (Grisso, 2013). Rather, qualitative descriptions of the adolescents' relative level of maturity more accurately convey the many findings in these types of evaluations (Salekin, 2015a). Grisso (2013) notes that the question of an adolescent's maturity may have multiple answers because of the various domains included in the concept of sophistication-maturity. Because maturity is a relative concept, there must be a comparison (similar-aged peers versus adults) to address the question of maturity relative to whom.

CHALLENGES IN ASSESSING SOPHISTICATION-MATURITY

Researchers and scholars have highlighted several challenges in assessing an adolescent's sophistication-maturity. For example, higher levels of maturity can be associated with correlates that weigh both in favor and against processing an adolescent in juvenile court (Salekin & Grimes, 2008). Adolescents with higher levels of maturity (e.g. cognitive skills, emotion regulation) may have better treatment results, consistent with the appropriateness of handling the case in juvenile court. Among other benefits, these adolescents may be able to use their greater maturity to change their antisocial beliefs and behaviors. However, a higher level of maturity is not exclusively associated with pro-social outcomes; it could be associated with more sophisticated criminal behavior that is less likely to desist—which may be more consistent with the case being processed in criminal court. The different implications of greater maturity highlight the importance of considering sophistication-maturity findings in the context of other constructs that inform the court's decision. For example, an adolescent's treatment amenability may be relevant to whether an adolescent with greater maturity is likely to use that maturity in a pro-social way. Adolescents with higher levels of maturity, characterized by better cognitive and decision-making capacities, may be better candidates for being processed in the juvenile justice system because of their likely amenability to treatment and reduced risk of re-offending. Evaluators should therefore consider an adolescent's maturity in the context of other factors whenever possible (Grisso, 2010–11).

Because there are many aspects to maturity, another challenge for evaluators involves determining which of those aspects are most relevant for a particular adolescent in a specific legal context. Certain aspects of maturity may be more relevant for transfer decisions than disposition decisions, and evaluators need to consider relevance in each context. The evaluator's task is further complicated because various aspects of maturity develop at different rates, so adolescents may be more mature in some respects and less so in others.

A final challenge involves determining what degree of maturity is relevant for the purposes of juvenile transfer. This relates to the comparison issue discussed previously. While some of the instruments that measure cognitive and emotional development have both adolescent and adult norms, there is no agreed-upon age reference point for the comparison. Arguments could be made for comparing adolescents to an 18-year-old (minimum age for criminal court jurisdiction is some states), 21-year-old (age of adulthood for many purposes), or a 25- or 30-year old (given recent research regarding the development of brain functions relevant to decision-making and planning) (Grisso, 2010–11). The average maturity level of young adults in the criminal justice system is likely substantially lower than the average maturity level of young adults in the general population, which raises the question of whether adolescents should be compared to samples of adults in the criminal justice system. Many of these questions remain unanswered, which may increase disagreement across evaluations because those conducting them are seeking answers to different questions.

CONCLUSION

In transfer decisions—and to some extent in dispositions—courts combine information about an adolescent's sophistication-maturity with information on dangerousness and treatment amenability. Evaluations of sophistication-maturity can be complex because the construct is multifaceted, and there are several unusual challenges associated with these evaluations. Nevertheless, mental health professionals can choose from certain validated or promising measures when assessing constructs relevant to sophistication-maturity. Using a measure that directly assesses the psycho-legal construct of sophistication-maturity (the RSTI) provides evaluators with legally relevant data that can inform certain aspects of the court's decisions.

CHAPTER EIGHT

Transfer and Reverse Transfer

This chapter addresses the legal questions of transfer and reverse transfer. The discussion includes the origins of the criteria for transfer and a review of the mechanisms for these actions, which develop the context in which a juvenile forensic mental health assessment is needed. It continues with a review of the underlying models for such evaluations. In the domains of authority cited throughout this book—law, science, ethics, and practice—there are a number of specific influences on the evaluation of transfer and reverse transfer. We review these as well. Some of this discussion elaborates upon material presented in earlier chapters (Chapters 2 and 3, this volume).

In the landmark case *Kent v. United States* (1966), the Supreme Court of the United States held that judges must consider specific relevant factors before transferring a youth from the juvenile to the criminal system or from criminal court back to juvenile court. These factors include nature of the offense (seriousness, violence, premeditation, and the like); the juvenile's level of sophistication and maturity; the juvenile's previous arrest and adjudication record; and the juvenile's likelihood of rehabilitation by means of treatments and services available within the juvenile system (Loving & Patapis, 2007).

TRANSFER TO CRIMINAL COURT

All states in the US have mechanisms that allow prosecution of a juvenile offender in criminal court (Davis, 2016; Griffin, Addie *et al.*, 2011; see generally Grigorenko, 2012; Heilbrun, DeMatteo *et al.*, 2016). These mechanisms include judicial waiver, prosecutorial waiver, and statutory exclusion-legislative waiver. In some states, there is more than one of these mechanisms available.

The Model Juvenile Court Act 2016, originally promulgated by the National Conference of Commissioners on Uniform State Laws in 1968, offers several criteria for juvenile transfer that may influence existing transfer mechanisms across the US. The Act holds that a juvenile can be prosecuted in criminal court if he or she is 16 or older at the time of the alleged offense—and if a hearing results in the findings that (1) there are sufficient grounds to believe the juvenile committed the offense; (2) the juvenile is not amenable to treatment; and (3) public safety concerns warrant a placement in a secure setting.

Judicial waiver is allowed in most US jurisdictions. The waiver hearing is held in juvenile court, typically on a motion of the prosecution, when the *Kent* criteria (or their jurisdiction-specific adaptation) are being considered. The decision is made by the court after arguments and the presentation of relevant evidence. Such evidence is typically presented to address the following elements: (1) probable cause that the juvenile committed the alleged offense; (2) the juvenile's threat to the community; (3) whether the youth is amenable to interventions that would address rehabilitation needs within the juvenile system; and (4) fit and amenability to existing adult treatment programs within the criminal justice system (Elrod & Ryder, 2011).

In some states, the criminal and juvenile courts can share jurisdiction (under specific circumstances) over a juvenile case in what is termed "concurrent jurisdiction." In these states (e.g. Florida), prosecutors have discretion regarding whether to charge cases meeting concurrent jurisdiction criteria in juvenile or criminal court (Elrod & Ryder, 2011). Prosecutors' decisions are usually based on the youth's age, history of prior delinquency, and the seriousness of the current offense.

A third transfer mechanism has been called by various terms: statutory exclusion, legislative waiver, and automatic waiver are the most frequent. It involves the automatic filing of charges in criminal court if the youth is younger than 18 but older than a threshold age specified by statute, and the alleged offense is of a kind also specified in this statute (see Davis, 2016). Some jurisdictions also specify in statute that once a youth is transferred to adult court, he or she will always be handled as an adult in future cases (King, 2016).

REVERSE TRANSFER TO JUVENILE COURT

Reverse transfer is the procedure that allows a youth who has been transferred from juvenile to criminal court via one of the mechanisms described in the previous section to appeal this decision and possibly have it reversed. Rather than having the case adjudicated in criminal court, the reverse transfer process addresses the possibility of returning the youth to juvenile court jurisdiction. Reverse transfer decisions are typically made during a criminal court hearing.

The criteria considered in the reverse transfer decision may be largely comparable to those employed in the transfer decision. Grisso (2013) observed that "[t]here is no broad consensus concerning the criteria and procedures for these reverse waiver evaluations. In general, though, it appears that clinicians are applying the same concepts and methods to reverse waiver hearings … [that they are] for waiver evaluations in juvenile court" (p. 250).

There is variability in the empirical evidence regarding the criteria employed (even if only implicitly) in making reverse transfer decisions. Investigators have cited

- gender, age, delinquency history, and offense severity (Singer, 1996);
- ethnicity, age, firearm involvement (in present offense), and delinquency history (Snyder, Sickmund *et al.*, 2000);
- delinquency history, role in index offense (i.e. primary or secondary), attorney type (public or private), and firearm involvement (Jordan & Myers, 2007); and
- age, severity of offense, delinquency history, and forensic mental health information (amenability and treatment recommendations).

(Riggs Romaine, 2010)

A recent review of reverse transfer statutes in the US (King, 2016) noted that 22 states have reverse transfer statutes. All 22 statutes include consideration of risk, 17 include amenability to treatment, and 13 include sophistication-maturity. The Wisconsin statute was identified as the only statute that does not explicitly reference or implicitly allow consideration of the three *Kent* criteria, and 15 statutes cited virtually identical factors for transfer and reverse transfer.

FEDERAL TRANSFER AND ADJUDICATION

The process of transferring justice-involved youth between the juvenile and criminal systems in the federal context in the US is guided by the Juvenile Justice and Delinquency Prevention Act, codified in Chapter 403 (Juvenile Delinquency) of Title 18 of the United States Code. The Act applies to juveniles who have been charged with committing a federal offense prior to the age of 18. For the purposes of proceedings and disposition, however, this federal law retains jurisdiction over offenders until they are 21 years old. Any individual who is indicted after the age of 21 (regardless of age at the time of the alleged offense) must be prosecuted as an adult in the federal system. This Act includes a provision for a prosecution motion to charge an individual as an adult if the youth is 15 or older and is alleged to have committed a qualifying offense.

RESEARCH ON TRANSFER AND REVERSE TRANSFER

Over the past 20 years, several researchers have examined the outcomes of youth who are transferred into the criminal system versus those who are retained in the juvenile system. Although there are some mixed findings, the weight of the empirical evidence strongly suggests that prosecuting youth in the criminal system is associated with a variety of negative outcomes. Some of the observed differences between transferred and retained youth relate to recidivism rates, time to recidivate, and longer-term outcomes.

An early study found that transferred youth were more likely to commit another violent offense compared to youth who were retained in the juvenile justice system, and youth who received prison sentences were twice as likely to commit a violent offense than youth who received other dispositions (Fagan, 1995). Another early study found mixed results regarding the transfer of youth and recidivism rates. Winner, Lanza-Kaduce *et al.* (1997)

found a recidivism rate of 42 percent for transferred youth compared to a recidivism rate of 43 percent for retained youth, although it took the retained youth a longer period of time to recidivate. After controlling for type of offense, Winner, Lanza-Kaduce *et al.* (1997) found that transferred youth had higher rates of recidivism than retained youth. In a later study by some of the same investigators, the recidivism rate for transferred youth was 49 percent versus a recidivism rate of 45 percent for retained youth (Lanza-Kaduce, Frazier *et al.*, 2002). However, when they limited their analyses to the best-matched cases (i.e. retained and transferred youth matched on age, gender, offense, and number of offenses), transferred youth recidivated 49 percent of the time while retained youth recidivated 37 percent of the time (Lanza-Kaduce, Frazier *et al.*, 2002). Finally, when the transferred youth and retained youth were matched on type of offense, the recidivism rate for transferred youth was 50 percent compared to a recidivism rate of 37 percent for retained youth (Lanza-Kaduce, Frazier *et al.*, 2002).

A more recent study found jurisdictional differences in judicial guideline departures in transfer cases in Pennsylvania and Maryland (Johnson & Kurlychek, 2012). Depending on the state, judges are provided with presumptive guidelines (legally mandated guidelines that judges are expected to follow) or voluntary guidelines (suggestions regarding sentencing for judges). Johnson and Kurlychek (2012) found that judges in Maryland (which has voluntary guidelines) departed from the guidelines more often than judges in Pennsylvania (which has presumptive guidelines). Status as a transferred youth was not related to receiving downward departures in Pennsylvania, although it was in Maryland. However, judges in both states were more likely to give transferred youth upward departures. For example, youth in Pennsylvania received departures that were 15 percent greater than the sentencing guidelines, while youth in Maryland received departures 20 percent greater than the recommended sentencing guidelines compared to adults close in age in the criminal system (Johnson & Kurlychek, 2012).

Other studies have focused on the longer-term effects of being transferred to criminal court. For example, Taylor (2015) found that juveniles prosecuted in criminal court have significantly lower incomes than juveniles adjudicated in juvenile court. Further, Hahn, Fuqua-Whitley *et al.* (2007) found that transferred youth have higher rates of interpersonal violence than retained youth following release.

RELEVANT MODELS OF FORENSIC MENTAL HEALTH ASSESSMENT

FMHA encompasses a variety of legal questions in criminal, civil, administrative, and juvenile law (Heilbrun, Grisso *et al.*, 2012). Three areas, generally, are the focus of evaluations conducted by forensic mental health experts:

1. *Past functioning*—investigating the mental state, motivations, behaviors, thoughts, and attitudes at an earlier time (e.g. mental state at the time of the offense; federal sentencing under 5K2 provisions; some mitigators in capital sentencing evaluations).
2. *Present functioning*—appraising an individual's current functioning and abilities in relation to a specific legal question (e.g. competence to stand trial; treatment needs as part of disposition recommendations in various juvenile and criminal evaluations).
3. *Future functioning*—evaluating the likelihood of some specific and legally relevant future outcome (e.g. risk assessment, favorable response to interventions).

(Heilbrun, Grisso *et al.*, 2012)

FMHA can be distinguished from clinical assessment, conducted for diagnostic and treatment-planning purposes, in several respects. Unlike the primary clinical goal of appraising for the purpose of intervention-planning, the primary FMHA goal is to inform the legal decision-maker about an evaluee's legally relevant capacities, abilities, and characteristics. The relationship between the evaluator and the evaluee differs accordingly, in that the evaluator's primary client is typically a legal actor (e.g. judge, attorney) rather than the individual who is evaluated, and the evaluator's allegiance is to the legal process (Heilbrun, Grisso *et al.*, 2012). Earlier in this book, we suggested that these forensic-clinical distinctions may be less pronounced in the context of juvenile transfer and disposition evaluations, as the primary goals of the assessment typically include the identification of treatment needs and recommendations regarding appropriate treatment targets (closer to the goals in clinical assessment). However, it is also important to note the differences between clinical and forensic assessment in the juvenile context, and to focus on legally relevant information and recommendations (see Chapter 6, this volume, for a discussion of making juvenile treatment recommendations). This applies to recommendations for juvenile rehabilitation, which use a different outcome in a justice context (primarily the reduction of reoffending risk) than a clinical context (focusing almost entirely on improvements in overall functioning and on symptomatic improvement). But it also applies to the appraisal of re-offense risk and sophistication-maturity, which are integral to transfer and reverse transfer evaluations but largely unconsidered in clinical contexts.

THEORETICAL MODELS OF FMHA

Psycho-legal scholars generally agree that FMHA should be guided by relevant legal statutes and case law, should incorporate standardized testing and validated measures whenever possible, and should gather data from multiple sources (e.g. interview, records, collateral informants, psychological tests, and specialized measures; Goldstein, 2003, 2007; Heilbrun, 2001; Heilbrun, Grisso *et al.*, 2012; Melton, Petrila *et al.*, 2007; Otto *et al.*, 2007). Selecting and applying a relevant model promotes each of these goals.

FMHA can generally be approached in two distinct ways. One approach identifies specific types of FMHA based on the relevant legal question(s), case law and statutory guidelines, practice literature, and ethical guidelines. An alternative approach posits that all types of FMHA share a common foundation, and can thus be described via overarching shared elements and guidelines (see, for example, Grisso, 2003; Heilbrun, Grisso *et al.*, 2012). A broadly applicable model is most valuable to the second approach. Other FMHA discussion taking this broad approach includes the identification of commonalities and guidelines that apply to each type of assessment (see, for example, Brodsky, 1991, 1999, 2004; Melton, Petrila *et al.*, 2007; Simon & Gold, 2004). Heilbrun (2001) described the foundational principles of FMHA, which have subsequently been applied to specific types of FMHA (e.g. neuropsychological assessment, capital sentencing) (Heilbrun, DeMatteo *et al.*, 2005; Heilbrun, Marczyk *et al.*, 2003). These guidelines have recently been adapted for use in juvenile forensic contexts (see Chapter 3, this volume; Heilbrun & Locklair, 2016).

There are three models discussed in this section. They have varying applicability to juvenile transfer evaluations, but is important to the discussion of how a model might be applied.

Morse

The simplest model of FMHA was proposed by Morse (1978) in the context of civil commitment. Based on his observation of questions frequently asked of evaluating experts in the course of civil commitment hearings, he proposed three major domains of interest: (1) the existence of a mental disorder; (2) the functional-legal capacities related to the legal question; and (3) the causal connection between the mental disorder (if present) and any deficits in functional-legal capacities. This model has the advantage of ease in application and communication: the evaluator focuses on clinical symptoms, functional-legal capacities, and the relationship between them. It does not incorporate situational influences and focuses on "main effects" rather than moderated relationships. (For example, the model would not account for situational variables such as the number of available beds for civilly committed individuals or the alternatives to involuntary commitment such as outpatient commitment.) Nevertheless, this model effectively describes key considerations and their relationship in the context of civil commitment.

It would not be straightforward to apply this model to juvenile evaluations of transfer or reverse transfer, however. The question of mental disorder in juvenile evaluations is not nearly as prominent as it is for adults who are being considered, usually on the basis of mental illness, for involuntary commitment. The absence of context as an explicit part of the model makes it more difficult to consider contingent responses to important questions (e.g. "this individual is currently appraised at high risk for re-offending, but appears amenable to relevant and available interventions—if he responds favorably, his re-offense risk will be lowered").

Accordingly, this model would be applied to the evaluation of transfer and reverse transfer in the following way. The functional-legal capacities would be identified as risk, treatment needs and amenability, and sophistication-maturity. The first section ("mental disorder") would need reconceptualization, as behavioral health symptoms are not the primary focus of transfer evaluation and may not be strongly related to capacities such as risk and sophistication-maturity. In addition, they may not be strongly related to "treatment needs and amenability" if the primary target outcome is reduced risk of re-offending. It is possible that this first section might be termed "Relevant Behavioral, Clinical, and Developmental Functioning" and comprise relevant historical and current influences in these areas. While it does not fit particularly well with the prominent aspects of transfer evaluations, this modification of the model would still guide the evaluator to consider a causal relationship between the youth's characteristics and the functional capacities of risk, treatment need and amenability, and sophistication-maturity.

The relatively poor fit of this model should not be surprising, since apparently it was not intended to be applied to FMHA generally. But its simplicity promotes relevant and easily understood communication. These are important considerations in applying a model that does fit better with juvenile transfer evaluations.

Grisso

A more comprehensive model for FMHA was offered by Grisso (1986). He observed that forensic evaluations were often limited by (1) insufficient legal knowledge on the part of the FMHA practitioner; (2) intrusion into the domain of legal decision-makers (e.g. by answering the ultimate legal question rather than limiting the evaluation to relevant psycho-legal constructs); and (3) overreliance on insufficient data or speculation rather than data-driven findings. To address these potential problems, he suggested greater familiarity with relevant law, more focus on functional-legal capacities, and the prioritization of empirical data. His original model was developed in part to facilitate these recommendations. This model had six components: (1) functional abilities (capacities and knowledge related to the legal question); (2) contextual (situational considerations defining the relevance of functional abilities); (3) causal inferences (describing the relationship between the functional abilities and the legal question); (4) interactive characteristic (whether the functional abilities meet the demands of the existing situation); (5) judgment (whether the person-situation incongruency is sufficient to warrant a legal finding and disposition; and (6) disposition (consequences of the legal finding) (Grisso, 1986). The revised model (Grisso, 2003a) reduced the number of components to five, eliminating "contextual" as a specific component although retaining "interactive" (so the evaluator should still consider context to describe whether the functional abilities are appropriate in that context).

The Grisso model is more complex, and better represents the potential contributions of behavioral science to legal decision-making. It shares two important features with the model described by Morse (1978): functional-legal capacities and causal inferences. The most important differences between the two models concern the appraisal of situational considerations ("context") and whether the functional-legal capacities are sufficient *within that context*. This is an analytic approach that is familiar to behavioral scientists, who are accustomed to asking questions about "main effects" (e.g. "How high is his risk?" or "Is there a rehabilitative placement available?"), but also about "interactions" (e.g. "Considering her risk status and intervention needs, is there a rehabilitative placement available that could address those needs?"). An important question in applying a model, however, is whether judges and attorneys are receptive to an analytic approach that goes beyond such main effects to consider the interactions. When they are, there is little question that Grisso's model is more comprehensive and provides better guidance for evaluators. When they are not, the attempt to introduce interactions into the analysis can be confusing and unwelcome.

In the context of transfer and reverse transfer evaluations, Grisso's (2003a) model would be applied as follows. The functional abilities would be defined as risk, treatment needs and amenability, and sophistication-maturity. (It is possible, as discussed in the next model, that sophistication-maturity could be held out as a separate consideration and not regarded as a core functional capacity.) Causal inferences might involve questions regarding the juvenile and criminal systems regarding the ultimate legal question (transfer or reverse transfer) and each of the functional-legal criteria. To what extent is the juvenile system likely to achieve the goal of preventing reoffending, given the appraised risk? To what extent is the criminal system likely to achieve that goal? To what extent is the juvenile system able to provide rehabilitative interventions to which the youth will be amenable? Interactive characteristics address whether the juvenile system would be able to reach the desired goal considering both the youth's appraised risk and the assessed treatment needs and amenability. This has a situational component, because the juvenile and criminal systems differ considerably in the availability of rehabilitative interventions, the peers with whom the individual would be placed, and the subsequent life consequences for a juvenile adjudication versus a criminal conviction, among other things. Applying Grisso's (2003a) model in this way has a number of implications, yielding both broad and detailed considerations that can guide the evaluator in transfer and reverse transfer cases.

Proposed Model

Although both the Morse and Grisso models have merits, neither was designed specifically for juvenile evaluations. Earlier in this book (Chapter 3, this volume), we proposed a model that adapts Grisso's (2003a) model to the juvenile context (see Figure 3.1). The proposed juvenile model is most specific to transfer and reverse transfer evaluations, as it focuses on risk, treatment needs and amenability, and seeks to integrate the information in these domains to yield a conclusion about rehabilitation potential.

Including both risk and risk-relevant needs in this model provides a parallel to the Risk-Need-Responsivity (RNR) model, which is a well-supported theoretical model of correctional rehabilitation planning and provision for adults and juveniles (Hoge & Andrews, 2010a). Amenability to treatment is also included, with the model linking risk, needs, and treatment amenability in this way: both re-offense risk and risk-relevant needs are important in deciding what program, with what services, at what level of security, in what location, and whether in the juvenile or criminal system.

It is not clear how sophistication-maturity should fit into this model. There are three possibilities, with two represented in Figure 3.1. First, sophistication-maturity findings could be used to inform the evaluator's conclusions about treatment amenability. Second, they could independently be applied toward the conclusion about rehabilitation potential without being considered as part of the treatment amenability findings. Third, findings regarding sophistication-maturity could be applied separately by the court, but not be considered within the model.

Since this proposed model is an adaptation of the broader model described by Grisso (2003a), the identification of functional, causal, and interactive components would be as described in the previous section discussing the Grisso model. The model does apply quite well to transfer and reverse transfer evaluations (not surprisingly, since that it what it was specifically adapted to do). Perhaps the most important unanswered question that remains is how sophistication-maturity would be considered: as part of treatment amenability, as part of rehabilitation potential more broadly, or separately at the time of disposition. To answer this question meaningfully, we need more empirical investigation of the sophistication-maturity construct in its relationship to treatment amenability, to rehabilitation potential (with and without being considered as part of treatment amenability), and to the quality of decision-making if it is considered separately from risk, needs, and amenability.

LAW, SCIENCE, ETHICS, AND PRACTICE AUTHORITY RELEVANT TO TRANSFER AND REVERSE TRANSFER

Much of the material in this section has been addressed broadly in earlier chapters in this book. In this section, we discuss its particular application to the evaluations of transfer and reverse transfer.

LAW

The broader legal considerations in juvenile disposition and transfer evaluations are outlined in Chapter 2 (this volume). There are several additional points that should be made in this context regarding the specific evaluation of transfer and reverse transfer. In *Kent v. United States* (1966), the Supreme Court delineated the importance of specific considerations in transfer and reverse transfer decisions: the youth's previous justice involvement, the nature and seriousness of the alleged offense, the likelihood of rehabilitation by means of treatments and services available within the juvenile system, and the youth's sophistication-maturity. These factors have consistently been incorporated into applicable transfer statutes, so they will almost always be important aspects of the transfer or reverse transfer evaluation. Given the evidence that states have largely developed statutory criteria for each of these evaluations that are very similar or identical (King, 2016), it is appropriate for evaluators to use similar criteria for each kind of evaluation.

One important consideration is how these criteria are translated into function-legal factors. *Kent* specifies both prior record and nature/seriousness of the offense. Both contribute to the larger appraisal of re-offending risk, and states have often been explicit in specifying that "public safety" (a clear proxy for re-offending risk) be a consideration. When *Kent* was decided in 1966, however, the fields of psychology and psychiatry did not have a reliable way to appraise this risk. Given the empirical and theoretical advances in risk assessment in the last 25 years, culminating in specialized measures such as the SAVRY and the YLS/CMI, it is a useful integration of law and science to include re-offense risk as a functional-legal criterion in the evaluation of transfer and reverse transfer.

Kent provides the basis for identifying treatment need and amenability as an important functional-legal criterion in transfer and reverse transfer evaluations. It also adds an important contextual consideration: the availability of rehabilitative services within the juvenile system that is likely to result in successful intervention with the youth. Whether that means within the juvenile system in the youth's jurisdiction, or within the juvenile system more broadly (to include out-of-jurisdiction placements) is a question that will more likely be answered through local (within-jurisdiction) policy and practice than by state statute. It is unlikely that a jurisdiction would routinely use out-of-state juvenile placements, given the cost and inefficiency of doing so. The question is whether extra-jurisdictional placement would be an alternative in very unusual cases—something about which an evaluator should seek information prior to forming an opinion about the prospect of rehabilitation through "available" placements.

The question of how appraised sophistication-maturity is considered in relation to the legal decision on transfer or reverse transfer remains unclear. While the field could clearly use more empirical evidence on whether sophistication-maturity affects treatment amenability, or affects risk and rehabilitation prospects more broadly, forensic evaluations of juveniles on transfer and reverse transfer must include sophistication-maturity among the domains that are appraised unless there is significant revision to existing case law and statutes.

SCIENCE

Much of the basis for the substantial improvement in policy and practice related to juvenile evaluations has been the greater empirical attention to domains such as risk and adolescent development. Important empirical evidence has also been obtained on interventions for justice-involved youth (see Heilbrun, DeMatteo *et al.*, 2016), although much remains to be done in this area. Sophistication-maturity (and its potential link to adolescent developmental evidence) appears to be the area most in need of programmatic research at present, particularly as applied in FMHA.

We advocate that the evaluations of transfer and reverse transfer be carefully informed by current empirical evidence. There are several prominent considerations linking scientific evidence with such evaluations. First, validated risk-need measures for adolescents are available and should be employed (DeMatteo, Wolbransky *et al.*, 2016). Tools such as the SAVRY (Borum, Bartel *et al.* 2006) and YLS/CMI 2.0 (Hoge & Andrews, 2010b) are consistent with applicable RNR theory, supported by empirical evidence, and constructive in their linkage of risk factors to intervention needs with the goal of re-offense risk reduction. Second, there is strong evidence that interventions that are family-based and include multiple systems are effective with justice-involved youth (Henggeler, 2016). Third, there is growing evidence that trauma and adverse experience have either direct or moderating influence on risk and likely response to interventions, particularly with females (Zelechoski, 2016), so evaluators should follow this literature carefully and adjust their evaluation procedures accordingly. It may be, for example, that this influence is sufficiently meaningful to justify a specialized risk-need measure for females, or for individuals who have experienced significant trauma. At a minimum, however, evaluators should obtain information on the evaluated youth's history of trauma and adverse experience, and consider that in drawing conclusions about risk, and treatment needs and amenability. Fourth, there is a continuing strong need for longitudinal research that seeks to identify youth at high risk for offending into early and mid-adulthood. Those who have not responded favorably to any of a range of interventions offered in the juvenile system, including both community-based and residential, and exhibit fairly stable risk factors for offending into adulthood, constitute the group that seems most appropriate for the criminal system within the meaning of *Kent*. But reliably identifying these individuals requires that the field develop a range of empirically supported interventions and identify stable risk factors in adolescence that portend high risk in adulthood. Both are active areas of scientific investigation (Cruise, Morin *et al.*, 2016; Henggeler, 2016;

Vincent, Kimonis *et al.*, 2016), so evaluators should follow the results of this developing literature carefully.

ETHICS

We would cite both broadly applicable ethical standards (e.g. *Ethical Principles of Psychologists and Code of Conduct* (EPPCC), American Psychological Association, 2010) and more specific forensic specialty guidelines (e.g. *Specialty Guidelines for Forensic Psychology* (SGFP), American Psychological Association, 2013) as authority for considering the ethical questions that arise in conducting juvenile evaluations. As they pertain specifically to transfer and reverse transfer evaluations, we see several ethical questions that psychologists should consider as part of conducting them. These questions are particularly salient because transfer evaluations involve potential movement between the juvenile and criminal systems, necessitating knowledge about both.

Beneficence and Non-maleficence

This ethical principle of psychology applies to the avoidance of unnecessary harm—not the avoidance of all harm—to the individual being evaluated. Even when the court or referring attorney are seen as the primary "clients" in transfer evaluations, it is still important to avoid the gratuitous harm to the evaluee that could result from a poorly informed decision to transfer a youth to the criminal system (or decline to transfer that youth back to the juvenile system). Conceptualizing transfer evaluations as part of decisions that will sometimes have particularly adverse consequences for youth is necessary and appropriate—so long as the evaluator is committed to providing thorough, impartial, and well-informed assessments for the court to consider.

Justice

Another ethical principle of psychology (used to connote "fairness" broadly, not only legal justice) prompts the consideration of whether an evaluator's potential biases and limitations of competence and expertise might contribute to a process that is unfair. It is important to point out that an evaluator who considers the transfer of *any* youth into the criminal system to be unfair would not meet the necessary criterion of impartiality; it is important for evaluators to accept the legal system's premise that some youth are appropriate for transfer. Predisposition in the other direction—the inclination, for instance, to use seriousness of charge as a substantial influence on other domains of the evaluation—would likewise be problematic. The clear trend in juvenile law in the last decade has been toward individualized decision-making, so evaluators should provide the court with an assessment that includes information that is clear and thorough.

We observe that seriousness of the charge sometimes appears to be used as a proxy for re-offense risk and for overall decision-making, particularly in evaluations of transfer and reverse transfer. This is seen most clearly when youth are charged with homicide. Offense severity is actually a poor proxy for future offense risk, with the various domains comprising specialized tools such as the SAVRY and YLS/CMI providing a much more accurate estimate of the likelihood of future offending. So when the focus of the evaluation is risk of future offending, treatment needs and amenability, and sophistication-maturity—as it is in transfer and reverse transfer evaluations—evaluators should be careful to ensure that these issues are evaluated without the "reverse halo effect" (a cognitive error in which the presence of one undesirable factor, such as a murder charge, is used to infer the presence of other undesirable factors which are actually unrelated) that can create this kind of subtle evaluative bias.

Respect for People's Rights and Dignity

This third ethical principle from the EPPCC (APA, 2010) raises an important point about the competence of evaluators who conduct transfer and reverse transfer evaluations. But this is not professional competence, which is discussed in the next section, but cultural competence. Frequently the personal backgrounds of evaluating psychologists and psychiatrists differ in sex, gender identity, race, ethnicity, culture, national origin, religion, sexual orientation, disability, language, and socioeconomic status from those of the youths they are evaluating. This can create various challenges for gathering relevant information accurately. It may be difficult for the youth to understand the evaluator's role, or believe that the evaluator will be fair. When language barriers exist, it may be difficult, even with the assistance of a qualified translator, to understand the youth adequately. Lack of cultural competence may cause subculturally normative behaviors to be interpreted as a reflection of personal psychopathology. It also may result in culturally inappropriate phrasing that does not yield accurate responding due to communication breakdown.

These are examples of problems that may result from insufficient cultural competence on the part of the evaluator in transfer and reverse transfer cases. There are many others. This underscores the importance of cultural competence in transfer evaluations, meaning that the evaluator (through some combination of training, experience, supervision, and consultation) must acquire knowledge and skill that are not available from the evaluator's personal experience. Simply put, it is very important to meaningfully understand the cultural influences on individuals who are evaluated—and the absence of such a meaningful understanding should cause the evaluator to decline to conduct the evaluation unless there is no better alternative.

Competence

The professional competence to provide a service is a fundamental ethical and practice tenet. In transfer and reverse evaluations, with the associated necessity for familiarity with both the juvenile and criminal systems, there are four areas in which evaluators should have acquired competence through training and experience: forensic, clinical (adult and adolescent), developmental, and correctional (both juvenile and criminal). First, evaluators should have experience conducting behavioral health evaluations at the request of courts and attorneys. This implies good familiarity with relevant law, legal procedures, report writing, depositions, testimony, and justice-involved populations. Second, they should have clinical training to identify both behavioral health and criminogenic influences; this training and experience should encompass both adults and adolescents. Familiarity with clinical child and family considerations is important as well in this area. Third, they should be familiar with human development and the relevant evidence describing changes from late childhood through early adulthood. It is valuable if they are particularly aware of how this evidence, often obtained with the general population of children and adolescents, applies to justice-involved youth. Finally, they should be aware of how the juvenile and criminal justice systems operate. This includes considerations such as the nature of placement or incarceration provided in each, the types of interventions offered, the differences between community-based and residential interventions, and the evidence about how justice-involved youth in general respond to being placed in both systems. This kind of professional competence can help to ensure that courts are well informed about the consequences of a transfer or reverse transfer decision.

Education and Training

This psychology ethical standard is cited to ensure that evaluators have acquired much of the professional competence needed for transfer and reverse transfer evaluations through formal education and training. It would be excessive, in our view, to expect that all evaluators have formal training in each of the four domains cited in the previous section. But it does seem reasonable to expect that there be specialized training in some of the areas (e.g. forensic, clinical) and knowledge acquired through experience, supervision, consultation, and continuing education in other areas (e.g. family, developmental, correctional). Without the foundation of specialization in at least two of these areas, evaluators would be at a substantial disadvantage in providing reliable and meaningful evaluations for the courts on the transfer questions.

Assessment

There are a number of standards for assessment in the EPPCC (APA, 2010) and a number of additional, more specialized guidelines in the SGFP (APA, 2013). We regard transfer and reverse transfer evaluations as among the most complex that are performed with juveniles, requiring the linkage of risk and risk-relevant needs; the provision of interpretation that is reconstructive, present-state, and predictive; and knowledge of both juvenile justice and criminal justice. Accordingly, we observe that the standards and guidelines from each of these documents apply consistently to the evaluation of transfer and reverse transfer.

There are some that are particularly salient. The SGFP guides the evaluator to identify and use legally relevant factors, requiring knowledge of the relevant statute that may provide similar (or identical) criteria for both. It further advises the use of relevant and validated assessment procedures. Some of these may be standard clinical assessment measures (e.g. IQ tests, achievement tests, objective measures of personality and psychopathology) that are relevant to risk, treatment needs and amenability, and sophistication-maturity (Archer & Baum, 2016), while others may be the specialized measures discussed throughout this book. Whatever measures are selected should be relevant to the functional legal criteria and generally well-validated, including for use with justice-involved youth.

Individual differences are increasingly relevant in transfer evaluations, given the trend toward individualized decision-making for youths seen in *Roper v. Simmons* (2005), *Graham v. Florida* (2010), *Miller v. Alabama* (2012), and *Montgomery v. Louisiana* (2016). Rather than using age or offense as largely determinative, it has become increasingly important to consider risk, treatment needs and amenability, and sophistication-maturity in detail and make an informed decision accordingly. Evaluations highlighting varying capacities within a single individual play an important role in such individualized decision-making by the court.

Finally, it is important to attend to the specialized forensic guideline on detailed and thorough documentation. The rules of evidence in criminal court, where reverse transfer hearings are likely to be held, are less flexible than those of juvenile court. The criminal court's expectation for detail in the report and possible testimony associated with reverse transfer evaluations may exceed that of the juvenile court. This is another reason for employing evaluators with experience in both criminal and juvenile court: knowledge about documentation and other procedural differences can be useful in providing the service that is most helpful to the legal decision-maker.

PRACTICE

This section focuses on the application of foundational principles of FMHA (Heilbrun, 2001; Heilbrun, Grisso *et al.*, 2009) in the version adapted to juveniles (Heilbrun & Locklair, 2016) as they apply to transfer and reverse transfer evaluations (see Chapter 3, this volume, for a broader discussion of their applicability). Given our earlier comment about the complexity of transfer evaluations, it should come as no surprise that we strongly suggest that evaluators apply all of these foundational principles (in their adapted juvenile form) to such evaluations. The following principles are particularly noteworthy in their application to transfer and reverse transfer, however.

Familiarity with the Legal System

These cases require that evaluators have a high degree of familiarity with both the juvenile justice system and the criminal justice system. It is insufficient to cite familiarity with "the legal system" broadly in these evaluations, because there is a need for great familiarity with the juvenile system to address questions such as whether placements are available that would provide rehabilitation in needed areas, the typical duration of such interventions, and whether they differ from what has been tried previously. Accordingly, this principle might best be understood as familiarity with both juvenile and criminal justice.

Avoiding an Adversarial Tone

The principle guiding the evaluator against becoming adversarial, but toward presenting and defending impartial opinions effectively, may vary somewhat in the context of juvenile versus criminal court. For example, an evaluator might expect a more vigorous cross-examination in a criminal court hearing, and a more active stance from the judge in asking questions and making comments in a juvenile court hearing. In neither context is an adversarial tone advisable for the evaluator—but particular preparation for a vigorous challenge on cross-examination (criminal court) or active questioning from the judge (juvenile court) might be indicated.

Notification of Purpose and Authorization

Evaluators are guided to provide appropriate notification of purpose and obtain appropriate authorization before beginning. This notification is somewhat more complex in cases of transfer or reverse transfer, because the court's transfer decision will determine not only where the individual might be placed if found legally culpable for the offense, but the *system* in which the placement will occur. This has ramifications that go beyond what can be explained in a fairly brief notification (e.g. the impact of a criminal conviction versus that of a juvenile adjudication). However, the youth must at least be notified that subsequent actions in adjudicating the case may occur in the juvenile or the criminal system.

Determining whether Notification is Understood

The expectations for understanding and assisting are higher in the criminal court, given the differences in evidentiary law, the age and greater maturity of adult defendants, and the more serious consequences for conviction. Evaluators in transfer and reverse transfer cases should be careful to address the referral questions. If these questions do not include competence to stand trial, then evaluators should not pursue this. However, a case in which a youth is notified about the purpose and nature of a transfer or reverse transfer evaluation and shows little meaningful understanding of this notification should raise a red flag for the evaluator. If the remainder of the evaluation uncovers extremely low intellectual functioning, extreme developmental immaturity, or symptoms of severe mental illness that appear to be limiting the youth's capacity to understand and assist, this information should certainly be conveyed to the referring attorney or to the court with the accompanying recommendation of a more thorough examination of the issue.

The Ultimate Legal Question

There is an important distinction between disposition evaluations, which inform the court about youths who will remain within the juvenile system if adjudicated delinquent, and transfer or reverse transfer evaluations, in which the court must decide which system will process the case. The judge in the latter case has the discretion to apply community and societal values toward this decision. This may even appear in the statutory language on transfer or reverse transfer.

This aspect of the decision is entirely a matter for the judge, who represents societal values as part of this process. Evaluators should take no position whatsoever on whether it is in "society's interest" to send a justice-involved youth to one system or the other. But if the evaluator draws an ultimate issue conclusion, such as the youth "should" or "should not" be transferred, then this evaluator has very likely conflated clinical-scientific findings (the appropriate focus of the evaluator) with societal values (the sole domain of the court). Hence transfer and reverse transfer evaluations are among the most appropriate evaluations in which to refrain from offering this kind of ultimate legal opinion as part of the evaluation. What is less intrusive but nonetheless very helpful is an appraisal of whether the youth would be a good candidate for rehabilitation in the juvenile system, given the available resources of the juvenile system, time remaining under juvenile jurisdiction, risk, needs, amenability to intervention, and sophistication-maturity.

CONCLUSION

This chapter addresses the evaluation of transfer and reverse transfer. As these are among the most complex evaluations that are provided for justice-involved youth, the broad and foundational considerations for evaluating juveniles that we have described throughout this book are applicable. We review the relevant law to identify the functional-legal criteria applicable to transfer and reverse transfer evaluations; these criteria are very similar or identical in many US jurisdictions. Three models are discussed as they apply to transfer and reverse transfer evaluations: those proposed by Morse, Grisso, and the present authors (a modification of the Grisso model). Finally, we review particularly relevant aspects of law, research, ethics, and practice that apply to these particular evaluations of justice-involved youth.

CHAPTER NINE

Evaluating Disposition and Placement

Once allegations against a juvenile are found to be substantiated by a juvenile court, the judge must determine a disposition. A disposition in juvenile court is similar in many respects to sentencing in the adult system, although there are several important differences that will be discussed in this chapter. There are typically several options available for juvenile court judges when deciding on an appropriate disposition for adolescents adjudicated in juvenile court. This chapter reviews the range of options that may be available, discussing a variety of disposition options ranging from diversionary programs to secure residential treatment facilities. This chapter also describes how disposition evaluations can most effectively be conducted and used in legal decision-making, integrating into this discussion a review of research on the effectiveness of dispositions in reducing recidivism.

DISPOSITIONAL OPTIONS

Juvenile courts use a bifurcated process in which the dispositional hearing occurs after the adjudication hearing. The adjudication hearing is subject to procedural rules regarding the admissibility of evidence and other legal matters, but the dispositional hearing is less structured. For example, hearsay testimony, which is typically excluded at the adjudication stage, can be introduced at the dispositional hearing. Permissible evidence at the disposition stage is broader in scope because the goal is for the judge to render a decision that incorporates all relevant data regarding a juvenile offender's current situation (del Carmen & Trulson, 2006). As such, juvenile court judges can use a variety of sources of information when making disposition determinations. A commonly used source of information at the disposition stage is the pre-disposition report, which is typically completed by a juvenile probation officer and includes information related to the facts of the case, the juvenile's functioning in relevant psycho-social domains (e.g. family life, school, employment), and any behavioral health needs the juvenile may have (del Carmen & Trulson, 2006). The judge considers all of this information in an effort to make an individualized decision regarding which disposition is most appropriate in a particular case.

There are several options for judges when deciding on an appropriate disposition for adolescents adjudicated in juvenile court—although the available dispositions vary by jurisdiction, with some jurisdictions having a wider range of available options. There are, however, several core dispositions that are available in most jurisdictions. One option that is rarely used is for the juvenile court judge to dismiss the case even if the juvenile has been adjudicated delinquent (del Carmen & Trulson, 2006). However, after a finding of delinquency, the vast majority of cases proceed to dispositional determinations, which can be grouped into three categories: (1) nominal, (2) conditional, and (3) custodial (Champion, Merlo *et al.*, 2013).

NOMINAL DISPOSITIONS

Nominal dispositions are the least punitive options available to a juvenile court judge—besides dismissing the case—and they typically involve judicial warnings and reprimands. In such dispositions, the judge verbally reprimands the juvenile in open court. Youths receiving nominal dispositions are usually released to the care of their parents or guardians (Champion, Merlo *et al.*, 2013), and they have no additional legal obligations to fulfill relating to the offense that brought them into contact with the justice system. This type of disposition is most commonly used with first-time, non-violent offenders (Abbott-Chapman, Denholm *et al.*, 2007), although juvenile court judges have wide discretion and can use nominal dispositions with any justice-involved youth at this stage.

There are two important benefits to nominal dispositions. First, by not requiring the juvenile to penetrate deeper into the juvenile justice system, the burden on the system is reduced, and probation officers and placement facilities can focus their efforts and (often limited) resources on higher-risk juveniles. Second, nominal dispositions prevent exposing low-risk juvenile offenders to higher-risk juvenile offenders. This is an important consideration because the empirical evidence is fairly convincing: mixing low-risk and higher-risk juvenile offenders can have pronounced negative effects on the low-risk offenders (Dishion & Andrews, 1995; Dishion,

McCord *et al.*, 1999; National Institute on Drug Abuse, 2003; Petrosino, Turpin-Petrosino *et al.*, 2000; Rhule, 2005). This influence is often referred to as "deviancy training" (see Dishion & Andrews, 1995).

CONDITIONAL DISPOSITIONS

Conditional dispositions for juveniles who have been adjudicated delinquent most commonly involve probation, imposing specific requirements with which the juvenile offenders must comply as part of the disposition (Champion, Merlo *et al.*, 2013; Sickmund & Puzzanchera, 2014). The conditions of this type of disposition are intended to address the specific criminogenic needs and sometimes clinical needs of juvenile offenders. For example, youths with substance use problems may be ordered to participate in substance abuse treatment, while those with anger problems may be required to participate in anger management training. Common conditions of probation supervision include regular school attendance, scheduled reporting to the probation officer, compliance with a strict curfew, refraining from substance use, and avoiding new contact with law enforcement. Conditions may also include more restrictive sanctions such as electronic monitoring or house arrest (Champion, Merlo *et al.*, 2013; del Carmen & Trulson, 2006), and restitution to the victim and community service (Furdella & Puzzanchera, 2015). Failure to comply with imposed conditions can lead to a harsher sanction by the court, which may include placement in a secure facility.

Probation is by far the most common disposition for adolescents who are adjudicated delinquent, with the most recent available data indicating that the proportion of cases in which probation is imposed has been increasing in recent years. Probation was ordered in 57 percent of cases in 1985, 61 percent of cases in 2010, and 64 percent of cases in 2013 (Furdella & Puzzanchera, 2015; Sickmund & Puzzanchera, 2014). In addition to the traditional form of probation in which the juvenile meets with a probation officer at regularly scheduled intervals, there are other forms of probation that may be used. For example, intensive supervised probation (ISP) is used more often with juveniles who are high risk. ISP involves more frequent contact with the probation officer; unannounced probation visits to the juvenile's home, school, or place of employment; increased contacts between probation staff and collateral sources (e.g. family, teachers, community members, friends); and strict curfew enforcement (del Carmen & Trulson, 2006). "Shock probation" is a term used to describe a type of disposition in which a juvenile is initially placed in a secure residential facility, but then is re-sentenced to probation after a short stay in the facility (del Carmen & Trulson, 2006). This type of disposition was designed to briefly expose ("shock") juvenile offenders to the realities of incarceration prior to imposing probation, as it was believed that giving juveniles a brief experience with incarceration will deter them from future offending behavior. As will be discussed later in this chapter, this type of intervention has not been shown to be effective in reducing recidivism. School-based probation is also available in some jurisdictions. These programs are similar to other juvenile probation programs, except that the probation supervision takes place in the school using an on-site juvenile probation officer (del Carmen & Trulson, 2006).

Conditional dispositions that are rooted in restorative justice principles are becoming increasingly popular. Such dispositions often require juvenile offenders to meet with the victim of their offenses as a way for the juveniles to accept responsibility for their actions (Champion, Merlo *et al.*, 2013), and for the victim to perhaps gain some measure of "closure" relating to the offense. A related disposition is restitution, which requires the juvenile to make financial reparations to the victim of his or her crime for property damage caused by the offense (del Carmen & Trulson, 2006). Community service has been used for years as a way for the youth to repay the community for the harm caused by his or her behavior.

CUSTODIAL DISPOSITIONS

Custodial dispositions result in the out-of-home placement of a juvenile offender following a judicial adjudication of delinquency. According to the 2014 National Center for Juvenile Justice Report, juvenile offenders adjudicated delinquent for serious offenses (e.g. homicide, robbery, aggravated assault) are the most likely to be placed in residential custody (Sickmund & Puzzanchera, 2014). While the proportion of cases in which probation is ordered has increased over the years, the number of delinquency cases in which residential placement is imposed has decreased over the same period of time. In 1985, 31 percent of adjudicated cases involved placement in a residential facility (Furdella & Puzzanchera, 2015). The percentage of cases in which residential placement was ordered decreased 29 percent between 2001 and 2010 (Sickmund & Puzzanchera, 2014). Data from the Office of Juvenile Justice and Delinquency Prevention (OJJDP) indicate that as of October 2012, there were 57,190 juvenile offenders housed in 1,985 facilities (Hockenberry, Sickmund *et al.*, 2015). The current number of juvenile offenders housed in residential facilities is the lowest since 1975, when there were 52,726 offenders in juvenile facilities (Hockenberry, Sickmund *et al.*, 2015). In 2013, 24 percent of cases in which a juvenile was adjudicated delinquent resulted in residential placement, which indicates that roughly one-quarter of all adjudicated juvenile cases result in residential placement (Furdella & Puzzanchera, 2015).

Custodial placements can be either non-secure or secure, depending on the level of restriction imposed on the juvenile. Non-secure custodial placements allow freedom of movement and include foster care, group homes, ranch/camp placements, and shelter care. First-time, non-violent, or lower-risk juvenile offenders are often considered to be more appropriate for placement in a non-secure setting. By contrast, secure custodial placements are the most restrictive dispositions available within the juvenile justice system, and they involve detention of the juvenile in a locked facility. Given the extreme liberty deprivation involved, placement in a secure facility is typically reserved for higher-risk juveniles or for juveniles who have not responded favorably to other interventions provided in non-secure placement.

There is a good deal of variety among placement facilities in terms of features, settings, and interventions. Most placement facilities include some educational/vocational component, and counseling related to common behavioral health concerns such as anger management, decision-making, and substance abuse. Some placement facilities also offer specialized treatment; for example, interventions may focus on sex offending behavior, drug dealing, or gang renunciation (del Carmen & Trulson, 2006).

The National Criminal Justice Treatment Practices (NCJTP) survey examined the types of services that were available to juveniles in residential facilities ($N = 315$ facilities), jails ($N = 1{,}395$ facilities), and community corrections ($N = 2{,}207$) (Taxman, Young *et al.*, 2007). Residential facilities reported that an average of 30.3 percent of facility staff were considered to be clinical, and the ratio of clinical staff to youth was approximately 2:10. The most frequently available programs across all settings were education/General Educational Development (GED) programs (73 percent of programs surveyed), intensive supervision (47.7 percent), sex offender therapy (44.3 percent), vocational training (37.5 percent), and transitional housing (18.3 percent). The survey also examined the availability and types of substance use treatment; results revealed that the majority of facilities (76.8 percent) provided some type of drug and alcohol education. The most common treatment modality for juvenile offenders with substance use needs was brief (1–4 hours/week) weekly substance abuse counseling provided in a group format, and approximately 40 percent of surveyed programs offered this type of treatment. Another 23.8 percent of surveyed facilities offered the equivalent of intensive outpatient substance use treatment (5–25 hours/week). However, data also indicated that substance use treatment at both levels of intensity was available to only small numbers of youths, serving an average of approximately 5 percent of juveniles in these facilities. Relatively few residential facilities (35.2 percent) and jails (5.8 percent) provided specific case management services designed to link juvenile offenders to substance use treatment in the community. However, more than half of the facilities (54.9 percent) provided drug-involved youths with referrals to community-based substance use treatment at discharge (see Taxman, Debus-Sherrill *et al.*, 2012; Young, Dembo *et al.*, 2007).

There are a few other variations relating to the disposition of juvenile court cases. Juvenile courts can handle juvenile matters formally (petitioned) or informally (non-petitioned). In formal case processing, a petition is filed requesting that the juvenile court hold an adjudicatory hearing or waiver hearing, whereas informal case handling may be used if a decision-maker, typically a police officer, probation officer, or prosecutor, believes that the juvenile can be held accountable and rehabilitated without formal court intervention. Formally processed delinquency cases typically involve more serious offenders, older adolescents, and adolescents with lengthier court histories than informally handled cases. If the case is handled informally, the juvenile agrees to comply with sanctions imposed by the court, which typically include community service, restitution, and/or probation. If the juvenile complies with the mandated conditions, the case is dismissed. If the juvenile fails to satisfy the conditions, then the case is typically petitioned for formal processing. Over the past few decades, there has been variability in the rates of formal processing of juvenile cases, with a slight decrease in recent years. Juvenile courts formally processed 46 percent of delinquency cases in 1985, 56 percent of cases in 2001, 54 percent of cases in 2010, and 55 percent of cases in 2013, which means that nearly half of delinquency cases are not formally petitioned in court (Furdella & Puzzanchera, 2015; Sickmund & Puzzanchera, 2014). Of the estimated 475,000 non-petitioned cases in 2013, 40 percent were dismissed, 23 percent received probation, and 37 percent received some other conditional disposition (Furdella & Puzzanchera, 2015).

Finally, some jurisdictions allow for blended sentencing, which means that adult and juvenile court sanctions are combined. Most commonly, blended sentencing results in a juvenile offender beginning the sentence in a juvenile placement facility before transferring to an adult correctional facility. The adult phase of the sentence can sometimes be waived or shortened if the juvenile completes his or her juvenile placement with satisfactory results (del Carmen & Trulson, 2006).

Juvenile placement facilities differ from adult jails and prisons in several meaningful ways. Consistent with the underlying philosophy of the juvenile justice system, juvenile placements are intended to be less restrictive and more focused on rehabilitation than adult correctional facilities.

As such, juvenile placements typically involve more programming focused on both criminogenic and clinical needs. Further, unlike adults who are incarcerated, juveniles may be released by placements whenever it is determined that the juvenile has been rehabilitated. This provides placements with a good deal of latitude. Finally, juvenile offenders typically must be released when they reach the upper age limit for the juvenile justice system, although in some cases juveniles can be transferred to the adult system once they reach the maximum age (del Carmen & Trulson, 2006). All states legislatively specify an age at which the juvenile "ages out" of the juvenile system, after which the juvenile justice system no longer has jurisdiction over the youth. In most states, the juvenile court has original jurisdiction over juveniles who were younger than 18 at the time of the offense, arrest, or referral to court (Sickmund & Puzzanchera, 2014). There are exceptions, however. In many states, for example, initial jurisdiction rests with the criminal court if the juvenile is married or otherwise emancipated.

JUVENILE DIVERSION PROGRAMS

In addition to the nominal, conditional, and custodial dispositions just discussed, juvenile offenders may be eligible for diversion programs. These programs serve as alternatives to the formal adjudication or placement of juvenile offenders (Chapin & Griffin, 2005), with a primary goal of minimizing the youth's penetration into the juvenile system. As noted earlier, exposing low-risk juvenile offenders to higher-risk juvenile offenders, even in treatment/rehabilitative contexts, can have negative and iatrogenic effects on the low-risk juveniles (see Dishion & Andrews, 1995), so using diversion to limit their exposure to higher-risk peers has clear benefits.

Diversion for juvenile offenders has a long history. In 1967, the President's Commission on Law Enforcement and Administration of Justice described the utilization of formal juvenile justice sanctions and placement as a "last resort" and suggested that youthful offenders be referred to community treatment via diversionary programs (Whitehead & Lab, 2001: 268). In the decades following the Commission's report, juvenile diversion programs for low-risk youth grew in popularity. Many viewed juvenile diversion programs as a response to concerns that the juvenile justice system was not effective in reducing recidivism (Dunford, Osgood *et al.*, 1982). Juvenile diversion programs serve several purposes, including decreasing the burden on juvenile courts and the juvenile justice system, reducing the stigma associated with justice involvement, reducing social control and coercion, decreasing costs, providing needed behavioral health services, and ameliorating the increase in offending behavior that is sometimes seen following residential placement (Chapin & Griffin, 2005; Palmer & Lewis, 1980; Whitehead & Lab, 2001).

Diversion programs can be classified into several categories, depending on the nature and timing of the diversion. True diversion occurs when juvenile offenders are handled informally (Whitehead & Lab, 2001), or in cases in which no formal or informal interventions are imposed. A second category—referral, service, and follow-up—describes cases in which juvenile offenders are referred to community services prior to adjudication (Whitehead & Lab, 2001). Finally, channeling to non-court institutions, such as a community treatment program, is a diversionary model in which youth are placed into an intervention program without being processed by the juvenile court (Whitehead & Lab, 2001).

Another classification scheme categorizes diversion programs as either informal or formal. Informal diversion refers to an arrangement under which juvenile offenders are required to avoid any new justice contact for a specific period of time, which is typically less than six months. If the juvenile completes the time period without new justice involvement, the offense that triggered the diversion is removed from the juvenile's record and the case is dismissed. By contrast, formal diversion refers to programs that require juvenile offenders to comply with specific conditions to achieve program completion (del Carmen & Trulson, 2006). These conditions often include mental health counseling, substance abuse treatment, and restitution. Formal diversion programs take many forms and can be operated by a variety of entities, including juvenile courts, probation departments, police agencies, and private organizations (del Carmen & Trulson, 2006). Examples of formal diversion programs include community service, teen courts, prison visitation programs (e.g. Scared Straight), and counseling-based programs that have an emphasis on areas such as family dysfunction, peer relationships, and restorative justice. In both informal and formal diversionary programs, successful completion of diversion programming typically results in the removal of any official record of the juvenile's offense (del Carmen & Trulson, 2006).

Juvenile diversion programs vary widely in terms of structure and emphasis, and some scholars have offered guidelines for effective diversion programs. For example, Griffin and Torbet (2002) suggest that core diversion elements include firm but flexible guidelines that simultaneously assist decision-makers and allow for discretion; a structure that allows for victim input; a written document outlining the diversion terms agreed to by the juvenile offender, the juvenile's parent or guardian and an intake officer; and mechanisms that address community and victim concerns via accountability, letters of apology, restitution, and engagement in pro-social or community service.

JUVENILE PREVENTION PROGRAMS

Although this chapter primarily addresses disposition and placement, which occur after a juvenile has been adjudicated delinquent, some focus on preventing initial contact with the juvenile justice system is necessary for an overall understanding of contemporary handling of at-risk juveniles. If the goal of diversion programs is to minimize a juvenile's penetration into the juvenile system, the goal of prevention programs is to preclude or limit any formal contact with the juvenile system. Preventing juveniles from coming into contact with the juvenile system serves many of the same purposes as diversion: reducing the burden on the juvenile system, decreasing costs, reducing the stigma associated with justice involvement, and preventing low-risk juveniles from mixing with higher-risk juveniles.

TYPES OF PREVENTION PROGRAMS

According to the public health model, the prevention of juvenile offending can occur at the primary/universal level and secondary/selective level. A third categorization, tertiary, describes interventions that are implemented after a juvenile is already in the justice system and is therefore only considered prevention to the extent that the intervention prevents recidivism (Bartol & Bartol, 2009; Flannery & Williams, 1999); tertiary prevention is better conceptualized as treatment. Primary/universal interventions seek to prevent juvenile offending among at-risk populations, secondary/selective interventions attempt to reduce the prevalence of offending among those who have engaged in some offending behavior, and tertiary interventions attempt to prevent recidivism through the provision of targeted treatment. This classification of prevention interventions provides a mechanism for identifying the types of interventions that can be used at various stages of youth offending (Mulvey, Arthur *et al.*, 1993).

Primary/Universal Prevention

The goal of primary/universal prevention strategies is to identify adolescents who may be at risk for engaging in antisocial behavior and address their criminogenic needs *before* they engage in offending behavior. The effectiveness of primary/universal prevention strategies therefore lies in recognizing existing static and dynamic risk factors, and ameliorating the negative effects of those risk factors and/or promoting the development of protective factors (DeMatteo & Marczyk, 2005; Mulvey, Arthur *et al.*, 1993). Whereas secondary/selective intervention strategies target high-risk *individuals*, primary/universal prevention strategies target high-risk *populations.*

Because primary/universal interventions focus on the prevention of antisocial behavior, these strategies are typically implemented at broad levels, such as the family, school, and community. The effectiveness of these broad-based interventions is based in part on the ability to reach a large number of at-risk adolescents. Family, school, and community levels are among the major intervention points for such primary/universal interventions.

Research suggests that family-based prevention efforts are an effective way of preventing antisocial behavior among adolescents (see Kumpfer & Alvarado, 2003). Family-based interventions can be divided into parent-focused interventions and family-supportive interventions. Whereas parent-focused interventions are designed to assist parents in recognizing warning signs for youth offending behavior, and/or training parents to effectively manage adolescent behavioral problems, family-supportive interventions provide social support services to families—typically from economically disadvantaged backgrounds (e.g. child care, medical assistance, counseling, assistance from other social service agencies). Some examples of family-focused prevention interventions include the Yale Child Welfare Research Program and the Strengthening Families Program (Bartol & Bartol, 2009). These strategies are typically used in collaboration with other intervention strategies, such as school-based interventions or community-based interventions. Combining interventions at multiple levels is consistent with the principles underlying Multisystemic Therapy (Henggeler & Borduin, 1990; Henggeler, Schoenwald *et al.*, 1998), which is discussed along with several other model programs later in this chapter.

School-based interventions can be effective because some risk factors for juvenile offending are school- or academically-related, including poor academic performance, low academic achievement, low commitment to school, school overcrowding, truancy, multiple school transitions, and associating with delinquent peers (Hawkins, Herrenkohl *et al.*, 2000). Some examples of school-based prevention efforts include Project Head Start, First and Best Teacher Project, Early Alliance, social skills training, and broad-based social interventions designed to alter the school environment (Bartol & Bartol, 2009; DeMatteo & Marczyk, 2005; Mulvey, Arthur *et al.*, 1993).

Finally, community-based preventive approaches focus on increasing community organization and making constructive activities available to adolescents, with a focus on at-risk adolescents. For example, recreational organizations such as the Police Athletic League and Boys and Girls Clubs, which include mentoring from adult role models and participation in structured activities, are associated with lower levels of adolescent offending behavior (e.g. Segrave & Chu, 1978). Other community-based primary/universal prevention programs include the Chicago Area Project, Neighborhood Watch, and Positive Youth Development Project (Bartol & Bartol, 2009).

Secondary/Selective Prevention

Secondary/selective prevention strategies attempt to reduce the prevalence of offending among those who have engaged in some offending behavior. These prevention efforts are more narrowly focused than primary/universal approaches because they are targeted at the smaller group of adolescents who have already had some contact with law enforcement. The goal of these approaches is to identify risk factors at the individual, family, and school levels, and provide social and clinical services that will reduce the likelihood that adolescents will engage in more serious antisocial behavior. Given limited resources, the effectiveness of these approaches is based partly on identifying and understanding the risk factors that distinguish between adolescent-limited offenders and life-course persistent offenders (Moffitt, 1993), or between those who will desist from limited juvenile involvement versus those who will escalate, at least during their adolescence.

Common secondary/selective intervention strategies include diversion programs, alternative and vocational education, family therapy, and skills training (see Bartol & Bartol, 2009; DeMatteo & Marczyk, 2005; Mulvey, Arthur *et al.*, 1993). Diversion programs were previously discussed, and these programs typically divert offending adolescents from the juvenile justice system into community- or school-based treatment programs. The use of alternative and vocational education programs, which provide job-related and educational training to adolescents with behavioral problems who have performed poorly in mainstream classroom settings, is another common approach. The family therapy and skills training approaches target the adolescent's family in addition to the adolescent, with the goal of reducing family-related risk factors and promoting healthier family function.

EFFECTIVENESS OF PREVENTION INTERVENTIONS AND JUVENILE COURT DISPOSITIONS

The litmus test when evaluating prevention interventions and juvenile court dispositions is whether juveniles continue to engage in antisocial behavior. As noted in Chapter 6 (this volume), interventions in the juvenile system are focused primarily on reducing recidivism as opposed to ameliorating distressing clinical symptoms, so the outcome of interest when researching the effectiveness of these interventions is the rate of re-offense. Accordingly, we turn to the social science literature relevant to outcomes for prevention programs and various juvenile court dispositions. There is an important distinction between *evidence-based practices*, which are individual intervention strategies that have been shown to be effective in reducing juvenile recidivism, and *evidence-based programs*, which are standardized programs that have been shown to be effective in reducing recidivism. We discuss both in the following sections.

PREVENTION INTERVENTIONS

There is convincing empirical evidence that some prevention efforts can prevent, limit, or reduce juveniles' contact with law enforcement and the juvenile justice system. Research has identified several shared features of successful or promising prevention approaches, including early implementation, the use of interventions that are consistent with developmental principles, implementation in multiple settings and across multiple systems, a focus on family dynamics, and sensitivity to multicultural issues (see Bartol & Bartol, 2009). Further, in a comprehensive review of prevention interventions and juvenile court dispositions, Howell (2009) described the following meta-analytically supported principles of effective juvenile prevention, court intervention, and correctional treatment programs: multimodal treatment, higher dosage of treatment, quality of treatment, and youth risk level (with programs having more risk-reduction impact on higher-risk juveniles).

Several specific intervention programs have been shown to be effective. Early education programs, such as Head Start, have shown positive results regarding antisocial behavior, school dropout, and employment success (see Schweinhart, Barnes *et al.*, 1993). Interventions targeting family- and school-based risk factors can reduce the likelihood that at-risk youth will engage in antisocial behavior during later childhood and adolescence (Tremblay, Pagani-Kurtz *et al.*, 1995). Based on meta-analytic evidence, Howell (2009) described several interventions as having above-average effects for youth who have not been adjudicated delinquent, including interpersonal skills training, parent training or counseling, and tutoring or remedial education. With respect to school-based prevention programs and strategies, research suggests that teaching social competency skills (e.g. self-control, stress management, responsible decision-making, social problem-solving, effective communication), utilizing behavioral classroom management, providing enhanced academic services, targeting younger children, and after-school programs have positive effects in preventing or reducing antisocial behavior (see Howell, 2009). Based on a meta-analysis of 165 studies of school-based prevention efforts, it appears that environmentally focused interventions, such as school-wide discipline management programs, are effective in reducing delinquent behavior (Wilson, Gottfredson *et al.*, 2001).

It is also important to identify prevention efforts that are not effective. In a comprehensive review, Howell (2009) categorized the Drug Abuse Resistance Education (DARE) program, prison visitation programs (e.g. Scared Straight), and zero tolerance policies as ineffective prevention strategies (see Melton, Petrila *et al.*, 2007, for a discussion of several juvenile prevention and rehabilitation programs/strategies). These interventions either failed to significantly reduce offending behavior (e.g. DARE), led to increases in offending behavior among certain subsets of adolescents (e.g. prison visitation programs), or led to disproportionate contact with the juvenile justice system (e.g. zero tolerance policies). (For a detailed discussion of the effects of zero tolerance policies, see Daly, Hildebrand *et al.*, 2016).

JUVENILE COURT DISPOSITIONS

Over the past 25 years, the response of the justice system to juvenile offending has become more punitive, as reflected in changes to jurisdictional authority (e.g. presumptive transfer), sentencing authority (e.g. mandatory sentencing, blended sentences), confidentiality (e.g. increased openness of juvenile court records and proceedings), and victims' rights. However, consistent with the rehabilitative focus of the juvenile system, there have also been promising developments in evidence-based interventions for high-risk and violent juvenile offenders placed in the community or residential institutions (see Bartol & Bartol, 2009; Elrod & Ryder, 2011; Skeem, Scott *et al.*, 2014). Zavlek (2005) provides an informative summary of the different intervention options that are available at different stages of the juvenile justice process—defined as pre-arrest (primary prevention), arrest (arrest/referral and intake/detention), adjudication (case filing/pre-trial release or detention and trial/adjudication and sentencing/disposition), disposition (sanction and sentence modification), and post-disposition (aftercare).

A number of programs and treatment models have been developed for justice-involved youth over the past few decades. Most of these interventions have not been systematically studied or, if they have been, have not received empirical research support for their effectiveness. But several treatment models have been shown to reduce behavioral problems and criminal recidivism among justice-involved youth. Before discussing them, we provide a broad overview of effective and ineffective treatment strategies.

Effective Interventions

There is a growing body of evidence regarding effective interventions for justice-involved juveniles. In terms of effective interventions at a broad level, Melton, Petrila *et al.* (2007) reviewed meta-analytic studies and concluded that effect sizes were larger (indicating higher levels of effectiveness) for interventions that are multimodal, skills-oriented, and community-based. Another summary of meta-analyses and comprehensive reviews concluded that community-based interventions are more effective than other approaches (Sheidow & Henggeler, 2005). These investigators also identified shared elements of effective programs: multimodal treatment; understanding risk factors, protective factors, and childhood and adolescent psychopathology; manualized interventions; and highly specified treatments with training, treatment, and quality/fidelity assurance protocols. Howell, Lipsey *et al.* (2014) found that counseling (e.g. individual, group, and family counseling; mentoring), skill building (e.g. cognitive/thinking skills, social skills, academic skills, vocational skills), multiple services (e.g. case management, service brokerage arrangements), and restorative justice (e.g. community service, restitution, victim-offender mediation) are associated with positive effects. In sum, matching interventions to the criminogenic needs of juvenile offenders is associated with the biggest reduction in offending. Several characteristics of interventions and programs that may lead to reductions in recidivism among justice-involved youth have included delivering services in youths' natural environments, using interventions that are flexible and individualized, emphasizing practical and attainable treatment goals, holding staff accountable for therapeutic outcomes, and utilizing highly trained and well supervised staff (Tate & Redding, 2005).

INTERVENTIONS WITH MIXED EVIDENCE

There is inconsistent evidence about the effects of institutions on recidivism, but reliable data suggest that institutional programs that rely heavily on skills-based, cognitive-behavioral therapeutic interventions are the mostly likely to reduce recidivism (see Howell, Lipsey *et al.*, 2014). There are several potential advantages of institutional treatment programs, including greater control over the juveniles' environment, longer duration of exposure to treatment, more frequent individual or group treatment sessions, and fewer concerns about attendance (Redding, Lexcen *et al.*, 2005). These investigators also cited several noteworthy concerns, however, such as (1) the provision of inadequate special education, which may exacerbate academic, developmental, and social deficits; (2) minimal family involvement; and (3) the potential for iatrogenic effects when mixing low-risk and higher-risk juveniles (Redding, Lexcen *et al.*, 2005). Howell, Lipsey *et al.* (2014) also described concerns relating to the treatment of juveniles in institutional settings, including exposure to antisocial peers, overuse and excessive duration of institutional placements, physical and emotional neglect and mistreatment, overcrowding, poor physical conditions, inadequate staffing, limited available services, and poor data management systems.

Ineffective or Iatrogenic Interventions

Research has also identified several intervention approaches as being generally ineffective or even harmful for justice-involved youth. The DARE Program, peer-led programs, and programs that are single-faceted and ill-matched to the development of skills in the natural environment are generally ineffectual in reducing offending behavior (Melton, Petrila *et al.*, 2007). Research also suggests that mixing low-risk and higher-risk youth is typically ineffective and potentially harmful for the lower-risk youth (e.g. Dishion & Andrews, 1995; Howell, Lipsey *et al.*, 2014). There is evidence that deterrence-based programs, such as shock treatments and prison visitation programs, are typically ineffective and may lead to iatrogenic harm (Lipsey, 1995; Lipsey & Wilson, 1998; Melton, Petrila *et al.*, 2007). In their review of meta-analyses of interventions for justice-involved youth, Howell, Lipsey *et al.* (2014) similarly concluded that negative effects are observed for interventions that focus primarily on deterrence (e.g. prison visitation programs) and discipline (e.g. boot camps).

EVIDENCE-BASED INTERVENTIONS

It is useful to consider whether treatment programs for justice-involved youth are utilizing empirically supported interventions. The National Criminal Justice Treatment Practices (NCJTP) survey examined the prevalence of ten evidence-based practices (EBPs) across 3,198 residential and community-based juvenile corrections programs (Taxman, Young *et al.*, 2007). The most commonly used EBP was family involvement in treatment (88.5 percent of programs), followed by the use of standardized assessments (80.3 percent); systems integration (77.9 percent), i.e. cooperation among judiciary, community corrections, and community-based treatment providers; use of engagement techniques (72.1 percent), e.g. motivational interviewing; addressing co-occurring disorders (71.3 percent); employment of qualified substance abuse treatment staff (69.7 percent), i.e. those with specialized training or credentials related to substance abuse treatment; assessment of treatment outcomes (59.0 percent); comprehensive services (41.8 percent), i.e. medical, mental health, substance abuse, and case management); continuing care (25.4 percent); and developmentally appropriate treatment (10.7 percent), i.e. specific programming for adolescents. On average, the surveyed programs reported adhering to approximately 5.5 of the ten identified EBPs (see Taxman, Young *et al.*, 2007; Taxman, Debus-Sherrill *et al.* 2012; Young, Dembo *et al.*, 2007).

Researchers have identified several model programs for at-risk and justice-involved youth. The Blueprints for Violence Prevention initiative, which was developed by the Center for the Study and Prevention of Violence at the University of Colorado-Boulder and supported by funding from OJJDP, is the most comprehensive evaluation of intervention programs to date (Mihalic, Fagan *et al.*, 2004). After developing criteria for evaluating program effectiveness and reviewing more than 600 treatment programs, the Blueprints for Violence Prevention initiative identified 11 model programs and 21 promising programs that prevent youth violence and treat youth with behavioral problems.

The 11 model programs identified by the Blueprints for Violence Prevention initiative are the Midwestern Prevention Project; Big Brothers Big Sisters of America; Functional Family Therapy; Life Skills Training; Multisystemic Therapy; Nurse-Family Partnership; Multidimensional Treatment Foster Care; Olweus Bullying Prevention Program; Promoting Alternative Thinking Strategies; The Incredible Years: Parent, Teacher, and Child Training Series; and Project Towards No Drug Abuse (Mihalic, Fagan *et al.*, 2004). A detailed review of all 11 model programs is beyond the scope of this chapter, so we focus on three model programs that have extensive empirical support for treating young offenders: Multisystemic Therapy,

Functional Family Therapy, and Multidimensional Treatment Foster Care. (For detailed reviews of several model and promising programs identified by the Blueprints for Violence Prevention initiative, see Brogan, Haney-Caron *et al.*, 2015; Daly, DeMatteo *et al.*, in press; Sheidow & Henggeler, 2005; and Underwood & Washington, 2016.)

Multisystemic Therapy

Multisystemic Therapy (MST) utilizes a multimodal approach for adolescents who are at risk for out-of-home placements and their families (Henggeler & Borduin, 1990; Henggeler, Melton *et al.*, 1992). Adolescent behavior is viewed as resulting from the interrelationships between the adolescent and his or her family, peers, school, and community. Over a period of several months, MST therapists attempt to reduce the likelihood that the juvenile will recidivate by restructuring the youth's environment in these areas: family (e.g. parental skills training, treating parental behavioral health problems), peers (e.g. promoting non-association with antisocial peers), and school/community (e.g. promoting education and/or job skills) (Henggeler, 1997).

MST has proven to be effective in terms of reducing recidivism and other justice-related outcomes. Some studies report reductions of 70 percent in re-arrest rates and reductions of 64 percent in out-of-home placements (National Mental Health Association, 2004), and there is evidence that the positive effects of MST last for more than ten years (Schaeffer & Borduin, 2005). Finally, in a meta-analysis of 11 MST outcome studies involving 708 juveniles, other investigators (Curtis, Ronan *et al.*, 2004) reported a medium effect size ($d = 0.55$) across different presenting problems and samples, and they also found that adolescents and families treated with MST were functioning better than 70 percent of youths and families in other treatments.

Functional Family Therapy

Functional Family Therapy (FFT) is a family-centered intervention for moderate-to-high risk youth and their families (Sexton & Alexander, 2000;

Shelton, 2005). By comparison with MST, FFT has a narrower scope and focuses solely on family dynamics (Celinska, Furrer *et al.*, 2013). Problematic behavior is viewed as resulting from dysfunctional family relationships (Trupin, 2007). As such, FFT seeks to enhance the family's motivation for change, enhance family members' strengths, and foster greater self-sufficiency and self-respect (Sexton & Alexander, 2000).

FFT has been found to effectively reduce recidivism rates among both at-risk and delinquent youth. For example, youth who received FFT had a 25 percent re-arrest rate, compared to a 45–70 percent re-arrest rate for youth processed in juvenile court or among youth who received no treatment or another treatment (Shelton, 2005). The National Mental Health Association (2004) reported that less than 10 percent of youth who received FFT were re-arrested during a five-year follow-up period, compared to 60 percent of youth who were processed in juvenile court over the same time period.

Multidimensional Treatment Foster Care

Whereas MST targets at-risk youth and FFT targets moderate-to-high risk youth, Multidimensional Treatment Foster Care (MTFC) targets high-risk youth. MTFC is often used as an alternative to residential, secure-care, or hospitalization treatment for youth with severe behavioral disorders (Elliot, 1998; Fisher & Chamberlain, 2000; Shelton, 2005). MTFC involves placing youth with trained and supervised families for 6–9 months to reduce the youth's antisocial behavior and increase pro-social engagement, with the goal of eventually returning the youth to his or her family of origin. Several interventions are typically used, including individualized behavioral management programs, close supervision of activities, and rewards and punishments for youth behavior. MTFC parents make regular reports to case managers regarding the youth's progress and maintain contact with behavioral-support specialists, physicians, teachers, probation officers, and employment supervisors (Fisher & Chamberlain, 2000).

MTFC significantly reduced offending, violence, and other negative behaviors among female youth in England and the United States (Rhoades, Chamberlain *et al.*, 2013). The National Mental Health Association (2004) reported that youth who received MTFC had significantly fewer days of incarceration and lower re-arrest rates than youth who did not receive services. Finally, female youth who received MTFC had significantly fewer days in locked settings and 42 percent fewer criminal referrals than the control group at a 12-month follow-up (Leve, Chamberlain *et al.*, 2005).

FUTURE DIRECTIONS

Various strategies have been proposed to reduce the number of adolescents in the juvenile system and decrease juvenile offending. For example, decriminalizing status offenses or divesting juvenile courts from jurisdiction over status offenses would eliminate some concerns about the negative effects of involvement with the juvenile justice system. In addition, MST, which has demonstrated success with at-risk populations, may be useful with status offenders. Finally, some school truancy programs that involve systematic progressive steps in response to adolescent misbehavior—for instance, letters to parents, then referrals to a school attendance officer or social service agency, followed by home visits by a school attendance officer and community law enforcement, and finally referral to the juvenile court—have demonstrated some positive effects (Elrod & Ryder, 2011).

One team (Redding, Lexcen *et al.*, 2005) offered an interesting proposal. They suggested viewing juvenile delinquent behavior and the often co-morbid behavioral health disorders seen in juvenile offenders as being analogous to a chronic, relapsing medical condition. Like others with such conditions, juvenile offenders need long-term supervision and support. Further, they argue that it is important to distinguish between minor setbacks and serious failures. Under this approach, any antisocial behavior by the juvenile should be met with a rapid and intensive treatment response.

Taxman, Debus-Sherrill *et al.* (2012) summarized the core components of three recent national initiatives that have drawn attention to juvenile justice programming designed to decrease the numbers of confined youths. First, the Annie E. Casey Foundation's Juvenile Detention Alternatives Initiative calls for collaboration among juvenile justice agencies, government entities, and community organizations. Such collaboration would use data to identify problematic practices and assess the impact of changes. This initiative also calls for the development of objective admission criteria for juvenile placement, non-secure alternatives to detention, flexible policies and practices to address special cases, and the improvement of confinement conditions through routine inspections and raised standards. Second, the MacArthur Foundation's Models for Change seeks to reduce juvenile involvement in the justice system by focusing on fundamental fairness, recognizing developmental and individual differences, and prioritizing each youth's potential, safety, personal responsibility, community responsibility, and system responsibility. Finally, the Robert Wood Johnson Foundation's Reclaiming Futures initiative calls for a focus on initial screening and assessment, service coordination, service engagement, and service completion.

CONDUCTING DISPOSITION EVALUATIONS

Ultimate dispositional determinations are judicial decisions. Like other decisions informed by FMHA, they are outside of the purview of forensic mental health professionals. Yet it is important for those who conduct evaluations of juveniles to be knowledgeable about the available dispositions and treatments in their jurisdiction. To the extent possible, treatment recommendations should be tailored to the specific needs of the individual juvenile offender within the context of available treatment settings. Treatment/placement facilities often have inclusion and exclusion criteria for juvenile offenders—for example, placement facilities may not accept juveniles with intellectual disabilities or those who were adjudicated delinquent for a sexual offense—so evaluators should be aware of any admission restrictions. Forensic mental health professionals should also be familiar with the practice literature regarding treatments for special subgroups of juvenile offenders, including juvenile sex offenders (e.g. Rich, 2011; Ryan, Hunter *et al.*, 2012), juvenile offenders with high levels of psychopathic traits (e.g. Ribeiro da Silvaa, Rijoa *et al.*, 2013; Salekin & Lynam, 2010), and juvenile homicide offenders (Bartol & Bartol, 2009). Specifically identifying the juvenile's treatment needs, with a focus on criminogenic factors (e.g. substance use treatment, anger management), and the context in which the treatment goals are most likely to be met (e.g. community-based MST; a secure residential facility that has clearly defined rules, monitoring to ensure compliance, and contingencies for non-compliance) will assist legal decision-makers when making disposition decisions and enhance the effective placement and treatment of youthful offenders.

At the system level, it is useful to consider best practices in juvenile justice processing. There are eight administrative tools and procedures that are particularly relevant to promoting evidence-based juvenile justice programming: (1) use of a valid risk assessment tool to assist with the determination of the appropriate level of care; (2) comprehensive assessment of the juvenile's treatment needs to determine the appropriate behavioral health treatment services, with a particular focus on criminogenic needs; (3) graduated assessments for juvenile offenders with more complex substance use and mental health needs; (4) use of disposition matrices that account for the juvenile's present offense and level of risk as a way to assign juvenile offenders to developmentally and risk-level appropriate levels of care; (5) comprehensive case management plans that integrate treatment services and supervision strategies; (6) quality assurance procedures designed to ensure that case management plans are followed appropriately; (7) data management information systems that are capable of tracking client services and outcomes; and (8) formalized court standards that support these seven tools and procedures (Howell, Lipsey *et al.*, 2014). Disposition evaluations provided by forensic mental health professionals can offer valuable information in the first four of these areas. Evaluators should be mindful of the empirically supported advantage in effectiveness of certain community-based alternatives. It is also useful to consider the advantages of recommending that low-risk offenders remain in the community with low-intensity services and supervision, moderate-risk offenders be placed in more structured community programs with intensive supervision as necessary, and high-risk juveniles be placed in residential corrections facilities. This is consistent with the Risk-Need-Responsivity model previously discussed.

There are a variety of considerations for mental health professionals who conduct evaluations of juveniles for disposition and placement purposes. The purpose of the evaluation is to gather data that will enable the judge to make an informed decision regarding an appropriate disposition for the juvenile offender. Therefore, the model we described in Chapter 3 is recommended as a guiding strategy for the evaluation. This model incorporates risk and needs, treatment amenability, and sophistication-maturity. These are the constructs that are most relevant to a disposition decision, although treatment amenability and sophistication-maturity are more explicitly associated with transfer and reverse transfer decisions. Being guided by Risk-Need-Responsivity principles is part of this model (see Andrews & Bonta, 2010a, Hoge & Andrews, 2010b, and Chapters 5–6, this volume). Among other things, this means that evaluators should focus on risk, need, and responsivity characteristics, which provide important data regarding an appropriate disposition.

The identification of a juvenile's risk and needs is important because it can affect the level of security that is needed and the type and level of treatment intensity that is provided, with higher-risk juveniles generally needing more secure settings and more intensive interventions. The evaluator should identify both static risk factors and dynamic risk factors, with the latter category also including behavioral health disorders that are relevant to risk and rehabilitation potential. However, as juvenile court judges—and indeed the juvenile justice system—are primarily interested in those factors that are relevant to risk of re-offense, it is particularly valuable to focus on dynamic risk factors and those behavioral health needs that are relevant to reoffending and rehabilitation potential. Amenability to treatment and sophistication-maturity (see Chapters 6–7, this volume, respectively) are the other elements in the evaluation model.

To assess a juvenile's risk and needs, treatment amenability, and sophistication/maturity, evaluators may benefit from following established principles of conducting FMHAs with juveniles (see Heilbrun & DeMatteo, 2012; Heilbrun & Locklair, 2016; and Chapter 3, this volume). Consistent with these principles of FMHA, data should be obtained from multiple sources, including self-report, testing, collateral records, and third parties. Gathering data from multiple sources places the evaluator in a better position to identify and resolve inconsistent information.

The interview should elicit information relevant to the juvenile's risk and needs, and (to the extent relevant) treatment amenability and sophistication-maturity. Covering the juvenile's functioning across psycho-social domains—family, school, social, substance use, employment, criminal, medical, and mental health—is useful for eliciting this type of information.

As discussed in Chapter 3, there is a variety of forensically relevant instruments that can be used to tap the major constructs of interest. Several well-validated measures provide a comprehensive assessment of risk and needs, and some also provide data on treatment planning. Evaluators should carefully choose measures that are appropriate given the purpose of the evaluation, and that are likely to withstand scrutiny if challenged.

In terms of records and third-party sources, evaluators should review all available and relevant records, which may provide useful information regarding the juvenile's risk and needs, treatment amenability, and sophistication-maturity. Records should ideally include those with information about schooling, behavioral and physical health, prior justice involvement, and prior placements. Third-party sources of information may include parents, teachers, treatment providers, and probation officers, among others.

CONCLUSION

Disposition decisions can have a substantial impact, positive or negative, on justice-involved youth. There are numerous considerations that influence a judge's disposition decision, and forensic mental health professionals can provide useful data to inform the court's decision. Evaluations of juveniles for disposition purposes should be sufficiently comprehensive to address the juvenile's risk and needs, and (to the extent relevant) treatment amenability and sophistication-maturity. These constructs are often cited as important considerations in many jurisdictions because they are relevant to recidivism risk and rehabilitation potential. Using the best practices outlined in this chapter is a useful way for evaluators to obtain reliable and valid data that may assist the court in determining the most appropriate disposition.

CHAPTER TEN

Juvenile Resentencing

Several recent decisions from the United States Supreme Court have effectively created a new type of sentencing evaluation in which juveniles who were tried as adults and initially sentenced to automatic life without parole must be resentenced. After discussing the Supreme Court decisions that created the need for this type of resentencing evaluation, this chapter builds on the material provided in previous chapters and outlines the appropriate steps for conducting these types of resentencing evaluations. At the time of this writing, these are very new types of evaluations, so their procedural and substantive aspects are still being worked out. However, there is an emerging practice literature that can be used to guide forensic mental health professionals who conduct these types of evaluations.

RELEVANT LAW

In several seminal cases, the United States Supreme Court has recognized that the differences between juveniles and adults in terms of developmental maturity—particularly the inclination toward sensation-seeking and risk-taking, and different approaches to decision-making—require the criminal justice system to treat juvenile offenders differently than adults in the imposition of a sentence following a determination of guilt in criminal court. For example, the Supreme Court held (in *Roper v. Simmons*, 2005) that defendants who committed capital offenses as juveniles could not be sentenced to death (see Chapter 2, this volume). Citing the lesser culpability of juvenile offenders, the Supreme Court held that a death sentence constitutes cruel and unusual punishment in violation of the Eighth Amendment, and that juvenile offenders should therefore be categorically excluded from the reach of the death penalty. The Supreme Court's decision in *Roper* ushered in a new era of jurisprudence in which the differences between juveniles and adults take center stage in determining appropriate sentences for offenders who commit their crimes as juveniles.

Five years after deciding *Roper*, the United States Supreme Court addressed the question of whether sentencing juvenile offenders to life without parole for non-homicide offenses violates the Eighth Amendment's prohibition against cruel and unusual punishment. In *Graham v. Florida* (2010), the Supreme Court held that imposing a sentence of life without parole on an offender who was under age 18 at the time of the offense constitutes cruel and unusual punishment in cases in which no homicide occurred.

At the time the Supreme Court decided *Graham*, case law from lower courts that had addressed a similar question was quite mixed. By the time *Graham* was decided in 2010, several jurisdictions had already held that sentencing juvenile offenders to life without parole was unconstitutional. For example, in *Workman v. Kentucky* (1968), the Kentucky Supreme Court held that sentencing a 14-year-old to life without parole for rape violated the prohibition against cruel and unusual punishment in the state constitution. *In re Nuñez* (2009), which was a decision from a California appellate court, held that sentencing a 14-year-old to life without parole for non-injurious kidnapping for ransom violated the prohibitions against cruel and unusual punishment in the state and federal constitutions. At least one court also held that sentencing a juvenile to life without parole for homicide was also unconstitutional. Specifically, in *Naovarath v. Nevada* (1989), the Supreme Court of Nevada held that sentencing a 13-year-old to life without parole for first-degree murder violated federal and state constitutional prohibitions against cruel and unusual punishment.

Other state and federal courts prior to *Graham*, however, had held that life without parole sentences for juvenile offenders did not violate any constitutional provisions. For example, in *Harris v. Wright* (1996), the United States Court of Appeals for the Ninth Circuit held that sentencing a 15-year-old to life without parole for murder did not constitute cruel and unusual punishment in violation of the Eighth Amendment. Several state courts reached similar decisions, including cases reviewed by the highest courts in Arizona (*Arizona v. Pierce*, 2010), Connecticut (*Connecticut v. Allen*, 2008), Delaware (*Wallace v. Delaware*, 2008), and Minnesota (*Minnesota v. Martin*, 2009).

Graham addressed the constitutionality of sentencing juvenile offenders to life without parole for non-homicide offenses. It was unclear at that time whether a sentence of life without parole for a homicide offense would run foul of the United States Constitution. In several post-*Graham* cases, lower courts throughout the United States held that imposing a sentence of life without parole on juvenile offenders convicted of homicide did not violate any state constitutional provisions. But without guidance from the United States Supreme Court, it was unclear if these decisions comported with the United States Constitution. The question of whether life without parole was an appropriate sentence for juvenile offenders convicted of homicide has clear importance, as the vast majority of juveniles who are serving life without parole sentences—more than 90 percent—received those sentences after being convicted of homicide (see Hechinger, 2011, for an informative analysis of the post-*Graham* but pre-*Miller* legal landscape). Fortunately, states did not have to wait long to receive guidance from the Supreme Court.

Two years after the landmark ruling in *Graham*, the United States Supreme Court addressed the question of whether life without parole for juvenile offenders convicted of homicide was constitutionally permissible. In *Miller v. Alabama* (2012), by a narrow 5–4 decision written by Justice Kagan, the Supreme Court held that a statutory scheme that makes a life without parole sentence mandatory for an individual who was a juvenile at the time of the offense, even a homicide offense, violates the Eighth Amendment's prohibition against cruel and unusual punishment. As with many cases from the Supreme Court, the contours of the *Miller* decision are important. The Supreme Court did not create a categorical prohibition against sentences of life without parole for all juvenile offenders. Rather, the Supreme Court in *Miller* confirmed that life without parole sentences for juvenile offenders are unconstitutional in cases in which no homicide occurred, and it held that life without parole sentences are also unconstitutional when the sentence is mandatory rather than discretionary, even when the juvenile offender has been convicted of homicide. Thus, because there is no absolute ban on life without parole sentences for juvenile offenders, the *Miller* decision left open the possibility that the sentencing court could impose a sentence of life without parole on a juvenile offender if the court has considered relevant factors.

An important question left unanswered by the decision in *Miller* was whether the ban on mandatory life without parole sentences for juvenile offenders should be applied retroactively for juveniles who received such sentences prior to the Supreme Court's *Miller* decision. This is particularly important because in 2010, when *Miller* was decided, there were more than 2,000 individuals serving mandatory life without parole sentences for homicides they committed as juveniles (Mills, Dorn *et al.*, 2016). Without clear guidance from the Supreme Court regarding the retroactivity of *Miller*, states reached differing conclusions about whether it should be applied retroactively. Following the *Miller* decision, at least six state supreme courts determined that resentencing was not required, citing *Miller* as a new rule that should be applied only to forthcoming cases (Scott, Grisso *et al.*, in press). However, courts in another 12 states determined that *Miller* represented a substantive rule of sentencing and thus required resentencing in all pre-*Miller* mandatory life without parole cases—effectively treating it as retroactive (Grisso & Kavanaugh, 2016).

In 2016, the United States Supreme Court resolved all questions regarding the retroactivity of the *Miller* decision in *Montgomery v. Louisiana* (2016). In *Montgomery*, the Supreme Court held by a 6–3 decision that *Miller* represented a new substantive rule that nullified all prior mandatory life without parole sentences for juvenile offenders. Writing for the majority, Justice Kennedy emphasized the infrequency with which life without parole sentences should be imposed on juvenile offenders, stating that life without parole should only be applied to "the rarest of juvenile offenders, those whose crimes reflect permanent incorrigibility," thus excluding "the vast majority of juveniles" (*Montgomery v. Louisiana*, 2016, p. 734). The Supreme Court provided states with two options: (1) provide parole hearings for all inmates who are currently serving mandatory life without parole sentences for crimes committed as a juvenile; or (2) resentence offenders who received a mandatory life without parole sentence for crimes committed as a juvenile.

THE CONTEXT OF POST-*MONTGOMERY* SENTENCING AND RESENTENCING EVALUATIONS

In its landmark decisions in *Roper*, *Graham*, and *Miller*, the United States Supreme Court was influenced by social science research related to the relatively immature brain development and behavioral functioning of adolescents (for a review of this literature, see Chapter 4, this volume). In general, this literature describes adolescents' relative deficits—compared to adults—in terms of sensation-seeking, risk taking, and self-regulation, all of which impair an adolescent's decision-making. The Supreme Court cited these relative deficits as reducing a juvenile offender's culpability, thereby making sentences of death (*Roper*) and mandatory life without parole (*Miller*) unconstitutional.

The United States Supreme Court's decisions in *Miller* and *Montgomery* did not specifically identify the characteristics of the rare juvenile offender who would presumably be an appropriate candidate to receive a sentence of life without parole in a homicide case. But the *Miller* decision delineated several age-related reasons that juvenile offenders require special protection in homicide cases (Grisso & Kavanaugh, 2016). Scott, Grisso *et al.* (in press) recently provided categorical summaries of these developmental factors: (1) *decisional*: juveniles' inclination toward sensation-seeking and risk-taking results in errors in judgment during decision-making; (2) *dependency*: juveniles' focus or reliance on those around them and the resultant difficulty avoiding negative influences (e.g. abusive family environment, peer influence); (3) *offense context*: the possible relationship of the aforementioned decisional and dependency factors to the youth's justice involvement; (4) *rehabilitation potential*: juveniles' greater capacity for change; and (5) *legal competency*: juveniles' immature capacity for making important legal decisions (e.g. *Miranda* waiver, interrogations, assisting legal counsel).

Although it is likely that these five factors will be utilized in the context of post-*Montgomery* resentencing decisions, courts have not yet offered any specific guidance regarding the application of these factors, or additional developmental evidence, in individual cases (Grisso & Kavanaugh, 2016). It will take some time for a meaningful body of relevant jurisprudence to develop in this area. However, Grisso & Kavanaugh (2016) provide an analysis of the situations in which these factors may be examined. They note that *Miller* hearings will probably have dual objectives in states that allow juvenile life without parole (LWOP) sentences: (1) to decide whether a juvenile exhibits the *irreparable corruption* required for the (rare) imposition of a sentence of life without parole under *Miller* and *Montgomery*; and (2) to impose an alternative sentence if life without parole is deemed inappropriate in a particular case.

For the first objective (i.e. sentencing and resentencing), Grisso and Kavanaugh (2016) assert that the *Miller* factors define a class of individuals who are protected from life without parole sentences; thus, most juvenile offenders will be excluded from such sentences by default. As such, the focus of an assessment to determine whether a juvenile should be eligible for a sentence of life without parole will be primarily on one factor: the offender's rehabilitation potential. It is important to note that only those juveniles who exhibit "irreparable corruption" (e.g. *Montgomery*, 2016, pp. 726, 734–6) are eligible for sentences of life without parole under *Miller* and *Montgomery*. A key question, therefore, is how the legal concept of irreparable corruption is operationalized, and the decisions in *Miller* and *Montgomery* suggest that irreparable corruption means that the offender cannot be rehabilitated by maturation or by psychological-behavioral interventions. According to Grisso and Kavanaugh (2016), because the presumption under *Miller* and *Montgomery* is that life without parole should rarely be imposed on juveniles, the burden will be on the prosecution in these cases to demonstrate that a specific juvenile falls into the rare category of irreparably corrupt youthful offenders and is therefore eligible for a sentence of life without parole.

This raises an obvious question: what type of evidence can be used to demonstrate that a juvenile is irreparably corrupt? Given that *Roper* deemed evidence of the brutality and violence of the crime to be too overwhelming, and that *Montgomery* noted that "children who commit even heinous crimes are capable of change" (*Montgomery v. Louisiana*, 2016, p. 736), it seems unlikely that evidence relating to the crime itself can be used to sufficiently establish that a juvenile offender is irreparably corrupt. Moreover, using the five criteria described by Scott, Grisso *et al.* (in press) to argue in favor of a sentence of life without parole will be challenging because some courts have already determined that the basis for juvenile life without parole sentencing is not predicated on the characteristics of youth, but solely on whether a juvenile is irreparably corrupt (*Veal v. State*, 2016). Other courts have determined that these factors may only be used as mitigating—and not aggravating—circumstances. For instance, in *Iowa v. Null* (2013), the Supreme Court of Iowa held that the developmental characteristics that contribute to mitigation under *Roper* and *Miller* cannot be cited as aggravating factors in support of an LWOP sentence for juvenile offenders. In another case, *Iowa v. Seats* (2015), the Supreme Court of Iowa reversed a juvenile's sentence of LWOP because the court "appeared to use [the juvenile's] family and home environment vulnerabilities together with his lack of maturity, underdeveloped sense of responsibility, and vulnerability to peer pressure as aggravating, not mitigating, factors" (p. 557). Given these considerations, Grisso & Kavanaugh (2016) note that it may be rare for prosecutors to seek a sentence of life without parole for juveniles due to the difficulties with meeting the burden of proof for "irreparable corruption" (see *Apprendi v. New Jersey*, 2000; *Blakely v. Washington*, 2004; *Ring v. Arizona*, 2002) and the likely backlogged dockets of *Miller* cases.

By contrast, Grisso and Kavanaugh (2016) assert that the second objective (i.e. alternative sentencing once life without parole has been ruled out) will be influenced by all five factors described by Scott, Grisso *et al.* (in press), which will be used primarily for mitigation purposes. It seems reasonable that life with the possibility of parole will be considered as an alternative sentence in these circumstances. However, given the wide variation among states in terms of the minimum years that must be served prior to parole eligibility, the length of life with parole possible sentences can differ considerably among jurisdictions. Scott, Grisso *et al.*'s (in press) survey indicated that these minimums range from 15 years to sentences that could be considered the functional equivalent of an LWOP sentence. Courts differ on whether lengthy minimum sentences for juvenile offenders are consistent with the *Graham* and *Miller* decisions. For example, the United States Court of Appeals for the Sixth Circuit upheld an 89-year minimum sentence for a juvenile offender based on the justification that *Graham* only prohibits specific life without parole sentences and not sentences that amount to the practical equivalent of life without parole (*Bunch v. Smith*, 2012). Other courts, however, have rejected lengthy minimum sentences for juvenile offenders, citing concerns that such sentences ignore the underlying principles of the *Graham* and *Miller* decisions, which focus on the unique capacity for rehabilitation among juvenile offenders (Scott, Grisso *et al.*, in press).

Miller's developmental factors will likely influence legal decision-making related to appropriate alternative sentencing because they can be used to determine where a specific juvenile falls with regard to maturity across several relevant domains. One case from the Supreme Court of Iowa held that *Miller*'s developmental principles should be considered in every juvenile case regardless of the type of crime, particularly in cases in which lengthy pre-parole eligibility sentences are likely (*Iowa v. Null*, 2013). Other jurisdictions, however, have rejected the use of the *Miller* criteria for this purpose and conceptualize them only as descriptors of a class of offenders that is protected from life without parole sentences (Grisso & Kavanaugh, 2016).

CONSIDERATIONS FOR FORENSIC MENTAL HEALTH PROFESSIONALS

Given the Supreme Court's decisions in *Miller* and *Montgomery*, forensic mental health professionals may be asked to evaluate the appropriateness of imposing a sentence of life without parole on an offender who committed a homicide as a juvenile. Alternatively, if it is determined that a sentence of life without parole is not appropriate for a given juvenile offender, an evaluator may be asked to evaluate the appropriateness of alternative sentencing options. Both types of evaluations are discussed in this section. After describing the relevant considerations for both types of evaluations, we highlight some of the substantial challenges that forensic mental health professionals may face when conducting *Miller* and *Montgomery* evaluations.

ELIGIBILITY FOR LIFE WITHOUT PAROLE (SENTENCING AND RESENTENCING)

Although *Miller* does not prohibit imposing a sentence of life without parole on a juvenile offender, the sentencing court must consider several factors when deciding if a sentence of LWOP is appropriate. At a minimum, for a juvenile offender to receive a sentence of LWOP, the offender must be among the small group of juvenile offenders who are considered to be "irreparably corrupt" (*Miller v. Alabama*, 2010; *Montgomery v. Louisiana*, 2016), meaning that the offender cannot be rehabilitated by maturation or by psychological-behavioral interventions. Thus, key questions for forensic mental health evaluators to consider are whether psychological data can meaningfully address this legal question and, if so, what types of data can help inform the court's decisions in these types of cases.

Some have argued that forensic mental health professionals cannot offer useful information to courts in *Miller* and *Montgomery* cases. For example, in *Graham*, the United States Supreme Court observed that "it is difficult even for expert psychologists to differentiate between the juvenile offender whose crime reflects unfortunate yet transient immaturity, and the rare juvenile offender whose crime reflects irreparable corruption" (*Graham v. Florida*, 2010, p. 68). Even national mental health organizations have recognized the limited ability of mental health professionals to opine on whether a juvenile offender is irreparably corrupt. An *amicus curiae* brief submitted in *Miller* by the American Psychological Association, American Psychiatric Association, and National Association of Social Workers (2012) stated:

> [T]here is no reliable way to determine that a juvenile's offenses are the result of an irredeemably corrupt character; and there is thus no reliable way to conclude that a juvenile—even one convicted of an extremely serious offense—should be sentenced to life in prison, without any opportunity to demonstrate change or reform. (p. 25)

There are, however, two constructs that can be assessed by mental health professionals that could potentially be relevant in *Miller* and *Montgomery* resentencing evaluations—treatment amenability and psychopathy.

Treatment Amenability

As noted in Chapter 6 (this volume), the relevant literature has not concretely defined the construct of treatment amenability as used in juvenile justice contexts, or reached a consensus on how treatment amenability should be assessed. But treatment amenability in juvenile justice contexts is typically conceptualized as focusing on reducing the likelihood that the juvenile will re-offend as opposed to ameliorating distressing clinical symptoms. As such, whereas treatment amenability in a clinical context focuses on clinical symptoms, treatment amenability in a juvenile context focuses primarily on criminogenic needs. To the extent that clinical symptoms are addressed, they should have criminogenic, risk reduction potential.

Scholars have suggested several different approaches to the assessment of treatment amenability among juveniles (see Chapter 6, this volume, for a more complete discussion), including Kinscherff's (2006) conceptualization of treatment amenability. Kinscherff (2006) recommends focusing on four factors when assessing treatment amenability:

1. Assess for and identify any static (i.e. fixed) factors that may have contributed to the juvenile's offending behavior, including the presence of prior offenses and the juvenile's age.
2. Assess for and identify any dynamic (i.e. changeable) factors that may have contributed to the offending behavior. Relevant considerations may include clinical, attitudinal, social, and environmental factors. Because dynamic factors are changeable, many can be conceptualized as treatment targets in the context of amenability assessment.
3. Gauge the presence of strengths and protective factors that may aid in treatment participation or outcome (e.g. family support, educational success, and the presence of pro-social attitudes).
4. Consider the recommended interventions based on the juvenile's risk and protective factors, and also describe the likely intervention-related outcomes (e.g. reduction in recidivism risk).

Using this conceptualization of treatment amenability, it is easy to see how such an evaluation would provide information related to the types of interventions that are likely to have the best chance of success with a particular juvenile offender. Yet it is more difficult to see that such an approach could be used to definitively determine that a youth is categorically unable to respond to any intervention and is thus "irreparably corrupt"—which is essentially the legal question at issue in juvenile life without parole sentencing cases.

There are relatively few standardized assessment measures designed to assess treatment amenability. One of the more commonly used measures is the Risk-Sophistication-Treatment Inventory, which is available as both a structured interview (RSTI) (Salekin, 2004b) and a self-report measure (RSTI-SR) (Iselin & Salekin, 2008). The RSTI includes three subscales relevant to treatment amenability: (1) responsibility and motivation to change (e.g. the offender takes responsibility for his or her actions); (2) psychopathology degree and type (e.g. insight into the cause of one's problems); and (3) consideration for and tolerance of others (e.g. considers and generally cares about others). The treatment amenability subscale of the RSTI is associated with older age of criminal behavior onset and has been negatively correlated with symptoms of conduct disorder; however, there is no indication that scores on the RSTI treatment amenability subscales can be used to definitively exclude a youth from the possibility of change—improvement resulting from targeted intervention (Salekin, MacDougall *et al.*, 2016).

Psychopathy

Another psychological construct that may be considered to be relevant in the *Miller* and *Montgomery* resentencing context is psychopathy. Psychopathy refers to a well-defined constellation of personality, behavioral, and affective characteristics, including glibness and superficial charm, a grandiose sense of self-worth, pathological lying, conning-manipulative behavior, lack of remorse-guilt, shallow affect, callousness-lack of empathy, need for stimulation, parasitic lifestyle, poor behavioral controls, early behavior problems, lack of realistic goals, impulsivity, irresponsibility, juvenile delinquency, promiscuous sexual behavior, many short-term relationships, and criminal versatility (Hare, 2003). The term psychopathy is currently used in the assessment and conceptualization of offenders (and occasionally non-offending populations), but it is not a formal diagnosis. Although psychopathy was initially identified among adults, later research found that the construct of psychopathy (or at least psychopathic traits) could also be identified among adolescents.

Psychopathy has often been considered to be a personality style that is resistant to change (see Frick & White, 2008; Salekin, 2002c), which, if true, would support the utility of psychopathy assessment as part of the determination related to an irreparably corrupt designation. However, there is evidence that individuals with psychopathic traits can benefit from treatment. For example, in one of the earlier studies to examine this issue (Caldwell, Skeem *et al.*, 2006), investigators found that adolescents with psychopathic features were significantly less likely to recidivate when they participated in an intensive treatment program, as compared with adolescents with psychopathic features who participated in treatment as usual. A recent comprehensive review of the literature concluded that "[t]here is no evidence that youths with psychopathic features are incapable of benefitting from treatment or that treatment is contraindicated" (Vincent, Kimonis *et al.*, 2016: 220). As such, relying on psychopathy to establish that a juvenile offender is irreparably corrupt does not appear to be empirically justified.

There are also several concerns related to the use of the term psychopathy in the context of juvenile forensic assessment, including prejudicial effects, instability of construct measurement, and overrepresentation of minority groups. First, research has demonstrated that simply describing juvenile defendants with the term "psychopath" leads research participants (and, by extension, possibly jurors) to perceive juvenile offenders as being higher risk and to make harsher punishment recommendations (see Boccaccini, Murrie *et al.*, 2008). Second, the measurement of psychopathy in juveniles is commonly unreliable over time and fails to indicate whether the juvenile will continue to exhibit psychopathic traits into adulthood (e.g. Cauffman, Skeem *et al.*, 2016). Finally, research suggests that minority groups are more likely to score highly on measures of psychopathy, which raises concerns about the cultural competence and inherent bias of commonly used psychopathy measures (see DeMatteo, Edens *et al.*, 2010; DeMatteo, Haney-Caron *et al.*, in press).

Taken together, these findings suggest that the constructs of treatment amenability and psychopathy may not have sufficient scientific support to meaningfully assist courts in making decisions about the appropriateness of sentences of life without parole for juvenile homicide offenders. With respect to treatment amenability, although forensic mental health professionals can testify (assuming the presence of appropriate supportive data) that a juvenile is likely to be amenable to treatment, there appears to be an insufficient scientific basis for concluding that a juvenile is irreparably corrupt and therefore eligible for a life without parole sentence. In an important respect, of course, the question of whether an individual is "irreparably corrupt" calls for a legal conclusion that is very close to the decision about whether a sentence of life without parole is justifiable. Evaluating psychologists and psychiatrists can provide relevant information about risk, needs, and amenability. But attempting to translate this information into a conclusion about whether an individual is "irreparably corrupt" raises the same difficulties that answering the ultimate legal question does in other contexts. Because irreparable corruption presumably has significant values embedded, answering this question for the court is likely to conflate the clinical-scientific information that *is* appropriate with the societal values that *are not* appropriate for expert forensic evaluation.

As for psychopathy, there are concerns regarding the overly prejudicial impact of the psychopathy label, instability of the adolescent psychopathy construct over time, and potential racial bias of some commonly used psychopathy measures. All caution against relying in a straightforward way on psychopathy when conducting resentencing evaluations.

ALTERNATIVE SENTENCING

Grisso & Kavanaugh's (2016) analysis suggests that the five *Miller and Montgomery* factors previously mentioned are most likely to be relevant in cases where a sentence of life without parole has been ruled out and an alternative sentencing decision needs to be made.

Decisional Factor

The first of *Miller* and *Montgomery*'s five developmental factors acknowledges the tendency for the decision-making of adolescents to be influenced by impulsivity, recklessness, and risk-taking. The decisional factor also focuses on the diminished autonomy in adolescent decision-making, given the susceptibility of adolescents to peer influence. As discussed in Chapter 4 (this volume), there are several important developmental processes occurring during adolescence that affect the decision-making capacity of adolescents. For example, brain development during this time, particularly the maturation of prefrontal executive functioning and limbic motivational-emotional processes, may be associated with a tendency toward sensation-seeking that may lead to greater risk-taking, particularly in the presence of peers (Luna & Wright, 2016). In addition, planning, self-governance, goal-directed behavior, values, and principles are among the domains that are evolving during adolescence (Steinberg, Dahl *et al.*, 2006). Capacities such as selective inhibition, inductive reasoning, and epistemic understanding also impact the decision-making of adolescents (Kuhn, 2009; Moshman, 2005).

In addition to a clinical interview, there are several measures that may assist with the assessment of an adolescent's decisional capacity (see Chapter 3, this volume, for a more detailed discussion of assessment approaches). These measures are particularly relevant when the individual is evaluated fairly soon after the offense. They become decreasingly relevant as the individual moves past young adulthood. The Consideration of Future Consequences Scale (CFCS) (Strathman, Gleicher *et al.*, 1994) is a 12-item self-report measure that is designed to assess an adolescent's ability to weigh both short-term and long-term consequences of behaviors. The CFCS also assesses how perceived outcomes may influence adolescent decision-making (Salekin, MacDougall *et al.*, 2016). The CFCS has demonstrated adequate test-reliability and internal consistency (Petrocelli, 2003; Strathman, Gleicher *et al.*, 1994), and it has been correlated with at least one other measure of future directedness—the Stanford Time Perspective Inventory (discussed below) (Salekin, MacDougall *et al.*, 2016; Zimbardo, 1990a).

The Psychosocial Maturity Inventory (PSMI Form D) (Greenberger, Josselson *et al.*, 1975) is a 30-item self-report measure designed to assess levels of personal responsibility. The PSMI includes three subscales: self-reliance (i.e. the ability to make independent decisions and perception of internal control), identity (i.e. sense of self and self-esteem), and work orientation (i.e. sense of accomplishment associated with goal attainment) (Salekin *et al.*, 2016). The PSMI has demonstrated acceptable reliability and validity (e.g. Cauffman & Steinberg, 2000; Colwell, Cruise *et al.*, 2005). Furthermore, the PSMI has been used to assess for constructs that are relevant to sophistication-maturity, such as autonomy and maturity of judgment (Salekin, MacDougall *et al.*, 2016).

The Stanford Time Perspective Inventory (STPI) (Zimbardo, 1990a) is a survey designed to assess the tendency of an individual to consider future and long-term consequences. The STPI included five predominant orientations: Past Regret, Future Achievement, Present Hedonistic, Present Fatalistic, and Time (Zimbardo, 1990a). Given the instability of the STPI's factor structure, a revised version—the Zimbardo Time Perspective Inventory (ZTPI)—was developed (Zimbardo & Boyd, 1999). The ZTPI consists of five factors: Past Negative, Past Positive, Present Hedonistic, Present Fatalistism, and Future. This scale takes into account both different times and emotions. The ZTPI has demonstrated high test-retest reliability (0.70 to 0.80), and acceptable convergent validity and discriminant validity; research also suggests that the five-factor structure accounts for 36 percent of the variance (Zimbardo & Boyd, 1999).

The Future Outlook Inventory (FOI) (Cauffman & Woolard, 1999) was developed by extracting items from the ZTPI, CFCS, and Life Orientation Task (Scheier & Carver, 1985). The 15-item FOI is intended to gauge both future orientation and perspective taking (Salekin, MacDougall *et al.*, 2016), so it is a useful measure when assessing an adolescent's decision-making abilities. In the normative sample, the FOI correlated with self-reports of risk perception among high school students and college students, and it demonstrated good internal consistency at six-month ($\alpha = 0.73$), 12-month ($\alpha = 0.70$), 18-month ($\alpha = 0.72$), and 24-month ($\alpha = 0.69$) follow-up time points (Cauffman & Woolard, 1999).

In addition to the direct assessment of adolescent decision-making using these measures, there are other assessment approaches that yield data that may be relevant. For example, laboratory tasks such as the Stroop Color and Word Test (Golden, 1978) and Go/No-Go Association Task (Nosek & Banaji, 2001) gauge impulsive responding and can detect deficiencies in self-regulation related to adolescents' impulsivity and risk-taking. These attributes make them useful measures when assessing the decisional factor described in *Miller* and *Montgomery*. Further, measures that assess intellectual functioning and achievement capacities can assist with the assessment of the decisional factor because those measures often include subscales that gauge capacities that are relevant for decision-making processes (e.g. abstract reasoning) (Grisso & Kavanaugh, 2016).

Dependency Factor

In *Miller* and *Montgomery*, the United States Supreme Court recognized that young people are susceptible to negative influences and pressures (e.g. environmental factors, family, and peers), and noted that adolescent offenders often lack the ability to control their environment or remove themselves from contexts in which criminal behavior may result.

As discussed in Chapter 4 (this volume), research related to social development has demonstrated that the active pursuit of peer approval and acceptance is a normative component of adolescent development (Cohen & Casey, 2014). Peer influence, including negative influence, is particularly salient during adolescence as youth begin spending more time with peers and less time with their families (DeMatteo & Marczyk, 2005; Haynie, 2002). Peer influence during adolescence comprises two related processes: social comparison (i.e. evaluating one's behavior by observing the behavior of others) and social conformity (i.e. imitation of the behavior of the peers). Social conformity is particularly important in adolescence because the tendency to model one's behavior on that of peers peaks around age 14 or 15 and then slowly declines during mid and late adolescence (Scott & Steinberg, 2008). Further, perceived peer rejection during adolescence often results in increased risk-taking behavior that is associated with efforts to gain acceptance from peers (Cohen & Casey, 2014; Steinberg &

Monahan, 2007). This may help explain why juveniles tend to commit more group-based crimes than their adult counterparts (Steinberg and Scott, 2003). Like the decisional considerations, dependency influences are particularly relevant for late adolescents and young adults if the question is future influence. They are consistently important in reconstructing the individual's motivation for the offense, however (see next section).

The Resistance to Peer Influence (RPI) (Steinberg & Monahan, 2007) measure can be a useful tool for assessing the dependency factor. The RPI is a 10-item self-report measure that assesses the ability to resist peer-influence. Respondents select one of two statements to describe their behavior, and then they rate how closely the statement approximates their behavior in life from 1 (really false) to 4 (really true). The RPI has been used to gauge autonomy in relation to sophistication and maturity, and it has been used in conjunction with the Psychosocial Maturity Inventory Form to provide supplemental information (Monahan, Steinberg *et al.*, 2009). An adolescent's family environment should also be assessed and considered in this context, as well as the adolescent's ability to separate from negative circumstances.

Offense Context Factor

This *Miller* and *Montgomery* factor is related to the first two factors (decisional and dependency) in that it refers to the circumstances of the offense, including the juvenile's role in the homicide and the manner in which social pressures may have affected the juvenile. Grisso & Kavanaugh (2016) note that the Supreme Court seemed to anticipate using data regarding the juvenile offender's decisional capacity and dependence on others to examine the offender's involvement in the offense, which may be relevant to mitigation. Particularly important factors include contextual influences on the youth's crime-related decision-making (e.g. peer pressure) and the level of planning required for the juvenile's involvement in the offense. Grisso & Kavanaugh (2016) also noted that information related to the offense can be classified into two categories: (1) characteristics of the youth (i.e. abilities, capacities, and environmental influences relevant to the decisional and dependency factors); and (2) information provided by witnesses, law enforcement, the defendant's peers, and the defendant.

Rehabilitation Potential Factor

We discussed rehabilitation-relevant considerations in our discussion of treatment amenability (above) and in Chapter 6 (this volume). Although many measures of recidivism risk are not directly related to this developmental factor, several may provide useful information regarding rehabilitation potential. For example, the Youth Level of Service/Case Management Inventory (YLS/CMI) (Hoge & Andrews, 2002; Hoge, 2005) was designed to assess risk factors in youthful offenders and to assist with treatment planning and placement recommendations. The risk assessment section comprises 42 items organized into eight subscales: family circumstances/parenting (e.g. inconsistent parenting), prior/current offenses/dispositions (e.g. prior probation), education/employment (e.g. disruptive classroom behavior), substance abuse (e.g. chronic drug use), peer relations (e.g. some delinquent friends), personality/behavior (e.g. poor frustration tolerance), attitudes/orientation (e.g. antisocial attitudes), and leisure/recreation (e.g. limited organized activities). A revised version of the YLS/CMI was published in 2010 (YLS/CMI 2.0) (Hoge & Andrews, 2010b) using a standardization sample that was demographically representative of the contemporary juvenile justice population. Information obtained using the YLS/CMI has clear implications for the *Miller* and *Montgomery* developmental factors, even independent of recidivism risk (e.g. responsivity and other case management sections). When evaluating individuals who are adults, the corresponding adult version of the YLS/CMI (the Level of Service/Case Management Inventory; Andrews, Bonta, & Wormith, 2005) is appropriate.

The primary outcome of interest in treatment amenability assessment is recidivism reduction. Clinical treatment outcomes can also be relevant, particularly when behavioral health conditions affect re-offending risk. Forensic mental health professionals conducting juvenile forensic assessments should assess for psychopathology that may have affected previous offending behavior, including serious mental illnesses such as mood disorders and psychotic disorders. Indeed, forensic mental health professionals should routinely assess for several disorders in the context of treatment amenability evaluations, including post-traumatic stress disorder and other trauma- and stress-related disorders; conduct, impulse-control, and other disruptive disorders; attention-deficit/hyperactivity disorder, specific learning disorders, and other neurodevelopmental disorders; mood disorders, and substance-related disorders (Kinscherff, 2006). In addition, Kinscherff suggests addressing several other important factors in the context of amenability assessments, including early onset of aggression, any established pattern of misconduct-rule breaking behavior, impulsivity, mood disturbance, anger control difficulties, the juvenile's perception of alienation from others, and psychotic symptoms.

Legal Competency Factor

Miller and *Montgomery* posited that mandatory sentencing does not consider that the juvenile offender might have been convicted of a lesser offense if not for incompetency associated with being young, including an inability to deal with police officers or prosecutors and the incapacity to assist an attorney in his or her own defense. Research demonstrates that adolescents are typically less competent than adults to make important legal decisions in contexts such as waiving *Miranda* rights (Goldstein, Kelley *et al.*, 2016), participating in interrogations (Goldstein, Condie *et al.*, 2003b; Kassin, Drizin *et al.*, 2010), and participating meaningfully in a trial (Kruh & Grisso, 2009). Thus, there is evidence supporting *Miller* and *Montgomery*'s supposition that juvenile offenders are particularly vulnerable to errors during legal processing.

Despite this research, Grisso & Kavanaugh (2016) note that it is difficult to determine how the legal competency factor will influence *Miller* and *Montgomery* cases. For example, could assessment data related to developmental capacities be used to demonstrate the possibility of prior due process violations? If so, will this evidence be used as mitigating evidence in the context of *Miller* and *Montgomery* alternative sentencing proceedings? As case law continues to develop, use of the legal competency factor by courts in *Miller* and *Montgomery* alternative sentencing proceedings will likely become clearer.

CONDUCTING *MILLER* AND *MONTGOMERY* FORENSIC MENTAL HEALTH ASSESSMENTS

Because the initial sentence of life without parole was mandatorily imposed, the offender may not have received a meaningful sentencing hearing in which evidence relating to the offender and offense was presented to the court. Therefore, the *Miller* and *Montgomery* resentencing hearing may be the first opportunity for the defense to present relevant mitigating evidence. As with some other types of forensic mental health assessments, *Miller* and *Montgomery* resentencing evaluations will typically involve interviews with the offender, collateral interviews, a review of relevant records, and psychological testing. In terms of the scope of the evaluation's content area, Kavanaugh (2014) provides a useful conceptualization of *Miller*'s clinically relevant factors (also relevant to *Montgomery*), which she groups into four categories.

Family and Home Environment

In *Miller*, the Supreme Court noted that imposing a mandatory sentence of life without parole on a juvenile offender precludes the sentencing court from considering the family and home environment of the offender, which may be dysfunctional and from which it may be difficult for the juvenile to escape. This category covers a broad scope of topics, including mental health, substance use, criminal history, and family history of abuse and neglect (Kavanaugh, 2014). In addition to interviewing the offender, evaluators can obtain useful information from interviewing the offender's family members and caretakers, and they should review records relating to the family and home environment.

Offender Age and Characteristics

The Supreme Court in *Miller* emphasized that individualized sentencing must consider the offender's age—and the characteristics and circumstances that are relevant to age. Along these lines, evaluators should consider the offender's behavioral health history, physical health history, academic and vocational history, and any interactions with the child welfare system (Kavanaugh, 2014). If the offender was evaluated during transfer proceedings, obtaining a copy of the evaluation can be informative. Data from these areas can help the sentencing court fashion a disposition that is informed by the totality of the circumstances that may have influenced the offender's decision-making.

Circumstances of the Offense

In *Miller*, the Supreme Court noted that the sentencing court should consider the circumstances of the homicide, including the extent of the offender's participation and the manner in which family and peer pressure might have influenced the offending behavior. The evaluator should therefore obtain detailed information regarding the offender's behavior before, during, and after the offense. Because the Supreme Court identified the influence of peers and adults on the offender and in relation to the offense as particularly relevant, evaluators should seek to understand the many pressures and influences on the convicted individual. Obtaining information regarding the offense serves two purposes—it enables the evaluator to place the offense in an appropriate developmental context, and it allows the evaluator to assess how the offender currently feels about the offense (Kavanaugh, 2014). In addition to interviews with the offender, the evaluator may want to interview co-defendants (if any) and review any relevant law enforcement and justice system records, including previous statements given by the offender (Kavanaugh, 2014).

Possibility for Rehabilitation

The Supreme Court in *Miller* noted that mandatory punishments do not require the sentencing court to consider the possibility that the offender may be rehabilitated, and it highlighted the "heightened capacity for change" among juvenile offenders (*Miller v. Alabama*, 2012, p. 2469). Kavanaugh (2014) notes that evaluators should consider (1) the programming and services that were available in the institutions in which the offender was held, and whether the offender participated in those opportunities; (2) statements from correctional personnel about the offender's progress and maturation during incarceration; and (3) evidence regarding the offender's mental state while incarcerated (e.g. mental health records). All of these data sources may be indicators of the individual's "rehabilitation, growth, and maturity" (Kavanaugh, 2014: 26), which are relevant considerations in resentencing contexts.

SPECIFIC CHALLENGES IN *MILLER* AND *MONTGOMERY* RESENTENCING CASES

Forensic mental health professionals may face substantial challenges when conducting *Miller* and *Montgomery* resentencing evaluations. One challenge is that the offender may have already served many years of the original sentence. For example, Henry Montgomery (of the *Montgomery* case) was a juvenile when the crime occurred in 1963 and is now entitled to a rehearing regarding his life without parole sentence that was imposed more than 50 years ago (Grisso & Kavanaugh, 2016). Conducting a resentencing evaluation in this context many years after the juvenile committed the offense makes it difficult to understand the convicted individual (e.g. developmental capacities) and relevant context-specific factors (e.g. peer and family influences) as they existed at the time of the offense. Reliance on multiple data sources that were contemporaneous with the offense can partially ameliorate some of these difficulties, but it is nevertheless challenging to assess and reconstruct many of the sentencing-relevant factors outlined in *Miller* and *Montgomery*. The longer the duration since the original sentencing, moreover, the more difficult it is.

Another challenge for evaluators involves whether the evaluation should assess the offender's *current* risk and rehabilitation potential, or the offender's risk and rehabilitation potential as they existed at the time of the initial sentencing. Given the potential length of time between the original sentence and the resentencing hearing, reconstructing an offender's risk and rehabilitation potential as they existed at the time of the initial sentencing seems questionable at best. Unfortunately, this question was not addressed in *Miller* or *Montgomery*, and it may not be clear in the jurisdiction in which the evaluation is being conducted. It is also something of a double-edged sword for offenders. On the one hand, an individual who was sentenced to life without parole may not have been motivated to engage in rehabilitative activities and may therefore be disadvantaged by a current evaluation. On the other hand, an individual who may have appeared to be a poor candidate for rehabilitation at the time of the first sentencing could benefit from evidence that he or she has since engaged in rehabilitative activities and could likely successfully transition to the community on parole (Grisso & Kavanaugh, 2016).

There is some question about whether a risk assessment is needed in the evaluation conducted by a forensic mental health professional in a *Miller* and *Montgomery* resentencing context. If the defense is seeking the offender's immediate release or release in the near future, then the offender's risk is a relevant consideration. If, however, the defense is not requesting a new sentence that would lead to the release of the offender in the near future, then conducting a risk assessment as part of the resentencing hearing may not provide information that is relevant to any decision that will be made shortly. To the extent that risk is linked with rehabilitation needs and potential, then a risk and needs analysis may provide useful information for future decision-making, although clearly another evaluation with current information would be needed when that individual is being considered for release.

CONCLUSION

The United States Supreme Court's decisions in *Miller* and *Montgomery* created a new type of sentencing evaluation for offenders who initially received mandatory sentences of life without parole for offenses they committed when they were younger than 18. Given a recent estimate that as many as 2,500 offenders are serving mandatory life without parole sentences for homicides they committed as juveniles (Mills, Dorn *et al.*, 2016), forensic mental health professionals will certainly become involved in resentencing hearings. The *Miller* decision provides some guidance for resentencing courts and forensic mental health professionals who become involved in resentencing hearings. Several aspects of these evaluations remain unclear at present. Because the body of jurisprudence relating to *Miller* and *Montgomery* resentencing cases is not yet sufficiently developed, it is also uncertain which factors will be most useful to courts. As case law continues to develop, forensic mental health professionals should receive more guidance regarding the legal and professional parameters of these resentencing evaluations.

CHAPTER ELEVEN

International Juvenile Justice Models and Trends

This chapter addresses relevant aspects of the scientific and professional literatures regarding juvenile justice, and the evaluation of disposition and transfer, in countries beyond the United States. We focus on Canada, Europe, Australia, and New Zealand in particular. This selection was partly because these jurisdictions have systems that resemble that of the US in some respects—although it will become clear in this discussion that there are a number of important differences. Such differences provide important context in considering possible areas for juvenile justice reform in the US. Adding additional countries to this comparison would have been desirable, but is beyond the scope of this book.

UNITED NATIONS CONVENTIONS ON JUVENILE JUSTICE

There are no universally accepted guidelines for the administration of juvenile justice. However, there have been multiple United Nations Conventions addressing important juvenile justice issues such as transfer, disposition, and treatment (Winterdyk, 2015). Such conventions are not binding on local, national, or international jurisdictions, but provide a framework from which to develop and implement juvenile justice systems around the world.

Numerous United Nations rules and guidelines related to juvenile justice were incorporated into the 1989 United Nations Convention on the Rights of the Child (CRC), a human rights treaty that delineates the political, civil, economic, health, social and cultural rights of children (including those who are justice-involved). The CRC *is* legally binding on the 196 countries and states that have ratified it. The US is the only United Nations member that has not ratified the CRC, being only a signatory (United Nations Human Rights Office of the High Commissioner, n.d.).

Many of the United Nations guidelines described in Table 11.1 are commonly referenced by the location of their development. For example, the United Nations Standard Minimum Rules for the Administration of

Table 11.1 Important United Nations Conventions with a Juvenile Justice Focus

Year	Rules/guidelines	Summary of focus
1985	United Nations Standard Minimum Rules for the Administration of Juvenile Justice (Beijing Rules)	The Beijing Rules were intended to provide a standard of minimum requirements for the administration of juvenile justice systems. Relevant goals were as follows: (1) to develop an age of responsibility, with consideration of emotional, intellectual, and psycho-social maturity; (2) to prioritize the well-being of the youth offender and design a justice system that reacts in proportion to the offense in question; and (3) to ensure that juvenile justice conditions maximize youths' ability to live a meaningful life in the community.
1990	United Nations Guidelines for the Prevention of Juvenile Delinquency (Riyadh Guidelines)	These guidelines for the prevention of juvenile delinquency emphasize the importance of early intervention, diversion programming, and multidisciplinary cooperation among juvenile justice stakeholders.
1990	United Nations Rules for the Protection of Juveniles Deprived of their Liberty (Havana Rules)	These rules aim to protect the rights of juveniles deprived of their liberty and endorse diversionary programs for youthful offenders under the age of 18.
1990	United Nations Standard Minimum Rules for Non-custodial Measures (Tokyo Rules)	These rules focus on non-custodial youth offender management and highlight the importance of community-based responses to juvenile offenders.
1996	Guidelines for Action on Children in the Criminal Justice System (Vienna Guidelines)	These guidelines focus on the importance of justice-involved youth rights and the establishment of a specific juvenile justice system.

Adapted from Winterdyk (2015). Reprinted with permission.

Juvenile Justice—or Beijing Rules—were developed by the United Nations Committee on Crime Prevention and Control, regional and interregional United Nations Institute, and interregional assembly for the seventh congress on "Youth, Crime and Justice" that was held in Beijing, China, in 1984 (International Juvenile Justice Observatory, 2016). These Guidelines establish an international context for many of the themes addressed in this book, including age of responsibility and associated maturity, diversion and community-based interventions, proportional response in the context of a specific juvenile justice system, and prospects for a meaningful life in the community. To some extent, these are currently considerations in the evaluation of disposition and transfer in the United States. They also provide interesting possibilities for modifying some aspects of juvenile justice proceedings in the US based on theory, practice, and evidence from other countries.

MODELS OF JUVENILE JUSTICE

Describing the salient aspects of juvenile justice systems in countries outside of the US facilitates a review of the evaluation of disposition and transfer evaluations in the larger context of juvenile systems in different jurisdictions. We offer a brief description of some of the current models of juvenile justice in a variety of countries (see Table 11.2). These countries do not adhere to a single model of juvenile justice. Table 11.2 provides a brief description of various models and their associated features. It is noteworthy that two of the models (the Crime Control Model, characteristic of countries such as the US and Hungary; and the Justice Model, which characterizes countries like Poland and Germany) emphasize due process and sanctioning/punishment of offending relative to other models. Of course, "punishment" is not an explicit goal of the juvenile justice system in the US, and its relative emphasis is mild when compared with the US criminal justice system. However, when contrasted with models from other countries described in Table 11.2, the US emphasis on juvenile punishment is relatively high. This can be contrasted with the Welfare Model (e.g. in the

Table 11.2 Juvenile Justice Models and Example Countries

Juvenile justice model	Emphasis/features	Country examples
Crime Control Model	Due process, protection of society, deterrence, punishment, legal maintenance of order	United States Hungary
Justice Model	Due process, individual responsibility, sanctioning of criminal behavior, education	Germany Poland
Modified Justice Model	Bifurcation of criminal justice system (diversion of lesser offenses and prosecution of more serious offenses), diminished individual responsibility, attention to special needs, punishment/sanctions related to offending behavior	Canada Ireland
Welfare Model	Individualized sentencing, informal juvenile justice system, treatment, rehabilitation	Australia Belgium New Zealand Netherlands
Participatory Model	Minimal formal intervention, education, resocialization	Japan Republic of Macedonia
Corporatist Model	Administrative decision making, diversion programs, inter-agency intervention	England Wales

Adapted from Winterdyk (2015). Reprinted with permission.

Netherlands, Australia, and New Zealand), in which sentencing is highly individualized and treatment/rehabilitation is prioritized more highly. Other models' features from this table include the diminished degree of formal intervention in favor of education and re-socialization (Participatory Model), the use of diversion from standard prosecution (Corporatist Model), and the bifurcation of proceedings according to offense severity, with minor offenders diverted into alternative programming (Modified Justice Model).

Several of these features have interesting implications for juvenile justice reform. But the models overlap in a number of respects. There is no single model that does not incorporate at least some features of other models. Countries guided by "what works" in juvenile justice might do well to consider the effective features of models beyond their own. Toward this end, we now take a closer look at some aspects of juvenile justice in Canada, Europe, Australia and New Zealand.

CANADA

The Canadian juvenile justice system operates under a model that emphasizes due process and bifurcation, so minor offenders are often diverted and those who commit more serious offenses are subject to sanctions (Winterdyk, 2015). The system also focuses on rehabilitation to a significant extent. It is subject to the Youth Criminal Justice Act (YCJA) of 2002 (Winterdyk & Miller, 2015). The YCJA has been described as having six primary components: (1) restraint (of both prosecution and sentencing decisions); (2) accountability (the importance of consequences that promote juvenile offender accountability, rehabilitation, and societal reintegration); (3) proportionality (consequences for juvenile offenders should consider the seriousness of the offense and the youth's level of responsibility); (4) protection of the public (intervening to lower the risk of future offending); (5) rehabilitation/addressing needs (both the nature of the offense and individualized needs are considered); and (6) structured discretion (juvenile justice system officials have discretion to carry out the Act's objectives) (Barnhorst, 2004).

Juveniles in Canada are handled through either the family court or a branch of the adult Provincial Court, depending upon the jurisdiction; both are considered to be designated youth courts (Winterdyk & Miller, 2015). Minor offenses are much less likely to result in custodial sentences under the YCJA. Apparently this Act has also increased the treatment resources available for youth with behavioral health difficulties (Winterdyk & Miller, 2015).

There is a mechanism for the transfer of juveniles to the adult court in Canada, although there is no "automatic" transfer (Winterdyk, 2015).

Rather, an "application" for adult sentencing must be filed and decided in a formal hearing (YCJA, 2002, s. 64[1], 71). The minimum age of responsibility (eligibility for the juvenile system) varies by jurisdiction, with 12 years being the lowest (Winterdyk, 2015). Juveniles must be at least 14 to be eligible for sentencing in the criminal court—and this must involve an offense for which an adult would receive a sentence greater than two years (YCJA, 2002, § 62). This age of eligibility varies across provinces, however; each Canadian province can set the specific age (between 14 and 16 years old) at which criminal court jurisdiction may apply (YCJA, 2002, § 61). When age and presumptive offense meet these criteria, the burden is on the youthful offender to demonstrate why he or she should be treated as a juvenile (Penney & Moretti, 2005).

Juvenile dispositions in Canada vary based on the seriousness of the offense. Some dispositions are relatively light in terms of the requirements on the juvenile and deprivation of liberty. These include judicial reprimand, absolute discharge (with the record expunged after one year), community service, and financial restitution provided to the victim. Dispositions that are moderately intensive in their requirements include probation and conditional discharge (record expunged after three years if the juvenile offender meets conditions of his or her sentence), and Intensive Support and Supervision programming. Finally, the most demanding and restrictive dispositions, generally provided for the most serious offenders, include custody (sometimes followed by supervision in the community) and Intensive Rehabilitation Custody and Supervision, which is close supervision and mandated treatment for serious/violent juvenile offenders (Winterdyk & Miller, 2015).

EUROPE

Diversion is important in the approach to juvenile offending in much of Europe. Education, restorative justice (and the concomitant consideration of victims), and rehabilitation are emphasized. With the exception of juveniles charged with serious offenses, the majority of juvenile offending in Europe (e.g. 80 percent of cases in Belgium; 70 percent of cases in

Germany) is handled outside of the court system through diversionary programming (Dünkel, 2015). The minimum age of eligibility for the juvenile system varies widely across Europe, ranging from 8 to 18 years of age with a modal minimum age of 14 (McAra & McVie, 2015).

There has also been some change in policy across Europe regarding the upper age limit for those eligible for the juvenile justice system. In light of research on social and neurocognitive development (discussed elsewhere in this book; see also Luna & Wright, 2016; Nagel, Guarnera *et al.*, 2016; Shulman & Steinberg, 2016), some European policy-makers have advocated an upper age limit between 21 and 24 years old—and the Netherlands has recently raised its upper age limit to 23 (Dünkel, 2015). This trend is consistent with a 2013 United Nations Office on Drugs and Crime proposal for a Model Law on Juvenile Justice, which suggested that jurisdictions extend the maximum age of juvenile court eligibility to 21 in light of evidence (e.g. Luna & Wright, 2016) that the brains of young adults are still developing at that age (United Nations Office on Drugs and Crime, 2013).

To be more specific about juvenile justice system functioning in Europe, we now discuss the various European regions separately. These regions include Northern Europe, Eastern Europe, Western Europe, Southern Europe, and Great Britain. As part of this discussion, we describe sample juvenile justice systems within each region.

Northern Europe

According to the United Nations classification Northern Europe comprises the Åland Islands, Channel Islands, Denmark, Estonia, Faeroe Islands, Finland, Guernsey, Iceland, Ireland, Isle of Man, Jersey, Latvia, Lithuania, Norway, Sark, Svalbard and Jan Mayen Islands, Sweden, and the United Kingdom of Great Britain and Northern Ireland. The administration of juvenile justice varies widely within this region. For example, Sweden refers to juvenile offenders aged 15–18 as "juvenile criminals" but does not allow transfer to adult court (Winterdyk, 2015). By contrast, Finland has three significant age categories: (1) youthful offenders under the age of 15 are not considered to be criminally responsible; (2) youthful offenders aged 15 to 17 are considered "children," eligible for lighter sentences; and (3) offenders between the ages of 18 and 21 are considered to be "juveniles." Personal responsibility, due process, and the sanctioning of offending are prominent aspects of this system in Finland; the Finnish system also excludes the eligibility of youth who are younger than 15. In contrast with both countries, Denmark does not have a formal juvenile justice system, and youthful offenders are handled on an individual basis (Winterdyk, 2015).

In Sweden, juvenile offenders under the age of 15 are primarily treated within the social services system. Those between the ages of 15 and 17 are managed by a combination of social services and judicial authorities; individuals between the ages of 18 and 20 are primarily the responsibility of the judicial system. Youth between the ages of 15 and 17 who have committed minor crimes often have their charges dropped via prosecutorial waiver, under the condition that social services be sought. Very few offenders under the age of 18 are sentenced to adult prison (no more than four per year between 1999 and 2006). However, a larger number are incarcerated in youth care facilities (Sarnecki, 2006).

Eastern Europe

There are ten countries that fall under the United Nations categorization of Eastern Europe: Belarus, Bulgaria, Czech Republic, Hungary, Moldova, Poland, Russia, Slovakia, and Ukraine. There is noteworthy variability across these countries as well. In Slovakia, for example, the minimum age of criminal responsibility is 14; those younger than 14 are not considered criminally responsible and hence not eligible for participation in the juvenile justice system. In addition, there is no blanket assumption that 14-year-olds are criminally responsible. Youth who are 14 must be evaluated to determine whether they can be held criminally responsible, using criteria similar to those appearing in various US sentencing laws (capacities for understanding the illegality of conduct and controlling behavior). Youthful offenders of this age are only sentenced if they display "the capacity of discernment concerning the wrongdoing" of their offending (Dünkel, 2015: 39). There is no mechanism in Slovakia for transfer from juvenile to adult court (Winterdyk, 2015). For youth who are 15 or older, the extent of criminal responsibility is based upon their intellectual and moral maturity. Juvenile offenders between the ages of 15 and 18 may also undergo psychological evaluations, but these are not mandated (Vráblová, 2012). Young adult offenders between the ages of 18 and 20 are considered to be a specialized cohort for whom punishment should be mitigated. They receive consideration with regard to incarceration; they can remain in juvenile placements or in the prison system to complete their education or vocational training, and can be released after they do so (Vráblová, 2012). Juvenile offenders in Slovakia generally receive sentences that are approximately half the length of the corresponding adult sentence, with a maximum sentence of seven years (except for the most serious offenses, for which a sentence of up to 15 years can be imposed) (Kusa & Nurse, 2015).

In the Republic of Macedonia, legislation introduced in 2013 modified the existing juvenile justice system so it is now a participatory model minimizing formal intervention and emphasizing the re-education of juvenile offenders (Winterdyk, 2015). The Polish age range for juvenile eligibility is 13 to 17, with offending responsibility based on the "mental and moral ability" of the juvenile offender (Winterdyk, 2015: 10). Poland operates under a justice model emphasizing individual responsibility, due process, individual rights, and sanctioning of criminal behavior (see Table 11.2).

Western Europe

There are nine countries in the United Nations categorization of Western Europe: Austria, Belgium, France, Germany, Liechtenstein, Luxembourg, Monaco, the Netherlands, and Switzerland. As in other regions of Europe, there is variability across these countries in the assumptions and process related to juvenile justice. The French system operates under a welfare model and emphasizes individualized sentencing, rehabilitation, and treatment. Juvenile offenders (eligibility age range: 13–18) are processed by specially trained juvenile justice judges and receive social services. There is no mechanism for transfer of French juvenile offenders to adult court (Winterdyk, 2015).

The German juvenile justice system follows a justice model that emphasizes individual responsibility, due process, individual rights, and sanctioning of criminal behavior (see Table 11.2). Germany's juvenile court system also has no provision for transfer to adult court. However, all "young adults" (ages 18–21) are reverse transferred to juvenile court (Dünkel, 2006), where they are treated as juveniles, if it is determined that their moral and psychological development is consistent with juvenile functioning. As of 2003, approximately 90 percent of young adults convicted of serious offenses were sentenced within the juvenile justice system (Dünkel, 2006). The German juvenile justice system operates under the provisions of the German Juvenile Justice Act 2008, which describes a sanction system for juvenile offenders. Formal sanctions are a last resort, with educational strategies the most commonly used intervention for juveniles. Minor offenses are often dismissed without the imposition of sanctions. All juvenile cases must be seen in juvenile court prior to the imposition of any diversion. Four levels of diversion are available in the German juvenile court system, ranging from diversion without any sanction to diversion with intervention (e.g. community service, mediation, education) (Dünkel, 2006). When incarceration is used, German juvenile offenders are housed in separate juvenile facilities for periods typically ranging from six months to five years. Serious offenses (those for which adults could be sentenced to more than ten years) carry a maximum sentence of ten years for juveniles.

Juvenile offenders in Belgium under the age of 16 are handled informally. Those 16 or older are subject to a welfare model (see Table 11.2) that focuses on treatment and rehabilitation. The Belgium juvenile justice system does allow the transfer of juvenile offenders to adult court (Winterdyk, 2015).

In the Netherlands, criminal law applicable to adults can be applied to juvenile offenders over the age of 16. Offense seriousness, offender characteristics, and the circumstances of the offense are considered by judges, who determine whether to apply the criminal law to 16–17-year-old offenders (Dünkel, 2015).

Southern Europe

The United Nations classification of Southern Europe includes Albania, Andorra, Bosnia and Herzegovina, Croatia, Gibraltar, Greece, the Holy See, Italy, Malta, Montenegro, Portugal, San Marino, Serbia, Slovenia, Spain, and the Republic of Macedonia. The age of juvenile eligibility in Italy is 14 to 18, with no mechanism for transfer to criminal court. Youth in the Italian juvenile system are handled using a model that mixes welfare and justice (Winterdyk, 2015).

In Spain, juvenile eligibility begins at the age of 14, with younger youth referred to social services. A specialized magistrate judge oversees juvenile justice matters. Considerations such as psycho-social stressors, treatment needs, and family conditions are taken into account. In addition, juvenile court prosecutors (unlike those in the adult court) have discretion regarding whether to pursue charges. Youthful offenders between the ages of 16 and 18 can be sentenced to more severe punishment (up to eight years of incarceration for the most serious offenses) than those between 14 and 16 (with a maximum of four years' incarceration for similar offenses). Youth who are incarcerated in juvenile facilities are transferred to adult facilities at age 23 if their sentence has not been completed (De La Cuesta, 2006).

Great Britain

Great Britain, which is included in the UN designation of Northern European countries, is discussed more specifically in this section. It includes England, Ireland, Scotland, Northern Ireland, and Wales. In England and Wales, the minimum age of juvenile eligibility is 10, extending to a maximum of 18. The model is described as mixed corporatist because it emphasizes administrative decision-making, diversion programs, and re-education of youthful offenders (Winterdyk, 2015). Transfer to the adult criminal court is available in England and Wales for extremely serious offenses; such transfer can be effected in youth as young as ten, although the court must apply special protections to youthful defendants (Dünkel, 2015). The Powers of Criminal Courts (Sentencing) Act 2000 provides that an individual under the age of 18 who has been convicted of murder is to be sentenced to detention at the government's discretion. The Act also states that juveniles convicted of other specified "serious" offenses for which adults could be sentenced to 14 or more years of incarceration can also receive up to the adult maximum for the offense, including a life sentence when applicable (Blakeman, 2009). Juvenile sentences vary in length and placement, with some offenders sentenced to detention in juvenile facilities. More serious offenders may be transferred, usually between the ages of 18 and 21, to an adult prison facility to complete their sentence (Blakeman, 2008).

In Ireland, the minimum age of eligibility for the juvenile system was raised in 2006 from 7 to 12. Processing relies upon a community-based model, with detention used as a last resort (Winterdyk, 2015). Irish juveniles are processed through the Children Court, which has jurisdiction through 18 years of age (previous legislation limited jurisdiction to 17-year-olds only, but this jurisdiction was expanded in 2001 to include 18-year-olds). The Children Court is part of a specialized and separate juvenile court system with the authority to deal summarily with juveniles charged with most offenses. These decisions are based on the age and maturity of the youth as well as other relevant considerations. Some offences cannot be summarily handled; these include offenses that must be tried by the Circuit Criminal Court. In these cases, juveniles are processed as adults in the adversarial system (Seymour, 2006).

Children in Scotland are eligible for the juvenile system when they are eight years old. Eligible youth can be referred to the Children's Hearings System for criminal offending. Juveniles may remain in the Children's Hearings System until the age of 18. However, the majority of youthful offenders between the ages of 16 and 18 are handled in the adult court (McAra & McVie, 2015). Children between the ages of 12 and 15 can also be prosecuted in the criminal court in cases involving serious offenses. The typical transitional age from the Children's Hearings System to adult court is 16—but there is an ongoing debate about the appropriateness of this age. Proponents argue that Scottish individuals can make the adult-like decisions to leave school and marry at the age of 16, so youthful offenders should also face criminal prosecution at this age. Critics have sought to raise the age of adult prosecution to 18, citing policies in other European countries and evidence that offenders between the ages of 16 and 18 exhibit many difficulties that would be better remedied within the juvenile system (McAra & McVie, 2015).

AUSTRALIA AND NEW ZEALAND

These countries operate under a welfare juvenile justice model (*parens patriae*) that emphasizes individualized sentencing, rehabilitation, and treatment (see Table 11.2). The particular juvenile justice model applied in Australia has changed over time, shifting from a welfare model to a justice model, and finally to its current iteration—a restorative justice model (O'Connell & O'Connell, 2015). Within Australia, the minimum age of criminal responsibility varies by jurisdiction, with two jurisdictions setting minimum ages below ten. Youthful offender access to legal counsel also varies by jurisdiction (Winterdyk, 2015).

New Zealand's minimum age of juvenile eligibility ranges from 10 (for murder and manslaughter only) to 14 (for other crimes). The maximum age of juvenile eligibility is 17. As in Australia, the juvenile justice system in New Zealand places a particular emphasis on restorative justice (Winterdyk, 2015). New Zealand has a separate juvenile court presided over by a specialized youth court judge. Strong emphasis is placed on diversion. A specialized youth justice division of the police department is trained to work with juvenile offenders, and approximately 75–80 percent of juvenile–police interactions result in diversionary measures (Foussard & Melotti, 2016). Only persistent or serious offenders are seen in criminal court, typically after police have judged diversion attempts to be ineffective—or diversion has been attempted several times for a particular youth. Before a youthful offender is seen in court, a family group conference must be held by police to convey the intention of trying the youth in juvenile court. The conference can sometimes result in a decision to use an additional diversionary approach in lieu of formal court proceedings (Foussard & Melotti, 2016).

The juvenile justice systems in both Australia and New Zealand include procedures for juvenile transfer to adult court (Winterdyk, 2015). But all Australian jurisdictions have diversion programs in operation (O'Connell & O'Connell, 2015). Among the challenges faced by the Australian juvenile system is the substantial overrepresentation of indigenous youth (O'Connell & O'Connell, 2015).

CONCLUSION

Six models of juvenile justice and multiple international jurisdictions have been considered in this chapter. Two of the models (Crime Control and Justice) emphasize components that are quite consistent with the re-offense risk and criminogenic need perspectives that have been discussed throughout this book as they apply to evaluations of juvenile transfer and disposition in the United States. Valuing the protection of society and deterrence are quite consistent with the formal appraisal of re-offense risk, and the reduction of such risk through addressing criminogenic needs. Other models more explicitly stress rehabilitation as a priority, but all six models share the priority of strengthening the functioning of youthful participants with the goal of having them return to responsible living without offending. Accordingly, the formal appraisal of juvenile risk and need will likely remain a very high priority in evaluations of youth in the United States—as well as countries such as Hungary, Poland, Germany, and others operating under approaches similar to the Crime Control or Justice models.

Another major theme recurring explicitly throughout the four remaining models (Modified Justice, Welfare, Participatory, and Corporatist) is the distinction between more serious offending, which is likely to receive dispositions that are more intensive and include a sanctioning component, and less serious offending leading to diversion into interventions that are less formal. Rather than using the offense itself as a proxy for the intensity of the intervention, a more empirically supported approach would involve using the formal appraisal of risk and needs to make the distinction between more intensive, secure dispositions (longer, residential) and diversion into briefer, community-based alternatives. Such a policy shift is difficult in jurisdictions using a model that includes an emphasis on sanctioning/punishing the offender. But this is an important consideration for debate in the area of juvenile justice reform, and would, if implemented, result in an even more prominent contribution of risk and need assessment to juvenile evaluations.

CHAPTER TWELVE

Recommendations for Law and Policy, Practice, and Research

The evaluation of justice-involved youth on the issues of disposition and transfer has seen substantial progress in relevance and reliability (*Daubert v. Merrell Dow Pharmaceuticals, Inc.*, 1993), particularly in the last two decades. Yet there is a great deal of work that remains before these evaluations consistently provide clear, accurate information about risk, rehabilitation, and sophistication-maturity. In this final chapter, we integrate the information from the previous chapters into a series of recommendations for law and policy, for practice, and for research.

These recommendations are prioritized by importance and based on the material discussed in the earlier chapters. They are presented in summary fashion, having been discussed in some detail above.

RECOMMENDATIONS FOR LAW AND POLICY

We begin with recommendations in the area of law and policy. Changes at this level—from minor adjustments to major reforms—should have a subsequent impact on practice, and will hopefully influence the empirical research conducted in the wake of such change.

PROMOTE DECISION-MAKING THAT IS INDIVIDUALIZED

There is a clear legal trend, seen in the US Supreme Court decisions in *Roper*, *Graham*, *Miller*, and *Montgomery*, away from mandated decisions and toward discretionary, individualized consideration in decisions regarding juveniles. While these cases concern the most serious kinds of offenses and punishments, it seems likely that one of the important influences on the Court's opinion in all of them (relatively less culpability stemming from developmental immaturity in adolescents) will be applied eventually to questions of transfer, reverse transfer, and possibly disposition.

If this trend were to expand, there could be several possible consequences. Statutes allowing automatic transfer based on charge would be modified in favor of those calling for judicial discretion (even courts that have narrowly construed *Roper* and its progeny have endorsed the desirability of judicial waivers over non-discretionary transfer mechanisms; see, for example, *People v. Patterson*, 2014). Statutes allowing prosecutorial discretion might also be modified in this fashion. At the very least, they would allow such decisions to be reviewed in a hearing, with the final decision made by the court. Reverse transfer laws that permit little judicial discretion (e.g. Kentucky: Ky. Rev. Stat. Ann. § 640.010, 2016) might be similarly revised.

This in turn would create more demand for individualized decision-making, much of it informed by transfer and reverse transfer evaluations. This kind of increased demand would make it even more important for the field to continue refining its knowledge and promoting specialized competence in the areas of juvenile forensic evaluation and treatment (Grisso, 2013).

STRATEGICALLY INCREASE THE AVAILABLE OPTIONS FOR JUSTICE-INVOLVED YOUTH

We resist the temptation to simply call for more assessment and treatment resources to be expended on justice-involved adolescents, for two reasons. First, the investment of resources in the juvenile system must compete with other priorities in the areas of criminal justice and public health. This is invariably a highly political process when advocating (as we do) a greater emphasis on rehabilitation that is commensurate with public safety. Consequently, in today's political and fiscal climate, current juvenile funding must be provided more strategically, emphasizing best practice and empirical evidence in a cost-conscious fashion.

In certain respects, the juvenile system aims to rehabilitate youth broadly, with a goal of promoting responsible, healthy living as a desirable outcome. But the juvenile system is not a substitute for other systems with primary attention to healthcare or social services. The juvenile court does not specialize in crisis intervention or mental health—to promote the delivery of such services, it is preferable to do so in these other respective systems, rather than diverting courts and juvenile agencies from their central functions. Tasking the juvenile system with these additional responsibilities would probably not improve their quality, but would certainly make them more coercive and stigmatizing. This argument may be extended to the development of additional problem-solving courts for juveniles (e.g. drug courts, gun courts, mental health courts). There are better ways of providing needed mental health and social services to many youths (see Melton, Petrila *et al.*, 2007, for a more extended discussion).

Our recommendation turns on the importance of investing in assessment and rehabilitative services *with the primary goal of reducing recidivism risk.* Risk factors that are empirically demonstrated to increase the risk of future offending, and interventions that reduce such risk factors and strengthen protective factors, are clearly within the domain of strategic investment. Making such a strategic change effectively will require research (to distinguish effective assessment and intervention) and practice (to implement certain aspects of legal and policy changes) priorities that are aligned with the change.

There are certain modifications that are worthy of immediate consideration. One involves blended sentencing, allowing youth to be placed in the juvenile system and then reviewed to determine the appropriateness of serving the balance of that sentence in the criminal system, maximizing both judicial discretion and exposure to the juvenile system, which is better designed to rehabilitate youth (Salekin & Grimes, 2016). A second concerns status offenders, who would benefit from a disposition that minimizes their penetration into the juvenile system. These are two examples of changes that would be largely cost-neutral, have important potential rehabilitative benefits, and not increase the risk to public safety. Considering other possible reforms in these terms can guide the strategic investment of resources into the juvenile system.

CONSIDER CROSSOVER YOUTH PRACTICE MODEL

An important advance in the assessment of risk and needs in justice-involved youth during the last decade has involved the increased awareness of the potential impact of trauma and adverse experience on risk of re-offending (see Zelechoski, 2016). The Crossover Youth Practice Model (CYPM) (Abbott & Barnett, 2015) explicitly incorporates influences including poverty, maltreatment, trauma and adverse experience, mental health, substance use, and antisocial behavior. Those who have experienced maltreatment and also engaged in delinquency are termed *crossover youth*, who may have involvement with both the child welfare and juvenile justice systems. Indeed, crossover youth may have formal involvement in multiple systems, including behavioral health, juvenile justice, education, child welfare, and low-income social healthcare. The model recommends system collaboration and information-sharing throughout case processing, facilitated by youth assent and guardian permission. It also promotes the use of multidisciplinary team meetings for the purposes of assessment, intervention-planning, and the delivery of relevant mental health and substance abuse services that are trauma-informed and gender-specific.

This represents a reasonable approach to a very challenging problem: providing rehabilitation for adolescents who are disadvantaged in numerous ways. We emphasize that the primary purpose of rehabilitation in the juvenile system is to reduce the risk of re-offending. But the information-sharing and coordinated service delivery envisioned by the CYPM is an alternative to designating the juvenile system as the primary provider of rehabilitative services that focus on other desirable outcomes. By keeping priorities within the appropriate system, but sharing information as feasible to maximize efficiency and effectiveness of all services, the CYPM promotes the delivery of services within their intended system, reducing redundancy and inefficiency.

DEVELOP MODEL LAW, SPECIALIZED ETHICAL STANDARDS, AND PRACTICE STANDARDS LINKING LEGAL PRACTICE TO CURRENT SCIENTIFIC EVIDENCE

The development of model law, ethical guidelines, and practice guidelines is a useful function of national organizations and more specialized organizations. For instance, on a national level within the United States, the American Bar Association could update its *Standards of Juvenile Justice* (ABA, 1982) as they have recently updated their *Criminal Justice Mental Health Standards* (ABA, 1984, 2016). More specialized organizations could provide psychologists and psychiatrists with updated standards on juvenile forensic evaluations. Collaboration across organizations in developing such standards is very useful. One advantage of such cross-organization collaboration is the opportunity to convey generalizable information to a larger constituency; while psychologists and psychiatrists have certain disciplinary differences in how they approach such evaluations and rehabilitative services, it might be feasible to focus on important common ground and produce a broad set of standards that could help to structure work in these areas.

Model law, and ethical and practice standards, would help move the field in a more unified direction by helping to resolve (or at least clarify) a number of issues. To what extent should conclusions about re-offense risk be informed by the use of a validated specialized risk measure for juveniles? How can applicable psycho-legal constructs be clarified so as to minimize the impact of morals and biases? Can international perspectives on transfer and disposition inform the debate about the extent to which the US juvenile system is rehabilitative versus retributive?

There are many additional considerations that could be addressed as part of such collaborative work developing model law and practice standards. One of the most important areas presently in need of attention is juvenile resentencing. With *Miller* and *Montgomery* clarifying that resentencing or parole consideration will be required for individuals who received mandatory life without parole sentences for offenses committed when they were younger than 18, there are important questions about how such evaluations should be conducted. Early attempts to answer these questions (see Chapter 10, this volume; Grisso & Kavanaugh, 2016) have offered some useful information, but additional questions must be addressed to provide consistent and informative evaluations on resentencing. For example, the question of timeframe—whether the evaluator focuses on the characteristics of the youth at the time of sentencing, or those of the older individual who is now being resentenced—will be enormously important in guiding the procedures, reasoning, and conclusions associated with the evaluation.

REFORM STATE TRANSFER LAWS

There are several ways in which current transfer laws could be modified. Three useful suggestions have been provided by Griffin (2008): (1) build in "fail-safes" to avoid unintended or unjust consequences in transfer cases; (2) provide more flexibility in sentencing transferred youth; and (3) mandate better tracking and reporting of basic information regarding juvenile transfers. Such "fail-safes" might include the availability of a hearing to challenge an automatic transfer or prosecutorial adult-charging decision in jurisdictions that do not presently provide this. "Flexibility in sentencing" could include a blended sentencing option allowing youth to spend placement time prior to the age of 18 in a juvenile facility, followed by a review of that sentence by the judge when the youth turns 18.

In many jurisdictions, criminal court judges are not nearly as familiar with the developmental and clinical evidence provided in transfer and reverse transfer evaluations as are juvenile court judges. This is a good justification for adjudicating reverse transfer decisions in juvenile court whenever possible. When this is not possible, one alternative involves developing specialty units within the offices of the prosecutor and the public defender, in which attorneys become very familiar with adolescent defendants and the important differences between youth and adults. It will be at least as important to have a small number of criminal court judges—each of whom is familiar with the important developmental, risk, needs, amenability, and sophistication-maturity considerations applicable to justice-involved youth—hearing cases involving reverse transfer.

Research has demonstrated that adolescents (particularly younger adolescents) in criminal court are less likely to exhibit the necessary capacities rendering them competent to stand trial (Larson & Grisso, 2016). Indeed, some youth who might meet that competence standard within the confines of juvenile court would not in criminal court, given the complex decisions stemming from serious charges in the less developmentally accommodating context of criminal court. States might consider requiring that competence-relevant abilities be examined as part of transfer and reverse transfer decisions.

IMPROVE CORRECTIONAL DISPOSITION OPTIONS FOR YOUTH WHO ARE ADJUDICATED IN THE CRIMINAL SYSTEM

Some transferred youth will remain in the criminal system, even when there are built-in mechanisms for individualizing this decision and considering important developmental, clinical, risk, needs, amenability, and sophistication-maturity findings. It is important that adult correctional systems, which will receive those youths sentenced to their custody, develop appropriate knowledge and specialized units for adolescents convicted of crimes in the adult system. One approach to this challenge would involve developing a specialized unit, either physically distinct from adult correctional facilities, or housed within one but without permitting interaction between youth and adult inmates. The programming in such a unit should be based on the educational, vocational, family, clinical, and criminogenic needs of justice-involved adolescents, influenced by programming in model juvenile rehabilitation placements. Staff should be selected for their knowledge and skill in working with adolescents. It can be particularly challenging to involve adolescents' families in their rehabilitation, as correctional facilities are often geographically remote and difficult to reach by public transportation, and frequently family members will have other difficulties that will limit their involvement in services for the youth's benefit. As technology increasingly enables communication over distances using common devices such as smartphones, this challenge may diminish.

At best, however, this option remains costly and more likely to create difficulty in access for family members, who are often an important part of the rehabilitative effort. We have noted the alternative of blended sentencing, which is likely to offer a more rehabilitative alternative within the juvenile system until the individual turns 18—and is less likely to have the placement options limited to a single, geographically remote site. This alternative has been cited by others as well (e.g. Salekin, MacDougall *et al.*, 2016) and appears promising in many respects.

RECOMMENDATIONS FOR PRACTICE

The next set of recommendations pertains to the practice of evaluating disposition, transfer, and reverse transfer. Some of these recommendations are linked to those in the law and policy area, while others raise important questions about future research that is needed.

PROVIDE AND PROMOTE TRAINING IN RELEVANT AREAS FOR EVALUATORS

Juvenile forensic evaluation requires specialized training, knowledge, and skills. Those conducting them should be competent in forensic, developmental, child–adolescent, clinical, and correctional areas (Ṣalekin, 2015a). While it is not reasonable to expect that good evaluators be highly specialized in each of these areas, we emphasize the importance of knowledge and skill in conducting psychological evaluations for the courts; applying theory and evidence about human development to these evaluations; recognizing clinical, criminogenic, and family contributions to adolescent offending; and understanding the operation of the juvenile justice and criminal justice systems in terms of placements and process.

Each of these areas requires a certain level of specialization, so any attempt to require that evaluators show meaningful specialization in all of them would dramatically shrink the pool of psychologists and psychiatrists available to conduct disposition and transfer evaluations. A more adaptive strategy would involve requiring that evaluators demonstrate specialization in two or three of these areas (e.g. a clinical forensic psychologist having substantial experience with adolescents) and develop competence in the remaining areas (e.g. juvenile, correctional, child and family). When necessary, such competence could be obtained through continuing education, supervision, and consultation after the completion of formal training. When evaluators can demonstrate a reasonable level of specialization or at least competence in all of these areas, our juvenile courts and justice-involved youth can be served by well-informed evaluations.

This may be particularly problematic when youth are initially charged in criminal court. When evaluators do not have competence in areas involving adolescents, families, developmental psychopathology, risk and needs, and the juvenile system, it becomes much more likely that the evaluation of reverse transfer will be missing important information and perspective. Indeed, an adult-specialized clinician might be practicing outside the bounds of his or her competence (see *Ethical Principles of Psychologists and Code of Conduct*, American Psychological Association, 2010). It would be far preferable to have the youth evaluated by a child–adolescent forensic clinician as part of criminal court proceedings (Larson & Grisso, 2016).

PROVIDE EVALUATIONS CONSISTENT WITH A LARGER FRAMEWORK AND FOUNDATIONAL PRINCIPLES

It is useful to structure disposition and transfer evaluations using a framework such as that described by Howell (2009; Howell, Lipsey *et al.*, 2014), which includes the following components: psycho-social history; behavioral health assessment; risk-need assessment; response to intervention; response to behavioral health treatment for youths in primary prevention programs or secondary prevention programs encountered in diversionary contexts; and response to sanctions including intermediate sanctions, community confinement, secure residential placements, and aftercare. These areas call for a good deal of historical information on previous interventions and responses, which is particularly valuable in appraising amenability to treatment.

Another approach to integrating broad, foundational information involves the consideration of principles of forensic mental health assessment adapted for juveniles, as described in Chapter 3 (this volume). In certain respects, the application of these principles yields a structure similar to that seen in Howell's model (previous paragraph), but it also provides more detail on the context, evaluation process, and communication of findings in testimony. An additional benefit to applying either involves the identification of information and evaluative techniques that might require additional competence on the evaluator's part. Understanding these evaluations in their broad context makes it easier to describe the abilities required to conduct them.

APPROACH REVERSE TRANSFER EVALUATION SIMILARLY TO TRANSFER EVALUATION

A review of the reverse transfer laws in the states that have this mechanism (Juvenile Justice GPPS website, n.d.; King, 2016; Salekin & Grimes, 2016) reveals that nearly all refer directly or indirectly to the three factors—risk, sophistication-maturity, and treatment amenability—that have achieved general acceptance as criteria associated with transfer evaluations (King, 2016). More empirical and practice scholarship is sorely needed on reverse transfer. But the similarity of transfer and reverse transfer statutory provisions supports the practice of approaching these two referral questions similarly (Dattilio & Fromm, 2011; Grisso, 2013; Salekin, 2015a).

PRIORITIZE RE-OFFENDING AS A TARGET OUTCOME IN EVALUATION AND INTERVENTION

The outcome that is most consistent with juvenile law and precedent involves re-offending. This does not mean that evaluators should fail to consider information in domains such as family, school, and behavioral health—only that the assessment of such domains is justified because they are relevant to re-offending. Using an approach that involves assessing risk factors and protective factors relevant to future offending, it is feasible to appraise risk, identify needs, and specify relevant interventions while describing amenability to such interventions. Such information is very useful to judges in making decisions that involve these areas, as we have discussed throughout this book.

This recommendation is consistent with the earlier law and policy recommendation on "strategically increasing the treatment options for justice-involved youth." If policy-makers decide that the investment of resources into the juvenile system will be primarily driven by the goal of reducing future offending, the link between legal decision-making and rehabilitation will be strengthened. As part of that process, it is particularly valuable to have juvenile evaluations oriented primarily toward the goal of reduced re-offending.

USE PSYCHOLOGICAL TESTS AND SPECIALIZED MEASURES THAT ARE RELEVANT AND RELIABLE FOR DISPOSITION OR TRANSFER

The availability of relevant psychological tests that are valid for juvenile assessment purposes is helpful. Even more useful, in our view, has been the development of validated measures of adolescent risk and need such as the Structured Assessment for Violence Risk in Youth (SAVRY) (Borum, Bartel *et al.*, 2006) and the Youth Level of Service/Case Management Inventory (YLS/CMI) (Hoge & Andrews, 2011). Carefully selecting measures that provide relevant and reliable information to the court strengthens the content of reports and their potential value considerably.

Practitioners should remain aware of the limitations of current knowledge and our means of assessing these domains, considering whether psychological tests and specialized instruments have been derived and validated through research with justice-involved adolescents—or at least applied to this group. The capacity to accurately measure the constructs involved in transfer and disposition varies, with strong supporting research available for some measures but less so for others (Larson & Grisso, 2016).

Collecting risk-relevant information has the potential to be very helpful to decision-makers. It is also subject to misuse. Research suggests that information obtained from risk assessment instruments is often used improperly—or not at all (Shook & Sarri, 2007; Young, Moline *et al.*,

2006). Conversely, legal decision-making that makes good use of reliable risk-relevant information improves public safety. It is incumbent on evaluators to convey risk information clearly and accurately, in a way that acknowledges its limitations, and in a fashion that helps to inform other relevant questions of need and amenability. Since reports do not invariably lead to testimony, this recommendation must be implemented by writing clear, accurate, and useful reports that stand alone, conveying necessary information without further elaboration from the evaluator.

ATTEND TO EMERGING STANDARDS IN THE EVALUATION OF JUVENILE RESENTENCING

It is now clear that reconsideration of juvenile life without parole sentences must be completed for all those who received such sentences. This demand is time-limited; following the resentencing (or release on parole) of all affected individuals, there will be no further need for evaluations and legal decisions pursuant to *Miller* and *Montgomery*. But there are currently numerous individuals affected, and it remains unclear how long it will take to complete this process. Accordingly, the development of clear standards and guidelines associated with this kind of evaluation must be an urgent priority.

One of the key questions for evaluators will be whether these cases will consider only the circumstances and characteristics of the youth at the time of sentencing, or whether they will include the time since sentencing and hence focus on present characteristics and capacities. Since there is justification for either, it may be that the evaluator should seek clarification from the referring attorney—and perhaps the presiding judge—about whether the decision will emphasize time of original sentencing, current condition, or both, and conduct the evaluation accordingly.

RECOMMENDATIONS FOR RESEARCH

The final set of recommendations involves research that would help to inform many of the important questions that have been raised in this book. In particular, we have selected recommended research topics that would provide information relevant to the recommendations in law and policy, and in practice, that we have offered in this final chapter.

COLLECT SYSTEMS-LEVEL DATA

There are numerous questions about the operation of the juvenile and criminal systems that could be addressed in part through the collection of systems-level data. Unfortunately, such data are frequently not available (Grisso, 2010–11). When youth are transferred between the juvenile and criminal systems, there will be questions of which system—or which combination of systems—can address rehabilitative goals most effectively.

For example, we have observed that unless criminal court judges, prosecutors, and defense attorneys are well-informed about developmental issues, the decisions made in criminal court regarding reverse transfer can miss important considerations. We made the same point about evaluators who provide reports for such hearings. Yet there is little empirical information about how well informed this decision is in jurisdictions in which the reverse transfer decision made in criminal court is entirely separate from decisions made in juvenile court. How does the quality of the evaluations compare? How extensive are the proceedings? To what extent are developmental differences, family considerations, educational needs, and other risk factors particularly important for adolescents incorporated into hearings? To what extent are hearings influenced by retributive versus rehabilitative considerations?

A similar recommendation involves studying system-level changes. We have recommended blended sentencing as an alternative to housing and rehabilitating justice-involved adolescents who are sentenced for convictions in the criminal system. If a jurisdiction were to change its applicable law to enable a sentencing court to use blended sentencing when it could not before, that change could be studied in a number of areas related to rehabilitation, public safety, and cost.

CONDUCT LONGITUDINAL OUTCOME RESEARCH

One of the most valuable study designs for addressing important questions raised in this book is the longitudinal approach. There is some research on the question of re-offending outcomes for youth who remain in the juvenile system versus those transferred to the criminal system. From a public safety perspective, this is important research that should be expanded. But there are additional questions that can be addressed through the use of the longitudinal design. Some are concerned with the process of transferring youth into criminal court, or declining to transfer them back. Is competence to stand trial explicitly addressed more often in criminal court, as one might expect given the more demanding context and more serious charges? Is the balance between retributive and rehabilitative influences comparable to that seen in juvenile court? Is risk assessment information used differently?

There are also rehabilitative questions about the alternatives and the intermediate outcomes of youth in the criminal system. Do youth receive placements following sentencing that are appropriate for their rehabilitative needs? To what extent are risk-relevant needs addressed in such placements through the delivery of relevant services? What are the indicators of favorable responding to such services? (An important longer-term indicator—re-arrest—is not available until the individual has been released from prison and followed for a designated period of time. But intermediate-term rehabilitative outcomes could be investigated earlier: adjustment to incarceration, acquisition of relevant skills, changes in expressed motivation, and various other relevant considerations.)

The field does not yet have validated methods for identifying youth who will continue offending and respond unfavorably to rehabilitation. This has been presented in terms such as "desistant versus life-course persistent" or callous/unemotional characteristics that presage the development of the full-blown psychopathy. Further research is needed in this area, and longitudinal designs appear to be one of the most effective approaches to carrying it out. But a number of other questions could be addressed as well, including the course and duration of change in youth who respond favorably to interventions. Data in these areas would contribute to the development of validated methods for answering questions on risk, amenability, and sophistication-maturity that are so important in transfer decisions (Grisso, 2010–11).

CONDUCT RESEARCH ON SPECIALIZED FORENSIC ASSESSMENT MEASURES

Specialized forensic assessment measures, addressing functional-legal capacities such as risk, need, amenability to treatment, and sophistication-maturity, offer significant advances in the ability of psychological and psychiatric evaluators to provide information to the court that is accurate, relevant, and supported by applicable scientific research. As research on existing measures continues, and as new measures are developed, this ability will continue to improve. It is among the most important areas of focus for research relevant to the evaluation of disposition and transfer.

Existing validated measures of risk and need, the SAVRY and LS/CMI, should continue to undergo validation research with juveniles of various ages and racial and ethnic backgrounds and both sexes. Their "field reliability" should be investigated as well, to determine whether they are subject to the kind of adversarial bias that can affect their results depending on whether the evaluator has been retained by the defense or the prosecution. It may be that a gender-specific version of one or both of these measures should be developed. Alternatively, it is possible that the basic measure, supplemented by additional information on family, trauma, abuse, and behavioral health problems, will provide a reasonable appraisal of risk and needs for females.

More research is also needed on the RSTI. Such research would include appraising its predictive validity (with respect to re-offending), developing norms for sophistication-maturity to anticipate blended sentences (and thus young adult offenders), and examining its field properties, similar to the proposed studies of the field properties of the SAVRY and YLS/CMI.

INVESTIGATE THE RISK RELEVANCE OF FACTORS IN THE DOMAINS OF BEHAVIORAL HEALTH, CRIMINOGENIC RISK, AND BOTH

The question of the contribution of behavioral health interventions to juvenile rehabilitation is framed differently if reducing the risk of re-offending is the highest priority of such rehabilitation. If this assumption is made, then the question focuses on the impact of symptoms of anxiety, mood, and psychosis, for example, on the risk of re-offending among adolescents.

On health and humanitarian grounds, behavioral health problems that grossly interfere with behavior necessary in daily living, or may result in self-harm, should be treated. But the question of prioritizing rehabilitation resources based on the relation of symptoms to risk of re-offending and other antisocial behavior may be complex. Many behavioral health symptoms may not have a direct effect on raising this risk, but may moderate it. Moreover, some behavioral health symptoms do have a direct relationship with re-offense risk in adolescents. This debate is currently ongoing for adults, and research is needed to disentangle these relationships in a younger population—so that risk may be estimated most accurately, and rehabilitative interventions designed and implemented most effectively with crossover youth and others with significant behavioral health challenges that are not also criminogenic.

INVESTIGATE THE IMPACT OF INTERVENTIONS IN THE DOMAINS OF BEHAVIORAL HEALTH, CRIMINOGENIC RISK, AND BOTH

Do behavioral health services and criminogenic interventions indeed have positive impacts on each other? Various commentators (Grisso, 1998; Kruh & Brodsky, 1997; Mulvey, 1984) have advocated the development of a valid and reliable offender-to-treatment matching methodology. Although this would be a massive undertaking, it is probably the most effective approach to investigating the construct of juvenile amenability. Program evaluation research is needed to maintain, develop, and tailor intervention programs that match a youth's treatment and developmental needs (Penney & Moretti, 2005). This approach might also yield new prospects for youth who are considered "not amenable" or poorly responsive to most interventions.

CONDUCT ADDITIONAL RESEARCH IN THE AREA OF SOPHISTICATION-MATURITY

Sophistication-maturity is clearly the construct that is most in need of empirical research attention among those we have reviewed in this book. In what respects does this legal construct correspond to developmental constructs such as psycho-social maturity? Is sophistication-maturity moderated by demographic factors? If it differs across racial/ethnic or gender lines, how can this be addressed so that unintended bias is reduced or eliminated?

The measurement of sophistication-maturity also needs a response style component, so that its use in the field is not overly contaminated by inaccuracies in self-reporting. The measurement of human intelligence may provide a useful model for the development of a new omnibus measure of sophistication-maturity, involving measurement facilitated by performance of tasks and observations of behavior, and compared to various peer groups of interest, rather than relying primarily on self-reporting.

CONCLUSION

This chapter has provided recommendations for action in the areas of law and policy, practice, and research on the evaluation of juvenile disposition and transfer. We have tried to identify important and related recommendations stemming from converging theory, empirical evidence, and practice standards that appear in our earlier discussion throughout the book. To the extent we have succeeded, we hope this book will provide meaningful contributions to those who adjudicate, defend, prosecute, evaluate, and rehabilitate adolescents who become involved with the juvenile and criminal justice systems.

REFERENCES

8 U.S.C. §§ 5031–42 (2016).

43 C.J.S. *Infants* §§ 38, 41–42, 59–60, 142–145, 156–157, 166, 381, 389–393, 395–397, 475–478 (2016).

46 Am. Jur. 2d. *Juvenile Courts and Delinquent and Dependent Children* § 25–33, 45–47, 59, 63–65, 102, 104, 126–127 (2016).

Abbott, S., & Barnett, E. (2015). *The Crossover Youth Practice Model (CYPM): CYPM in brief: Behavioral health and crossover youth.* Retrieved from the Georgetown University, McCourt School of Public Policy, Center for Juvenile Justice Reform website: http://cjjr.georgetown.edu/wp-content/uploads/2015/08/CYPM-Behavioral-Health-Brief-Final-8_6_16.pdf?utm_content=kirk.heilbrun%40drexel.edu&utm_source=VerticalResponse&utm_medium=Email&utm_term=Read&utm_campaign=New%20Issue%20Brief%20on%20Behavioral%20Health%20%26%20Crossover%20Youthcontent.

Abbott-Chapman, J., Denholm, C., & Wyld, C. (2007). Pre-service professionals' constructs of adolescent risk-taking and approaches to risk management. *Journal of Sociology, 43*, 241–261.

Abram, K. M., Teplin, L. A., King, D. C., Longworth, S. L., Emanuel, K. M., Romero, E. G., *et al.* (2013). *PTSD, trauma, and comorbid psychiatric disorders in detained youth.* Juvenile Justice Bulletin. Washington, DC: US Department of Justice, Office of Justice Programs, Office of Juvenile Justice and Delinquency Prevention.

American Bar Association (1980). *Standards for juvenile justice.* Washington, DC: Author.

American Bar Association (1982). *Standards for juvenile justice.* Retrieved October 15, 2015 from http://www.americanbar.org/content/dam/aba/migrated/sections/criminaljustice/PublicDocuments/JJ_Standards_Summary_Analysis.authcheckdam.pdf.

American Bar Association (1984). *Criminal justice mental health standards.* Washington, DC: Author. Retrieved from http://www.americanbar.org/publications/criminal_justice_section_archive/crimjust_standards_mentalhealth_toc.html.

American Bar Association (2015). *Resolution. Model Act governing the confidentiality and expungement of juvenile delinquency records.* Retrieved from http://www.americanbar.org/content/dam/aba/administrative/house_of_delegates/resolutions/2015_hod_annual_meeting_103A.docx.

American Bar Association (2016). *Criminal justice mental health standards (revised).* Washington, DC: Author. Retrieved from http://www.americanbar.org/groups/criminal_justice/standards.html

American Bar Association and Institute of Judicial Administration (1981). *Standards of juvenile justice: A summary and analysis.* Retrieved from http://www.americanbar.org/content/dam/aba/migrated/sections/criminaljustice/PublicDocuments/JJ_Standards_Summary_Analysis.authcheckdam.pdf.

American Medical Association (2001). *Principles of medical ethics.* Retrieved from http://www.ama-assn.org/ama/pub/physician-resources/medical-ethics/code-medical-ethics/principles-medical-ethics.page.

American Psychiatric Association (2013a). *Principles of medical ethics with annotations especially applicable to psychiatry.* Retrieved from http://www.psychiatry.org/practice/ethics.

American Psychiatric Association (2013b). *Diagnostic and statistical manual of mental disorders* (5th ed.). Washington, DC: Author.

American Psychological Association (2010). *Ethical principles of psychologists and code of conduct.* Retrieved from http://www.apa.org/ethics/code/principles.pdf.

American Psychological Association (2013). Specialty guidelines for forensic psychology. *American Psychologist, 68*, 7–19. doi: 10.1037/a0029889

American Psychological Association, American Psychiatric Association, and National Association of Social Workers (2012). Brief for amicus curiae: *Miller v. Alabama* and *Jackson v. Hobbs*. Washington, DC: Author. Retrieved December 23, 2016 from http://www.apa.org/about/offices/ogc/amicus/miller-hobbs.pdf.

Andrews, D. A., & Bonta, J. (2010a). *The psychology of criminal conduct* (5th ed.) Cincinnati, OH: Anderson.

Andrews, D. A., & Bonta, J. (2010b). Rehabilitating criminal justice policy and practice. *Psychology, Public Policy, and Law, 16*, 39–55. doi: 10.1037/a0018362

Andrews, D., Bonta, J., & Hoge, R. (1990). Classification for effective rehabilitation: Rediscovering psychology. *Criminal Justice and Behavior, 17*, 19–52. http://dx.doi.org/10.1177/0093854890017001004

Andrews, D., Bonta, J., & Wormith, J.S. (2004). Level of Service/Case Management Inventory. North Tonawanda, NY: Multi-Health Systems.

Archer, R. & Baum, L. (2016) Forensic uses of clinical assessment instruments. In K. Heilbrun, D. DeMatteo, & N. Goldstein (eds), *APA handbook of psychology and juvenile justice* (pp. 425–443). Washington, DC: American Psychological Association.

Ashford, J. B. (1988). Assessing treatability in drug offenders. *Behavioral Sciences and the Law, 6*, 139–148.

Baglivio, M. T., & Epps, N. (2015). The interrelatedness of adverse childhood experiences among high-risk juvenile offenders. *Youth Violence and Juvenile Justice, 14*, 1–20. doi: 10.1177/1541204014566286

Baglivio, M., & Jackowski, K. (2013). Examining the validity of a juvenile offending risk assessment instrument across gender and race/ethnicity. *Youth Violence and Juvenile Justice, 11*, 26–43.

Barbot, B., & Hunter, S. R. (2012). Developmental changes in adolescence and risks for delinquency. In E. L. Grigorenko (ed.), *Handbook of juvenile forensic psychology and psychiatry* (pp. 11–34). New York: Springer.

Barnhorst, R. (2004). The youth criminal justice act: New directions and implementation issues. *Canadian Journal of Criminology and Criminal Justice, 46*, 231–250.

Barnoski, R. (2004, March). *Assessing risk for re-offense: Validating the Washington State Juvenile Court Assessment*. Retrieved from http://www.wsipp.wa.gov/RcportFile/869.

Barnoski, R., & Markhussen, S. (2005). Washington State Juvenile Court Assessment. In T. Grisso, T. Vincent, & D. Seagrave (eds), *Mental health screening and assessment in juvenile justice* (pp. 271–282). New York: Guilford Press.

Barnum, R. (1987). Clinical evaluation of juvenile defendants facing transfer to adult court. *Journal of the American Academy of Child and Adolescent Psychiatry, 26*, 922–925.

Barnum, R. (1990). Self-incrimination and denial in the juvenile transfer evaluation. *Bulletin of the American Academy of Psychiatry and the Law, 18*, 413–428.

Barriga, A., Sullivan-Cosetti, M., & Gibbs, J. (2009). Moral cognitive correlates of juvenile delinquents. *Criminal Behavior and Mental Health, 19*, 253–264.

Bartol, C. R., & Bartol, A. M. (2009). *Juvenile delinquency and antisocial behavior: A developmental perspective*. Upper Saddle River, NJ: Pearson Education.

Begle, A. M., Hanson, R. F., Danielson, C. K., McCart, M. R., Ruggiero, K. J., Amstadter, A. B., *et al.* (2011). Longitudinal pathways of victimization, substance use, and delinquency: Findings from the National Survey of Adolescents. *Additive Behaviors, 36*, 682–889. doi: 10.1016/j.addbeh.2010.12.026

Berkheiser, M. (2005). Capitalizing adolescence: Juvenile offenders on death row. *University of Miami Law Review, 59*, 135–202.

Beyth-Marom, R., Austin, L., Fischhoff, B., Palmgren, C., & Jacobs-Quadrel, M. (1993). Perceived consequences of risky behaviors: Adults and adolescents. *Developmental Psychology, 29*, 549–563.

Bilchik, S. (1999, Dec.). *Opening remarks (summary of proceedings).* National Assembly, Drugs, Alcohol Abuse, and the Criminal Offender, Washington, DC.

Bishop, D. M. (2009). Juvenile transfer in the United States. In J. Junger-Tas & F. Dünkel (eds), *Reforming juvenile justice* (pp. 85–104). New York: Springer.

Blakeman, I. (2009). The youth justice system of England and Wales. In G. Lord (ed.), *Resource material series no. 78* (pp. 80–93). Retrieved from http://www.unafei.or.jp/english/pdf/RS_No78/No78_00All.pdf.

Boccaccini, M. T., Murrie, D. C., Clark, J., & Cornell, D. (2008). Describing, diagnosing and naming psychopathy: How do youth psychopathy labels influence jurors? *Behavioral Sciences and the Law, 26*, 487–510. doi: 10.1002/bsl.821

Borum, R. (2006). Assessing risk for violence among juvenile offenders. In S. N. Sparta & G. P. Koocher (eds), *Forensic mental health assessment of children and adolescents* (pp. 11–29). New York: Oxford University Press.

Borum, R., & Grisso, T. (2007). Developmental considerations for forensic assessment in delinquency cases. In A. M. Goldstein (ed.), *Forensic psychology: Emerging topics and expanding roles* (pp. 553–570). Hoboken, NJ: Wiley.

Borum, R., & Verhaagen, D. (2006). *Assessing and managing violence risk in juveniles*. New York: Guilford.

Borum, R., Bartel, P. A., & Forth, A. E. (2005). Structured assessment of violence risk in youth. In T. Grisso, G. Vincent, & D. Seagrave (eds), *Mental health screening and assessment in juvenile justice* (pp. 311–323). New York: Guilford Press.

Borum, R., Bartel, P., & Forth, A. (2006). *Manual for the Structured Assessment for Violence Risk in Youth (SAVRY)*. Odessa, FL: Psychological Assessment Resources.

Borum, R., Lodewijks, H., Bartel, P. A., & Forth, A. E. (2010). Structured Assessment of Violence Risk in Youth (SAVRY). In R. K. Otto & K. Douglas (eds), *Handbook of violence risk assessment* (pp. 63–80). New York: Routledge.

Brannen, D. N., Salekin, R. T., Zapf, P. A., Salekin, K. L., Kubak, F. A., & DeCoster, J. (2006). Transfer to adult court: A national study of how juvenile court judges weigh pertinent Kent criteria. *Psychology, Public Policy, and Law, 12*, 332–355. doi: 10.1037/1076-8971.12.3.332

Brief for American Psychological Association & Missouri Psychological Association as Amici Curiae Supporting Respondent, *Roper v. Simmons*, 542 U.S. 551 (2005) (No. 03-633).

Brief for American Psychological Association, American Psychiatric Association & National Association of Social Workers as Amici Curiae Supporting Petitioners, *Miller v. Alabama,* 132 S. Ct. 2455 (2012) (Nos. 10-9646, 10-9647), 2012 WL 174239.

Brodsky, S. L. (1991). *Testifying in court: Guidelines and maxims for the expert witness*. Washington DC: American Psychological Association.

Brodsky, S. L. (1999). *The expert expert witness: More maxims and guidelines for testifying in court*. Washington, DC: American Psychological Association.

Brodsky, S. L. (2004). *Coping with cross-examination and other pathways to effective testimony*. Washington, DC: American Psychological Association.

Brodsky, S. L. (2013). *Testifying in court: Guidelines and maxims for the expert witness* (2nd ed.). Washington, DC: American Psychological Association.

Brogan, L., Haney-Caron, E., NeMoyer, A., & DeMatteo, D. (2015). Applying the Risk-Needs-Responsivity (RNR) model to juvenile justice. *Criminal Justice Review*, *40*, 277–302.

Butcher, J., Williams, C., Graham, J., Archer, R., Tellegen, R., Ben-Porath, Y., & Kaemmer, B. (1992). *MMPI-A: Manual for administration, scoring and interpretation*. Minneapolis, MN: University of Minnesota Press.

Caldwell, M., Skeem, J., Salekin, R., & Van Rybroek, G. (2006). Treatment response of adolescent offenders with psychopathy features: A 2-year follow-up. *Criminal Justice and Behavior*, *33*, 571–596. doi: 10.1177/0093854806288176

Casey, B. J. (2015). Beyond simple models of self-control to circuit-based accounts of adolescent behavior. *Annual Review of Psychology*, *66*, 295–319.

Casey, B. J., Jones, R. M., & Hare, T. A. (2008). The adolescent brain. *Annals of the New York Academy of Sciences*, *1124*, 111–126.

Cauffman, E., & Woolard, J. (1999). "The Future Outlook Inventory." Unpublished manuscript.

Cauffman, E., & Steinberg, L. (2000). (Im)maturity of judgment in adolescence: Why adolescents may be less culpable than adults. *Behavioral Sciences and the Law*, *18*, 741–760. doi: 10.1002/bsl.416

Cauffman, E., Lexcen, F. J., Goldweber, A., Shulman, E. P., & Grisso, T. (2007). Gender differences in mental health symptoms among delinquent and community youth. *Youth Violence and Juvenile Justice*, *5*, 287–307. doi: 10.1177/1541204007301292

Cauffman, E., Shulman, E., Steinberg, L., Claus, E., Banich, M., Graham, S., & Woolard, J. (2010). Age differences in affective decision making as indexed by performance on the Iowa Gambling Task. *Developmental Psychology, 46*, 193–207.

Cauffman, E., Skeem, J., Dmitrieva, J., & Cavanagh, C. (2016). Comparing the stability of psychopathy scores in adolescents versus adults: How often is "fledgling psychopathy" misdiagnosed? *Psychology, Public Policy, and Law, 22*, 77–91. doi: 10.1037/law0000078.

Celinska, K., Furrer, S., & Cheng, C. (2013). An outcome-based evaluation of functional family therapy for youth with behavioral problems. *OJJDP Journal of Juvenile Justice, 2*, 23–36.

Chambers, R. A., Taylor, J. R., & Potenza, M. N. (2014). Developmental neurocircuitry of motivation in adolescence: A critical period of addiction vulnerability. *American Journal of Psychiatry, 160*, 1041–1052.

Champion, D. J., Merlo, A. V., & Benekos, P. J. (2013). *The juvenile justice system: Delinquency, processing, and the law* (7th ed.). Boston, MA: Pearson Education.

Chandler, M., Lalonde, C., Sokol, B., & Hallett, D. (2003). Personal persistence, identity development, and suicide. *Monographs of the Society for Research in Child Development, 68*. Retrieved from http://web.uvic.ca/~lalonde/manuscripts/2003-Monograph.pdf.

Chapin, D. A., & Griffin, P. A. (2005). Juvenile diversion. In K. Heilbrun, N. E. S. Goldstein, & R. E. Redding (eds), *Juvenile delinquency: Prevention, assessment, and intervention* (pp. 161–178). New York: Oxford University Press.

Chapman, J. F. (2012). The juvenile forensic court clinic in theory and practice. In E. L. Grigorenko (ed.), *Handbook of juvenile forensic psychology and psychiatry* (pp. 201–214). New York: Springer.

Chassin, L., Mansion, A., Nichter, B., & Pandika, D. (2016). Substance use and substance use disorders as risk factors for juvenile offending. In K. Heilbrun, D. DeMatteo, & N. E. S. Goldstein (eds), *APA handbook of psychology and juvenile justice* (pp. 277–305). Washington, DC: American Psychological Association. http://dx.doi.org/10.1037/14643-013

Cheesman, F. (2011). *A decade of NCSC research on blended sentencing of juvenile offenders: What have we learned about "who gets a second chance*?" Retrieved from National Center for States Courts website at http://www.ncsc.org/~/media/Microsites/Files/Future%20Trends/Author%20PDFs/Cheesman.ashx.

Chein, J., Albert, D., O'Brien, L., Uckert, K., & Steinberg, L. (2011). Peers increase adolescent risk taking by enhancing activity in the brain's reward circuitry. *Developmental Science, 14*, F1–F10.

Chen, D. R., & Salekin, R. T. (2012). Transfer to adult court: Enhancing clinical forensic evaluations and informing policy. In E. L. Grigorenko (ed.), *Handbook of juvenile forensic psychology and psychiatry* (pp. 105–126). New York: Springer. doi: 10.1007/978-1-4614-0905-2_8

Childs, K. K., Frick, P. J., & Gottlieb, K. (2016). Sex differences in the measurement invariance and factors that influence structured judgments of risk using the Structured Assessment of Violence Risk in Youth (SAVRY). *Youth Violence and Juvenile Justice, 14*, 1–17. doi: 10.1177/1541204014547722

Cleckley, H. (1941). *The mask of sanity*. St Louis, MO: Mosby.

Cohen, A. O., & Casey, B. J. (2014). Rewiring juvenile justice: The intersection of developmental neuroscience and legal policy. *Trends in Cognitive Sciences, 18*, 63–65.

Cohen, A., Breiner, K., Steinberg, L., Bonnie, R., Scott, E., Taylor-Thompson, K., … Casey, B. J. (2016). When is an adolescent an adult? Assessing cognitive control in emotional and nonemotional contexts. *Psychological Science, 27*, 549–562.

Cohen, D., & Strayer, J. (1996). Empathy in conduct-disordered and comparison youth. *Developmental Psychology, 32*, 988–998.

Cohen-Gilbert, J. E., & Thomas, K. M. (2013). Inhibitory control during emotional distraction across adolescence and early adulthood. *Child Development, 84*, 1954–1966.

Colwell, L. H., Cruise, K. R., Guy, L. S., McCoy, W. K., Fernandez, K., & Ross, H. H. (2005). The influence of psychosocial maturity on male juvenile offenders' comprehension and understanding of the Miranda warning. *Journal of the American Academy of Psychiatry and the Law, 33*, 444–454.

Committee on Ethical Guidelines for Forensic Psychologists. (1991). Specialty guidelines for forensic psychologists. *Law and Human Behavior, 15*, 655–665.

Conroy, M. A. (2012). Assessing juveniles for risk of violence. In E. L. Grigorenko (ed.), *Handbook of juvenile forensic psychology and psychiatry* (pp. 227–238). New York: Springer.

Conroy, M. A., & Murrie, D. (2007). *Forensic assessment of violence risk: A guide for risk assessment and risk management*. Hoboken, NJ: John Wiley & Sons.

Cornell, D., & Heilbrun, A. (2016). School-based risk factors, bullying, and threat assessment. In K. Heilbrun, D. DeMatteo, & N. E. S. Goldstein (eds), *APA handbook of psychology and juvenile justice* (pp. 233–255). Washington, DC: American Psychological Association. http://dx.doi.org/10.1037/14643-011

Cottle, C., Lee, J., & Heilbrun, K. (2001). The prediction of criminal recidivism in juveniles. *Criminal Justice and Behavior, 28*, 367–394.

Cox, J. M., Goldstein, N. E. S., Dolores, J., Zelechoski, A. D., & Messenheimer, S. (2012). The impact of juveniles' ages and levels of psychosocial maturity on judges' opinions about adjudicative competence. *Law and Human Behavior*, *36*, 21–27. doi: 10.1037/h0093953

Crites, E. L., & Taxman, F. S. (2013). The responsivity principle: Determining the appropriate program and dosage to match risk and needs. In F. S. Taxman & A. Pattavina (eds), *Simulation strategies to reduce recidivism* (pp. 143–166). New York: Springer.

Cruise, K. R., Fernandez, K., McCoy, W. K., Guy, L. S., Colwell, L. H., & Douglas, T. R. (2008). The influence of psychosocial maturity on adolescent offenders' delinquent behavior. *Youth Violence and Juvenile Justice*, *6*, 178–194. doi: 10.1177/1541204007313229

Cruise, K., Morin, S., & Affleck, K. (2016). Residential interventions with justice-involved youths. In K. Heilbrun, D. DeMatteo, & N. E. S. Goldstein (eds), *APA handbook of psychology and juvenile justice* (pp. 611–639). Washington, DC: American Psychological Association. http://dx.doi.org/10.1037/14643-028

Curtis, N. M., Ronan, K. R., & Borduin, C. M. (2004). Multisystemic treatment: A meta-analysis of outcome studies. *Journal of Family Psychology*, *18*, 411–419.

Daly, B., DeMatteo, D., Hildebrand, A., Baker, C., & Fisher, J. (in press). Psychosocial treatment and prevention in the adolescent years: Evidence-based psychosocial treatment and prevention programs in the adolescent period (from middle to late adolescence) for ODD and CD. In J. E. Lochman & W. Matthys (eds), *The Wiley handbook of disruptive and impulse-control disorders*. Hoboken, NJ: Wiley.

Daly, B., Hildebrand, A., Haney-Caron, E., Goldstein, N., Galloway, M., & DeMatteo, D. (2016). Disrupting the school-to-prison pipeline: Strategies to reduce the risk of school-based zero tolerance policies resulting in juvenile justice involvement. In K. Heilbrun, D. DeMatteo, & N. E. S. Goldstein (eds), *APA handbook of psychology and juvenile justice* (pp. 257–276). Washington, DC: American Psychological Association. doi: 10.1037/14643-012

Dattilio, F. M., & Fromm, L. (2011). Juvenile delinquency and decertification. In E. Y. Drogin, F. M. Dattilio, R. L. Sadoff, & T. G. Gutheil, *Handbook of forensic assessment: Psychological and psychiatric perspectives* (pp. 227–254). Hoboken, NJ: John Wiley & Sons. http://dx.doi.org/10.1002/9781118093399.ch11

Davis, S. M. (2016). *Rights of juveniles 2d: The juvenile justice system*. New York: Thomson Reuters.

Dawes, R. M., Faust, D., & Meehl, P. E. (1989). Clinical versus actuarial judgment. *Science, 243*, 1668–1674

De La Cuesta, J. L. (2006) The new Spanish penal system on delinquency. In E. L. Jensen & J. Jepsen (eds), *Juvenile law violators, human rights, and the development of new juvenile justice systems* (pp. 99–113). Portland, OR: Hart.

deKemp, R., Overbeek, G., De Wied, M., Engels, R., & Scholt, R. (2007). Early adolescent empathy, parental support, and antisocial behavior. *Journal of Genetic Psychology, 168*, 5–18.

del Carmen, R. V., & Trulson, C. R. (2006). *Juvenile justice: The system, process, and law*. Belmont, CA: Thomson Wadsworth.

DeLisi, M., Beaver, K. M., Vaughn, M. G., Trulson, C. R., Kosloski, A. E., Drury, A. J., ... Wright, J. P. (2010). Personality, gender, and self-control theory revisited: Results from a sample of institutionalized juvenile delinquents. *Applied Psychology in Criminal Justice, 6*, 31–46.

DeMatteo, D., & Marczyk, G. (2005). Risk factors, protective factors, and the prevention of antisocial behavior among juveniles. In K. Heilbrun, N. E. S. Goldstein, & R. E. Redding (eds), *Juvenile delinquency: Prevention, assessment, and intervention* (pp. 19–44). New York: Oxford University Press.

DeMatteo, D., Edens, J. F., & Hart, A. (2010). The use of measures of psychopathy in violence risk assessment. In R. K. Otto & K. S. Douglas (eds), *Handbook of violence risk assessment* (pp. 19–40). New York: Routledge.

DeMatteo, D., Haney-Caron, E., Mowle, E., & Edens, J. F. (in press). The use of measures of psychopathy in violence risk assessment. In R. K. Otto & K. S. Douglas (eds), *Handbook of violence risk assessment* (2nd ed.). New York: Routledge/Taylor & Francis.

DeMatteo, D., Wolbransky, M., & LaDuke, C. (2016). Risk assessment with juveniles. In K. Heilbrun, D. DeMatteo, & N. E. S. Goldstein (eds), *APA handbook of psychology and juvenile justice*. Washington, DC: American Psychological Association. doi: 10.1037/14643-017

Development Services Group, Inc. (2015). *Status offenders*. Retrieved from Office of Juvenile Justice and Delinquency Prevention website: http://www.ojjdp.gov/mpg/litreviews/Deinstituionalization_of_Status_Offenders.pdf.

Dishion, T. J. (2012). Juvenile forensic psychology and psychiatry: The movement toward data-based innovations. In E. L. Grigorenko (ed.), *Handbook of juvenile forensic psychology and psychiatry* (pp. 579–584). New York: Springer.

Dishion, T. J., & Andrews, D. W. (1995). Preventing escalation in problem behaviors with high-risk young adolescents: Immediate and 1-year outcomes. *Journal of Consulting and Clinical Psychology*, *63*, 538–548.

Dishion, T. J., McCord, J., & Poulin, F. (1999). When interventions harm: Peer groups and problem behavior. *American Psychologist*, *54*, 755–764.

Dohrn, B. (2002). The school, the child, and the court. In M. K. Rosenheim, F. E. Zimring, D. S. Tanenhaus, & B. Dohrn (eds), *A century of juvenile justice* (pp. 267–309). Chicago: University of Chicago Press.

Dosenbach, N., Nardos, B., Cohen, A., Fair, D., Power, J., Church, J, … Schlaggar, B. (2010). Prediction of individual brain maturity using fMRI. *Science*, *329*, 1358–1361. http://dx.doi.org/10.1126/science.1194144

Dowden, C., & Andrews, D. A. (1999). What works in young offender treatment: A meta-analysis. *Forum on Corrections Research*, *11* (2), 21–24.

Drake, E. K., Aos, S., & Miller, M. G. (2009). Evidence-based public policy options to reduce crime and criminal justice costs: Implications in Washington State. *Victims and Offenders*, *4*, 170–196. doi: 10.1080/15564880802612615

Dreyfuss, M., Caudle, K., Drysdale, A. T., Johnston, N. E., Cohen, A. O., Somerville, L. H., … Casey, B. J. (2014). Teens impulsively react rather than retreat from threat. *Developmental Neuroscience*, *36*, 220–227.

Dunford, F. W., Osgood, D. W., & Weichselbaum, H. F. (1982). *National evaluation of diversion projects: Executive summary*. Washington, DC: Office of Juvenile Justice and Delinquency Prevention.

Dünkel, F. (2006). Juvenile justice in Germany. In E. L. Jensen & J. Jepsen (eds), *Juvenile law violators, human rights, and the development of new juvenile justice systems* (pp. 115–153). Portland, OR: Hart.

Dünkel, F. (2015). Juvenile justice and crime policy in Europe. In F. E. Zimring, M. Langer, & D. S. Tanenhaus (eds), *Juvenile justice in global perspective* (pp. 9–62). New York: New York University Press.

Dupée, S. M. (2002). Juveniles tried as adults. In N. G. Ribner (ed.), *The California School of Professional Psychology handbook of juvenile forensic psychology* (pp. 77–92). San Francisco, CA: Jossey-Bass.

Eaton, D. K., Kann, L., Kinchen, S., Shanklin, S., Ross, J., Hawkins, J., … Wechsler, H. (2008). Youth risk behavior surveillance—United States, 2007. *Morbidity and Mortality Weekly Report 57*, 1–131. Retrieved from http://www.cdc.gov/mmwr/preview/mmwrhtml/ss5704a1.htm.

Edelman, P. (2002). American government and the politics of youth. In M. K. Rosenheim, F. E. Zimring, D. S. Tanenhaus, & B. Dohrn (eds), *A century of juvenile justice* (pp. 310–338). Chicago: University of Chicago Press.

Edens, J. F., Campbell, J. S., & Weir, J. M. (2007). Youth psychopathy and criminal recidivism: A meta-analysis of the psychopathy checklist measures. *Law and Human Behavior, 31*, 53–75.

Elliott, D. S. (ed.) (1998). *Blueprints for violence prevention: Multidimensional treatment foster care*. Denver, CO: C & M Press.

Elliott, D. S., Huizinga, D., and Morse, B. (1986). Self-reported violent offending: A descriptive analysis of juvenile violent offenders and their offending careers. *Journal of Interpersonal Violence, 1*, 472–514.

Elrod, P., & Ryder, R. S. (2011). *Juvenile justice: A social, historical, and legal perspective*. Sudbury, MA: Jones & Bartlett.

Erikson, E. (1968). *Identity: Youth and crisis*. New York: W. W. Norton.

Ernst, M., & Spear, L. P. (2009). Reward systems. In M. De Haan & M. R. Gunnar (eds), *Handbook of developmental social neuroscience* (pp. 324–341). New York: Guilford Press.

Ernst, M., Nelson, E. E., Jazbec, S., McClure, E. B., Monk, C. S., Leibenluft, E., ... Pine, D. S. (2005). Amygdala and nucleus accumbens in responses to receipt and omission of gains in adults and adolescents. *Neuroimage, 25*, 1279–1291.

Ernst, M., Pine, D. S., & Hardin, M. (2006). Triadic model of the neurobiology of motivated behavior in adolescence. *Psychological Medicine, 36*, 299–312.

Ewing, C. P. (1990). Juveniles or adults? Forensic assessment of juveniles considered for trial in criminal court. *Forensic Reports, 3*, 3–13.

Fabian, J. M. (2011). Applying *Roper v. Simmons* in juvenile transfer and waiver proceedings: A legal and neuroscientific inquiry. *International Journal of Offender Therapy and Comparative Criminology, 55*, 732–755.

Fagan, J. (1995). Separating the men from the boys: The comparative advantage of juvenile versus criminal court sanctions on recidivism among adolescent felony offenders. In J. Howell, K. Krisberg, J. Hawkins, & J. Wilson (eds), *Serious, violent and chronic juvenile offenders: A sourcebook* (pp. 238–260). Thousand Oaks, CA: Sage.

Fair, D., Dosenbach, N., Church, J., Cohen, A., Brahmbhatt, S., Miezin, F., ... Schlaggar, B. (2007). Development of distinct control networks through segregation and integration. *Proceedings of the National Academy of Sciences, USA, 104*, 13507–13512. http://dx.doi.org/10.1073/pnas.0705843104

Farrington, D. P. (1998). Predictors, causes, and correlates of male youth violence. *Crime and Justice, 24*, 421–475l.

Farrington, D. P., & Hawkins, D. (1991). Predicting participation, early onset and later persistence in officially recorded offending. *Criminal Behavior and Mental Health, 1*, 1–33.

Farrington, D. P., & Welsh, B. C. (2006). A half century of randomized experiments on crime and justice. *Crime and Justice*, *34*, 55–132. doi: 10.1086/500057

Fazel, S., Singh, J. P., Doll, H., & Grann, M. (2012). Use of risk assessment instruments to predict violence and antisocial behaviour in 73 samples involving 24,827 people: Systematic review and meta-analysis. *BMJ*, *345*, e4692.

Feld, B. C. (1988). The juvenile court meets the principle of offense: Punishment, treatment, and the difference it makes. *Boston University Law Review*, *68*, 821–915.

Feld, B. C. (2003). Competence, culpability, and punishment: Implications of *Atkins* for executing and sentencing adolescents. *Hofstra Law Review*, *32*, 463–552.

Feld, B. C. (2006). The inherent tension of social welfare and criminal social control: Policy lessons from the American juvenile court experience. In E. L. Jensen & J. Jepsen (eds), *Juvenile law violators, human rights, and the development of new juvenile justice systems* (pp. 407–442). Portland, OR: Hart.

Feldman, S., & Weinberger, D. (1994). Self-restraint as a mediator of family influence on boys' delinquent behaviour: A longitudinal study. *Child Development*, *65*, 195–211.

Figner, B., Mackinlay, R. J., Wilkening, F., & Weber, E. U. (2009). Affective and deliberative processes in risky choice: Age differences in risk taking in the Columbia Card Task. *Journal of Experimental Psychology: Learning, Memory, and Cognition*, *35*, 709–730.

Figurelli, G. A., Hartman, B. W., & Kowalsky, F. X., Jr (1994). Assessment of change in scores on personal control orientation and use of drugs and alcohol of adolescents who participate in a cognitively oriented pretreatment intervention. *Psychological Reports*, *75*, 939–944.

Fischer, K., & Bidell, T. (2006). Dynamic development of action and thought. In W. Damon & R. Lerner (eds), *Handbook of child psychology*, Vol. 1 (pp. 313–399). Hoboken, NJ: Wiley.

Fisher, P. A., & Chamberlain, P. (2000). Multidimensional treatment foster care: A program for intensive parenting, family support, and skill building. *Journal of Emotional and Behavioral Disorders*, *8*, 155–164.

Flannery, D. J., & Williams, L. (1999). Effective youth violence prevention. In T. Gullotta & S. J. McElhaney (eds), *Violence in homes and communities: Prevention, intervention, and treatment*. Thousand Oaks, CA: Sage.

Forth, A., Kosson, D., & Hare, R. (2003). *The Hare Psychopathy Checklist: Youth Version, Technical manual*. North Tonawanda, NY: Multi-Health Systems.

Foussard, C., & Melotti, G. (2016). *Addressing juvenile justice priorities in the Asia-Pacific region*. Retrieved from http://www.oijj.org/sites/default/files/oijj_asia-pacific_council_2016.pdf.

Fox, B., Perez, N., Cass, E., Baglivio, M., & Epps, N. (2015). Trauma changes everything: Examining the relationship between adverse childhood experiences and serious, violent, and chronic juvenile offenders. *Child Abuse and Neglect*, 46, 163–173. doi: 10.1016/j.chiabu.2015.01.011

Frick, P., & White, S. (2008). Research review: The importance of callous-unemotional traits for the development of aggressive and antisocial behavior. *Journal of Child Psychology and Psychiatry*, *49*, 359–375. doi: 10.1111/j.1469-7610.2007.01862.x

Fried, C. S., & Reppucci, N. D. (2001). Criminal decision making: The development of adolescent judgment, criminal responsibility, and culpability. *Law and Human Behavior*, *25*, 45–61. doi: 10.1023/A:1005639909226

Furdella, J., & Puzzanchera, C. (2015). *Delinquency cases in juvenile court, 2013*. Washington, DC: Office of Juvenile Justice and Delinquency Prevention.

Gaa, J. P. (1977). The effect of individual goal-setting conferences on academic achievement and modification of locus of control orientation. *Psychology in the Schools*, *16*, 591–598.

Galvan, A., Hare, T. A., Parra, C. E., Penn, J., Voss, H., Glover, G., & Casey, B. J. (2006). Earlier development of the accumbens relative to orbitofrontal cortex might underlie risk taking behavior in adolescents. *Journal of Neuroscience*, *26*, 6885–6892.

Gammelgard, M., Weizmann-Henelius, G., Koivisto, A., Eronen, M., & Kaltiala-Heino, R. (2012). Gender differences in violence risk profiles. *Journal of Forensic Psychiatry and Psychology*, *23*, 76–94. doi: 10.1080/14789949.2011.639898

Gardner, M. (2014). *Understanding juvenile law* (4th ed.). New Providence, NJ: Matthew Bender.

Gardner, M., & Steinberg, L. (2005). Peer influence on risk taking, risk preference, and risky decision making in adolescence and adulthood: An experimental study. *Developmental Psychology*, *41*, 625–635.

Geier, C. F., Terwilliger, R., Teslovich, T., Velanova, K., & Luna, B. (2010). Immaturities in reward processing and its influence on inhibitory control in adolescence. *Cerebral Cortex*, *20*, 1613–1629.

Gendreau, P., Little, T., & Goggin, C. (1996). A meta-analysis of the predictors of adult offender recidivism: What works! *Criminology*, *34*, 575–608. doi: 10.1111/j.1745-9125.1996.tb01220.x

Gillen, C. T. A., MacDougall, E. A. M., Salekin, R. T., & Forth, A. E. (2015). The validity of the Risk-Sophistication-Treatment Inventory–Abbreviated (RSTI-A): Initial evidence in support of a measure designed for juvenile evaluations. *Psychology, Public Policy, and Law, 21*, 205–212. doi: 10.1037/law0000044

Giorgi-Guarnieri, D., Janofsky, J., Keram, E., Lawsky, S, Merideth, P., Mossman, D., Schwartz-Watts, D., Scott, C., Thompson, J., & Zonana, H. (2002). American Academy of Psychiatry and the Law. AAPL practice guideline for forensic evaluation of defendants raising the insanity defense. *Journal of the American Academy of Psychiatry and the Law*, 30, S3–S40. PMID:12099305

Godwin, C. D., & Helms, J. L. (2002). Statistics and trends in juvenile justice and forensic psychology. In N. G. Ribner (ed.), *The California School of Professional Psychology handbook of juvenile forensic psychology* (pp. 1–28). San Francisco, CA: Jossey-Bass.

Gogtay, N., Giedd, J., Lusk, L., Hayaski, K., Greenstein, D., Vaituzis, A.C., … Thompson, P. (2004). Dynamic mapping of human cortical development during childhood through early adulthood. *Proceedings of the National Academy of Sciences, 101*, 8174–8179. doi: 10.1073/pnas.0402680101

Gold, L., Anfang, S., Drokteinis, A., Metzner, J., Price, M., Wall, B., … Zonana, H. (2008). AAPL practice guideline for the forensic evaluation of psychiatric disability. *Journal of the American Academy of Psychiatry and the Law, 36*, S3–50.

Golden, C. (1978). *A manual for the clinical and experimental use of the Stroop Color and Word Test*. Available at: http://nsuworks.nova.edu/cps_facbooks/47.

Goldstein, A. M. (ed.). (2003). *Handbook of psychology, Vol. 11: Forensic psychology*. Hoboken, NJ: Wiley. http://dx.doi.org/10.1002/0471264385.wei1101

Goldstein, A. M. (ed.). (2007). *Forensic psychology: Emerging topics and expanding roles*. Hoboken, NJ: Wiley. http://dx.doi.org/10.1300/J158v07n02_01

Goldstein, N., Condie, L., Kalbeitzer, R., Osman, D., & Geier, J. (2003a). Juvenile offenders' confessions: Risk factors and recommendations. *Law and Human Behavior, 34*, 3–38. doi: 10.1007/s10979-009-9188-6

Goldstein, N., Condie, L., Kalbeitzer, R., Osman, D., & Geier, J. (2003b). Juvenile offenders' *Miranda* rights comprehension and self-reported likelihood of false confessions. *Assessment, 10*, 359–368. doi: 10.1177/1073191103259535

Goldstein, N., Kelley, S. M., Peterson, L., Brogan, L., Zelle, H., & Riggs Romaine, C. (2016). Evaluation of *Miranda* waiver capacity. In K. Heilbrun, D. DeMatteo, & N. E. S. Goldstein (eds), *APA handbook of psychology and juvenile justice* (pp. 467–488). Washington, DC: American Psychological Association. http://dx.doi.org/10.1037/14643-022

Greenberger, E., & Sorenson, A. B. (1974). Toward a concept of psychosocial maturity. *Journal of Youth and Adolescence, 3*, 329–358. doi: 10.1007/BF02214746

Greenberger, E., Josselson, R., Knerr, C., & Knerr, B. (1975). The measurement and structure of psychosocial maturity. *Journal of Youth and Adolescence, 4*, 127–143. doi: 10.1007/BF01537437

Grieger, L., & Hosser, D. (2014). Which risk factors are really predictive? An analysis of Andrews and Bonta's "Central Eight" risk factors for recidivism in German youth correctional facility inmates. *Criminal Justice and Behavior, 41*, 613–634.

Griffin, P. (2008). *Different from adults: An updated analysis of juvenile transfer with recommendations for reform*. Pittsburgh, PA: National Center for Juvenile Justice.

Griffin, P., & Torbet, P. (2002). *Desktop guide to good juvenile probation practice*. Pittsburgh, PA: National Center for Juvenile Justice.

Griffin, P., Addie, S., Adams, B., & Firestine, K. (2011). *Trying juveniles as adults: An analysis of state transfer laws and reporting*. Washington, DC: Office of Juvenile Justice and Delinquency Prevention.

Grigorenko, E. L. (ed.). (2012) *Handbook of juvenile forensic psychology and psychiatry*. New York: Springer.

Grisso, T. (1986). *Evaluating competencies: Forensic assessments and instruments*. New York: Plenum. http://dx.doi.org/10.1007/978-1-4899-5046-8

Grisso, T. (1998). *Forensic evaluations of juveniles*. Sarasota, FL: Professional Resource Press.

Grisso, T. (2000). Forensic clinical evaluations related to waiver of jurisdiction. In J. Fagan & F. Zimring (eds), *The changing borders of juvenile justice* (pp. 321–352). Chicago: University of Chicago Press.

Grisso, T. (2003a). *Evaluating competencies: Forensic assessments and instruments* (2nd ed.). New York: Kluwer Academic/Plenum.

Grisso, T. (2003b). Forensic evaluation in delinquency cases. In A. M. Goldstein, *Handbook of psychology: Volume 11: Forensic psychology* (pp. 315–334). Hoboken, NJ: John Wiley & Sons.

Grisso, T. (2005). *Evaluating juveniles' adjudicative competence: A guide for clinical practice*. Sarasota, FL: Professional Resource Press.

Grisso, T. (2010–11). Clinicians' transfer evaluations: How well can they assist judicial discretion? *Louisiana State University Law Review, 71*, 157–189.

Grisso, T. (2013). *Forensic evaluation of juveniles* (2nd ed.). Sarasota, FL: Professional Resource Press.

Grisso, T., & Kavanaugh, A. (2016). Prospects for developmental evidence in juvenile sentencing based on *Miller v. Alabama*. *Psychology, Public Policy, and Law*, *22*, 235–249. http://dx.doi.org/10.1037/law0000090

Grisso, T., Vincent, G., & Seagrave, D. (eds). (2005). *Mental health screening and assessment in juvenile justice*. New York: Guilford Press.

Grose-Fifer, J., Rodrigues, A., Hoover, S., & Zottoli, T. (2013). Attentional capture by emotional faces in adolescence. *Advances in Cognitive Psychology*, *9*, 81–91.

Grossberg, M. (2002). Changing conceptions of child welfare in the United States, 1820–1935. In M. K. Rosenheim, F. E. Zimring, D. S. Tanenhaus, & B. Dohrn (eds), *A century of juvenile justice* (pp. 3–41). Chicago: University of Chicago Press.

Grove, W., & Meehl, P. (1996). Comparative efficiency of informal (subjective, impressionistic) and formal (mechanical, algorithmic) prediction procedures: The clinical-statistical controversy. *Psychology, Public Policy, and Law*, *2*, 293–323.

Grove, W., Zald, D., Lebow, B., Snitz, B., & Nelson, C. (2000). Clinical versus mechanical prediction: A meta-analysis. *Psychological Assessment*, *12*, 19–30.

Guerra, N. G., Hoge, R. D., & Boxer, P. (2008). Introduction. In R. D. Hoge, N. G. Guerra, & P. Boxer (eds), *Treating the juvenile offender* (pp. 1–14). New York: Guilford Press.

Guerra, N. G., Williams, K. R., Tolan, P. H., & Modecki, K. L. (2008). Theoretical and research advances in understanding the causes of juvenile offending. In R. D. Hoge, N. G. Guerra, & P. Boxer (eds), *Treating the juvenile offender* (pp. 54–78). New York: Guilford Press.

Guy, L. S., Nelson, R. J., Fusco-Morin, S. L., & Vincent, G. M. (2014). What do juvenile probation officers think of using the SAVRY and YLS/CMI for case management, and do they use the instruments properly? *International Journal of Forensic Mental Health*, *13*, 227–241.

Hahn, R., Fuqua-Whitley, D., Wethington, H., Lowy, J., McGowan, A., Liberman, A., Crosby, A., Fullilove, M., Johnson, R., Moscicki, E., Price, L., Snyder, S. R., Tuma, F., Cory, S., Stone, G., Mukhopadhaya, K., Chattopadhya, S., & Dahlberg, L. (2007). Effects on violence of laws and policies facilitating the transfer of youth from the juvenile to the adult justice system. *Morbidity and Mortality Weekly Report*, *56*, 1–11.

Hamilton, M. (2015). Risk-needs assessment: Constitutional and ethical challenges. *American Criminal Law Review, 52*, 231–286.

Hare, R. D. (2003). *The Hare Psychopathy Checklist–Revised (PCL-R)* (2nd ed.). Toronto, Canada: Multi-Health Systems.

Hare, T. A., Tottenham, N., Galvan, A., Voss, H. U., Glover, G. H., & Casey, B. J. (2008). Biological substrates of emotional reactivity and regulation in adolescence during an emotional go-no go task. *Biological Psychiatry, 63*, 927–934.

Harris, A. (2008). The social construction of "sophisticated" adolescents: How judges integrate juvenile and criminal justice decision-making models. *Journal of Contemporary Ethnography, 37*, 469–506. doi: 10.1177/0891241607309886

Hart, S., & Logan, C. (2011). Formulation of violence risk using evidence-based assessments: The structured professional judgment approach. In P. Sturmey & M. McMurran (eds), *Forensic case formulation* (pp. 83–106). Chichester: Wiley-Blackwell.

Hawkins, J. D., Herrenkohl, T. I., Farrington, D. P., Brewer, D., Catalano, R. F., & Harachi, T. W. (1998). A review of predictors of youth violence. In R. Loeber & D. P. Farrington (eds), *Serious and violent juvenile offenders: Risk factors and successful interventions* (pp. 106–146). Thousand Oaks, CA: Sage.

Hawkins, J. D., Herrenkohl, T. I., Farrington, D. P., Brewer, D., Catalano, R. F., Harachi, T. W., & Cothern, L. (2000). *Predictors of youth violence.* Juvenile Justice Bulletin. Washington, DC: Office of Juvenile Justice and Delinquency Prevention. Retrieved from US Department of Justice, Office of Justice Programs, Office of Juvenile Justice and Delinquency Prevention website: https://www.ncjrs.gov/pdffiles1/ojjdp/179065.pdf.

Haynie, D. (2002). Friendship networks and delinquency: The relative nature of peer delinquency. *Journal of Quantitative Criminology, 18*, 99–134.

Hechinger, S. R. (2011). Juvenile life without parole: An antidote to Congress's one-way criminal law ratchet? *New York University Review of Law and Social Change, 35*, 408–495.

Heilbrun, K. (2001). *Principles of forensic mental health assessment.* New York: Plenum.

Heilbrun, K. (2009). *Evaluation for risk of violence in adults.* New York: Oxford University Press.

Heilbrun, K., & DeMatteo, D. (2012). Toward establishing standards of practice in juvenile forensic mental health assessment. In E. L. Grigorenko (ed.), *Handbook of juvenile forensic psychology and psychiatry* (pp. 145–156). New York: Springer.

Heilbrun, K., & Locklair, B. (2016). Forensic assessment of juveniles. In K. Heilbrun, D. DeMatteo, & N. Goldstein (eds), *Handbook of psychology and juvenile justice* (pp. 345–364). Washington, DC: American Psychological Association. http://dx.doi.org/10.1037/14643-016

Heilbrun, K., Brooks Holliday, S., & King, C. (2013). Evaluation for risk of violence in adults. In R. Roesch & P. Zapf (eds), *Forensic assessments in civil and criminal law: A handbook for lawyers* (pp. 74–87). New York: Oxford University Press.

Heilbrun, K., DeMatteo, D., & Goldstein, N. E. S. (eds) (2016). *APA handbook of psychology and juvenile justice*. Washington, DC: American Psychological Association. http://dx.doi.org/10.1037/14643-000

Heilbrun, K., DeMatteo, D., Marczyk, G., & Finello, C. (2005). Applying principles of forensic mental health assessment to capital sentencing. *Widener Law Review, 11*, 93–118.

Heilbrun, K., Douglas, K., & Yasuhara, K. (2009). Violence risk assessment: Core controversies. In J. Skeem, K. Douglas, & S. Lilienfeld (eds), *Psychological science in the courtroom: Controversies and consensus* (pp. 333–357). New York: Guilford Press.

Heilbrun, K., Goldstein, N., & Redding, R. E. (eds) (2005). *Juvenile delinquency: Prevention, assessment, and intervention*. New York: Oxford University Press.

Heilbrun, K., Grisso, T., & Goldstein, A. (2009). *Foundations of forensic mental health assessment*. New York: Oxford University Press.

Heilbrun, K., Grisso, T., Goldstein, A. M., & LaDuke, C. (2012). Foundations of forensic mental health assessment. In R. Roesch & P. A. Zapf (eds), *Forensic assessment in criminal and civil law* (pp. 1–15). New York: Oxford University Press.

Heilbrun, K., Lee, R., & Cottle, C. (2005). Risk factors and intervention outcomes. In K. Heilbrun, N. Goldstein, & R. E. Redding (eds), *Juvenile delinquency: Prevention, assessment, and intervention* (pp. 111–133). New York: Oxford University Press.

Heilbrun, K., Leheny, C., Thomas, L., & Huneycutt, D. (1997). A national survey of U.S. statutes on juvenile transfer: Implications for policy and practice. *Behavioral Sciences and the Law, 15*, 125–149.

Heilbrun, K., Marczyk, G. R., DeMatteo, D., Zillmer, E. A., Harris, J., & Jennings, T. (2003). Principles of forensic mental health assessment implications for neuropsychological assessment in forensic contexts. *Assessment, 10*, 329–343. http://dx.doi.org/10.1177/1073191103258591

Heilbrun, K., Shah, S., Foster, E., Keesler, M., & Brooks, S. (2014). Empathy, acceptance of responsibility, and compelled testimony in juvenile transfer hearings: Legal context and empirical evidence. *Court Review, 50*, 21–31.

Heilbrun, K., Yasuhara, K., & Shah, S. (2010). Approaches to violence risk assessment: Overview and critical analysis. In R. Otto & K. Douglas (Eds.), *Handbook of violence risk assessment* (pp. 1–17). New York: Routledge.

Heilbrun, K., Yasuhara, K., Shah, S., & Locklair, B. (in press). Approaches to violence risk assessment: Overview, critical analysis, and future directions. In R. Otto & K. Douglas (eds), *Handbook of violence risk assessment* (2nd ed.). New York: Routledge.

Hempel, I., Buck, N., Cima, M., & van Marie, H. (2013). Review of risk assessment instruments for juvenile sex offenders: What is next? *International Journal of Offender Therapy and Comparative Criminology, 57*, 208–228. doi: 10.1177/0306624X11428315

Henggeler, S. (1989). *Delinquency in adolescence.* Thousand Oaks, CA: Sage.

Henggeler, S. (1997). *Treating serious antisocial behavior in youth: The MST approach.* Washington, DC: US Department of Justice.

Henggeler, S. (2016). Community-based interventions for juvenile offenders. In K. Heilbrun, D. DeMatteo, & N. E. S. Goldstein (eds), *APA handbook of psychology and juvenile justice* (pp. 575–595). Washington, DC: American Psychological Association. http://dx.doi.org/10.1037/14643-026

Henggeler, S., & Borduin, C. (1990). *Family therapy and beyond: A multisystemic approach to treating the behavior problems of children and adolescents.* Pacific Grove, CA: Brooks/Cole.

Henggeler, S., Melton, G. B., & Smith, L. A. (1992). Family preservation using multisystemic therapy: An effective alternative to incarcerating serious juvenile offenders. *Journal of Consulting and Clinical Psychology, 60*, 953–961.

Henggeler, S., Schoenwald, S., Borduin, C., Rowland, M., & Cunningham, P. (2009). *Multisystemic therapy for antisocial behavior in children and adolescents* (2nd ed.) New York: Guilford Press.

Henngeler, S., Schoenwald, S., Borduin, C., Rowland, M., & Cunningham, P. (1998). *Multisystemic treatment of antisocial behavior in children and adolescents.* New York: Guilford Press.

Hinshaw, S. P. (1992). Externalizing behavior problems and academic underachievement in childhood and adolescence: Causal relationships and underlying mechanisms. *Psychological Bulletin, 111*, 127–155.

Hockenberry, S., Sickmund, M., & Sladky, A. (2015). *Juvenile residential facility census, 2012: Selected findings*. Washington, DC: Office of Juvenile Justice and Delinquency Prevention.

Hoge, R. (2001). *The juvenile offender: Theory, research, and applications*. Boston, MA: Kluwer.

Hoge, R. (2005). Youth Level of Service/Case Management Inventory. In T. Grisso, G. Vincent, & D. Seagrave (eds), *Mental health screening and assessment in juvenile justice* (pp. 283–294). New York: Guilford Press.

Hoge, R. (2008). Assessment in juvenile justice systems. In R. D. Hoge, N. G. Guerra, & P. Boxer, *Treating the juvenile offender* (pp. 54–78). New York: Guilford Press.

Hoge, R. (2012). Assessment in juvenile justice systems: An overview. In E. L. Grigorenko (ed.), *Handbook of juvenile forensic psychology and psychiatry* (pp. 157–168). New York: Springer.

Hoge, R. (2013). Evaluation of juveniles' risks and needs. In R. Roesch & P. A. Zapf (eds), *Forensic assessments in criminal and civil law: A handbook for lawyers* (pp. 237–263). New York: Oxford University Press.

Hoge, R. (2016). Risk, need, and responsivity in juveniles. In K. Heilbrun, D. DeMatteo, & N. E. S. Goldstein (eds), *APA handbook of psychology and juvenile justice* (pp. 179–196). Washington, DC: American Psychological Association. http://dx.doi.org/10.1037/14643-009

Hoge, R., & Andrews, D. A. (1996). *Assessing the youthful offender: Issues and techniques*. New York: Plenum.

Hoge, R., & Andrews, D. A. (2002). *Youth Level of Service/Case Management Inventory*. Toronto, Canada: Multi-Health Systems.

Hoge, R., & Andrews, D. A. (2010a). *Evaluation for risk of violence in juveniles*. New York: Oxford University Press. http://dx.doi.org/10.1093/med/9780195370416.001.0001

Hoge, R., & Andrews, D. A. (2010b). *Youth Level of Service/Case Management Inventory 2.0*. Toronto, Canada: Multi-Health Systems.

Hoge, R., & Andrews, D. A. (2011). *Youth Level of Service/Case Management Inventory 2.0 (YLS/CMI 2.0): Users' manual*. North Tonawanda, NY: Multi-Health Systems.

Howell, J. C. (2009). *Preventing and reducing juvenile delinquency: A comprehensive framework*. Thousand Oaks, CA: Sage.

Howell, J. C., Lipsey, M. W., & Wilson, J. J. (2014). *A handbook for evidence-based juvenile justice systems*. Lanham, MD: Lexington Books.

International Juvenile Justice Observatory. (n.d.). *United Nations standard minimum rules for the administration of juvenile justice* (The Beijing Rules). Retrieved from http://www.oijj.org/en/preguntas-frecuentes#152483-0.

Iselin, A. M. R. & Salekin, R. T. (2008). Risk-Sophistication-Treatment Inventory: Self-Report. Unpublished instrument. Tuscaloosa, AL: Department of Psychology, University of Alabama.

Iselin, A. M. R., DeCoster, J., & Salekin, R. T. (2009). Maturity in adolescent and young adult offenders: The role of cognitive control. *Law and Human Behavior, 33*, 455–469.

Jennings, W. G., & Gonzalez, J. M. R. (2016). Gangs. In K. Heilbrun, D. DeMatteo, & N. E. S. Goldstein (eds), *APA handbook of psychology and juvenile justice* (pp. 307–325). Washington, DC: American Psychological Association.

Jensen, E. L. (2006). An historical overview of the American juvenile justice system. In E. L. Jensen & J. Jepsen (eds), *Juvenile law violators, human rights, and the development of new juvenile justice systems* (pp. 83–98). Portland, OR: Hart.

Jensen, E. L., & Jepsen, J. (eds) (2006). *Juvenile law violators, human rights, and the development of new juvenile justice systems*. Portland, OR: Hart.

Jensen, L., & Arnett, J. (2012). Going global: New pathways for adolescents and emerging adults in a changing world. *Journal of Social Issues, 68*, 473–492.

Johnson, B. D., & Kurlychek, M. C. (2012). Transferred juveniles in the era of sentencing guidelines: Examining judicial departures for juvenile offenders in adult criminal court. *Criminology, 50*, 525–564.

Johnson, S. B., Blum, R. W., & Giedd, J. N. (2009). Adolescent maturity and the brain: The promise and pitfalls of neuroscience research in adolescent health policy. *Journal of Adolescent Health, 45*, 216–221.

Jolliffe, D., & Farrington, D. (2004). Empathy and offending: A systematic review and meta-analysis. *Aggression and Violent Behavior, 9*, 540–550.

Jung, S., & Rawana, E. P. (1999). Risk and need assessment of juvenile offenders. *Criminal Justice and Behavior, 26*, 69–89. doi: 10.1177/0093854899026001004

Junger-Tas, J., & Dünkel, F. (2009). *Reforming juvenile justice*. New York: Springer.

Juvenile Justice and Delinquency Prevention Act, 18 U.S.C. §§ 5031-42 (2016).

Juvenile Justice Geography, Policy, Practice & Statistics (n.d.). Retrieved from http://www.jjgps.org/.

Juvenile Law Center (2014a). *Failed policies, forfeited futures: A national scorecard on juvenile records*. Retrieved from http://juvenilerecords.jlc.org/juvenilerecords/documents/publications/scorecard.pdf.

Juvenile Law Center (2014b). *Juvenile records: A national review of state laws on confidentiality, sealing and expungement*. Retrieved from http://juvenilerecords.jlc.org/juvenilerecords/documents/publications/national-review.pdf.

Juvenile right to jury trial chart (2014). Retrieved from National Juvenile Defender Center website: http://njdc.info/wp-content/uploads/2014/01/Right-to-Jury-Trial-Chart-7-18-14-Final.pdf.

Kalogerakis, M. (1992). Violent juveniles. In M. Kalogerakis (ed.), *Handbook of psychiatric practice in juvenile court* (pp. 111–120). Washington, DC: American Psychiatric Association.

Kandel, E., Mednick, S. A., Kirkegaard-Sorensen, L., Hutchings, B., Knop, J., Rosenberg, R., & Schulsinger, F. (1988). IQ as a protective factor for subjects at high risk for antisocial behavior. *Journal of Consulting and Clinical Psychology*, *56*, 224–226.

Kashani, J. H., Jones, M. R., Bumby, K. M., & Thomas, L. A. (1999). Youth violence: Psychosocial risk factors, treatment, prevention, and recommendations. *Journal of Emotional and Behavioral Disorders*, *7*, 200–210.

Kassin, S., Drizin, S., Grisso, T., Gudjonsson, G., Leo, R., & Redlich, A. (2010). Police-induced confessions: Risk factors and recommendations. *Law and Human Behavior*, *34*, 3–38.

Kaukiainen, A., Björkqvist, K., Lagerspetz, K., Österman, K., Salmivalli, C., Rothberg, S., & Ahlbom, A. (1999). The relationship between social intelligence, empathy, and three types of aggression. *Aggressive Behavior*, *25*, 81–89.

Kavanaugh, A. (2014). Retaining a forensic mental health expert in *Miller*. *The Champion*, *38* (9), 22–27.

Keenan, K., Loeber, R., Zhang, Q., Stouthamer-Loeber, M., & van Kammen, W. B. (1995). The influence of deviant peers on the development of boys' disruptive and delinquency behavior: A temporal analysis. *Development and Psychopathology*, *7*, 715–726.

Kentucky Rev. Stat. Ann. § 640-010 (West 2016).

Kessler, C. L., & Kraus, L. J. (2007). *The mental health needs of young offenders: Forging paths toward reintegration and rehabilitation*. Cambridge: Cambridge University Press.

Kessler, R. C., Berglund, P., Demler, O., Jin, R., Merikangas, K. R., & Walters, E. E. (2005). Lifetime prevalence and age-of-onset distributions of DSM-IV disorders in the National Comorbidity Survey Replication. *Archives of General Psychiatry*, *62*, 593–602.

Kim, B. S. K., Omizo, M. M., & D'Andrea, M. J. (1998). The effects of culturally consonant group counseling on the self-esteem and internal locus of control among Native American adolescents. *Journal for Specialists in Group Work, 23*, 145–163.

King, C. M. (2016). The three core psycholegal constructs for juvenile transfer evaluations are likewise evident in reverse transfer laws. Manuscript submitted for publication.

Kinscherff, R. (2006). Forensic assessment of amenability to rehabilitation in juvenile delinquency. In S. N. Sparta & G. P. Koocher (eds), *Forensic mental health assessment of children and adolescents* (pp. 311–329). New York: Oxford University Press.

Kinscherff, R. (2016). Distinguishing and assessing treatment needs and amenability to rehabilitation. In K. Heilbrun, D. DeMatteo, & N. E. S. Goldstein (eds), *APA handbook of psychology and juvenile justice* (pp. 385–404). Washington, DC: American Psychological Association. http://dx.doi.org/10.1037/14643-018

Koehler, J. A., Lösel, F., Akoensi, T. D., & Humphreys, D. K. (2013). A systematic review and meta-analysis on the effects of young offender treatment programs in Europe. *Journal of Experimental Criminology, 9*, 19–43. doi: 10.1007/s11292-012-9159-7

Koocher, G., & Kinscherff, R. (2016). Ethical issues in psychology and juvenile justice. In K. Heilbrun, D. DeMatteo, & N. E. S. Goldstein (eds), *APA handbook of psychology and juvenile justice* (pp. 693–714). Washington, DC: American Psychological Association. http://dx.doi.org/10.1037/14643-031

Krisberg, B., & Wolf, A. M. (2005). Juvenile offending. In K. Heilbrun, N. E. S. Goldstein, & R. E. Redding (eds), *Juvenile delinquency: Prevention, assessment, and intervention* (pp. 67–84). New York: Oxford University Press.

Kroger, J. (2003). What transits in an identity status transition? *Identity: An International Journal of Theory and Research, 3*, 197–220.

Kruh, I., & Brodsky, S. (1997). Clinical evaluations for transfer of juveniles to criminal court: Current practices and future research. *Behavioral Sciences and the Law, 15*, 151–165. http://dx.doi.org/10.1002/(SICI)1099-0798(199721)15:2<151::AID-BSL267>3.0.CO;2-U

Kruh, I., & Grisso, T. (2009). *Evaluation of juveniles' competence to stand trial.* New York: Oxford.

Kuhn, D. (2009). Adolescent thinking. In R. Lerner & L. Steinberg (eds), *Handbook of adolescent psychology* (pp. 152–186). Hoboken, NJ: Wiley.

Kumpfer, K. L., & Alvarado, R. (2003). Family-strengthening approaches for the prevention of youth problem behaviors. *American Psychologist*, *58*, 457–465.

Kusa, D., & Nurse, A. M. (2015). Juvenile justice in Slovakia. In J. A. Winterdyk (ed.), *Juvenile justice: International perspectives, models, and trends* (pp. 295–320). Boca Raton, FL: Taylor & Francis.

Landsheer, J. A., & van Dijkum, C. (2005). Male and female delinquency trajectories from pre through middle adolescence and their continuation in late adolescence. *Adolescence*, *40*, 729–748.

Lanza-Kaduce, L., Frazier, C. E., Lane, J., & Bishop, D. M. (2002). *Juvenile transfer to criminal court study: Final report.* Tallahassee, FL: Florida Department of Juvenile Justice.

Larson, K., & Grisso, T. (2016). Transfer and commitment of youth in the United States: Law, policy, and forensic practice. In K. Heilbrun, D. DeMatteo, & N. E. S. Goldstein (eds), *APA handbook of psychology and juvenile justice* (pp. 445–466). Washington, DC: American Psychological Association. doi: 10.1037/14643-019

Leistico, A. M. R., & Salekin, R. T. (2003). Testing the reliability and validity of the Risk, Sophistication-Maturity, and Treatment Amenability Instrument (RST-i): An assessment tool for juvenile offenders. *International Journal of Forensic Mental Health*, *2*, 101–117. doi: 10.1080/14999013.2003.10471182

Lerman, P. (2002). Twentieth-century developments in American's institutional systems for youth in trouble. In M. K. Rosenheim, F. E. Zimring, D. S. Tanenhaus, & B. Dohrn (eds), *A century of juvenile justice* (pp. 74–110). Chicago: University of Chicago Press.

Leve, L., Chamberlain, P., & Reid, J. (2005). Intervention outcomes for girls referred from juvenile justice: Effects on delinquency. *Journal of Consulting and Clinical Psychology*, *73*, 1181–1185.

Levick, M., & Feirman, J. (2016). Children in the justice system: The legal framework. In K. Heilbrun, D. DeMatteo, & N. E. S. Goldstein (eds), *APA handbook of psychology and juvenile justice* (pp. 23–42). Washington, DC: American Psychological Association. http://ds.doi.org/10.1037/14643-002

Lipsey, M. W. (1995). What do we learn from 400 research studies on the effectiveness of treatment with juvenile delinquents? In J. McGuire (ed.), *What works: Reducing reoffending* (pp. 63–78). Chichester: Wiley.

Lipsey, M. W. (2009). The primary factors that characterize effective interventions with juvenile offenders: Synthesis of research. *Victims and Offenders*, *4*, 124–147.

Lipsey, M. W., & Derzon, J. H. (1998). Predictors of violent or serious delinquency in adolescence and early adulthood. In R. Loeber & D. P. Farrington (eds), *Serious and violent juvenile offenders: Risk factors and successful interventions* (pp. 86–105). Thousand Oaks, CA: Sage.

Lipsey, M. W., & Wilson, D. B. (1998). Effective intervention for serious juvenile offenders: A synthesis of research. In R. Loeber & D. P. Farrington (eds), *Serious and violent juvenile offenders: Risk factors and successful interventions* (pp. 313–345). Thousand Oaks, CA: Sage.

Lodewijks, H. P. (2008). *Violence risk assessment in adolescents in the Dutch juvenile justice system: Studies on the reliability and predictive accuracy of the SAVRY*. Amsterdam: Vrije Universiteit.

Loeber, R., & Farrington, D. P. (eds). (1998). *Serious and violent juvenile offenders: Risk factors and successful interventions*. Thousand Oaks, CA: Sage.

Loeber, R., & Farrington, D. P. (2011). *Young homicide offenders and victims: Risk factors, prediction, and prevention from childhood*. New York: Springer.

Loeber, R., Farrington, D. P., Stouthamer-Loeber, M., Moffitt, T. E., & Caspi, A. (1998). The development of male offending: Key findings from the first decade of the Pittsburgh youth study. *Studies on Crime and Crime Prevention*, *7*, 141–171.

Loving, J. L., & Patapis, N. S. (2007). Evaluating amenability to treatment: Integrating statutes and case law into clinical practice. *Journal of Forensic Psychology Practice*, *7*, 67–78.

Luciana, M., Conklin, H., Hooper, C., & Yager, R. (2005). The development of nonverbal working memory and executive control processes in adolescents. *Child Development*, *76*, 697–712.

Luna, B., & Wright, C. (2016). Adolescent brain development: Implications for the juvenile justice system. In K. Heilbrun, D. DeMatteo, & N. E. S. Goldstein (eds), *APA handbook of psychology and juvenile justice* (pp. 91–116). Washington, DC: American Psychological Association.

Luna, B., Marek, S., Larsen, B., Tervo-Clemmens, B., & Chahal, R. (2015). An integrative model of the maturation of cognitive control. *Annual Review of Neuroscience*, *38*, 151–170.

McAra, L., & McVie, S. (2015). The Scottish juvenile justice system: Policy and practice. In J. A. Winterdyk (ed.), *Juvenile justice: International perspectives, models, and trends* (pp. 263–294). Boca Raton, FL: Taylor & Francis.

McGrath, R. J. (1991). Sex-offender risk assessment and dispositional planning: A review of empirical and clinical findings. *International Journal of Offender Therapy and Comparative Criminology*, *35*, 328–350.

McPherson, S. B. (2012). Major principles in a minor context: Forensic practices involving adolescents. In E. L. Grigorenko (ed.), *Handbook of juvenile forensic psychology and psychiatry* (pp. 69–82). New York: Springer.

Marczyk, G. R., Heilbrun, K., Lander, T., & DeMatteo, D. (2003). Predicting juvenile recidivism with the PCL: YV, MAYSI, and YLS/CMI. *International Journal of Forensic Mental Health*, *2*, 7–18.

Marczyk, G. R., Heilbrun, K., Lander, T., & DeMatteo, D. (2005). Juvenile decertification: Developing a model for classification and prediction. *Criminal Justice and Behavior*, *32*, 278–301.

Marsh, T. (2007). *Juvenile law*. Clifton Park, NY: Thomson Delmar Learning.

Melton, G. B., & Kimbrough-Melton, R. J. (2006). Integrating assessment, treatment, and justice: Pipe dream or possibility? In S. N. Sparta & G. P. Koocher (eds), *Forensic mental health assessment of children and adolescents* (pp. 11–29). New York: Oxford University Press.

Melton, G., Petrila, J., Poythress, N., & Slobogin, C. (1987). *Psychological evaluations for the courts: A handbook for mental health professionals and lawyers*. New York: Guilford Press.

Melton, G., Petrila, J., Poythress, N., & Slobogin, C. (1997). *Psychological evaluations for the courts: A handbook for mental health professionals and lawyers* (2nd ed.). New York: Guilford Press.

Melton, G., Petrila, J., Poythress, N., & Slobogin, C. (2007). *Psychological evaluations for the courts: A handbook for mental health professionals and lawyers* (3rd ed.). New York: Guilford Press.

Mihalic, S., Fagan, A., Irwin, K., Ballard, D., & Elliott, D. (2004). *Blueprints for violence prevention.* Washington, DC: Office of Juvenile Justice and Delinquency Prevention.

Miller, P., & Eisenberg, N. (1988). The relation of empathy to aggressive and externalizing/antisocial behavior. *Psychological Bulletin*, *103*, 324–344.

Mills, J. R., Dorn, A., & Hritz, A. C. (2016). Juvenile life without parole in law and practice: The end of superpredator era sentencing. *American University Law Review*, *65*, 535–605.

Mills, K., Goddings, A., Clasen, L., Giedd, J., & Blakemore, S. (2014). The developmental mismatch in structural brain maturation during adolescence. *Developmental Neuroscience*, *36*, 147–160.

Millstein, S. G., & Halpern-Felsher, B. L. (2001). Perceptions of risk and vulnerability. In B. Fischoff, E. O. Nightingale, & J. G. Ianotta (eds), *Adolescent risk and vulnerability: Concepts and measurement* (pp. 15–49). Washington, DC: National Academy Press.

Model Juvenile Court Act (1968), U.L.A. (2015).

Moffitt, T. (1993). Adolescence-limited and life-course-persistent antisocial behavior: A developmental taxonomy. *Psychological Review, 100*, 674–701.

Moffitt, T. (2003). Life-course persistent and adolescent-limited antisocial behavior: A 10-year research review and a research agenda. In B. B. Lahey, T. E. Moffitt, & A. Caspi (eds), *Causes of conduct disorder and juvenile delinquency* (pp. 49–75). New York: Guilford.

Monahan, J. (ed.). (1980). *Who is the client? The ethics of psychological intervention in the criminal justice system.* Washington, DC: American Psychological Association.

Monahan, J., & Skeem, J. (2015). Risk assessment in criminal sentencing. *Annual Review of Clinical Psychology*. Retrieved from http://papers.ssrn.com/sol3/papers.cfm?abstract_id=2662082.

Monahan, J., Steadman, H. J., Silver, E., Appelbaum, P. S., Robbins, P. C., Mulvey, E. P., Roth, L. H., Grisso, T., & Banks, S. (2001). *Rethinking risk assessment: The MacArthur study of mental disorder and violence.* New York: Oxford University Press.

Monahan, K. C., Steinberg, L., Cauffman, E., & Mulvey, E. P. (2009). Trajectories of antisocial behavior and psychosocial maturity from adolescence to young adulthood. *Developmental Psychology, 45*, 1654–1668.

Moretti, M., Odgers, C., & Jackson, M. (eds). (2004). *Girls and aggression: Contributing factors and intervention principles*. New York: Kluwer Academic/Plenum.

Morse, S. (1978). Law and mental health professionals: The limits of expertise. *Professional Psychology, 9*, 389–399. http://dx.doi.org/10.1037/0735-7028.9.3.389

Moshman, D. (2005). *Adolescent psychological development: Rationality, morality, and identity*. Mahwah, NJ: Erlbaum.

Mossman, D., Noffsinger, S., Ash, P., Fierson, R., Gerbasi, J., Hackett, M., … Zonana, H. (2007). AAPL practice guideline for the forensic psychiatric evaluation of competence to stand trial. *Journal of the American Academy of Psychiatry and the Law, 35*, S3–72.

Mulvey, E. P. (1984). Judging amenability to treatment in juvenile offenders. In N. D. Reppucci (ed.), *Children, mental health, and the law* (pp. 195–210). Beverly Hills, CA: Sage.

Mulvey, E. P., & Iselin, A. M. R. (2008). Improving professional judgments of risk and amenability in juvenile justice. *The Future of Children, 18*, 35–57.

Mulvey, E. P., Arthur, M. W., & Reppucci, N. D. (1993). The prevention and treatment of juvenile delinquency: A review of the research. *Clinical Psychology Review, 13*, 133–167.

Mulvey, E., Steinberg, L., Fagan, J., Cauffman, E., Piquero, A., Chassin, L., … Losoya, S. (2004). Theory and research on desistance from antisocial activity among serious adolescent offenders. *Youth Violence and Juvenile Justice*, *2*, 213–236. http://dx.doi.org/10.1177/1541204004265864

Mulvey, E., Steinberg, L., Piquero, A., Besana, M., Fagan, J., Schubert, C., & Cauffman, E. (2010). Trajectories of desistance and continuity in antisocial behavior following court adjudication among serious adolescent offenders. *Development and Psychopathology*, *22*, 453–475. doi: 10.1017/S0954579410000179

Nagel, A., Guarnera, L., & Reppucci, N.D. (2016). Adolescent development, mental disorder, and decision making in delinquent youths. In K. Heilbrun, D. DeMatteo, & N. E. S. Goldstein (eds), *APA handbook of psychology and juvenile justice* (pp. 117–138). Washington, DC: American Psychological Association. http://dx.doi.org/10.1037/14643-006

National Academy of Sciences (2013). *Reforming juvenile justice: A developmental approach*. Washington, DC: National Academy Press.

National Archive of Criminal Justice Data (n.d.). Retrieved from https://www.icpsr.umich.edu/icpsrweb/NACJD/index.jsp.

National Center for Juvenile Justice (n.d.). Juvenile justice geography, policy, practice & statistics. Retrieved from http://www.jjgps.org/.

National Child Traumatic Stress Network (2008). *Judges and child trauma: Findings from the National Traumatic Stress Network/National Council of Juvenile and Family Court Judges Focus Groups*, Service Systems Brief, Vol. 2, No. 2. Los Angeles: Author.

National Council of Juvenile and Family Court Judges (2005). *Juvenile delinquency guidelines: Improving court practice in juvenile delinquency cases*. Reno, NV: Author.

National Crime Records Bureau (2013). *Crime in India 2013*. Retrieved from http://www.ncrb.gov.in/.

National Gang Center (n.d.). *National youth gang survey analysis*. Retrieved from https://www.nationalgangcenter.gov/Survey-Analysis.

National Institute on Drug Abuse (2003). *Preventing drug use among children and adolescents: A research-based guide for parents, educators, and community leaders* (2nd ed.). Washington, DC: US Department of Health and Human Services.

National Juvenile Defender Center & Juvenile Law Center (2009). *Toward developmentally appropriate practice: Juvenile court training curriculum* (2nd ed.). Retrieved October 20, 2015 from http://www.modelsforchang.net/publications/255.

National Mental Health Association (2004). *Mental health treatment for youth in the juvenile justice system: A compendium of promising practices.* Chicago: Author.

Nelson, E. E., Leibenluft, E., McClure, E., & Pine, D. S. (2005). The social re-orientation of adolescence: A neuroscience perspective on the process and its relation to psychopathology. *Psychological Medicine, 35,* 163–174.

Nosek, B., & Banaji, M. R. (2001). The go/no-go association task. *Social Cognition, 19,* 161–176.

O'Connell, M., & O'Connell, E. (2015). Youth justice and youth crime in Australia. In J. A. Winterdyk (ed.), *Juvenile justice: International perspectives, models, and trends* (pp. 55–87). Boca Raton, FL: Taylor & Francis.

Odgers, C. L., Moretti, M. M., & Reppucci, N. D. (2005). Examining the science and practice of violence risk assessment with female adolescents. *Law and Human Behavior, 29,* 7–27.

Office of Justice Programs. (n.d.). *National criminal justice reference service: Juvenile justice.* Retrieved from https://www.ncjrs.gov/App/Topics/Topic.aspx?Topicid=122.

Office of Juvenile Justice and Delinquency Prevention (2012). *OJJDP statistical briefing book.* Retrieved from http://www.ojjdp.gov/ojstatbb/structure_process/qa04105.asp.

Office of Juvenile Justice and Delinquency Prevention (n.d.). *Compendium of national juvenile justice datasets.* Retrieved from http://www.ojjdp.gov/ojstatbb/.

Ogloff, J. R., Wong, S., & Greenwood, A. (1990). Treating criminal psychopaths in a therapeutic community program. *Behavioral Sciences and the Law, 8,* 181–190.

Olver, M. E., Stockdale, K. C., & Wormith, J. S. (2009). Risk assessment with young offenders: A meta-analysis of three assessment measures. *Criminal Justice and Behavior, 36,* 329–353.

Olver, M. E., Stockdale, K. C., & Wormith, J. S. (2014). Thirty years of research on the Level of Service Scales: A meta-analytic examination of predictive accuracy and sources of variability. *Psychological Assessment, 26,* 156–176.

Orbis Partners. (2007). *Long-term validation of the Youth Assessment and Screening Instrument (YASI) in New York state juvenile probation.* Ottawa: Author.

Otto, R. K., & Douglas, K. S. (eds) (2010). *Handbook of violence risk assessment.* New York: Routledge.

Otto, R. K., & Heilbrun, K. (2002). The practice of forensic psychology: A look toward the future in light of the past. *American Psychologist, 57,* 5–18. doi: 10.1037/0003-066X.57.1.5

Otto, R. K., Borum, R., & Epstein, M. (2012). Evaluation of children in the juvenile justice system. In D. Faust (ed.), *Coping with psychiatric and psychological testimony* (pp. 754–774). New York: Oxford University Press.

Otto, R. K., Slobogin, C., & Greenberg, S. A. (2007). Legal and ethical issues in accessing and utilizing third-party information. In A. M. Goldstein (ed.), *Forensic psychology: Emerging topics and expanding roles* (pp. 190–208). Hoboken, NJ: Wiley.

Page, G. L., & Scalora, M. J. (2004). The utility of locus of control for assessing juvenile amenability to treatment. *Aggression and Violent Behavior, 9*, 523–534.

Palmer, T. B., & Lewis, R. V. (1980). A differentiated approach to juvenile diversion. *Journal of Research in Crime and Delinquency, 17*, 209–229.

Parker, R. N., Negola, T., Haapanen, R., Miranda, L., & Asencio, E. (2008). Treating gang-involved offenders. In R. D. Hoge, N. G. Guerra, & P. Boxer, *Treating the juvenile offenders* (pp. 171–192). New York: Guilford Press.

Parrott, C., & Strongman, K. (1984). Locus of control and delinquency. *Adolescence, 19*, 459–471.

Patterson, G. R., DeBaryshe, B. D., & Ramsey, E. (1989). A developmental perspective on antisocial behavior. *American Psychologist, 44*, 329–335.

Penney, S., & Moretti, M. (2005). The transfer of juveniles in adult court in Canada and the United States: Confused agendas and compromised assessment procedures. *International Journal of Forensic Mental Health, 4*, 19–37.

Pennsylvania Juvenile Act, 42 Pa. Cons. Stat. § 6301 et seq. (2013).

Perrault, R. T., Paiva-Salisbury, M., & Vincent, G. M. (2012). Probation officers' perceptions of youths' risk of reoffending and use of risk assessment in case management. *Behavioral Sciences and the Law, 30*, 487–505.

Petanjek, Z., Judaš, M., Šimić, G., Rašin, M. R., Uylings, H. B. M., Rakic, P., & Kostović, I. (2011). Extraordinary neoteny of synaptic spines in the human prefrontal cortex. *Proceedings of the National Academy of Sciences, 108*, 13281–13286.

Petrocelli, J. V. (2003). Factor validation of the consideration of future consequences scale: Evidence for a short version. *Journal of Social Psychology, 143*, 405–413.

Petrosino, A., Turpin-Petrosino, C., & Finckenauer, J. O. (2000). Well-meaning programs can have harmful effects! Lessons from experiments of programs such as Scared Straight. *Crime and Delinquency, 46*, 354–379.

Quinn, M., Rutherford, R. B., Leone, P. E., Osher, D. M., & Poirier, J. M. (2005). Youth with disabilities in juvenile corrections: A national survey. *Exceptional Children, 71*, 339–345.

Quinsey, V. L. (1988). Assessment of the treatability of forensic patients. *Behavioral Sciences and the Law*, *6*, 443–452.

Rauschecker, J., & Marler, P. (1987). What signals are responsible for synaptic changes in visual cortical plasticity? In J. Ranschecker & P. Marler (eds), *Imprinting and cortical plasticity* (pp. 193–200). New York: Wiley.

Raznahan, A., Shaw, P. W., Lerch, J. P., Clasen, L. S., Greenstein, D., Berman, R., … Giedd, J. N. (2014). Longitudinal four dimensional mapping of subcortical anatomy in human development. *Proceedings of the National Academy of Sciences of the United States of America*, *111*, 1592–1597.

Redding, R. E., & Arrigo, B. A. (2005). Multicultural perspectives on delinquency etiology and intervention. In C. Frisby & C. Reynolds (eds), *Comprehensive handbook on multicultural school psychology* (pp. 710–743). Hoboken, NJ: Wiley.

Redding, R. E., & Hensl, K. B. (2011). Knowledgeable judges make a difference: Judicial beliefs affect juvenile court transfer decisions. *Juvenile and Family Court Journal*, *62*, 15–24. doi: 10.1111/j.1755-6988.2011.01063.x

Redding, R., & Mrozoski, B. (2005). Adjudicatory and dispositional decision making in juvenile justice. In K. Heilbrun, N. Goldstein, & R. E. Redding (eds), *Juvenile delinquency: Prevention, assessment, and intervention* (pp. 232–256). New York: Oxford University Press.

Redding, R. E., & Murrie, D. C. (2007). Judicial decision making about forensic mental health evidence. In A. M. Goldstein (ed.), *Forensic psychology: Emerging topics and expanding roles* (pp. 683–707). Hoboken, NJ: John Wiley & Sons.

Redding, R., Goldstein, N., & Heilbrun, K. (2005). Juvenile delinquency: Past and present. In K. Heilbrun, N. Goldstein, & R. E. Redding (eds), *Juvenile delinquency: Prevention, assessment, and intervention* (pp. 3–18). New York: Oxford University Press.

Redding, R. E., Lexcen, F. J., & Ryan, E. P. (2005). Mental health treatment for juvenile offenders in residential psychiatric and juvenile justice settings. In K. Heilbrun, N. Goldstein, & R. E. Redding (eds), *Juvenile delinquency: Prevention, assessment, and intervention* (pp. 282–309). New York: Oxford University Press.

Resnick, M. D., Ireland, M., & Borowsky, I. (2004). Youth violence perpetration: What protects? What predicts? Findings from the National Longitudinal Study of Adolescent Health. *Journal of Adolescent Health*, *35*, 424. doi: 10.1016/j.jadohealth.2004.01.011

Rhoades, K. A., Chamberlain, P., Roberts, R., & Leve, L. D. (2013). MTFC for high-risk adolescent girls: A comparison of outcomes in England and the United States. *Journal of Child and Adolescent Substance Abuse*, *22*, 439–449.

Rhule, D. M. (2005). Take care to do no harm: Harmful interventions for youth problem behavior. *Professional Psychology: Research and Practice*, *36*, 618–625.

Ribeiro da Silvaa, D., Rijoa, D., & Salekin, R. T. (2013). Child and adolescent psychopathy: Assessment issues and treatment needs. *Aggression and Violent Behavior*, *18*, 71–78.

Ribner, N. G. (ed.). (2002). *The California School of Professional Psychology handbook of juvenile forensic psychology*. San Francisco, CA: Jossey-Bass.

Rich, J., Harris, E., Bloom, S., Rich, L., & Corbin, T. (2016). Intervening in the community to treat trauma in young men of color. In K. Heilbrun, D. DeMatteo, & N. E. S. Goldstein (eds), *APA handbook of psychology and juvenile justice* (pp. 597–609). Washington, DC: American Psychological Association. http://dx.doi.org/10.1037/14643-027

Rich, P. (2011). Understanding, assessing, and rehabilitating juvenile sexual offenders. Hoboken, NJ: John Wiley & Sons.

Richardson, D., Hammock, G., Smith, S., Gardner, W., & Signo, M. (1994). Empathy as a cognitive inhibitor of interpersonal aggression. *Aggressive Behavior*, *20*, 275–289.

Riggs Romaine, C. L. (2010). *Juvenile decertification in Philadelphia County: A model for jurisdiction-specific research* (Doctoral dissertation). Retrieved from https://idea.library.drexel.edu/islandora/object/idea%3A3289/datastream/OBJ/download/Juvenile_decertification_in_Philadelphia_County__a_model_for_jurisdiction-specific_research.pdf.

Roesch, R., & Zapf, P. (eds). (2012). *Forensic assessments in civil and criminal law: A handbook for lawyers*. New York: Oxford University Press.

Rogoff, B., Baker-Sennett, J., & Matusov, E. (1994). Considering the concept of planning. In M. Haith, J. Benson, R. Roberts, & B. Pennington (eds), *The development of future-oriented processes* (pp. 353–373). Chicago: University of Chicago Press.

Rosenberg, D. R., & Lewis, D. A. (1995). Postnatal maturation of the dopaminergic innervation of monkey prefrontal and motor cortices: A tyrosine hydroxylase immunohistochemical analysis. *Journal of Comparative Neurology*, *358*, 383–400.

Rosenheim, M. K. (2002). The modern American juvenile court. In M. K. Rosenheim, F. E. Zimring, D. S. Tanenhaus, & B. Dohrn (eds), *A century of juvenile justice* (pp. 341–359). Chicago: University of Chicago Press.

Rosenheim, M. K., Zimring, F. E., Tanenhaus, D. S., & Dohrn, B. (eds). (2002). *A century of juvenile justice*. Chicago: University of Chicago Press.

Rotter, J. B. (1966). Generalized expectancies for internal versus external control of reinforcement. *Psychological Monographs, 80,* 1–28.

Ryan, E. P., Hunter, J. A., & Murrie, D. C. (2012). *Juvenile sex offenders: A guide to evaluation and treatment for mental health professionals.* New York: Oxford University Press.

Ryba, N. L., Cooper, V. G., & Zapf, P. A. (2003a). Assessment of maturity in juvenile competency to stand trial evaluations: A survey of practitioners. *Journal of Forensic Psychology Practice, 3,* 23–46. doi: 10.1300/J158v03n03_02

Ryba, N. L., Cooper, V. G., & Zapf, P. A. (2003b). Juvenile competence to stand trial evaluations: A survey of current practices and test usage among psychologists. *Professional Psychology: Research and Practice, 34,* 499–507.

Salekin, R. (2002a). Clinical evaluation of youth considered for transfer to adult criminal court: Refining practice and directions for science. *Journal of Forensic Psychology Practice, 2,* 55–72.

Salekin, R. (2002b). Juvenile transfer to adult court: How can developmental and child psychology inform policy decision making? In B. L. Bottoms, M. B. Kovera, & B. D. McAuliff (eds), *Children, social science, and the law* (pp. 203–232). Cambridge: Cambridge University Press. doi: 10.1017/CBO9780511500114.009

Salekin, R. (2002c). Psychopathy and therapeutic pessimism: Clinical lore or clinical reality? *Clinical Psychology Review, 22,* 79–112. doi: 10.1016/S0272-7358(01)0083-6.

Salekin, R. (2004a). *Risk-Sophistication-Treatment Inventory.* Lutz, FL: Psychological Assessment Resources.

Salekin, R. (2004b). *Manual for the Risk-Sophistication-Treatment Inventory.* Lutz, FL: Psychological Assessment Resources.

Salekin, R. (2012). Risk-Sophistication-Treatment Inventory—Abbreviated. Unpublished clinical rating measure. Tuscaloosa, AL: Department of Psychology, University of Alabama.

Salekin, R. (2015a). *Forensic evaluation and treatment of juveniles: Innovation and best practice.* Washington, DC: American Psychological Association. doi: 10.1037/14595-000

Salekin, R. (2015b). Psychopathy in childhood: Toward better informing the DSM-5 and ICD-11 conduct disorder specifiers. *Personality Disorders: Theory, Research, and Treatment, 7,* 180–191.

Salekin, R., & Grimes, R. (2008). Clinical forensic evaluations for juvenile transfer to adult criminal court. In R. Jackson (ed.), *Learning forensic assessment* (pp. 313–346). New York: Routledge.

Salekin, R., & Grimes, R. (2016). Clinical forensic evaluations for juvenile transfer to adult criminal court. In R. Jackson & R. Roesch (ed.), *Learning forensic assessment: Research and practice* (pp. 294–323). New York: Routledge.

Salekin, R., & Iselin, A. M. (2010). The Risk-Sophistication-Treatment Inventory—Self Report. Unpublished manuscript.

Salekin, R., & Lynam, D. R. (2010). *Handbook of child and adolescent psychopathy*. New York: Guilford Press.

Salekin, R., MacDougall, E. A. M., & Harrison, N. A. (2016). Developmental maturity and sophistication-maturity: Learning more about its purpose and assessment. In K. Heilbrun, D. DeMatteo, & N. E. S. Goldstein (eds), *APA handbook of psychology and juvenile justice* (pp. 405–424). Washington, DC: American Psychological Association. doi: 10.1037/14643-019

Salekin, R., Price, K. M., Tant, K. E., Adams, E. W., Ang, X., & Rosenbaum, J. (2012). Evaluation for disposition and transfer of juvenile offenders. In R. Roesch & P. A. Zapf (eds), *Forensic assessments in criminal and civil law* (pp. 249–263). New York: Oxford University Press.

Salekin, R., Rogers, R., & Ustad, K. L. (2001). Juvenile waiver to adult criminal courts: Prototypes for dangerousness, sophistication-maturity, and amenability to treatment. *Psychology, Public Policy, and Law*, *7*, 381–408. doi: 10.1037/1076-8971.7.2.381

Salekin, R., Salekin, K. L., Clements, C. B., & Leistico, A.-M. R. (2005). Risk–Sophistication–Treatment Inventory. In T. Grisso, G. M. Vincent, & S. Daniel (eds), *Mental health screening and assessment in juvenile justice* (pp. 341–356). New York: Guilford Press.

Salekin, R., Tippey, J. G., & Allen, A. D. (2012). Treatment of conduct problem youth with interpersonal callous traits using mental models: Measurement of risk and change. *Behavioral Sciences and the Law*, *30*, 470–486. doi: 10.1002/bsl.2025

Salekin, R., Yff, R. M. A., Neumann, C. S., Leistico, A.-M. R., & Zalot, A. A. (2002). Juvenile transfer to adult courts: A look at the prototypes for dangerousness, sophistication-maturity, and amenability to treatment through a legal lens. *Psychology, Public Policy, and Law*, *8*, 373–410. doi: 10.1037/1076-8971.8.4.373

Sarnecki, J. (2006). Responses to juvenile crime: The Swedish perspective. In E. L. Jensen & J. Jepsen (eds), *Juvenile law violators, human rights, and the development of new juvenile justice systems* (pp. 187–211). Portland, OR: Hart.

Schaeffer, C. M., & Borduin, C. M. (2005). Long-term follow-up to a randomized clinical trial of multisystemic therapy with serious and violent juvenile offenders. *Journal of Consulting and Clinical Psychology*, *73*, 445–453.

Scheier, M. F., & Carver, C. S. (1985). Optimism, coping, and health: Assessment and implications of generalized outcome expectancies. *Health Psychology*, *4*, 219–247.

Schetky, D., & Benedek, E. (2002). *Principles and practice of child and adolescent forensic psychiatry*. Washington, DC: American Psychiatric Publishing.

Schmidt, F., Campbell, M., & Houlding, C. (2011). Comparative analyses of the YLS/CMI, SAVRY, and PCL:YV in adolescent offenders: A 10-year follow-up into adulthood. *Youth Violence and Juvenile Justice*, *9*, 23–42. doi: 10.1177/1541204010371793

Schwalbe, C. S. (2007). Risk assessment for juvenile offenders: A meta-analysis. *Law and Human Behavior*, *31*, 449–462.

Schwalbe, C. S. (2008a). Strengthening the integration of actuarial risk assessment with clinical judgment in an evidence based practice framework. *Children and Youth Services Review*, *30*, 1458–1464. doi: 10.1016/j.childyouth.2007.11.021

Schwalbe, C. S. (2008b). A meta-analysis of juvenile justice risk assessment instruments: Predictive validity by gender. *Criminal Justice and Behavior*, *35*, 1367–1381.

Schwalbe, C. S., Fraser, M. W., Day, S. H., & Cooley, V. (2006). Classifying juvenile offenders according to risk or recidivism: Predictive validity, race/ethnicity, and gender. *Criminal Justice and Behavior*, *33* (3), 305–324.

Schweinhart, L. J., Barnes, H. V., & Weikart, D. P. (1993). *The High/Scope Perry Preschool Study through age 27*. Ypsilanti, MI: High/Scope Educational Foundation.

Scott, E., & Steinberg, L. (2008). *Rethinking juvenile justice: Adolescent development and the regulation of youth crime*. Cambridge, MA: Harvard University Press.

Scott, E., Grisso, T., Levick, M., & Steinberg, L. (in press). "Children are different:" The Supreme Court and the transformation of juvenile sentencing. *Temple Law Review*. Retrieved from http://modelsforchange.net/publications/778/The_Supreme_Court_and_the_Transformation_of_Juvenile_Sentencing.pdf.

Segrave, J. O., & Chu, D. B. (1978). Athletics and juvenile delinquency. *Review of Sports and Leisure*, *3*, 1–24.

Sexton, T. L., & Alexander, J. F. (2000). *Functional family therapy*. Washington, DC: US Department of Justice.

Seymour, M. (2006). *Juvenile justice in the Republic of Ireland.* Retrieved from http://esc-eurocrim.org/files/juvenile_justice_in_the_republic_of_ireland.doc.

Sheidow, A. J., & Henggeler, S. W. (2005). Community-based treatments. In K. Heilbrun, N. E. S. Goldstein, & R. E. Redding (eds), *Juvenile delinquency: Prevention, assessment, and intervention* (pp. 257–281). New York: Oxford University Press.

Shelton, D. (2005). Patterns of treatment services and costs for young offenders with mental disorders. *Journal of Child and Adolescent Psychiatric Nursing, 18*, 103–112.

Shoenberg, D. (2012). Introduction. In E. L. Grigorenko (ed.), *Handbook of juvenile forensic psychology and psychiatry* (pp. 1–10). New York: Springer.

Shook, J. J., & Sarri, R. C. (2007). Structured decision making in juvenile justice: Judges' and probation officers' perceptions and use. *Children and Youth Services Review, 29* (10), 1335–1351.

Shufelt, J. L., & Cocozza, J. J. (2006). *Youth with mental health disorders in the juvenile justice system: Results from a multi-state prevalence study* (pp. 1–6). Delmar, NY: National Center for Mental Health and Juvenile Justice.

Shulman, E., & Steinberg, L. (2016). Human development and juvenile justice. In K. Heilbrun, D. DeMatteo, & N. E.S. Goldstein (eds), *APA handbook of psychology and juvenile justice* (pp. 69–90). Washington, DC: American Psychological Association. doi: 10.1037/14643-004

Sickmund, M., & Puzzanchera, C. (eds). (2014). *Juvenile offenders and victims: 2014 national report.* Retrieved from Office of Juvenile Justice and Delinquency Prevention website http://www.ojjdp.gov/ojstatbb/nr2014/downloads/NR2014.pdf.

Simon, R. & Gold, L. (eds). (2004). *Textbook of forensic psychiatry.* Washington, DC: American Psychiatric Publishing.

Singh, J. P., Grann, M., & Fazel, S. (2011). A comparative study of violence risk assessment tools: A systematic review and metaregression analysis of 68 studies involving 25,980 participants. *Clinical Psychology Review, 31*, 499–513.

Sisk, C. L., & Zehr, J. L. (2005). Pubertal hormones organize the adolescent brain and behavior. *Frontiers in Neuroendocrinology, 26*, 163–174.

Skeem, J. L., Scott, E., & Mulvey, E. P. (2014). Justice policy reform for high-risk juveniles: Using science to achieve large-scale crime reduction. *Annual Review of Clinical Psychology, 10*, 709–739. doi: 10.1146/annurev-clinpsy-032813-153707

Slobogin, C. (2016). Preventive justice for adolescents. In K. Heilbrun, D. DeMatteo, & N. E. S. Goldstein (eds), *APA handbook of psychology and juvenile justice* (pp. 45–65). Washington, DC: American Psychological Association. http://dx.doi.org/10.1037/14643-003

Slobogin, C., & Fondacaro, M. (2011). *Juveniles at risk: A plea for preventive justice*. New York: Oxford University Press. http://dx.doi.org/10.1093./acprof:oso/9780199778355.001.0001

Snyder, H., & Sickmund, M. (1999). Juvenile offenders and victims: 1999 national report. Washington, DC: National Center for Juvenile Justice. Retrieved October 11, 2015 from https://www.ncjrs.gov./html/ojjdp/nationalreport99/toc.html.

Somerville, L. H., Hare, T., & Casey, B. J. (2011). Frontostriatal maturation predicts cognitive control failure to appetitive cues in adolescents. *Journal of Cognitive Neuroscience, 23*, 2123–2134.

Sowell, E. R., Thompson, P. M., Leonard, C. M., Welcome, S. E., Kan, E., & Toga, A. W. (2004). Longitudinal mapping of cortical thickness and brain growth in normal children. *Journal of Neuroscience, 24*, 8223–8231.

Spear, L. P. (2000). The adolescent brain and age-related behavioral manifestations. *Neuroscience and Biobehavioral Reviews, 24*, 417–463.

Spice, A., Viljoen, J. L., Gretton, H. M., & Roesch, R. (2010). Psychological assessment for adult sentencing of juvenile offenders: An evaluation of the RSTI and the SAVRY. *International Journal of Forensic Mental Health, 9*, 124–137. doi: 10.1080/14999013.2010.501846

Stagman, S., & Cooper, J. (2010). *Children's mental health: What every policy-maker should know*. New York: National Center for Children in Poverty.

Steinberg, L. (2007). Risk taking in adolescence: new perspectives from brain and behavioral science. *Current Directions in Psychological Science, 16*, 55–59.

Steinberg, L. (2008). A social neuroscience perspective on adolescent risk-taking. *Developmental Review, 28*, 78–106.

Steinberg, L. (2010). A dual systems model of adolescent risk taking. *Developmental Psychobiology, 52*, 216–224.

Steinberg, L., & Cauffman, E. (1996). Maturity of judgment in adolescence: Psychosocial factors in adolescent decision making. *Law and Human Behavior, 20*, 249–272. doi: 10.1007/BF01499023

Steinberg, L., & Monahan, K. C. (2007). Age differences in resistance to peer influence. *Developmental Psychology, 43*, 1531–1543. doi: 10.1037/0012-1649.43.6.1531

Steinberg, L., & Scott, E. (2003). Less guilty by reason of adolescence: Developmental immaturity, diminished responsibility, and the juvenile death penalty. *American Psychologist*, 58, 1009–1018. http://dx.doi.org/10.1037/0003-066X.58.12.1009

Steinberg, L., Albert, D., Cauffman, E., Banich, M., Graham, S., & Woolard, J. (2008). Age differences in sensation seeking and impulsivity as indexed by behavior and self-report: Evidence for a dual systems model. *Developmental Psychology, 44*, 1764–1778.

Steinberg, L., Cauffman, E., Woolard, J., Graham, S., & Banich, M. (2009). Are adolescents less mature than adults? Minors' access to abortion, the juvenile death penalty, and the alleged APA "flip-flop." *American Psychologist, 64*, 583–594.

Steinberg, L., Dahl, R., Keating, D., Kupfer, D., Masten, A., & Pine, D. (2006). The study of developmental psychopathology in adolescence: Integrating affective neuroscience with the study of context. In D. Cicchetti & D. Cohen (eds), *Developmental psychopathology* (Vol. 2, pp. 710–741). New York: Wiley.

Steinberg, L., Grisso, T., Scott, E., & Bonnie, R. (2016). Don't treat young adults as teenagers. *New York Times*. April 29. Retrieved December 12, 2016 from http://www.nytimes.com/2016/05/01/opinion/sunday/dont-treat-young-adults-as-teenagers.html.

Strathman, A., Gleicher, F., Boninger, D. S., & Edwards, C. S. (1994). The consideration of future consequences: Weighing immediate and distant outcomes of behavior. *Journal of Personality and Social Psychology, 66*, 742–752. doi: 10.1037/0022-3514.66.4.742

Tate, D. C., & Redding, R. E. (2005). Mental health and rehabilitative services in juvenile justice: System reforms and innovative approaches. In K. Heilbrun, N. E. S. Goldstein, & R. E. Redding (eds), *Juvenile delinquency: Prevention, assessment, and intervention* (pp. 134–160). New York: Oxford University Press.

Taxman, F. S., Debus-Sherrill, S., & Watson, C. A. (2012). Services for youth in closed settings: Gaps in services. In E. Grigorenko (ed.), *Handbook of juvenile forensic psychology and psychiatry* (pp. 281–296). New York: Springer.

Taxman, F. S., Young, D., Wiersema, B., Rhodes, A., & Mitchell, S. (2007). National Criminal Justice Treatment Practices Survey: Methods and procedures. *Journal of Substance Abuse Treatment, 32*, 225–238.

Taylor, M. (2015). Juvenile transfers to adult court: An examination of long-term outcomes of transferred and non-transferred juveniles. *Juvenile and Family Journal, 66*, 29–47.

Teplin, L. A., Abram, K. M., McClelland, G. M., Dulcan, M. K., & Mericle, A. A. (2002). Psychiatric disorders in youth in juvenile detention. *Archives of General Psychiatry, 59*, 1133–1143.

The right to counsel in status offense cases. (2010). Retrieved from American Bar Association website http://www.americanbar.org/content/dam/aba/migrated/child/PublicDocuments/right_to_counsel_factsheet.authcheckdam.pdf

Thornberry, T. R, & Krohn, M. D. (2003). *Taking stock of delinquency: An overview of findings from contemporary longitudinal studies*. New York: Kluwer/Plenum.

Tolan, P. H. (1987). Implications of age of onset for delinquency risk. *Journal of Abnormal Child Psychology, 15*, 47–65.

Tremblay, R. E., Pagani-Kurtz, L. C., Masse, L. C., Vitaro, F., & Pihl, R. O. (1995). A bimodal preventive intervention for disruptive kindergarten boys: Its impact through mid-adolescence. *Journal of Consulting and Clinical Psychology, 63*, 560–568.

Trupin, E. (2007). Evidence-based treatment for justice involved youth. In C. L. Kessler & L. J. Kraus (eds), *The mental health needs of young offenders: Forging paths toward reintegration and rehabilitation* (pp. 340–367). West Nyack, NY: Cambridge University Press.

Underwood, L. A., & Washington, A. (2016). Mental illness and juvenile offenders. *International Journal of Environmental Research and Public Health, 13*, 228–241.

United Nations Human Rights Office of the High Commissioner (n.d.). Status of ratification interactive dashboard [select Convention on the Rights of the Child from drop-down menu]. Retrieved from indicators.ohchr.org.

United Nations Office on Drugs and Crime. (2013). *Justice matters involving children in conflict with the law: Model law on juvenile justice and related commentary*. New York: United Nations.

Urquhart, T. A., & Viljoen, J. L. (2014). The use of the SAVRY and YLS/CMI in adolescent court proceedings: A case law review. *International Journal of Forensic Mental Health, 13*, 47–61.

van der Put, C. E., van der Laan, P., Stams, G., Dekovic, M., & Hoeve, M. (2011). Promotive factors during adolescence: Are there changes in impact and prevalence during adolescence and how does this relate to risk factors? *International Journal of Child, Youth and Family Studies, 2*, 119–141.

Van Leijenhorst, L., Zanolie, K., Van Meel, C. S., Westenberg, P. M., Rombouts, S., & Crone, E. A. (2010). What motivates the adolescent? Brain regions mediating reward sensitivity across adolescence. *Cerebral Cortex, 20*, 61–69.

Vieira, T. A., Skilling, T. A., & Peterson-Badali, M. (2009). Matching court-ordered services with youths' treatment needs: Predicting treatment success with young offenders. *Criminal Justice and Behavior, 36*, 385–401.

Viljoen, J., Brodersen, E., Shaffer, C., & McMahon, R (2016). Risk reduction interventions for adolescent offenders. In K. Heilbrun, D. DeMatteo, & N. E. S. Goldstein (eds), *APA handbook of psychology and juvenile justice* (pp. 517–543). Washington, DC: American Psychological Association. http://dx.doi.org/10.1037/14643-024

Viljoen, J. L., Elkovitch, N., Scalora, M. J., & Ullman, D. (2009). Assessment of reoffense risk adolescents who have committed sexual offenses. *Criminal Justice and Behavior, 36*, 981–1000. doi: 10.1177/0093854809340991

Viljoen, J. L., Mordell, S., & Beneteau, B. L. (2012). Prediction of adolescent sexual reoffending: A meta-analysis of the J-SOAP-II, ERASOR, J-SORRAT-II, and Static-99. *Law and Human Behavior, 36*, 423–438.

Viljoen, J. L., Scalora, M., Cuadra, L., Bader, S., Chavez, V., Ullman, D., & Lawrence, L. (2008). Assessing risk for violence in adolescents who have sexually offended: A comparison of the J-SOAP-II, J-SORRAT-II, and SAVRY. *Criminal Justice and Behavior, 35*, 5–23. doi: 10.1177/0093854807307521

Viljoen, J. L., Wingrove, T., & Ryba, N. L. (2008). Adjudicative competence evaluations of juvenile and adult defendants: Judges' views regarding essential components of competence reports. *International Journal of Forensic Mental Health, 7*, 107–119. doi: 10.1080/14999013.2008.9914408

Vincent, G. M. (2015). Application and implementation of risk assessment in juvenile justice for the courts. *Science in the Courtroom, 1*. Retrieved from http://www.macoe.org/sites/macoe.org/files/Vincent_2015.pdf.

Vincent, G. M., Chapman, J., & Cook, N. E. (2011). Risk–needs assessment in juvenile justice: Predictive validity of the SAVRY, racial differences, and the contribution of needs factors. *Criminal Justice and Behavior, 38*, 42–62.

Vincent, G. M., Guy, L. S., & Grisso, T. (2012a). *Risk assessment in juvenile justice: A guidebook for implementation.* Models for Change, National Youth Screening and Assessment Project. Retrieved from http://njjn.org/uploads/digital-library/Risk_Assessment_in_Juvenile_Justice_A_Guidebook_for_Implementation.pdf.

Vincent, G. M., Guy, L. S., Fusco, S. L., & Gershenson, B. G. (2012b). Field reliability of the SAVRY with juvenile probation officers: Implications for training. *Law and Human Behavior, 36*, 225–236. doi: 10.1037/h0093974

Vincent, G. M., Guy, L. S., Gershenson, B. G., & McCabe, P. (2012c). Does risk assessment make a difference? Results of implementing the SAVRY in juvenile probation. *Behavioral Sciences and the Law, 30*, 384–405.

Vincent, G., Kimonis, E., & Clark, A. (2016). Juvenile psychopathy: Appropriate and inappropriate uses in legal proceedings. In K. Heilbrun, D. DeMatteo, & N. E. S.

Goldstein (eds), *APA handbook of psychology and juvenile justice* (pp. 197–232). Washington, DC: American Psychological Association. doi: 10.1037/14643-010

Vincent, G. M., Terry, A., & Maney, S. (2009). Risk/needs tools for antisocial behavior and violence among youthful populations. In J. Andrade (ed.), *Handbook of violence risk assessment and treatment: New approaches for forensic mental health practitioners* (pp. 377–423). New York: Springer.

Vitopoulos, N. A., Peterson-Badali, M., & Skilling, T. A. (2012). The relationship between matching service to criminogenic need and recidivism in male and female youth: Examining the RNR principles in practice. *Criminal Justice and Behavior*, *39*, 1025–1041.

Vráblová, M. (2012). *Alternatives to custody for young offenders: National report for young offenders: Slovakia.* Retrieved from http://www.oijj.org/sites/default/files/baaf_slovakia1.pdf.

Wachter, A. (2014). *Statewide Risk Assessment in Juvenile Probation.* JJGPS StateScan. Pittsburgh, PA: National Center for Juvenile Justice.

Wasserman, G. A., Keenan, K., Tremblay, R. E., Cole, J. D., Herrekohl, T. I., Loeber, R. & Petechuk, D. (2003). *Risk and protective factors of child delinquency.* Washington, DC: US Department of Justice, Office of Justice Programs, Office of Juvenile Justice and Delinquency Prevention.

Wasserman, G. A., McReynolds, L. S., Lucas, C. P., Fisher, P., & Santos, L. (2002). The voice DISC-IV with incarcerated male youths: Prevalence of disorder. *Journal of the American Academy of Child and Adolescent Psychiatry*, *41*, 314–321.

Wasserman, G., McReynolds, L., Ko, S., Katz, L., & Carpenter, J. (2005). Gender differences in psychiatric disorders at juvenile probation intake. *American Journal of Public Health*, *95*, 131–137.

Wasserman, G., McReynolds, L., Schwalbe, C., Keating, J., & Jones, S. (2010). Psychiatric disorder, comorbidity, and suicidal behavior in juvenile justice youth. *Criminal Justice and Behavior*, *37*, 1361–1376. http://dx.doi.org/10/1177/0093854810382751

Waterman, A. (1982). Identity development from adolescence to adulthood: An extension of theory and a review of research. *Developmental Psychology*, *18*, 341–358.

Waterman, A. S. (2004). Finding someone to be: Studies on the role of intrinsic motivation in identity formation. *Identity*, *4*, 209–228.

Weinberger, D., & Gomes, M. (1995). Changes in daily mood and self-restraint among undercontrolled preadolescents: A time-series analysis of "acting out." *Journal of the American Academy of Child and Adolescent Psychiatry*, *34*, 1473–1482.

Weinberger, D. A., & Schwartz, G. E. (1990). Distress and restraint as superordinate dimensions of self-reported adjustment: A typological perspective. *Journal of Personality, 58*, 381–417. doi: 10.1111/j.1467-6494.1990.tb00235.x

Weiner, I., & Hess, A. (2006). *The handbook of forensic psychology*. Hoboken, NJ: John Wiley & Sons.

Weisz, J. R. (1986). Contingency and control beliefs as predictors of psychotherapy outcomes among children and adolescents. *Journal of Consulting and Clinical Psychology, 54*, 789–795.

Weithorn, L. A. (2006). The legal contexts of forensic assessment of children and families. In S. N. Sparta & G. P. Koocher (eds), *Forensic mental health assessment of children and adolescents* (pp. 11–29). New York: Oxford University Press. http://dx.doi.org/10.1093/med:psych/9780195145847.003.0002

Welsh, J. L., Schmidt, F., McKinnon, L., Chattha, H. K., & Meyers, J. R. (2008). A comparative study of adolescent risk assessment instruments: Predictive and incremental validity. *Assessment, 15*, 104–115. doi: 10.1177/1073191107307966

Westen, D., Klepser, J., Ruffins, S. A., Silverman, M., Lifton, N., & Boekamp, J. (1991). Object relations in childhood and adolescence: The development of working representations. *Journal of Consulting and Clinical Psychology, 59*, 400–409. doi: 10.1037/0022-006X.59.3.400

White, J., & Jones, R. (1996). Identity styles of male inmates. *Criminal Justice and Behavior, 23*, 490–504.

Whitehead, J. T., & Lab, S. P. (2001). *Juvenile justice: An introduction* (3rd ed.). Cincinnati, OH: Anderson.

Wigfield, A., Eccles, J., Schiefele, U., Roeser, R., & Davis-Kean, P. (2006). Development of achievement motivation. In N. Eisenberg, W. Damon, & R. Lerner (eds), *Handbook of child psychology* (Vol. 3) (pp. 933–1002). Hoboken, NJ: Wiley.

Williams, K. R., Tuthill, L., & Lio, S. (2008). A portrait of juvenile offending in the United States. In R. D. Hoge, N. G. Guerra, & P. Boxer (eds), *Treating the juvenile offender* (pp. 15–32). New York: Guilford Press.

Wilson, D. B., Gottfredson, D. C., & Najaka, S. S. (2001). School-based prevention of problem behaviors: A meta-analysis. *Journal of Quantitative Criminology, 17*, 247–272.

Winner, L., Lanza-Kaduce, L., Bishop, D. M., & Frazier, C. E. (1997). The transfer of juveniles to criminal court: Reexamining recidivism over the long term. *Crime and Delinquency, 43*, 548–563.

Winterdyk, J. A. (2015). Introduction: Juvenile justice in the international arena. In J. A. Winterdyk (ed.), *Juvenile justice: International perspectives, models, and trends* (pp. 1–24). Boca Raton, FL: Taylor & Francis.

Winterdyk, J. A., & Miller, A. (2015). Juvenile justice and young offenders: A Canadian overview. In J. A. Winterdyk (ed.), *Juvenile justice: International perspectives, models, and trends* (pp. 107–136). Boca Raton, FL: Taylor & Francis.

Witt, P. H. (2003). Transfer of juveniles to adult court: The case of H. H. *Psychology, Public Policy, and Law, 9*, 361–380.

Witt, P. H., & Dyer, F. J. (1997). Juvenile transfer cases: Risk assessment and risk management. *Journal of Psychiatry and Law, 25*, 581–614.

Woolard, J. L., Vidal, S., & Fountain, S. (2015). Juvenile offenders. In B. L. Cutler & P. A. Zapf (eds), *APA Handbook of forensic psychology: Volume 2: Criminal investigation, adjudication, and sentencing outcomes* (pp. 33–58). Washington, DC: American Psychology Association.

Wynkoop, T. F. (2008). Neuropsychology in the juvenile justice system. In R. L. Denney & J. P. Sullivan (eds), *Clinical neuropsychology in the criminal forensic setting* (pp. 295–325). New York: Guilford Press.

Young, D., Dembo, R., & Henderson, C. (2007). A national survey of substance abuse treatment for juvenile offenders. *Journal of Substance Abuse Treatment, 32*, 255–266.

Young, D., Moline, K., Farrell, J., & Bierie, D. (2006). Best implementation practices: Disseminating new assessment technologies in a juvenile justice agency. *Crime and Delinquency, 52*, 135–158. http://dx.doi.org/10.1177/0011128705281752

Youth Criminal Justice Act, 2002 S.C., ch. 1 (Can.).

Youth Law Center, Juvenile Law Center, & American Bar Association (2000). *Understanding adolescents: A juvenile court training curriculum*. Retrieved from http://www.modelsforchange.net/publications/178.

Zara, G., & Farrington, D. P. (2013). Assessment of risk for juvenile compared with adult criminal onset: Implications for policy, prevention, and intervention. *Psychology, Public Policy, and Law, 19*, 235–249. doi: 10.1037/a0029050

Zavlek, S. (2005). *Planning community-based facilities for violent juvenile offenders as part of a system of graduated sanctions*. Retrieved from the National Criminal Justice Reference Service website https://www.ncjrs.gov/pdffiles1/ojjdp/209326.pdf.

Zelechoski, A. (2016). Trauma, adverse experience, and offending. In K. Heilbrun, D. DeMatteo, & N. E. S. Goldstein (eds), *APA handbook of psychology and juvenile justice* (pp. 326–342). Washington, DC: American Psychological Association. doi: 10.1037/14643-015

Zimbardo, P. G. (1990a). *Stanford Time Perspective Inventory manual.* Stanford, CA: Stanford University, Department of Psychology.

Zimbardo, P. G. (1990b, August). *Strategies for coping with social traps: Time perspective influences.* Paper presented at the meeting of the American Psychological Association, Boston, MA.

Zimbardo, P. G., & Boyd, J. N. (1999). Putting time in perspective: A valid, reliable individual-differences metric. *Journal of Personality and Social Psychology, 77,* 1271–1288. doi: 10.1037/0022-3514.77.6.1271

Zimring, F. (2005). *American juvenile justice.* New York: Oxford University Press. http://dx.doi.org/10.1093/acprof:oso/97801951811166.001.0001

Zottoli, T. M., Daftary-Kapur, T., & Zapf, P. A. (2015). We don't always mean what we say: Attitudes toward statutory exclusion of juvenile offenders from juvenile court jurisdiction. *Journal of Forensic Psychology Practice, 15,* 423–448. doi: 10.1080/15228932.2015.1099335

CASES

INDEX

Printed in Japan
落丁、乱丁本のお問い合わせは
Amazon.co.jp カスタマーサービスへ

11775290R00196